American Ethnic and Cultural Studies

John C. Walter and Johnnella E. Butler, Series Editors

T0366848

American Ethnic and Cultural Studies

The American Ethnic and Cultural Studies series presents critical interdisciplinary, cross-disciplinary, and comparative studies of cultural formations and expressions of racialized peoples of North America. Focusing on African Americans, American Indians, Asian Americans, Chicanos/as, and Latinos/as, and on comparative works among these groups and racialized Euro-Americans, the series also explores new and changing configurations of race and ethnicity as shaped by gender, class, and religion in global and domestic contexts. Informed by research in the humanities, arts, and social sciences; transnational and diasporic studies; film studies; legal studies; and public policy, environmental, urban, and rural studies, books in the series will aim to stimulate innovative approaches in scholarship and pedagogy.

Color-line to Borderlands: The Matrix of American Ethnic Studies
Edited by Johnnella E. Butler

Being Buddhist in a Christian World: Gender and Community
in a Korean American Temple
Sharon A. Suh

Complicating Constructions: Race, Ethnicity, and Hybridity in American Texts
Edited by David S. Goldstein and Audrey B. Thacker

COMPLICATING CONSTRUCTIONS

RACE,
ETHNICITY,
AND HYBRIDITY
IN AMERICAN
TEXTS

EDITED BY DAVID S. GOLDSTEIN

AND AUDREY B. THACKER

UNIVERSITY OF WASHINGTON PRESS   *Seattle & London*

© 2007 by the University of Washington Press
Printed in the United States of America
Designed by Audrey Seretha Meyer
12 11 10 09 08 07 5 4 3 2 1

University of Washington Press
P.O. Box 50096, Seattle, WA 98145 U.S.A.
www.washington.edu/uwpress

Library of Congress Cataloging-in-Publication Data

Complicating constructions : race, ethnicity, and hybridity in American texts / edited
by David S. Goldstein and Audrey B. Thacker.
    p. cm. — (American ethnic and cultural studies)
Includes index.
ISBN 13: 978-0-295-98835-1

1. American literature—Minority authors—History and criticism.   2. American
literature—19th century—History and criticism.   3. American literature—20th
century—History and criticism.   4. Race in literature.   5. Ethnicity in literature.
6. Minorities in literature.   7. Ethnic groups in literature.   8. Multiculturalism
in literature.   I. Goldstein, David S.   II. Thacker, Audrey B.
PS153.M56C65   2007
810.9'3552—dc22   2006032916

To our most important teachers,
our parents:
Fran and Bob Goldstein
and Rita and Gilbert Cooperman,
with love

CONTENTS

I

Re-Constructing Race and Ethnicity:
Identity Imposed or Adopted

II

Re-Contexualizing Race and Ethnicity:
Texts in Historical and Political Perspective

III

Re-Considering Race and Ethnicity:
Meta-Issues in Theory and Criticism

ACKNOWLEDGMENTS

W E HAVE BEEN ACCOMPANIED ON THIS long journey by more gifted individuals than we can name here, but we are no less grateful to all who have assisted.

Foremost among those whom we must specially acknowledge are our essay contributors, who patiently endured multiple requests for revisions and a process longer than any of us could have envisioned. We have relied mightily on their intellects and tolerance, and they have given far more than any editors had a right to ask. Alexandra Schultheis's essay, "Traumatic Legacy in Darryl Pinckney's *High Cotton*," was published in a substantially different form in her book, *Regenerative Fictions: Postcolonialism, Psychoanalysis, and the Nation as Family* (Palgrave McMillan, 2004) and appears here with her kind permission. Jeffrey Partridge's "Re-viewing the Literary Chinatown" in this volume is a modified version of chapter 7 in his book *Beyond Literary Chinatown* (University of Washington Press, 2007).

Jacquelyn Ray and Michael Cook provided invaluable editorial assistance.

The University of Washington Press staff has been extraordinarily helpful and professional. We especially wish to thank our sponsoring editor, Jacqueline Ettinger, and copyeditor, Molly Wallace.

We also are very pleased to acknowledge the enduring support of our families, friends, and colleagues.

INTRODUCTION

DAVID S. GOLDSTEIN

THE ESSAYS IN THIS VOLUME RE-EXAMINE IN innovative ways the concepts of "race" and "ethnicity" as manifested in and challenged by a variety of American texts.[1] Unlike most critics currently publishing either on constructions of race and ethnicity or on ethnic American literature, these essayists pull together both conversations by using American texts (both those that have been understood to be "ethnic" and those generally considered "non-ethnic") to interrogate the concepts themselves. Rather than beginning with an unquestioned assumption about the meanings of "race" and "ethnicity" in their studies of American texts, the scholars represented in this volume instead examine the interplay between texts themselves and "race" and "ethnicity" as concepts, treating "race" and "ethnicity" as problematic and shifting terms. In so doing, these writers represent the cutting edge in American literary studies, American studies more broadly, and ethnic studies, engaging issues that have never been so timely and crucial.

More than a century after W. E. B. Du Bois presciently predicted that the problem of the twentieth century would be the color line, academic scholarship in the field of race and ethnicity continues to increase expo-

nentially. One of the most-often cited texts in ethnic and American studies is *Racial Formation in the United States: From the 1960s to the 1990s*
(1994), in which authors Michael Omi and Howard Winant trace the
links between race and the American nation-state. Some influential texts,
such as bell hooks's *Black Looks: Race and Representation* (1992), examine in fresh ways the representation of race in American culture. A growing body of scholarship on whiteness as a socially constructed marker,
including *Displacing Whiteness: Essays in Social and Cultural Criticism*
(1997), edited by Ruth Frankenberg,[2] and *The Making and Unmaking of
Whiteness* (2001), edited by Birgit Brander Rasmussen and others,
extends and complements studies of race. None of these texts, however,
focuses specifically on literature.

On the other hand, excellent studies of ethnic American literature
proliferate, typically concentrating on specific ethnic groups. Rachel C.
Lee's *The Americas of Asian American Literature: Gendered Fictions of
Nation and Transnation* (1999) and *The Black Columbiad: Defining
Moments in African American Literature and Culture* (1994), edited by
Werner Sollors and Maria Diedrich, exemplify this group. *The Ethnic
Canon: Histories, Institutions, and Interventions* (1995), edited by David
Palumbo-Liu, is one of the few critical works to focus on more than one
ethnic literary tradition. *Postcolonial Theory and the United States: Race,
Ethnicity, and Literature* (2000), edited by Amritjit Singh and Peter
Schmidt, specifically examines the relationships between American literature and racial and ethnic studies, but necessarily (and effectively)
delves deeply into the single theoretical approach—postcolonialism—
rather than analyzing broadly and comparatively among literary
approaches.

Some of these studies interrogate the changing concepts of "race"
and "ethnicity" in theoretical and cultural terms, but do not focus
specifically on concrete texts. Others examine race and ethnicity in American texts but with little attention to the fluidity of the terms themselves.
Still others focus only on what has traditionally been called "ethnic" American literature or only on racial constructions in European American (i.e.,
so-called "non-ethnic") literary works. This volume, on the other hand,
examines how American texts, including literary works traditionally
defined as "ethnic" *and* those considered "non-ethnic" or "mainstream,"
force us to re-examine what "race" and "ethnicity" have meant histori-

cally and presently. Along the lines of Patricia McKee's influential study, *Producing American Races: Henry James, William Faulkner, Toni Morrison* (1999), which discusses how three major American authors construct race, this volume is broad in scope in terms of time, textual genre, topic, and theoretical approach, and treats a variety of authors and texts. Ranging from the early nineteenth century to the late twentieth, from poetry, fiction, and drama to film and television, from racist rhetoric to racial hybridity, from close readings of individual texts to considerations of theoretical meta-issues, the essays collected in this volume vigorously analyze "race" and "ethnicity" as they are constructed in—and, conversely, as they have influenced—understandings of writers and readers in their own times and in ours. As disparate as they are, these essays, taken collectively, provide an initial, extended interrogation of "race" and "ethnicity" as a variety of American texts have inscribed those concepts. To our knowledge, no other volume takes this innovative approach.

The Mythology and Reality of "Race"

Most scholars probably are ahead of the general public in recognizing that "race" is socially constructed and holds no significant meaning in biological or genetic terms. As early as 1942, in the midst of Nazi atrocities, Ashley Montagu argued in his landmark book, *Man's Most Dangerous Myth: The Fallacy of Race*, that race in public discourse has been predicated upon mistaken assumptions, misinformation, and poor science, with tragic results.[3] Montagu lucidly explains how categories of so-called "races" of human beings were developed for social, political, and economic reasons, fueled by a misapplication of Linnaeus's methodical classification, in the eighteenth century, of living organisms into the now-familiar kingdom, genus, species, and so forth. Just as Darwin's ideas about natural selection are routinely misapplied to social phenomena, Linnaeus's contributions to biological classification, which were followed by elaboration later that century by Georges L. L. Buffon and then Johann Blumenbach, have been misapplied to suggest that natural, meaningful "racial" categories of human beings exist, as if each "race" were equivalent to a subspecies. Linnaeus, Buffon, and Blumenbach all understood that modern humans constitute a single, biologically indivisible species, *homo sapiens* (Montagu 100). Their categorizations of human differences were exercises based on conjectured associations between physical appearances and climate, not on organic, generic differences among human beings. Two centuries later, most Americans nevertheless continue to think, speak, and act as if "race" were the basis of a meaningful taxonomy.

Anyone producing scholarship in a field that deals with the concept of race—including teachers and scholars of American literature, for this literature cannot be understood without understanding the role of race as a social phenomenon—needs to understand very clearly why race carries no scientific meaning,[4] and though the following propositions are doubtless familiar to most critical race scholars, they nonetheless bear repeating.

Diversity within categories far exceeds diversity between categories. Suppose, hypothetically, one catalogues each member of two of the most popular racial categories in current use—white (or Caucasian) and black (or Negroid)—on a selected physical trait, such as height. One likely will find that the tallest black person is taller than the tallest white person. The difference in height, however, between the shortest black person and the tallest black person is far greater than the difference between the tallest white person and the tallest black person. In other words, each racial group exhibits enormous diversity on every imaginable phenotypical trait, including the one most obvious in discussions of race: skin color. Racial groups, however, differ from one another only slightly at the extremes. Therefore, those who explain differences between person A who is black and person B who is white by referring to their respective races, in a biological or genetic sense, speak nonsense.

Genetic differences between races are statistically insignificant. If "races" existed in a biological sense, then one would expect that an examination of the chromosomes of representatives from each race would differ, for chromosomes carry the DNA codes that underlie our genetic makeup. As it turns out, however, such is not the case. Philosopher Anthony Appiah describes a hypothetical experiment that belies the myth of genetic difference between races: If one were randomly to select two persons who supposedly are Caucasian and then to compare the same, randomly selected locus on each person's chromosomes, the chances of difference between the two are about 14.3 percent. If one were randomly to select two persons from the world population at large, Appiah continues, the chances that the two specimens will differ are about 14.8 percent, only half of a percentage point (about 3.5 percent) higher—hardly a meaningful difference. Appiah concludes that "given only a person's race, it is hard to say what his or her biological characteristics will be, except in the 'grosser' features of color, hair, and bone" (31).[5] If we cannot count on genetics to explain even fundamental, phenotypical differences between individuals of two so-called races, we hardly can expect genetics to explain racial differences in abilities, beliefs, or behaviors.

Clearly, despite the terms of public discourse about race, "race" has no biological meaning. It is a myth. But it is a powerful myth.

Because most people in the industrialized West, including the United States, believe that race does mean something, they historically have behaved as if it does. The result, of course, is that the belief in racial categories has itself created, maintained, and perpetuated those categories. Race is a social construction; it means something only because we collectively believe, and behave as if, it means something. The red light of a traffic signal means "stop" not because red inherently carries "stopness," but because we tacitly agree to behave as if red means "stop." Analogously, we have tacitly agreed that black skin will stand for certain meanings, white skin will stand for other meanings, and so forth. Of course, as our essayists make clear, those meanings are more contested and fluctuating than the simple example of a traffic signal.

Although this essay is an inadequate venue in which to recount the vast literature on the centuries-long development of racial thinking in the West, we would like to make a few points that pertain especially to this volume.

First, the constant fluctuation in the last three hundred years in the number and description of racial categories promulgated in Europe and the United States, let alone the enormous variations of attributes ascribed to each of those categories, demonstrates the confusion about and absurdity of such categorizations. The great majority of Westerners historically have operated with the consensus—an inaccurate one, as we have noted—that racial categories are meaningful, but rarely have they achieved consensus regarding the meanings themselves, except that self-described whites have almost always assumed their superiority to the other supposed races.[6] That is why our essayists do not begin with assumed consensus about the meanings of race, racial categories, or ethnicity, but rather use their chosen literary and visual texts dialectically to generate and interrogate meanings of race and ethnicity.

Second, Americans have constructed their social institutions, sometimes intentionally and sometimes unintentionally, to reflect and reiterate racial distinctions. The burgeoning, complementary fields of Critical Legal Theory and Critical Race Theory, for example, examine the largely hidden ways in which common and statutory law, and related institutions such as the police, reinscribe racial inequalities.[7] Insofar as the schools in which American literature is studied and taught constitute one such social institution, they are not immune from the consequences of racial thinking, nor is the literary canon itself, as the last several decades of critique of the canon in literary studies suggest. We shall return to this latter point in this essay's next section.

Third, racial categorization, based though it is on faulty assumptions about human populations, profoundly affects real human beings in the United States and elsewhere. The black teenager lynched by a white mob clearly benefits not at all from the fact that racial categories have no biological reality. The choice to intern Japanese Americans but not German Americans or Italian Americans during World War II highlights not only the difference between physically "marked" persons of a supposed race and the "unmarked" persons of white ethnic groups, but also the underlying belief that "inscrutable" and "sneaky" Asians are too risky to be permitted basic civil rights. Even beyond these obvious and egregious examples of the consequences of racial categorization, one also can find more covert, and therefore sometimes more insidious—or at least more common—consequences, such as in the daily privileges that accrue to persons seen as "white."[8]

Fourth, because categorizations based on race depend upon physical markers such as skin color, "race" cannot be considered simply one kind of ethnicity, and racially defined groups cannot be considered simply one kind of ethnic group. A number of respected scholars of race and ethnicity have made such claims,[9] but, as Michael Omi and Howard Winant persuasively argue, race operates in our society in ways that distinguish it sharply from ethnicity. At the very least, the physical marker of skin color has made racially-defined groups inassimilable in ways that white ethnic groups never have been. Our essayists not only share this perspective, but also illuminate it in new ways.

The Significance of Literature

History, as historians like Hayden White have reminded us, is not the past. Rather, it is our *story* of the past, a story we tell ourselves in order to make the past speak to us. Because it is a story, it changes according to the time, place, and perspective in which it is told, and thereby remains fresh and relevant to us today. For example, stories about the Civil War tend to mean much more to southerners than to northerners in the United States. Although both regions share a common past, their stories about that past differ markedly. The Euro-American story of "westward expansion" necessarily takes a divergent form, perhaps "eastern encroachment," when told by American Indians. History, as story, tells us who we imagine ourselves to have been and who we imagine ourselves to be.

As literary critics, we believe in the power of stories and in the power of literature more specifically. A nation's literature documents its self-imaginings, its self-definitions. Taken as a whole, the body of American literary texts, encompassing both the most arcane chapbook of poetry and the most wildly popular novel of the day, dialectically reflects and influences the broad range of American experiences. Any modern-day Tocqueville wanting to assay the range of ideas and values of the American people would do well to survey its literature, including its most revered and most reviled, its most canonized and most marginalized texts. American literature provides a lens nonpareil through which one can begin to understand America.[10] Because we believe that America remains incomprehensible without understanding race and ethnicity, we argue for careful, critical attention to the ways in which American literary texts inscribe and critique race and ethnicity.

We need not say much here about the related issue of canon formation and the ways in which groups of privilege have used the canon to perpetuate their own values and their own hegemony. Numerous, fine analyses of the politics of canon formation and canon deconstruction proliferate.[11] Suffice it to say here that examination of only those literary works that have been traditionally canonized will lead primarily to an understanding of the most privileged groups in America. On the other hand, neglecting these works also misleads, inasmuch as they represent, for complex reasons, what Americans have considered to be their finest achievements. The recognition that artistic merit has not been the sole criterion for a work's admission to the canon does not mean that the work has no merit or is unworthy of study for other reasons. We therefore include in this volume essays that study recognized classics like Jack London's *The Valley of the Moon* (1913), but also Etsu Inagaki Sugimoto's *A Daughter of the Samurai* (1925), and even the odious white-supremacist tract, *The Turner Diaries* (1978).

Moreover, because American literary texts not only reflect but also influence American society (the influence of Harriet Beecher Stowe's *Uncle Tom's Cabin* [1852] on the abolitionist movement comes to mind), their study helps illuminate both the lifeways of Americans of prior generations and the trajectory of America's culture. In the study of race and ethnicity, social constructions that, as we have argued, lie so deep in the heart of American society, literary analyses are especially critical.

We assert, in short, that we need to understand race and ethnicity to understand America, and we therefore need to understand how race and ethnicity are constructed in, reiterated by, and critiqued through America's literature.

Organization of the Book

We have organized the essays into three sections: "Re-Constructing Race and Ethnicity: Identity Imposed or Adopted," "Re-Contextualizing Race and Ethnicity: Texts in Historical and Political Perspective," and "Re-Considering Race and Ethnicity: Meta-Issues in Theory and Criticism." The essays in the first section examine the ways various American texts raise new questions and issues regarding racial or ethnic identity. The second section comprises essays that contribute to the growing scholarship on the historical development of racial concepts in the West, using a variety of American texts. Essays that explore how critics might respond to newly complicated understandings of race and ethnicity constitute the third section. Each essay is followed by its own endnotes, and list of works cited. A comprehensive index, following a short set of biographical notes about the contributors, provides a convenient method for finding references to particular topics.

The essays constituting the volume's first section, "Re-Constructing

Race and Ethnicity: Identity Imposed or Adopted," look at representations of race in a variety of nineteenth- and twentieth-century texts, complicating rather than simplifying the ways that race has intersected with personal and collective identities, citizenship, and colonialism. Racial or ethnic hybridity—the idea that ethnic and even racial identities, more fluid and situational than previously thought, can be shifted and blended in countless ways—preoccupies several of these essayists.[12]

Leading the first section, Jesse Alemán examines the work of nineteenth-century novelist María Amparo Ruiz de Burton as a "brand of resistance" to the racial identities constructed by Anglos for the Mexicans of California. Ruiz de Burton's novels, written during the westward expansion of the United States following the Mexican-American War, critique, according to Alemán, the "dominant narrative of Anglo American nationhood." Moreover, American critics' disregard of these novels signifies a continuing marginalization of Mexican Americans, who are seen as racially ambiguous and therefore difficult to integrate into an American racial schema. Alemán analyzes the myriad ways Ruiz de Burton's narratives complicate ideas of race and caste in old California.

Andrea Tinnemeyer also examines race, class, and history in California, focusing on Bret Harte's *Gabriel Conroy*, a novel that reverses the Treaty of Guadalupe Hidalgo, which resulted in the annexation by the United States of what is now California and parts of other Western states. Specifically, she notes how this work's depiction of California after the Mexican-American War forces issues of citizenship and nationhood. Anglos perceived the newly annexed population of non-white "racial other" to be a potential threat and corrupter of family. Tinnemeyer suggests a kind of racial cannibalism as a way in which these California whites consumed other groups' lands and expressed the savagery of Manifest Destiny. The idea of the cannibal in this case is not a colonized, indigenous people acting in defiance of the colonizer but rather the white settler who consumes the lives and identities (racial and cultural) of those he or she colonizes.

Shifting from the problematic racial identity of characters to the problematic racial identity of intended audience, Ariel Balter's essay, "The Color of Money in *The Autobiography of an Ex-Colored Man*," argues that James Weldon Johnson addresses middle-class, white America to reach them but also to critique them. Johnson's inevitable problem is the double-consciousness made acute and apparent in the case of the Ex-Colored Man who moves in and out of black and white racial groups. Balter argues that, throughout the novel, the meanings of race, sexuality, and economics vary according to the character's racial identity, and thus none of these issues can be discussed alone.

In "Passing as the 'Tragic Mulatto': Constructions of Hybridity in Toni Morrison's novels," AnnaMarie Christiansen addresses Toni Morrison's attempt to palliate African Americans' "double-consciousness," which Morrison accomplishes in part through a creative re-figuring of the tragic mulatto motif. Morrison's insistence upon subjectivity and validation of cultural exploration outside of the narrow options defined by the dominant white culture, Christiansen maintains, "becomes a space of creativity in which new identity is formed from cultural fragmentation." While mulattos tend to occupy ambiguous roles in Morrison's work, these minor characters become important when we examine how they become implicated through Morrison's construction of race within the communities she writes about. Christiansen argues that, despite society's efforts to place them in a static role, the mulatto figures in Morrison's work are no longer tragic as mulattos were often presented historically, but rather powerful as creators of their own narratives, pasts, and futures.

Jeffrey Partridge examines a different manifestation of hybridity: the ways in which the title character of Gish Jen's *Mona in the Promised Land* self-consciously constructs her own ethnic identity, resisting the confines of her racial categorization. Partridge argues that Jen's novel deconstructs the "literary Chinatown," in which works of Asian American writers are read variously as exotica, as attempts to regain a lost heritage, or as attempts to assimilate. Jen's Mona Chang creates an identity that Partridge believes "valorizes choice, change and creolization as phenomena that are part of the American experience." For example, the formation of Camp Gugelstein—the young characters' experiment in multiracial living—offers "the pan-ethnic interaction and its resultant multicultural hybridity . . . that provide a provocative re-visioning of race and ethnicity." Partridge believes the final scenes of the novel, in which Mona marries her Jewish lover Seth and considers changing her name to Changowitz—a hybridization of her own Chinese surname and a common Jewish suffix—symbolize her power to fashion her own "multicultural hybridity."

In contrast to this multicultural hybridity, an anti-Semitic, white-supremacist text, the so-called *Turner Diaries*, teaches us a great deal about the underpinnings of ethnic essentialism, according to Joe Lockard. Tracing the origins of William Pierce's racist novel (apparently an inspiration to Oklahoma City bomber Timothy McVeigh) to head-body discourses emerging from the Enlightenment, Lockard provocatively suggests that "the classical legacy of head-body discourses on race still flows powerfully beneath current American debates pertaining to race."

"Re-Contextualizing Race and Ethnicity: Texts in Historical and Political Perspective," the second section in this volume, shifts the discussion to the "real world" implications of American racial ideologies. Edwin J. McAllister uses anti-immigrant (primarily anti-Chinese) fiction from the Western frontier to demonstrate how literature can illuminate the enigmatic and irrational fears harbored by Americans long gone. In his study of turn-of-the-century fiction, McAllister shows that guilt over the genocide of American Indians transferred whites' animosity to the newly arriving Chinese. From stirring fear of smallpox infection to raising an alarmist specter of a Chinese takeover of the United States, these texts lead us to re-examine how race informs our understanding of Western history.

Author Georgina Dodge argues that two twentieth-century autobiographies by Americans of color, Etsu Sugimoto's *A Daughter of the Samurai* and Ernesto Galarza's *Barrio Boy*, challenge both the myth that all immigrant stories are like white immigrant stories and the recent scholarship in autobiography studies. Rather than narratives of assimilation, the autobiographies she studies show that for racially-identified immigrants, "the story of becoming American is one of negotiating individual and community identities within racist culture," Dodge writes. She asserts that despite the myth of immigrant assimilation, race often forms an unacknowledged barrier to immigrants of color.

Tracy Floreani also takes a comparative approach, showing how Gwendolyn Brooks's novel, *Maud Martha*, and the television situation comedy, *I Love Lucy*, variously depict consumerism after World War II and how ethnic identity and class inform consumer desires. Focusing on parallel scenes of childbirth in these two texts, Floreani contrasts the experiences of the African American character Maud, with her intensely realistic, vivid childbirth reverberating through the neighborhood, and middle-class, white Lucy, whose childbirth takes place behind closed doors, packaged and delivered for the viewing public to consume.

Moving from textual analysis to larger issues of theory and criticism, Part 3 begins with William Over's essay on the ways whiteness theory illuminates readings of African American drama—and how those dramas reveal flaws in contemporary whiteness theory. Like the construction of other "races," the construction of whiteness has profoundly inscribed American history, as well as the literature that attempts to reflect and make sense of that history.[13] Over argues that modern black dramatists recognize "that the reified division of racial identities must give way to a genuinely historical and dialectical approach to the representation of race." Not bound by guilt or hegemony so closely linked to the monolithic race divisions of the past, they see beyond an objectification of race and a deterministic future. Knowledge and identity have become contextual and complex, and thus permeable.

Similarly using literature to critique theory, Alexandra W. Schultheis's reading of Darryl Pinckney's *High Cotton* points out serious inadequacies in applying psychoanalytic literary theory to texts with sensibilities outside a white mainstream. Focusing specifically on the uses and limitations of pscyhoanalysis in addressing African American masculine subjectivity, Schultheis finds the novel's greatest contribution to be its struggle between dangerous reification of patriarchy and racial categorization on one hand and progressive recognition of the power of those metaphors on the other.

Derek Parker Royal, concerned to articulate postmodernism and ethnic studies, proposes a revision of the Jewish American literary canon. Against claims that recent Jewish American writing lacks the potency of the generation of Mailer and Bellow, Royal argues that postmodern Jewish American texts, such as those by Stanley Elkin, Cynthia Ozick, and Philip Roth, invigorate both Jewish American literature and ethnic American literature more broadly. Their struggles with ethnic identity—fluid and problematic rather than established and firm—reflect not a failing but a modernization of Jewishness in America, renewing its relevancy for the new century.

Bringing diverse texts and perspectives to bear on Du Bois's classic concept of "double-consciousness," Sheree Meyer, Chauncey Ridley, and Olivia Castellano explore how an individual learns to live within the tensions of his or her cultural context. By bringing into conversation with one another Pearl Abraham's *The Romance Reader*, Rudolfo Anaya's *Bless Me, Ultima*, and Zora Neale Hurston's *Their Eyes Were Watching God*, the authors study each protagonist's attempt to resolve those tensions. They find that each protagonist ultimately rejects the imposition of double-consciousness in favor of a personal and individualized identity, reflecting the authors' own experiences in their collaboration.

Finally, José L. Torres-Padilla examines how postmodern gestures like hybridity (discussed by Christiansen and Partridge, for example), which so often lead to resistant and interestingly complicated identities, sometimes fail. He argues that one such text, the well-received *Yo-Yo Boing!* by Giannina Braschi, falters in its code-switching between the Spanish and English of New York's Puerto Rican community. Rather than creating a synthetic and resistant hybridization of cultures, languages, and identities, Braschi creates portraits of characters and communities that "yo-yo" between, but do not progressively transcend, the two cultures, ultimately preserving the status quo. Torres-Padilla's analysis reminds us that postmodernism's promise for fresh, unoppressive constructions of ethnicity is no guarantee of liberating art or criticism.

Neither the authors represented in this volume nor its editors would suggest that this collection represents an exhaustion of, or a conclusion to, scholarly dialogues on race, ethnicity, and American texts. Rather, to the contrary, we hope that we have created a more complicated picture of the necessarily complex ways in which race and ethnicity interact with American texts of all sorts. Indeed, we hope that the ideas presented herein lead readers to feel less certain, less easy, and more careful and circumspect about their own understandings of "race" and "ethnicity" as concepts. Those of us who love literature know its power to shake, at least occasionally, our faith in what we think we know. In an era in which those socially constructed taxonomies play out in genuine material struggles in the United States and around the world, dialogues like the ones represented in this book grow increasingly crucial.

Notes

1. Although the problematic and fluctuating definitions of "race" and "ethnicity" are precisely the motivation for this volume, for simplicity we here

use "ethnicity" to denote the voluntary self-description of individuals who, because of shared experiences or perceived common backgrounds, consider themselves a definable group. We use "race" to denote the principally exclusionary, socially-imposed categorizations of individuals based upon characteristics ascribed to them principally in association with physical markers, such as skin color. We discuss these terms further in this introductory essay.

2. See also her classic text, *White Women, Race Matters* (1993), in which she persuasively argues what should have been obvious to all of us: race shapes not only the lives of women of color, but also of white women.

3. Montagu's classic book not only remains in print, but now is in its sixth edition.

4. Toni Morrison persuasively argues in *Playing in the Dark* (1993) that American literary history, just like American history itself, cannot be understood without considering the profound but largely unacknowledged role of race.

5. Appiah, "The Uncompleted Argument: Du Bois and the Illusion of Race."

6. Human beings' remarkable capacity to maintain even simultaneous, contradictory stereotypes about racial groups—e.g., blacks are both lazy and violent; Asians are both sneaky and passive—lends credence to the notion of cognitive dissonance.

7. See, for example, Delgado and Stefancic, eds., *Critical Race Theory* (2000).

8. For an illuminating catalogue of some of these privileges, see Peggy McIntosh's widely-cited essay, "White Privilege and Male Privilege," available in several essay collections, including *Race, Class, and Gender*, edited by Andersen and Collins.

9. Nathan Glazer, Daniel Patrick Moynihan, and Milton Gordon number among those who exemplify this perspective, although not always in the same manner.

10. Throughout this volume, we use "United States" to refer specifically to the nation-state, and the more ambiguous "America" to refer to the imagined land of the people who call themselves Americans. These terms resist firm definitions.

11. Ruoff and Ward, eds., *Redefining American Literary History* (1990), exemplifes the best of these. See Palumbo-Liu, ed., *The Ethnic Canon* (1995), for excellent analyses of sometimes separate, sometimes integrated canons of "ethnic" American literature (as if there is an American literature that is not "ethnic").

12. "Hybridity," going well beyond the idea of miscegenation with which Americans have been obsessed for centuries, now carries varying meaning in postcolonial studies, cultural studies, diaspora studies, postmodernism, and even the science fiction idea of the cyborg. For a remarkably thorough and useful discussion of the development of competing ideas of hybridity, see Hutnyk, "Hybridity." For an enlightening critique of the hybridity concept, focusing on England but useful for Americanists, too, see Young, *Colonial Desire: Hybridity in Theory, Culture and Race* (1995). Kawash follows up, in *Dislocating the Color Line: Identity, Hybridity, and Singularity in African-American Narrative* (1997), noting that the hybridity concept bears the problem of being associated historically with the socially feared "problem" of miscegenation. Moreover, Kawash points out that "the very notion of hybridity is already predicated on conditions named by the essentializing division it seeks to counter, that is, the color line" (5).

13. For example, as Jacobson argues in *Whiteness of a Different Color* (1998), Jews and other European immigrants were, for economic, social, and political reasons, considered outside the white race until the middle decades of the twentieth century, when racial politics shifted to a sharper "black" and "white" distinction, whereupon Jews "became" white.

Works Cited

Appiah, Anthony. "The Uncompleted Argument: Du Bois and the Illusion of Race." *"Race," Writing, and Difference.* Ed. Henry Louis Gates, Jr. Chicago: University of Chicago Press, 1986. 21–37.

Delgado, Richard, and Jean Stefancic, eds. *Critical Race Theory: The Cutting Edge.* 2nd ed. Philadelphia: Temple University Press, 2000.

Frankenberg, Ruth, ed. *Displacing Whiteness: Essays in Social and Cultural Criticism.* Durham, NC: Duke University Press, 1997.

———. *White Women, Race Matters: The Social Construction of Whiteness.* Minneapolis: University of Minnesota Press, 1993.

hooks, bell. *Black Looks: Race and Representation.* Boston: South End, 1992.

Hutnyk, John. "Hybridity." *Ethnic and Racial Studies* 28.1 (Jan. 2005): 79–102.

Jacobson, Matthew Frye. *Whiteness of a Different Color: European Immigrants and the Alchemy of Race.* Cambridge, MA: Harvard University Press, 1998.

Kawash, Samira. *Dislocating the Color Line: Identity, Hybridity, and Singularity in African-American Narrative.* Stanford, CA: Stanford University Press, 1997.

Lee, Rachel C. *The Americas of Asian American Literature: Gendered Fictions of Nation and Transnation.* Princeton, NJ: Princeton University Press, 1999.

McIntosh, Peggy. "White Privilege and Male Privilege: A Personal Account of Coming to See Correspondences through Work in Women's Studies." *Race, Class, and Gender: An Anthology.* 4th ed. Ed. Margaret L. Andersen and Patricia Hill Collins. Belmont, CA: Wadsworth, 2001. 95–105.

McKee, Patricia. *Producing American Races: Henry James, William Faulkner, Toni Morrison.* Durham, NC: Duke University Press, 1999.

Montagu, Ashley. *Man's Most Dangerous Myth: The Fallacy of Race.* 6th ed. Walnut Creek, CA: AltaMira Press, 1997.

Morrison, Toni. *Playing in the Dark: Whiteness and the Literary Imagination.* New York: Vintage, 1993.

Omi, Michael, and Howard Winant. *Racial Formation in the United States: From the 1960s to the 1990s.* 2nd edition. New York: Routledge, 1994.

Palumbo-Liu, David, ed. *The Ethnic Canon: Histories, Institutions, and Interventions.* Minneapolis: University of Minnesota Press, 1995.

Rasmussen, Birgit Brander, Eric Klinenberg, Irene J. Nexica, and Matt Wray, eds. *The Making and Unmaking of Whiteness.* Durham, NC: Duke University Press, 2001.

Ruoff, A. LaVonne Brown, and Jerry W. Ward, Jr., eds. *Redefining American Literary History.* New York: MLA, 1990.

Singh, Amritjit and Peter Schmidt, eds. *Postcolonial Theory and the United States: Race, Ethnicity, and Literature.* Jackson: University Press of Mississippi, 2000.

Sollors, Werner, and Maria Diedrich. *The Black Columbiad: Defining Moments in African American Literature and Culture.* Cambridge, MA: Harvard University Press, 1994.

White, Hayden. *Metahistory: The Historical Imagination in Nineteenth-Century Europe.* Baltimore: Johns Hopkins University Press, 1973.

Young, Robert J. C. *Colonial Desire: Hybridity in Theory, Culture and Race.* New York: Routledge, 1995.

I

Re-Constructing Race and Ethnicity:
Identity Imposed or Adopted

1 Citizenship Rights and Colonial Whites

The Cultural Work of María
Amparo Ruiz de Burton's Novels

JESSE ALEMÁN

N 1856, THE CAPTAIN OF SAN DIEGO'S MILITARY post headed out to Temecula, California, after hearing rumors that Cahuilla Indians under Juan Antonio and Luiseños under Manuelito Cota had gathered to organize against Indian taxation, inept Indian Agents, and the threat posed by Anglo squatters. The San Diegans were still reeling from the Antonio Garra uprising and feared another revolt led by Juan Antonio, so the U.S. captain made the trek to Temecula to keep the natives in check. The captain listened to the Indian complaints but afterwards warned Juan Antonio that he and his men "would be punished if they caused difficulties. . . . [S]ix hundred well-armed men, with plenty cannon, could be brought against him immediately" if Antonio did not return to his village (Phillips 133). Antonio did, only to receive another visit from the captain after Mormons attempted to incite the Cahuillas into a conflict with the anti-Mormon Americans who continued neglecting Indian affairs. He warned Antonio again: "you will mind your own business, and keep your people quiet and peaceable. I will come to see you again soon. The government is watching you, and if you do wrong you will be punished" (qtd. in Phillips 153). Apparently, the captain's paternalistic intimidation worked. Juan Antonio never led his revolt, though whites remained suspicious of him until he died of smallpox. The U.S. captain, by the way, was Henry S. Burton, husband of the Californiana novelist, María Amparo Ruiz de Burton.

Along with many of her Californio contemporaries, most notably Mariano G. Vallejo, María Amparo Ruiz de Burton registered her opposition to Anglo colonization of the Southwest through the memory of displacement, but unlike other Californios, Ruiz de Burton's brand of resistance came in the form of two novels, *Who Would Have Thought It?* (1872) and *The Squatter and the Don* (1885). The fact that her two works remained relatively unnoticed in American literary studies for over one hundred years speaks to Ruiz de Burton's exclusion from American literary history and more generally to the marginalization of Mexican Americans in the construction of American history. The recent republication of her novels thus redresses the historical erasure of Mexican Americans in the nineteenth century, and it would not be an exaggeration to say that these novels both shake to its foundation the American literary tradition and its attendant narrative of nationhood. While *Who Would Have Thought It?* questions the cultural, literary, and moral centrality of the American Northeast, for instance, *The Squatter and the Don*, published a year after Helen Hunt Jackson's *Ramona* (1884), challenges the Northeast's colonial and literary appropriation of the West. As it is, unabashed literary critiques of Anglo America rarely find their way into the annals of U.S. literary history, and it does not help that Ruiz de Burton's novels decenter the imaginary geopolitical heart of the nation by exposing the cultural hypocrisy of the North. Compound her social critique with her social position as a Californiana and the reasons for her obscurity in American literary history begin to add up.[1]

Because of its critical perspective on U.S. nation-building, it is tempting to read her work as part of a genealogy of Chicana literature. But Ruiz de Burton's life and work cannot be easily cast as proto-Chicana, as José Aranda, Jr., has pointed out. She was, after all, a landed Californiana, whose marriage to Captain Henry S. Burton following the Mexican American War situated her in an ambiguous position between Californio elite, the upstart Yankees, and California's Native American population, as her husband's short trip to Temecula suggests. So, even though the republication of her novels by Rosaura Sánchez and Beatrice Pita bodes well for Chicano/a literary studies, both narratives nevertheless play out problematic ethno-racial romances that claim white racial identity for Californios at the expense of nonwhite racial Others, Native Americans and blacks in particular. *Who Would Have Thought It?*, for instance, recounts the story of Lola Medina, who, after being born into Indian captivity and dyed dark, becomes increasingly white as the narrative progresses, and *The Squatter and the Don* makes a more explicit case for racial assimilation as it concludes with the marriage between Mercedes Alamar, a Californinana, and Clarence Darrell, an Anglo. Both novels, in other words, actively participate in the belief of many Californio elites that they could profit from Anglo economic and cultural expansion into California in much the same way Californios profited from Spanish and Mexican colonization of Indian lands. Such is the paradox of Ruiz de Burton's work: it challenges the Anglocentricism of Northeastern America by arguing that upper-class Californios are white.[2] No wonder her novels have yet to find a place in literary studies. They scramble the otherwise clearly constructed ethno-racial lines that frame and separate American and Chicano/a literary histories.

Indeed, Ruiz de Burton's novels reveal the lengths to which landed Californios were willing to travel to secure, and perhaps even improve, their social position in response to the nineteenth-century's shifting racial code, but there is nevertheless something radical in Ruiz de Burton's re-figuring of whiteness in the U.S. to include Hispano identity, since, with this repositioning, her novels emphasize whiteness as a construct historically contingent on legal positioning, regional location, and class status. In other words, whiteness comes into a crisis in Ruiz de Burton's narratives as they imagine Hispano racial whiteness but also emphasize the cultural difference between Hispanos and Anglos, especially in the context of Spanish and Anglo American colonialism. In contrast to the vulgar materialism of Anglo expansion, backed by racist Northerners, a corrupt, secularized government, and a national obsession with industry, Ruiz de Burton's novels imagine Hispano colonial identity as a more culturally refined whiteness that deserves to profit from Manifest Destiny but does not deserve its social stain. With her claim to racial whiteness, Ruiz de Burton shows that Hispanos are not like Indians and Mexicans, but with her claim to cultural difference, she shows that Hispanos are not like Anglos either. She puts her novels to cultural work, then, to narrate the contradictory historical emergence of white Hispano ethnicity in the U.S.'s imaginary citizenship, a citizenship status built in contrast to Anglo America but ultimately (per)formed at the expense of non-white racial Others.

Given the tenuous relationship between racial identity, citizenship status, and land-ownership rights following the Mexican American War, Ruiz de Burton's construction of Mexican whiteness is a characteristic response to the colonial conditions in California. Many Californios emphasized their *sangre azul*, their pure, "blue" Spanish blood, as a way of distinguishing their regional, Californio identity from the rest of Mexico's mestizo citizenry as well as from California's Indian population (Haas 37). After enjoying the privileged class status Spanish colonialism and Mexican neocolonialism afforded them, Californio *criollos* found their social, racial, and economic position in California on the decline after 1848. The nation's industrial reconstruction following the Civil War only compounded their problems, since it brought California's pastoral economy to an end and precipitated the relegation of Californios to a wage-labor class previously occupied by mestizo and Indian workers. As Albert Camarillo explains, "Mexican men, women, and children were initially drawn into the Anglo labor market when traditional pastoral occupations began to disappear during the 1870s. By the 1880s, as other working-class sectors left the community and as the expanding local economy increasingly necessitated a large pool of cheap labor, Chicanos entered the market en masse" (78). California's economy shifted from pastoral to industrial because landownership shifted from Californios to Anglo Americans, with the help of the 1851 Land Law's challenge to Spanish/Mexican land titles. To add further insult to injury, the 1855 Vagrancy Act, commonly known as the "Greaser Act," pauperized Californios by forcing "idle" Mexicans—namely those who could not find work—to a pay a vagrancy fine in cash or through indentured labor. The seemingly secure status of "white" citizenship conferred onto Mexican men at the 1849 California Constitutional Convention, in other words, rapidly gave way to other white men claiming citizenship and land rights in the West, Anglo Americans. By 1870, Camarillo concludes, "the Spanish-surname work force was steadily becoming a downwardly mobile, unskilled, displaced working class" (86).

The 1849 Convention, however, did save the Californios from being treated as poorly as Native Americans. Californio delegates insured the social status of white Mexican men at the expense of women and Native Americans whose non-white racial identity, the Convention unanimously concluded, excluded Indians from enjoying full citizenship rights in the state. Certainly, landed Californios must have tasted the bitter irony of the 1855 Vagrancy Act, considering many of them had previously supported and profited from a similar act targeting Native Americans. Indeed, the 1850 Indenture Act picked up where the Spanish mission and Californio rancho systems left off by allowing local governments to hire out as involuntary indentured servants any Native American or mestizo arrested for vagrancy. Never mind that most Native Americans were "vagrant" in urban areas because they were displaced from their rural locations, the Indenture Act ostensibly created a slave-labor system that, besides providing a cheap labor source, maintained the residual hierarchy between Californios and Native Americans. As Tomás Almaguer puts it, the legal use of indentured Indian servants was the remaining signal that Californios, despite their tenuous status in the state, still held a social position above Native Americans (a delusory belief at best, considering Californios fell victim to the Greaser Act five years later). With the enactment of the Indenture Act, Almaguer explains, Indians "remained in the grasp of the Mexican rancho system where they labored in a state of debt peonage and virtual slavery. Indians were also continually victimized by both Mexican and Anglo slave traffickers, who kidnapped and sold upwards of four thousand Indian children to Mexican ranchers and Anglo settlers between 1852 and 1867" (149).

As with much of the Southwest, then, Californios and Anglos competed for political and economic power during the state's shifting colonial status, with Native Americans bearing the brunt of the colonial conflict, and Ruiz de Burton novels in particular enact California's colonial contradiction, a contradiction that responds to Californio dispossession at the hands of Anglo American colonialism by invoking a legacy of Spanish/Mexican colonial whiteness that positions the Mexican American gentry above Indians and blacks. Published in Philadelphia in 1872, *Who Would Have Thought It?* raises fundamental questions about what it means to be American and, more specifically, what it means to be white in the United States, a theme made more significant considering the book's place of publication. Set mainly in the Northeast during the Civil War and Reconstruction, but including significant narrative events in the Southwest during the Mexican American War, two intersecting narrative plots shape the novel's overall geo-racial cartography. First, the novel recounts the coming-of-age of Lola Medina, a wealthy Mexican American orphan born in Indian captivity, raised in New England by the Norvals, and eventually re-united with her father in Mexico, where she stays, happily ever after, once her Yankee lover, Julian Norval, joins her. While Lola comes of age, the novel also covers the rise and fall of Mrs. Norval, the cruel republican mother who treats Lola miserably, plots against Mr. Norval to exploit Lola's wealth, and, in the process, falls into an affair with the Reverend Hackwell, until the matron finally succumbs to brain fever.

Of course, as with most historical romances, *Who Would Have Thought It?* has its share of contrived plots, melodramatic moments, stock characters, and crucial misunderstandings that help or hinder the narrative's multiple marriage plots. It is no coincidence, however, that the touchstones of Ruiz de Burton's satire are Northerners who have fallen from republican grace. Early in the narrative, for instance, Mrs. Cackle, a provincial New Englander, literally and figuratively recounts the complex legacy of conquest in the West as she gives voice to the brand of jingoistic patriotism at the center of the novel's social critique:

> "To me they are all alike—Indians, Mexicans, or Californians—they are all horrid. But my son Beau says our just laws and smart lawyers will soon *'freeze them out.'* That as soon as we take their lands from them they will never be heard of anymore, and then the Americans, with God's help, will have all the land that was righteously acquired through a just war and a most liberal payment of money." (11)

Never mind their own differences based on region, cultural practices, colonial history, nationalism(s), or racial caste categories (to name a few), Mrs. Cackle has no problem literally homogenizing Indians, Mexicans, and Californios. They are simply "horrid." The order in which she lists these groups is likewise important: "Indians, Mexicans, and Californians" figuratively recounts the actual order of conquest as a result of Anglo westward expansion. Moreover, even though she recognizes westward expansion as a literal legal process and capitalistic venture, she nevertheless upholds the figurative construction of expansion as divine Manifest Destiny—God willed it; Yankees bought it. Mrs. Cackle, in other words, expresses the mainstream racist and colonialist logic promulgated by many Northerners during the nation's most rapid period of expansion.

But if Mrs. Cackle is unsympathetic to the plight of Indians, Mexicans, or Californios, she is herself treated unsympathetically in the novel, as her name suggests. Indeed, the novel goes to great lengths to disprove Mrs. Cackle's account, hoping to show instead that "the natives" of Spanish decent, as the narrative often describes them, are not at all like those "horrid" Indians or Mexicans Mrs. Cackle imagines. Hispanos, the novel argues, are civilized whites, an argument that certainly "turn[s] the Anglo American racial aesthetic on its head," as Anne Goldman puts it (62). Take the problem of Lola Medina's racial identity. Born in Indian captivity in the Southwest around 1847 and dyed dark, Lola's arrival in the North undoubtedly marks a moment when the margins converge onto the center of western expansion to undermine its racial codes. Indian, black, or white European are the only categories the New Englanders have to identify Lola's racial ambiguity. Her dark skin signifies "blackness" to the group, but Lola's "well-cut" nose, lips, and "superb" eyes, along with her white palms, convince Mattie Norval otherwise (17). Her red shawl and reticence, moreover, signal "Indian" to the group, since, as Lavinia Sprig puts it, "Indians are as proud and surly as they are treacherous" (20). Her manners and fluency in English, however, mark her as white European, at least according to Dr. Norval, while her full name—María Dolores Medina—highlights her as a "foreigner" in New England. In other words, within their geo-racial paradigms, the Northerners cannot conceptualize a dark-skinned body with claims to racial whiteness in the U.S., a historical problem Lola herself represents in the narrative as she introduces the New Englanders to the reality of *mestizaje* in the U.S. following the Mexican American War.

And the newly created Mexican American population was indeed a problem for Anglo America during and after the War. In fact, most historians of the Mexican American War agree that the U.S. did not pursue the "all of Mexico movement," which had wide support from Northern industrialists, Western (Mississippi valley region) expansionist, and Southern slave interests, primarily because the U.S. government did not want to grant citizenship to Mexico's roughly eight million mestizos, and because the Wilmont Proviso prohibited slavery in Mexican territory. "The addition of a people alien 'in language and race, in habits, usages and associations' would only be 'repugnant' to Americans and contrary to the spirit of their institutions," John Schroeder explains, citing an 1847 Whig editorial (123–24). Instead of eight million, the Treaty of Guadalupe Hidalgo turned eighty thousand Mexican citizens into Americans, but for some Americans, like Florida Representative Edward C. Cabell, eighty thousand mestizos were enough to threaten the U.S.'s race-based definitions of citizenship. "And shall we, . . . by an act of congress," Cabell asked in 1848, "convert the black, white, red, mongrel, miserable population of Mexico—the Mexicans, Indians, Mulattoes, Mestizos, Chinos, Zambos, Quinteros—into free and enlightened American citizens, entitled to all privileges which we enjoy?" (qtd. in Horsman 242–43).

At least on a symbolic level, then, the circumstances of Lola's birth mark her as one of the eighty thousand Mexican American citizens who, after 1848, found themselves "orphans" in the U.S.[3] The expansion of the U.S.'s borders, though, also means the expansion of the nation's racial codes, and through the story of Lola Medina, Ruiz de Burton stretches the definition of whiteness in the U.S. to include Hispano identity. Going from black to white, and seen as Indian and Spanish, Lola passes through various stages of racial identity—black, Indian, brown, "spotted" white, and, finally, "pure" white. Lola's racial ambiguity thus draws on two competing racial codes: an Anglo American one that defines race as white or black, and a Spanish/Mexican caste system that recognizes multiple levels of hybrid racial identity. Of course, the narrative's project emphasizes Lola's "pure" whiteness, but as Lisabeth Haas explains, in colonial Spanish America, "whiteness was . . . not a singular or static category but included a range of color. 'White' lineage could be purchased from the crown with gold or other goods through a decree called *gracias al sacar* (thanks to be taken out, removed, or freed)" (31). In this sense, perhaps much to the fear of Senator Cabell, the transformation of Lola's racialized body situates her—and the body of Hispanos she represents—within the U.S.'s imaginary citizenship by replacing the U.S.'s black/white racial paradigm with the Spanish/Mexican process of *gracias al sacar*, suggesting that all of Mexico's "miserable population" has the potential to become white citizens.[4]

But the potential for Lola's racial and cultural whiteness rests on the racialization of Others. The richer Lola gets, for instance, the whiter she gets, leading Emma Hackwell to comment enviously, "I think Lola might teach us the secret of that Indian paint that kept her white skin under cover, making it whiter by bleaching it" (232). The secret is Spanish/ Mexican colonialism in North America. After all, Lola and her mother are dyed dark because they are Indian captives, and even though the Mexican American War indeed made Mexican citizens vulnerable to native attacks, as José Aranda has observed, not just any Mexican citizens were targeted. The Indians carry Doña Theresa off her Sonoran hacienda, emphasizing the intersecting colonial conflicts that make up the "secret" of Lola's Indian paint: the U.S.'s expansion into Mexico displaced Mexican landowners and made them vulnerable to Native American attacks, but indigenous groups attacked landholders such as Doña Theresa in the first place precisely because they dispossessed Native Americans of their land and natural resources.

The history behind Lola's wealth, in fact, bears this point out, since her money comes directly from her mother's use of Indian labor to mine native resources. Dr. Norval explains:

> "She picked it up, and, as she had some knowledge of precious stones, she saw it was a large diamond, though only partly divested of its rough coating. Then, she looked about for similar pebbles, and found many more. . . . Afterwards the Indians brought her emeralds and rubies, seeing that she liked pretty pebbles. Thus she made a fine collection, for she took only the largest and those which seemed to her most perfect." (28)

Enacting in miniature the history of Spanish colonization of the Americas, Doña Theresa uses the wealth she gains from indigenous exploitation to rescue (*sacar*) Lola from the threat of Indian identity. And for Doña Theresa, this threat to Spanish "purity" is both biological and cultural. She implicitly fears the fate of Lola's sexual interaction with Indians, but she seems equally concerned with Lola's religious fate: "Thank God, Lolita is away from those horrid savages! Please do not forget that she must be baptized and brought up a Roman Catholic," she explains to Dr. Norval (36). As Californios put it in the nineteenth century, Doña Theresa wants Lola to grow up *gente de razón* instead of *gente sin razón*, the two opposing cultural markers that distinguished Spanish *criollos* from Native Americans, white citizens from dark-skinned laborers, in Spanish colonial California. The categories of *"de razón"* and *"sin razón,"* Lisabeth Haas explains, developed from sixteenth-century theological debates on whether or not Indians had souls and "were used inter-changeably with the ethnic and national categories *español* and *indio*, and in this sense implied an insurmountable divide between civilization and savagery" (31). In effect, Doña Theresa's Spanish/Mexican caste system replaces the racialist logic that Mrs. Cackle and the rest of the Yankees used to define their Anglo American identity in contrast to "horrid" Indians, Mexicans, and Californios. Indeed, indigenous labor eventually allows Lola to "purchase" her whiteness not from the Spanish crown, as was usually the case with the *gracias al sacar* process, but from Dr. Norval's Northern bankers, suggesting that Californio colonial mentality in the novel is actually quite akin to Anglo American colonialism when it comes to fashioning whiteness by racializing and oppressing Others.

While the confluence of religion and labor distinguishes Lola from the Indians, though, Catholicism itself is not the sole harbinger of white *"razón."* The narrative must still negotiate the anti-Catholicism of the Protestant Northeast, where the influx of Irish immigrants created a host of alternative Anglo American anxieties regarding "savagery." Thus, Ruiz de Burton must also work to distance white Mexican Catholics from the Irish Catholic maids Lola encounters in the Norval house. Relegated to the servant's quarters by Mrs. Norval, Lola would rather sleep on the floor outside of Dr. Norval's bedroom with the family dog than share a bed with one of the Irish servants: "Lola had refused to share the bed with either of the two servants, and both had resented the refusal as a most grievous insult. . . . Hannah, the chambermaid, was not so repulsive to look upon. Still, the thought of sharing her bed was to Lola very terrible" (30). Lola's cultural gentility cringes from having to share a room, let alone a bed, with Irish servants; she is after all the daughter of a Don. The Irish maids, however, with their broken English, dirty socks, "corrugated" knees, and loud snoring are obviously déclassé, racialized whites that, although meant as comic relief, put in relief the "natural," cultured whiteness hidden beneath Lola's dyed skin (31).

And this is exactly the dubious distinction Ruiz de Burton is making. As Noel Ignatiev argues, Irish immigrants learned to *become* white by making conscious political choices that collectively situated them within white supremacist discourses and practices. Labor politics and economic competition in particular, Ignatiev notes, created racial tension between Irish Americans and blacks in the U.S., ultimately leading many Irish Americans to support slavery as a way of protecting their own positions as wage laborers in free territories such as Boston and Philadelphia. In 1844, they helped elect President Polk, a Democrat who led the country to war with Mexico; they often contributed to the mobocracy of violent voting arenas to help maintain the slave state; and many Irish, according to Iganatiev, generally supported an ideology of "white solidarity" (77). This, Ignatiev concludes, is how the Irish "became" white—in an attempt to overcome the racism and anti-Catholicism they encountered in Anglo America, Irish Americans sought their economic and political stability at the expense of black freedom. "The vast majority [of Irish] clung to the Democratic Party," Ignatiev explains, "which continued to protect them from the nativists and guarantee them a favored position over those whom they regarded as the principal threat to their position, the free black people of the North (the only group as 'free' of either property or marketable skills as the Irish)" (87).

As servants in the Norval house, the Irish maids have thus secured a wage-labor status that distinguishes them from free blacks in the North, but, as laborers, they have yet to establish themselves fully as "whites" vis à vis the nouveau riche Norvals. Obviously, Lola out-classes them economically, culturally, and racially, as she does many of the Northerners in the narrative. Lola is already white, Ruiz de Burton would have us believe, and is just temporarily beset by her blackface; her grace, gentility, and language-use perform the "natural" whiteness beneath her dark skin. Of course, what the narrative conceals is its own formation of white Mexican identity. After all, much like the Irish, Californios had to reposition themselves as white in Anglo America to secure the country's real and imaginary citizenship rights. They did this by distinguishing themselves from Indians and blacks, whose status as indentured servants or slave laborers left them with no rights in the U.S. Californios also brokered on their class status, hoping that their material and cultural capital would buy them entry into the emerging Anglo nation. This class hierarchy ultimately informs the racial hierarchy that distinguishes Lola from the Norvals and the Irish maids. Lola's status as white depends on the degree to which she is economically distant from the Irish servants, and even though Mrs. Norval sees no difference between Lola's racialized status and the economic status of the servants, Lola, and the novel as a whole, find the comparison utterly repugnant. Rather, the Norvals and their Irish maids, the novel implies, have much to learn from Lola about being white.[5]

Blackness, though, is the prevailing anxiety of Ruiz de Burton's narrative about whiteness. Along with her class envy, Mrs. Norval, as with many of the book's Northerners, simply hates Lola because she looks black. "And would that little nigger be so rich, and her girls so poor?" Mrs. Norval thinks to herself (49). Put off by Lola's refusal to share her bed, the Irish cook likewise responds, "Niggers ain't my most particliest admirashun" (30). While Lola herself never utters such blatantly racist comments, she obviously regrets her dark skin, mainly because she rightly thinks Julian finds it unattractive: Explaining the "stain" of her skin, she tells Julian, "I wanted to tell you this many times, for though I didn't care whether I was thought black or white by others, I hated to think that *you* might suppose I was Indian or black" (100). While Lola's dark skin exposes the North's racism, it also reveals a peculiar Mexican racial anxiety for being categorized as Indian or black. In other words, Lola's blackface enacts the contradictory cultural logic of minstrelsy. Blackface performances in the nineteenth century, Eric Lott contends, reveal white, male working-class fears and desires of blackness that crossed racial boundaries while simultaneously reinforcing them in contradictory public displays of black cultural appreciation and appropriation. "What was on display in minstrelsy," Lott explains, "was less black culture than a structured set of white responses to it which had grown out of northern and frontier social rituals and were passed through an inevitable filter of racist presupposition" (101).

In the case of Lola's blackface, it undermines Anglo American racism but then replaces it with a Spanish/Mexican racial caste system that nevertheless situates whiteness as the highest identity marker. It thus resolves the fear of Californio racialization by enacting it and resolving it through a process of racialization that eventually positions Mexicans within the nation's white imagined community. Indeed, in much the same way minstrelsy eventually reinforced working-class white privilege, Ruiz de Burton aligns Mexicans with white Southerners not only to draw on the discourse of victimized whiteness, as David Luis-Brown notes (817–18), but to reconstruct whiteness altogether as an old world marker of cultured gentility. For Ruiz de Burton, low-down, scheming Anglo politicians and socialites determine the nation's modern political policies in the North, so the South, with its attendant racial codes, becomes the last bastion of national honor and old world order in the U.S. The narrative, for instance, valorizes the nameless Confederate soldier who befriends Isaac and eventually releases him from prison based on Isaac's promise "not to bear arms against the Confederacy" (191). The virtue, honesty, and trust the nameless Confederate soldier extends to Isaac contrasts sharply with the cowardice of the Cackles, the duplicity of Reverend Hackwell, and the political shenanigans of Congressmen Le Grand Gunn, who is responsible for Isaac's over-extended stay in the Southern prison camp in the first place. This might explain why the narrative conceals the harsh conditions of the prison camps in the South, as Sánchez and Pita point out (xxiii–xxvi). Short of being openly pro-Confederacy, the novel goes to great lengths to see the South as a victim of the North's liberal capitalism and politics. The plight of Dr. Norval makes this quite clear. A Northern Democrat, Dr. Norval finds himself run out of the country after he openly advocates an alternative to Southern succession and civil war. Representative of the Peace Democrats, Dr. Norval supports the Union but also sees the hypocrisy behind its claim to democratic liberty. He considers Lincoln's suspension of the Writ of Habeas Corpus as an infringement on the right to free speech and finds the racism behind Northern abolitionists, including his wife, doubly hypocritical, leading him to believe, as did many Southerners, that the government is securing the freedom of blacks at the expense of white citizenship rights. As Dr. Norval puts it when he explains his sympathy for Lola, "I—a good-for-nothing Democrat, who doesn't believe in Sambo but believe[s] in Christian charity and human mercy—I feel pity for the little thing" (18).

The absence of slavery in the novel more tellingly reveals the narrative's attempt to valorize the South. It is difficult to imagine why a novel set during the Civil War includes very little about slavery, unless of course, the issue of slavery raised problems for the novel's larger cultural work of re-imagining Mexican whiteness in opposition to Northern Anglo Saxonism. The novel may in fact eschew slavery to take on issues of national racism, but in the process, it re-circulates its own racist paradigms of blackness by aligning Hispano whiteness with the displaced white Southern identity. Take Caesar ("Sar" for short), for example, Ruiz de Burton's version of the "happy darky" who whistles "merrily" as he cleans "his master's pistols" (190). Besides simply offering dubious representations of blacks, Ruiz de Burton's narrative actively participates in the Reconstructionist myth that the old world order of the South, especially for blacks, was much better before the Civil War. Indeed, as Isaac finds "a friend in [the] rebel" soldier, he also gains Sar as a personal body servant: "Sprig did not find it necessary to tell Sar to go for the clothes. Sar had been an attentive listener to the officer's recital, and started off after him at a trot. 'Here, massa, put 'em on, for de Lo's sake, an' look like a gin'leman ag'in'" (190). Sar, in effect, re-makes Isaac into a Southern gentleman!

Her argument with the Colossus of the North, then, leads Ruiz de Burton to romanticize the South as a way of symbolically aligning the old world Hispano culture of the Southwest, built by the exploitation of Indian labor, land, and resources, with the South's old world traditions, which, of course, were built by slavery. In much the same way the Northerners in the novel define their civilized whiteness in contrast to those savagely "horrid" Indians, Mexicans, and Californians, Ruiz de Burton's novel constructs the civility of Hispano whiteness in contrast to Native Americans "savagery" and black slaves, repeating in effect the same racialist logic that displaced Hispanos themselves from the U.S.'s imaginary citizenship. We might even say this is the contradictory price for re-imagining the nation and expanding its racial cartography. With *Who Would Have Thought It?*, Ruiz de Burton deploys a scathing critique of the North, creating an imaginary socio-literary intervention that re-figures white Hispanos as the ideal American citizenry of republican beliefs that have since given over to Anglo American liberal self-interest. She in effect Mexicanizes the nation's social, racial, and literary cartography as a way of positioning Hispanos at the forefront of the nation's—indeed, the Americas'—formation, but positioning Hispanos within the nation means positioning Others without, as the novel's treatment of Native, Irish, and African Americans makes clear. Perhaps the greatest irony of the novel's social critique, then, is that it comes back on itself, despite the novel's attempt to forget the neo-colonial history and racism of Hispanos in the Southwest.

Enter Victoriano Alamar, son of the eponymous Don of *The Squatter and the Don* (1885), who says to his father, "I wish we were squatters"

(74). As a member of California's nineteenth-century Hispanic landed gentry, Victoriano laments the encroachment of Anglo squatters into California. He "wishes" he was a squatter because Anglo squatters, under the 1851 Land Law, legally dispossessed the Californios of their land ownership titles and, after parceling out the large Spanish/Mexican land tracts, "settled" California. Ironically, Victoriano, and *The Squatter and the Don* as a whole, seems to "forget" that the Alamars, and Californios in general, are themselves "squatters" on Indian-owned lands, which were parceled out into missions, presidios, pueblos, and ranchos and "settled" by the Spanish/Mexican government. As Benedict Anderson puts it, "All profound changes in consciousness, by their very nature, bring with them their characteristic amnesias. Out of such oblivions, in specific historical circumstances, spring narratives" (204). Victoriano's historical "amnesia" indeed highlights the "oblivion" caused by the "profound changes" in colonial consciousness that frame Ruiz de Burton's second novel, and perhaps the most significant cause of the novel's amnesia is the shifting relationship between racial identity and land laws in the nineteenth century. After all, Victoriano wishes he were a squatter because the squatters are Anglo, and as the novel goes to great lengths to prove, Californios such as the Alamars are indeed white.

As with *Who Would Have Thought It?*, then, *The Squatter and the Don* actively participates in the belief of Californio elite that they could profit from Anglo expansion into California, just as they profited from Spanish and Mexican colonization of Indian lands. Indeed, the novel as a whole makes an explicit case for racial assimilation as it concludes with the marriage between Mercedes Alamar, a Californiana, and Clarence Darrell, an Anglo. "Such a merger," Manuel M. Martín Rodríguez explains, "seem[s] to be the easiest way for the Californios to retain land and privileges in a changed social order" (44). However, the novel also reproduces the contradictory cultural critique of Ruiz de Burton's first narrative: it makes claims to racial whiteness to maintain the colonial distinction between Californios, Indians, and Mexicans, but it also creates a cultural distinction between the two competing forms of colonial identity in the novel, Californio whiteness and the whiteness of Anglo Americans. In fact, the narrative goes through a dual process of "forgetting" Spanish colonialism's own "stains" while re-figuring and refining Manifest Destiny itself to make it more appealing to the Californio colonial mentality.

For instance, when Don Mariano critiques the formation of the U.S. land commission and their distribution of land, he ironically draws a comparison between Californio colonialism and Anglo Manifest Destiny. As Don Mariano sees it, Congress formed the land commission because Anglo settlers could not stand the idea that only a few Californio families owned large tracts of California land. "Such good-for-nothing, helpless wretches are not fit to own such lordly tracts of land. It was wicked to tolerate the waste, the extravagance of the Mexican government, in giving such large tracts of land to a few individuals," Don Mariano explains, mimicking the racialist mentality behind the formation of the land commission (163). Yet, as he rightly points out, the land commission distributed "millions upon millions of acres of land" to privately-owned railroad companies (163). One colonial consciousness replaces another, Don Mariano shows, as the argument for industrial "prosperity" dispossesses the "lazy, thriftless, [and] ignorant" Californios of their land (162).

But out of this colonial shift springs Don Mariano's historical amnesia. Comparing Spanish land grants with the land commission's grants to the railroad industry, Don Mariano explains to Clarence:

> "Yes, but that was exactly the same motive which guided the Spanish and the Mexican governments—to give large tracts of land as an inducement to those citizens who would utilize the wilderness of the government domain—utilize it by starting ranchos which afterwards would originate 'pueblos' or villages, and so on. . . . The landowners were useful in many ways, though to a limited extent they attracted a population by employing white labor. They also employed Indians, who thus began to be less wild. Then in times of Indian outbreaks, the landowners with their servants would turn out as in feudal times in Europe, to assist in the defense of the missions and the sparsely settled country threatened by the savages. Thus, you see, that it was not a foolish extravagance, but a judicious policy which induced the viceroys and Spanish governors to begin the system of large land grants." (163)

Rhetorically, Don Mariano reverses the usual stereotypes that distinguish Spanish/Mexican colonialism's "foolish extravagance" from the virtuous industriousness of Anglo America's Manifest Destiny. Spanish/

Mexican land grants had a moral and social purpose, the Don argues; Anglo Manifest Destiny, however, is a morally bankrupt obsession with industry. Of course, Don Mariano neglects to mention how missions functioned as panopticons of colonial discipline and punishment, as Lisabeth Haas shows (19–29). He likewise forgets about the clashes between Spanish missionaries and second generation Californios, who, by 1821, Sánchez reminds us, espoused the liberal rationalist arguments of the day as a way of securing and secularizing mission land grants after Mexico gained its independence from Spain (*Telling Identities* 96–141). Most importantly, though, he sweeps under the carpet of Californio coloniality the wholesale dispossession and enslavement of Native Americans. He hints at it—after all, why are there "Indian outbreaks"? But for the most part, Don Mariano suffers from a historical amnesia, one that results from his attempt to align his racial rights to landownership with Manifest Destiny without necessarily aligning himself with the colonial culture of Anglo materialism.

The neocolonial business venture Don Mariano proposes to the Anglo squatters on his land, one of his many (failed) ventures in *The Squatter and the Don*, by the way, likewise shows the Don's attempt to profit from a more refined version of Manifest Destiny. As he sees it, Anglo colonization would be profitable for squatters and Californios alike if they exploited California's natural resources for raising cattle and growing fruit, so Don Mariano offers the squatters a homestead on his land as long as they agree to raise cattle, grow fruit, or fence their grain, despite the "no fence law" (91). Indeed, "no fence law" distinguishes Don Mariano's form of colonialism from the colonial culture of the Anglo squatters: their land occupation is unproductive, wasteful, and, according to Don Mariano's argument, "unnatural," since cattle cannot read the no fence law in the first place, and in the second, grain is not native to California. Don Mariano's version of Manifest Destiny, though, proves to be culturally productive for everyone. He gets his large land tract "cultivated" and "civilizes" the squatters in the process by ensuring them a homestead, a livelihood, and, of course, interest-free loans on cattle or wood (88–9).

But there is no civilizing the squatters, as Matthews exclaims, "I ain't no '*vaquero*' to go '*busquering*' around and *lassoing* cattle" (89). Ironically, neither is Don Mariano. "I don't go '*busquering*' around *lassoing*, unless

I want to," the Don explains, "You can hire an Indian boy to do that part" (89). So goes Don Mariano's neocolonial venture, which rests on two fundamental differences. Culturally, it distinguishes white Californios from Anglo squatters, who are too self-centered and provincial to capitalize on the Don's plan; racially, however, it distinguishes the Californios and Anglos from the Indians, on whose back the labor of the Don's plan fully rests. Land-owning Indians simply are not an option in the Don's plan; instead, the Don seeks to transfer the use value of Indian labor from the Mexican rancho system to the Anglo American homestead. His venture thus repeats in miniature the race-based codes of land ownership and labor that denied Indians their civic and property rights after 1848 and relegated them to a class of indentured servants. Certainly, as John M. González says, the Don's plan proves that "Californios traded upon their status as an elite class in post-1848 California to construct a peace structure that at some fundamental political level granted them rights and privileges as white citizens, and that these political concessions resulted in real material advantages from the resultant control of indigenous and mestizo labor" (36).

And as the mediating act between Californios and Anglos, the marriage between Clarence Darrell and Mercedes Alamar ultimately bridges the gap between two colonial mentalities. Their marriage affirms the whiteness of Californio identity, but, unlike his father, Clarence is no Anglo squatter. Rather, he is a white settler, which is quite a different thing altogether, the novel would have us believe. So it is quite fitting that Clarence's land, money, and cattle rarely materialize in the novel, even though, by the end of the narrative, he is the one with the most material wealth. He wants to keep a secret the land he purchases from the Don—that is, immaterial. Via a telegraph order, Clarence's investor purchases the farm on which the Darrells first lived, after its owner loses heavily in stocks, but that farm never appears in the narrative (142). He likewise purchases Arizona mines through his investor, but the mines, their laborers, or previous owners remain suspiciously absent in the narrative as well, and when Clarence uses his own capital to open a bank, he appoints George Mechlin as the bank's president and Gabriel Alamar as its teller. Even Clarence's money is immaterial, since he invests much of it in stocks and rarely handles his own financial transactions, which explains why he must receive occasional updates from his investor, Hubert Haverly. And when he does make his own purchases, the cattle he buys from Don Mariano literally disappear in the snow (301) while the Alamars symbolically disappear off of their own land grant after Clarence buys it from Doña Josefa (332).

In effect, the immateriality of Clarence's material possessions highlights perhaps the most profound form of narrative amnesia: the novel tries to forget that Clarence is an Anglo profiting from Manifest Destiny. Instead, the narrative consolidates the privileges of Clarence's racial whiteness with the cultural whiteness of Californios as a way of arguing for their sociocultural position above Anglo squatters. "Only remember, the Darrells are not squatters," the Don admonishes his family, and yet the narrative would like to forget that Clarence makes out quite well with the Don's daughter, cattle, and land; he simply does it with a little more finesse (110). The marriage between Clarence and Mercedes thus reconstructs whiteness, changing it from an Anglo identity marker to a Californio one, which allows the novel as a whole to make an argument for Californio citizenship rights based on their white cultural capital. Indeed, several other marriages likewise consolidate Californio culture with genteel Anglo capital in strategic geo-racial alliances that connect the Southwest with the Northeast's most refined Anglo entrepreneurs and the South's myth of white gentility. As with Clarence Darrell, Mr. Mechlin purchases a homestead on the Don's land, and, as if to symbolize the economic merger between Californio lands and Northern banks, George Mechlin marries Elvira Alamar and Gabriel Alamar marries Elizabeth Mechlin in a "double loop" ceremony that binds the North and the Southwest in two harmonious marriages twice securing the economic stability of the Alamar family while allowing the Mechlins a way of entering California's residual ruling class (115).[6] To be sure, intermarriage between Californios and Anglos, Leonard Pitt explains, "made the Yankee conquest [of California] smoother than it might otherwise have been" (125), and Ruiz de Burton's own marriage to Captain Henry S. Burton following the Mexican American War may in fact prove Pitt right. But the marriage between Gabriel Alamar and Lizzy Mechlin in particular suggests that the "double loop" wedding functions less as historical mimesis—since marriage between Californio men and Anglo women rarely occurred in colonial California—and more as a socially symbolic act that crosses the nation's geo-racial terrain to consolidate Northern banking interests with Southwestern landowners. The dual marriage, along with the marriage between Clarence and Mercedes and the budding romance between Victoriano Alamar and Alice Darrell, imagines an almost incestuous community of Californians whose cultural capital and material wealth happily consolidate Yankee industriousness, Southern sensibilities (for Mrs. Darrell is a Southerner after all), and Californio gentility to signal the emergence of a new social class of white American citizens.

Of course, as the novel plays itself out, Anglos and Californios alike lose their civil rights to free enterprise and private land ownership to corrupt Yankee congressmen, railroad monopolies, and big-money politics. Californians become the "white slaves" of corporate colonialism and its power to buy congress (344). Ironically, the appeal to collective white slavery comes at a time when the nation is reconstructing itself following the end of black slavery. And this is the catch to the novel's geopolitical restructuring of whiteness. In much the same way that the Don's neocolonial venture relies on Indian labor, the narrative's re-mapping of whiteness forgets about black freedom. "Ruiz de Burton strategically emphasizes regional exploitation [of Californios, Southerners, and squatters] in a capitalist world system so as to create a discourse of white unity that obscures exploitation by race and class," Luis-Brown explains (817–18). Consider Mrs. Darrell's black servant Tisha, for example. As with the narrative's "lazy" Indians, Tisha's stereotypical role in the novel alone raises problems for Ruiz de Burton's narrative, but her status in the Darrell house in particular functions as the racial unconscious to the narrative's political critique and reconstruction of whiteness. Tisha remains a servant to Mrs. Darrell despite emancipation. In fact, the privilege attached to white rights in California depends on the labor of people like Tisha as well as their noncitizen status. So when the Darrells arrive in San Diego, they repeat in miniature the very social hierarchy the novel as a whole advocates in its alliance between California and the South: "'In the Phaeton I will take Alice, her lap dog and our two satchels, and last but not least, Webster will take the Concord with Willie in the front seat and Tisha in the back in state, with the cockatoos and canaries and parcels,' said Clarence, patting Tisha on the head" (105). Put in the back with the pets and the luggage, Tisha is simply another commodity to the Darrells, one that maintains their social status precisely because they paternalistically position her at the bottom of the socioeconomic scale. Not surprisingly, Tisha even takes to calling Victoriano Alamar "Massa Tano" in what is surely a symbolic moment that signals a merger between the legacy of white privilege and slavery in the South and Southwest.[7]

Ruiz de Burton's novels make quite apparent what American studies scholars such as David Roediger, Eric Lott, and Noel Ignatiev have been arguing recently: whiteness is not a natural racial category but a cultural identity marker contingent on class status, labor politics, market capitalism, legality, and public performances. Whiteness, in other words, emerges from cultural dyads of difference: free versus slave; civilized versus savage; citizen versus noncitizen; upper versus lower class, to name a few. As George Lipsitz explains, "More than the product of private prejudices, whiteness emerged as a relevant category in American life largely because of realities created by slavery and segregation, by immigration restriction and Indian policy, by conquest and colonialism" (370). Oddly enough, recent studies of whiteness also reproduce the very binaries of racial difference that construct white identity as a privileged category in the first place; that is, the emphasis on whiteness as the opposite of blackness, via labor, class, or sexuality, recirculates the notion that there are only two clear-cut racial categories in the U.S.—white or black. "Scholars studying both 'whiteness' and 'blackness' in modern U.S. society," George Sánchez argues, "have to account for the myriad ways that these two racial categories are projected onto the bodies of individuals who are neither 'white' nor 'black'" (390).[8] Indeed, scholars must consider the way white *latinidad* raises the contradictions of racial formation in the U.S. altogether.

Consider the colonial identities that characterize Ruiz de Burton's life and work. Already established in the Californio ruling class, Ruiz de Burton, as with many of her upper-class *criollo* contemporaries, had to negotiate a new position within the emerging American ruling class, a class that was by no means accepting of California Mexicans. Thus arises the problem of whiteness—Californios distinguished themselves from Native Americans and blacks in an attempt to align themselves with the very colonial ideologies that threatened to displace them racially, economically, and legally in the U.S. After the 1848 Treaty, Aranda explains, "racist cultural practices in the U.S. soon found their way into laws that openly discriminated against people of Mexican descent, in

employment, housing, the purchasing of property, and legal representation. . . . [T]hese racist practices conjoined with pre-existing racist practices in Mexican culture to encourage not only the internalization of new
racist ideologies but also the creation of an additional social policing
mechanism that exaggerated the already privileged status of 'whiteness'
within Mexican American communities." This latter point is essential
in contextualizing Ruiz de Burton's racial politics, given that she saw
herself as a "white" Mexican (5). Such contradictory politics make it difficult to read Ruiz de Burton's work strictly as a "counter-history of the
subaltern, the conquered Californio population," as Sánchez and Pita
argue (7), for while it does recount the dispossession and displacement
of Californios, the cultural work of her novels seeks to legitimate Californios' claims to the same colonial privileges of Anglo Americans. Even
if we consider Ruiz de Burton's narrator in *The Squatter and the Don* "as
a subaltern supplementary subject," as José David Saldívar puts it (170),
we must still reconcile narrator's subalternity with the narrative's colonial contradiction—its argument that Californios should be included in,
rather than excluded from, the acquisition of new wealth in the Southwest. So goes the historical amnesia that emerges from the shifts in colonial consciousness. Ruiz de Burton's work stretches the nation's
geopolitical terrain of whiteness to include Californios but simultaneously consolidates whiteness by excluding Native Americans and blacks
from the same suffrage Ruiz de Burton seeks for Californios.

Notes

I would like to thank José F. Aranda Jr. and Amelia de la Luz Montes for
their continuous support of my work and their dedication to Ruiz de Burton
studies; I also owe a great debt to Manuel G. Gonzales and Hector Torres for
encouraging this essay and offering their keen comments and suggestions.
Finally, I am grateful to the scholars of the Recovering the U.S. Hispanic
Literary Project for hearing, reading, and offering feedback on perhaps too
many versions of this essay, which has been published previously in two
revised forms.

    1. Several studies have initiated the process of generating criticism on
Ruiz de Burton's work. Sánchez and Pita (Introduction) deserve special consideration for recovering Ruiz de Burton's two novels and writing compelling

introductions to both texts, as well as essays on Ruiz de Burton and José Martí. González ("Romancing Hegemony") has written a lucid essay on *The Squatter and the Don* and its reconstruction of whiteness as a privileged marker of Californio identity while Martín Rodríguez ("Textual and Land Reclamations") offers a similar analysis of the novel, focusing on the class status of the Californios. Luis-Brown's article ("White Slaves") considers *The Squatter and the Don* and *Ramona* in the context of whiteness and class status, and Saldívar (*Border Matters*) offers an analysis of the novel in the context of nineteenth-century American colonial cultural production. Montes ("Es Necesario") has done the important work of recovering Ruiz de Burton's copious letters and reading them in light of her novelistic production, and I have explored the theoretical dynamics of history, romance, and law in *The Squatter and the Don* (Alemán, "Novelizing National Discourses"). Goldman considers Ruiz de Burton's use of satire and sentimentality in *Who Would Have Thought It?*, and Fisher ("Captive Mexicana") has produced a convincing discussion of Ruiz de Burton's first novel as a narrative of bourgeoisie domestic desire. Aranda ("Contradictory Impulses") has done much to further Ruiz de Burton studies in an article that troubles the subaltern approach to Ruiz de Burton's life and works.

2. This paradox is not exclusive to Ruiz de Burton and her work. It may in fact be the central paradox of being Mexican American, that of being a United States citizen yet being excluded from the real and imaginary citizenship of the United States. For instance, Menchaca convincingly "documents cases in which people of Mexican descent [in the United States] were compelled to argue in court that they should be treated as Caucasians in order to gain the legal rights of full citizens" ("Chicano Indianism" 583). Moreover, Gutiérrez (*Walls and Mirrors*) has shown how, throughout the nineteenth and twentieth centuries, some Mexican American social organizations have rhetorically positioned themselves nationally and ethnically with Anglo Americans instead of Mexican immigrants during times of national and legal crisis. Finally, many early twentieth-century Mexican American writers, such as María Cristina Mena, Nina Otero-Warren, Fabiola Cabeza de Baca, and Jovita Gonzalez, emphasized Mexican American cultural whiteness, leading Raymund Paredes to claim pejoratively that such writers suffered from "hacienda syndrome" ("Evolution" 52). As with much of Chicano/a social and literary history, then, Ruiz de Burton seeks to re-position herself and her collective social identity by discursively constructing an ethnic space in Anglo America that will guarantee Mexican Americans full rights as United States citizens.

3. As Aranda notes, the Indian abduction of Lola's mother, Doña Theresa,

speaks volumes about the historical moment of her captivity, since it occurs on the eve of the Mexican American War: "This is undoubtedly a very deliberate use of irony to mark the disruption of regional power that enabled Native American groups to take action against Mexican settlers. Dr. Norval's rescue of Lola Medina figures here as poetic justice, since it was his nation that made Mexican citizens vulnerable to native retaliation in the first place" ("Contradictory Impulses" 577). Moreover, it occurs to historian Richard R. Stenberg ("Polk Accused") that the Polk administration considered using U.S. Indians to invade Mexico as a way of covertly drawing Mexico into war. One Mr. Duff Green, an 1845 Tyler-appointed ambassador to Mexico, seems to have been the mastermind behind this intrigue, but there is no indication that his covert operations ever went into effect. Nevertheless, this is part of the "political unconscious," as Jameson puts it, that underlies such a simple narrative event as Doña Theresa's abduction and Lola's birth in captivity.

4. We might even say Lola's removal from Indian captivity is triply-voiced, as it also recalls the way Indian captivity narratives deploy racial categories along the distinction between "civilization" and "savagery." In all three cases, going from black to white, Indian to white, or "savage" to "civilized," Lola performs the various categories that comprise the Spanish/Mexican *casta* system. This is why I see her (de)racialization as an enactment of *mestizaje*, if not on a literal, biological level, then at least on a figurative, cultural level.

5. Interestingly enough, unlike Ruiz de Burton, the Irish American regiment established to fight in the Mexican American War did see Catholicism as a common cultural bond between Irish and Mexicans. Two-hundred Irishmen deserted the U.S. Army and fought on the Mexican side, forming the famous San Patricio Corps. The majority of Irish Americans may have learned how to become Anglo, as Ignatiev argues (*How the Irish*), but a handful of them learned to become Mexican, too. For more on the San Patricio Corps, see Hogan (*Irish Soldiers*), Miller (*Shamrock and Sword*), and Wynn (*San Patricio Soldiers*).

6. "The double loop," Luis-Brown reminds us, "refers to the ceremonial lasso tossed over the heads of bride and groom in traditional Mexican Catholic wedding ceremonies" ("White Slaves" 816). While Luis-Brown overlooks this very literal moment when the narrative connects the Alamars with the Mechlins in a socially symbolic "double loop" romance, his article does perceptively point out that the lassoing of Mr. Darrell by Gabriel Alamar symbolizes a violent marriage between squatters and Dons ("White Slaves" 816).

7. This symbolic collusion between Californios and the slave labor system

of the South resonates with historical significance. It raises the specter of legislated Indian servitude in California, which allowed Mexican ranchers and Yankee newcomers to traffic in an Indian slave trade that closely resembled the chattel slavery of blacks in the South. As Pierson B. Reading, a Sutter ranch employee, put it in 1844, "The Indians of California make as obedient and humble slaves as the Negroes in the south, . . . for a mere trifle you can secure their services for life" (qtd. in Hurtado, *Indian Survival* 74–75). In effect, Ruiz de Burton's novel imagines the same thing: while the squatters can potentially profit from Indian labor under the Don's homesteading plan, Victoriano Alamar gains a black servant when he aligns himself with the Darrells. And his re-alignment may speak to a larger cultural moment of national reconstructions of the South and Southwest. As Gillman notes in her discussion of *Ramona* and José Martí: "In the 1880s the myth of the Old South emerged in response to the economic and political threat of the 'New Negro' and the 'New South,' just as the invention of the romantic, Spanish heritage . . . coincided with the decline of the Californios . . . as an economic and political power and with the need to maintain a racial-national dichotomy between the high-class 'Spanish' and the low-class 'Mexican Indian'—the latter group constituting a growing social and economic threat to Anglo-American hegemony" ("Ramona"106).

8. Any thorough historical analysis of the ambiguous racial formation, categorization, and ethnic construction of Mexican Americans soundly challenges current studies of "whiteness," a term that has become synonymous with "Anglo American-ness" in white studies. Consider Eric Lott's study of blackface minstrelsy (*Love and Theft*). Insightful as it is, Lott's discussion of minstrelsy during the mid-nineteenth century considers the Mexican American War as simply the precursor to the ensuing crisis over slavery. His project elides completely how the specter of Mexican whiteness in popular and political culture radically influenced the debate of whiteness as a labor and citizenship category.

Works Cited

Alemán, Jesse. "Novelizing National Discourses: History, Romance, and Law in *The Squatter and the Don*." *Recovering the U.S. Hispanic Literary Heritage*. Vol. 3. Ed. María Herrera-Sobek and Virginia Sánchez Korrel. Houston: Arte Público, 2000. 38–49.

Almaguer, Tomás. *Racial Fault Lines: The Historical Origins of White Supremacy in California*. Berkeley: University of California Press, 1994.

Anderson, Benedict. *Imagined Communities: Reflections on the Origin and Spread of Nationalism*. Revised ed. New York: Verso, 1991.

Aranda, José F., Jr. "Contradictory Impulses: María Amparo Ruiz de Burton, Resistance Theory, and the Politics of Chicano/a Studies." *American Literature* 70 (1998): 551–79.

Camarillo, Albert. *Chicanos in a Changing Society: From Mexican Pueblos to American Barrios in Santa Barbara and Southern California, 1848–1930*. Cambridge, Mass: Harvard University Press, 1996.

Fisher, Beth. "The Captive Mexicana and the Desiring Bourgeois Woman: Domesticity and Expansionism in Ruiz de Burton's *Who Would Have Thought It?*" *Legacy* 16.1 (1999): 59–69.

Gillman, Susan. "Ramona in 'Our America.'" *José Martí's "Our America": From National to Hemispheric Cultural Studies*. Ed. Jeffrey Belnap and Raúl Fernández. Durham: Duke University Press, 1998. 91–111.

Goldman, Anne E. "'Who Ever Heard of a Blue-Eyed Mexican?': Satire and Sentimentality in María Amparo Ruiz de Burton's *Who Would Have Thought It?*" *Recovering the U.S. Hispanic Literary Heritage*. Vol. 2. Ed. Erlinda Gonzales-Berry and Chuck Tatum. Houston: Arte Público, 1996. 59–79.

González, John M. "Romancing Hegemony: Constructing Racialized Citizenship in María Amparo Ruiz de Burton's *The Squatter and the Don*." *Recovering the U.S. Hispanic Literary Heritage*. Vol. 2. Ed. Erlinda Gonzales-Berry and Chuck Tatum. Houston: Arte Público, 1996. 23–39.

Gutiérrez, David G. *Walls and Mirrors: Mexican Americans, Mexican Immigrants, and the Politics of Ethnicity*. Berkeley: University of California Press, 1995.

Haas, Lisabeth. *Conquests and Historical Identities in California, 1769–1936*. Berkeley: University of California Press, 1995.

Hogan, Michael. *The Irish Soldiers of Mexico*. Guadalajara, MX: Fondo Editorial Universitario, 1997.

Horsman, Reginald. *Race and Manifest Destiny: The Origins of American Racial Anglo-Saxonism*. Cambridge, MA: Harvard University Press, 1981.

Hurtado, Albert L. *Indian Survival on the California Frontier*. New Haven, CT: Yale University Press, 1988.

Ignatiev, Noel. *How the Irish Became White*. New York: Routledge, 1995.

Jameson, Fredric. *The Political Unconscious: Narrative as a Socially Symbolic Act*. Ithaca, NY: Cornell University Press, 1981.

Lipsitz, George. "The Possessive Investment in Whiteness." *American Quarterly* 47 (1995): 369–87.

Lott, Eric. *Love and Theft: Blackface Minstrelsy and the American Working Class.* New York: Oxford University Press, 1993.

Luis-Brown, David. "White Slaves and the 'Arrogant Mestiza': Reconfiguring Whiteness in *The Squatter and the Don* and *Ramona.*" *American Literature* 69 (1997): 813–39.

Martín Rodríguez, Manuel M. "Textual and Land Reclamations: The Critical Reception of Early Chicano/a Literature." *Recovering the U.S. Hispanic Literary Heritage.* Vol. 2. Ed. Erlinda Gonzales-Berry and Chuck Tatum. Houston: Arte Público, 1996. 40–57.

Menchaca, Martha. "Chicano Indianism: A Historical Account of Racial Repression in the United States." *American Ethnologist* 23 (1993): 583–603.

Miller, Robert Ryal. *Shamrock and Sword: The St. Patrick's Battalion in the U.S. Mexican War.* Norman: University of Oklahoma Press, 1989.

Montes, Amelia M. de la Luz. "Es Necesario Mirar Bien: Nineteenth-Century Letter Making and Novel Writing in the Life of María Amparo Ruiz de Burton." *Recovering the U.S. Hispanic Literary Heritage.* Vol. 3. Ed. María Herrera-Sobek and Virginia Sánchez Korrol. Houston: Arte Público, 2000. 16–37.

Paredes, Raymund A. "The Evolution of Chicano Literature." *Three American Literatures: Essays in Chicano, Native American, and Asian-American Literature for Teachers of American Literature.* Ed. Houston A. Baker, Jr. New York: MLA, 1982. 33–79.

Phillips, George Howard. *Chiefs and Challengers: Indian Resistance and Cooperation in Southern California.* Berkeley: University of California Press, 1975.

Pita, Beatrice. "Engendering Critique: Race, Class, and Gender in Ruiz de Burton and Martí." *José Martí's "Our America": National to Hemispheric Cultural Studies.* Ed. Jeffrey Belnap and Raúl Fernández. Durham: Duke University Press, 1998. 129–44.

Pitt, Leonard. *The Decline of the Californios: A Social History of the Spanish-Speaking Californians, 1846–1890.* Berkeley: University of California Press, 1966.

Roediger, David R. *The Wages of Whiteness: Race and the Making of the American Working Class.* New York: Verso, 1991.

Ruiz de Burton, María Amparo. *Who Would Have Thought It?* 1872. Ed. Rosaura Sánchez and Beatrice Pita. Houston: Arte Público, 1995.

———. *The Squatter and the Don.* 1885. Ed. Rosaura Sánchez and Beatrice Pita. Houston: Arte Público, 1992.

Saldívar, José David. *Border Matters: Remapping American Cultural Studies.* Berkeley: University of California Press, 1997.

Sánchez, George J. "Reading Reginald Denny: The Politics of Whiteness in the Late Twentieth Century." *American Quarterly* 47 (1995): 388–394.

Sánchez, Rosaura. *Telling Identities: The Californio Testimonios.* Minneapolis: University of Minnesota Press, 1995.

———. "Dismantling the Colossus: Martí and Ruiz de Burton on the Formulation of Anglo América." *José Martí's "Our America": From National to Hemispheric Cultural Studies.* Ed. Jeffrey Belnap and Raúl Fernández. Durham, NC: Duke University Press, 1998. 115–28.

Sánchez, Rosaura and Beatrice Pita. Introduction. *The Squatter and the Don.* By María Amparo Ruiz de Burton. Ed. Rosaura Sánchez and Beatrice Pita. 2nd ed. Houston: Arte Público, 1992. 7–49.

———. Introduction. *Who Would Have Thought It?* By María Amparo Ruiz de Burton. Ed. Rosaura Sánchez and Beatrice Pita. Houston: Arte Público, 1995. vii–lxv.

Schroeder, John H. *Mr. Polk's War: American Opposition and Dissent, 1846–1848.* Madison: University of Wisconsin Press, 1973.

Stenberg, Richard R. "Polk Accused." *The Mexican War: Was it Manifest Destiny?* Ed. Ramón Eduardo Ruiz. New York: Holt, Rinehart, and Winston, 1963. 65–76.

Wynn, David J. *The San Patricio Soldiers: Mexico's Foreign Legion.* El Paso: Texas Western Press, 1984.

2 Testifying Bodies

Citizenship Debates in Bret Harte's Gabriel Conroy

ANDREA TINNEMEYER

PUBLISHED IN 1876, *GABRIEL CONROY*, BRET Harte's obscure novel[1] of multiple disguises, hustlers, two-timing women, cannibals, legal and illegal fights over mining rights, and the Indian and Chinese Questions mimics posturings occurring mid-century on a national scale. Harte moved to California in 1854 on the heels of the Gold Rush and worked for local newspapers such as the San Francisco *Golden Era* before gaining notoriety for his own writing as editor and contributor to *The Overland Monthly*. The year 1854 was pivotal in the Southwest because it marked the California Supreme Court decision of *People v. Hall* regarding the racial and national identity of Chinese immigrants. It was also the year of the Gadsden Purchase, a predictable consequence of the United States-Mexican War, which had ended a mere six years prior.[2]

The Gadsden Purchase revisited citizenship issues raised by the peace treaty between Mexico and the United States and reopened the debate over eligibility requirements. As recently as 1790, the United States had declared that citizenship was exclusively reserved for "free white persons" (Almaguer 24). On the surface, the Treaty of Guadalupe Hidalgo, which ended the United States-Mexican War, appeared to extend citi-

zenship to all former Mexican citizens, but because it threatened to challenge the "white only" composition of United States citizenry, ratification
stalled over the Indian Question. Harte attempts to answer the multifaceted Indian Question—which also applied to Mexicans (mestizos) and
Chinese—through the character of Grace Conroy, who takes on a mestiza identity to avoid a social fall resulting from an unwed pregnancy
and the barred testimony of Ah Fe, a Chinese immigrant who could exon-
erate a murder suspect. Harte further challenges the racial composition
of United States citizens in a fictional account (John Doe alias Gabriel
Conroy v. Jane Roe alias Julie Conroy) of the murder trial of George W.
Hall that occasioned the California Supreme Court decision of 1854. Tying
these two plotlines together—the racial masquerade of Grace Conroy
and the murder trial of Victor Ramirez—is the political aftermath of the
United States-Mexican War.

    Gabriel Conroy fictionalizes the United States-Mexican War's reper-
cussions in California and dwells particularly on the legal and racial implications of legislation like Article IX that extended United States
citizenship to all former Mexican citizens. Harte's novel reflects the War's
tumultuous impact on Native Americans, Chinese, and Mexican Americans, who jockeyed for positions of political and social legitimacy
through vexed engagements with whiteness and racial otherness.
Through the course of this essay, I will examine how Harte's novel critiques the United States-Mexican War's impact on United States race
relations both by decentering whiteness through legal maneuvers for
citizenship rights and by disrupting the family romance, which served
as a cradle for national consolidation.[3]

    Set in a newly formed mining town overcrowded with gamblers and
charlatans, all making multiple false claims about their familial relationships in order to inherit a silver mine, Harte's *Gabriel Conroy* provides a fictional petri dish for observing the legacies of Manifest Destiny
in the Treaty of Guadalupe Hidalgo (1848), the Foreign Miners' Tax
(1850), the Gadsden Purchase (1854), and *People v. Hall* (1854). The novel
chronicles the lives of fictional survivors of a catastrophe based on that
of the Donner Party, a group of would-be settlers who were forced to
turn to cannibalism in order to survive a harsh winter in the Sierra Nevada
in February, 1847. Harte's characters include: Gabriel Conroy, his sister
Grace (a.k.a. Doña Dolores Salvatierra, a.k.a. Mrs. Peter Dumphy),

Philip Ashley (a.k.a. Arthur Poinsett), Peter Dumphy (the cannibal and, not coincidentally, a lawyer), Julie Devarges (a.k.a. Grace Conroy), and Victor Ramirez (Julie's jilted lover whose death occasions the novel's sensational court case). Three events transpiring between members of the emigrant party significantly impact the subplots of the novel: before he dies, renowned scientist Dr. Devarges bequeaths his silver mine claim to Grace Conroy; Grace leaves the party with Philip Ashley, her lover who impregnates and subsequently abandons her; and Devarges's ex-wife, Julie, impersonates Grace and then marries Grace's brother, Gabriel, in the hopes of reclaiming the silver mine. The real Grace Conroy assumes a *mestiza* identity as Doña Dolores Salvatierra, and only returns to reclaim her identity as Grace when her brother is put on trial for the death of Julia's ex-lover, Victor Ramirez. Indeed, Ramirez's death (a bizarre suicide—he falls upon his own knife) culminates in a lengthy murder trial in which Harte, in effect, puts United States legislative acts on trial.

All in the Family

Although both family and national romances in the nineteenth century expanded to include differences in gender, they did not accommodate differences in race. Indeed, for Anglo Americans the family romance was a homogenizing myth intent upon insulating and protecting the family from racial difference.[4] Ensuring legitimacy and inheritance necessitated measures to safeguard the republican family from any external (read racialized) sexual threat.[5] Ironically, although racial difference was imagined by Anglo Americans as a corrupter of family and, therefore, national romances, the rigorous campaign for circumscribing whiteness within the familial unit posed an even greater threat by inadvertently encouraging the transgression of powerful social taboos specific to the family. For Harte, these taboos come in the characteristically western form of the con, characters posing as family members to secure rights to the silver mine. These multiple maskings and unmaskings undermine the sanctity of the Anglo American family, and, in so doing, reveal the extent to which this source of national identity is ultimately corruptible by the same forces shaping the new wealth in the post-1848 Southwest.

Prior to the United States-Mexican War in 1848, the practice of absorbing people of color into the citizenry of the United States was an unspoken necessity to populate the landscape with individuals loyal to the nation who would take up arms against any enemy and fight, at least for the land they occupied. Mexico, and Spain before it, employed similar tactics to assure their literal presence in regions distant from the capital or center of government.[6] In the view of the United States and Mexican governments, the Southwest was a relatively barren region whose geographic proximity to both nations made it a contested territory by default. Both nations would wrestle for a stronghold in the region—Mexicans by offering citizenship and land grants, and the United States by Manifest Destiny. To fortify their claim to the Southwestern territory, both governments were willing to accept members of the other nation into their citizenry, and this drive to occupy the contested landscape meant a sanctioning (whether direct or indirect) of interracial marriage.[7] After the war, in post-1848 United States, there was no longer a need to recruit people wholesale into the citizenry, and the incidence of interracial marriage, quietly tolerated in the past out of necessity, was no longer permitted.

Through the doubling of United States territory, Manifest Destiny brought about the crisis that William Snyder, an attorney who lobbied for a national standard of marital laws, and others address. Former Mexican territories like California and Colorado would pose the greatest threat to the domestic model because matrimonial law was based upon Mexican laws.[8] The church first instituted marriage laws by publishing lists of relatives forbidden to join in marriage. States passed legislation to prohibit and punish instances of incestuous unions between people of consanguinity and affinity. In cases of incest, rulings in southern courts in general reveal the connection assumed between family and nation. Judges were reticent to intrude upon or undermine patriarchal rule. As further testament to the bond between family and nation, the Mississippi high court in 1872 characterized incest as a transgression against "domestic virtues" and "the obligations of a citizen" (Bardaglio 33). In the South in particular, where slavocracy conflated family and racial servitude, and where countless slave owners raped and impregnated black female slaves, the policy against incest became all the more complex and insidious.

The insular properties associated with the family romance are predicated in part on the specter of the racial other. Yet the guarded, homogenizing function of the family romance to maintain and reproduce whiteness fostered the very practices it sought to avoid. The strategic incorporation and deployment of racial otherness, whether of Native American or Mexican identity, signifies the consequences of a national preoccupation with the republican family. Populated by Californios, mestizos, Indians, and Chinese, California adopted its own state constitution to determine how it would legislate citizenship after the treaty, which granted United States citizenship to all individuals eligible for Mexican citizenship.[9] Article VIII of the treaty states: "Those who shall prefer to remain in the said territories, may either retain their title and rights as Mexican citizens, or acquire those of citizens of the United States" (reported in Griswold del Castillo 189).

The Legality of Whiteness

Article IX created a dilemma for Californios that centered on the status of Indians, who, under the Mexican Constitution of 1824, had been granted Mexican citizenship.[10] According to the 1848 peace treaty, then, all Indians in former Mexican territory (which included California) were eligible for United States citizenship, a policy at odds with Article XI of the treaty naming the United States government as the agent responsible for policing the border and protecting its citizenry against Indian raids. One year after the treaty, California's State Constitutional Convention debated how racial lines were to be drawn; such decisions involved the extension of enfranchisement and other citizenship rights. At the convention's close, Mexicans were defined socially as "white" and extended citizenship while California Indians were deemed "nonwhite" and were therefore ineligible for citizenship.[11] The 1854 case of *People v. Hall* classified Chinese as "Indians" and therefore nonwhite (Almaguer 9, 10).

The adoption of a "white" heroine into a Mexican family—Harte's Grace Conroy as Doña Dolores into the Salvatierra family—should be read as a domesticated version of the Treaty of Guadalupe Hidalgo, particularly Article IX declaring the "incorporation" of former Mexican citizens into the United States. The aftermath of the United States-Mexican War enables the consumption of mestizo identity by Harte's Grace Conroy. In an inverse relationship, the rapid de-peopling of Native Americans and Mexicans from the national landscape further authenticated characters like Grace Conroy to "go native." In a photonegative version of the Treaty, where adoption serves as a domesticated version of incorporation, the racial and political identities of the adoptees (in this case, Grace) in Harte's novel mirror those of Mexicans, ostensibly welcomed into the United States national family. Strikingly, the central dilemma of racial identification facing Grace Conroy, a dilemma concerning the ownership of whiteness, reflects the very real predicament confronting Mexicans and Native Americans after the California State Constitutional Convention created the term, "white Mexican."

California's subsequent interpretations of the Treaty's very broad, ambiguous terms for United States citizenship placed racial categories in flux. Specifically, the category of "white" was dislodged from a fixed racial and social position as many upper class Californios, those who declared their European ancestry through pure Spanish bloodlines, claimed status as white persons. What I argue in my reading of the legislative acts particular to post-1848 California is that whiteness is expunged from its position as a static racial, social, and legal category by the dynamic interplay between Mexicans and Native Americans. Indeed, California passed laws to "disenfranchise Mexicans of Indian descent and to allow only white Mexicans full political rights" (Menchaca 588). What followed, according to ethnologist Martha Menchaca, was both phenomenal and utterly disheartening: "The conquered Mexican population learned that it was politically expedient to assert their Spanish ancestry . . . [conversely] it became politically expedient for American Indians to pass for Mexican mestizos if they wished to escape the full impact of the discriminatory Indian legislation" (587). The legal posturings of people of both Native American and Mexican descent chronicled by Menchaca are replicated in hyperbolic form in *Gabriel Conroy* to such an extent that even the titular character's identity is called into question on the witness stand.

Grace Conroy and People v. Hall

Like the original state court case that culminated in *People v. Hall*, the fictional court case that places Gabriel Conroy on trial for murdering Victor Ramirez pivots on the eyewitness testimony of a Chinese immigrant. George W. Hall, a white man accused of murdering Ling Sing, was originally found guilty based on the testimony of three Chinese witnesses. On appeal to the state supreme court, the original ruling was overturned precisely because of the racial identity of the eyewitness. The Supreme Court of California ruled that because Chinese were not white, a convoluted argument briefly quoted below, they were ineligible to testify against white people:

> We are of the opinion that the words "white," "Negro," "mulatto," "Indian," and "black person," wherever they occur in our Constitution and laws, must be taken in their generic sense, and that, even admitting the Indian of this continent is not of the Mongolian type,[12] that the words "black person," in the 14th section, must be taken as contradistinguished from white, and necessarily excludes all races other than the Caucasian. (*People v. Hall*)

This same negative dialectic, in which "Caucasian" is defined primarily by "all races other than the Caucasian," would later be applied against Mexican inhabitants of the Southwest following the United States-Mexican War, except for a chosen few who had carried the doubly inflected title of "white Mexican." In a chapter entitled, "What Ah Fe Does Not Know," Gabriel Conroy's lawyer intends to interrogate Ah Fe "to establish the fact of Gabriel's remoteness from the scene of the murder by some corroborating incident or individual that Ah Fe could furnish in support of the detailed narrative he had already given. But it did not appear that any Caucasian had been encountered or met by Ah Fe at the time of his errand" (134).

In keeping with *People v. Hall*, Ah Fe is prohibited from testifying, even though here it is on behalf of a white man accused of murder. We witness Harte's treatment of the ruling in the parade of immigrants (Irish, French, and German) whose testimony, accepted by the court because the immigrants are "white," is utterly useless and tangential at best to the case. The German immigrant's testimony, however, is most telling as an indicator of Harte's political agenda: "[The German immigrant] believes a Chinaman as good as any other man" (465). In one succinct sentence, Harte alludes to and dismisses the Supreme Court findings, which describe the Chinese as "[a people] whose mendacity is proverbial; a race . . . nature has marked as inferior, and . . . incapable of progress or intellectual development beyond a certain point" (McClain 550). Though Harte does not explicitly reference the degree to which the rejection of Ah Fe's testimony is linked to the "Indian Question," the Chinese community at the time would certainly have understood this connection. Members of the Chinese community had reacted to the *Hall* decision by distinguishing themselves from "these Indians [who] know nothing about the relations of society; they know no mutual respect; they wear neither clothes nor shoes; they live in wild places and in caves" (Bancroft letter from Lai Chun-Cheun). There was solid legal reason for the Chinese in mid-nineteenth-century California to want to distance themselves from Native Americans. As noted earlier, Native Americans were denied United States citizenship, targeted during the Indian Removal era in the 1830s, and treated as the basis on which Mexican residents could claim their whiteness.

Violence, represented by the death of Victor Ramirez, occasions the novel's moment of revelation where the characters' "true" identities are revealed, their crimes exposed. I read the court scene as the passage in which Manifest Destiny, in all of its guises and forms, appears naked and ugly, exposed for both narrator and reader alike to ridicule. Given the history of legislation designed to authorize and perpetuate Manifest Destiny, it is appropriate that Harte should set the novel's final showdown in the courtroom where, like the aftermath of Manifest Destiny, the victimized and displaced Mexican is virtually ignored. The occasion of the trial—Victor Ramirez's mysterious death—is overshadowed by the ridiculous posturing of Anglo American characters relating to ownership of the infamous silver mine.

Grace Conroy figures prominently in the novel by offering, in the guise of racial masquerade and the appropriation of Mexican land grants by "legal" means, the most in-depth examination of Manifest Destiny's impact after the war. Indeed, it is no accident that the novel tethers the subplot of ownership disputes over the silver mine with the recovery of Grace Conroy. Gabriel Conroy unwittingly settles on the silver mine and, through his foolish actions and thoughts, represents the watered-down version of an Anglo American who receives the spoils from Manifest Destiny, but remains ignorant of the means employed to gain them. When at the novel's conclusion Grace secures the title to the mine based on her inheritance from José Salvatierra, her adoptive father, we witness the duplicitous mechanisms of Manifest Destiny—in the form of the geographic incorporation of Mexican territory, signified by the silver mine, and the racial incorporation of Mexican identity, signified by Grace's guise as Doña Dolores Salvatierra—and how these two forms of incorporation function together.

Grace Conroy enacts an imperialist consumption of Mexican racial and cultural traits when she disguises herself and lives as Doña Dolores Salvatierra. I argue that Hartes takes his cue in his representation of Grace from national documents like the Treaty of Guadalupe Hidalgo. I read Article IX of the Treaty, the section that figures Mexicans in the United States after the war, as a type of racial incorporation and racial erasure. The United States did not just stop at incorporating half of Mexico's territory, it also took its people, its citizens. And in doing so, the United States made manifest a kind of racial and cultural ownership of Mexicans, to be deployed whenever it served the interests of the nation.

Examining the imperialist rhetoric of Article IX of the Treaty of Guadalupe Hidalgo reveals the extreme degree to which Manifest Destiny permeated the Mexican War, both fueling patriotic fervor before the war, and later justifying the violence after peace was met. Witness the manner in which the Article imagines "the Mexicans who, in the territories aforesaid, shall not preserve the character of citizens of the Mexican Republic . . . [to be] *incorporated* into the Union of the United States" (190, emphasis mine). Tellingly, this concept of incorporation does not account for racial difference—nor does it figure Mexicans as agents of their own nationalities. Although the language of the article is couched as a choice, ostensibly giving Mexicans the decision either to retain Mexican citizenship or else to become United States citizens, the application of this article denied that such a choice existed at all. Incorporation does not imply choice—it in fact implies an unspoken violence, an action that occurs in direct disregard of someone's choice.

It's Mine!

Harte exposes how the Treaty's rhetoric negatively impacted the identities of Mexicans by denying them entry into the "American family." Mrs. Julie Devarges, the widow of Dr. Devarges, intends to use the Spanish report "show[ing] both [Conroy] sisters to be dead and leav[ing] [Gabriel Conroy's] identity in doubt" to discredit Gabriel Conroy and make claims on her deceased husband's silver mine (71). The identity of Grace Conroy, Gabriel's older sister who leaves the emigrant party with Arthur Poinsett to search for relief, remains a mystery throughout much of the novel because the Spanish report legally disinherits her from her own identity. When Grace first appears in front of Don José Salvatierra, commander of the Presidio of San Geronimo, she enlists his aid in finding her family. From the translation of a Mexican official document, she learns that among the bodies of the deceased was one identified as Grace Conroy (52). Upon hearing that she is officially dead and that Philip Ashley, the father of her unborn child, is "not found," Grace faints at the feet of Don José. The next time she appears in the narrative it is in the guise of Doña Dolores Salvatierra, the daughter of Don José and a Native American woman. I want to trace out Grace's transformation into Doña Dolores as an indicator of the failure of the republican family romance.

When Grace originally leaves the emigrant party with Philip Ashley, a false biological relationship between the two is manufactured to protect Grace's reputation. At Philip's insistence that Grace's beauty "offers an explanation of [their] companionship that the world will accept more readily than any other, and the truth to many would seem scarcely as natural," she takes his name (35). But what momentarily appears to be a marriage proposal turns instead into an insidious creation of familial ties—Philip declares that Grace shall be his sister (35). This benign covering for an illicit love affair offers no protection to Grace once she has been impregnated and summarily abandoned by Philip. In her pregnant condition, to repeat the lie that she and Philip are brother and sister would be not only to condemn both her and her child to the scandal of incest but their child as the product of an incestuous affair. This tenuous status exists not only for Grace's baby, but also for Grace herself. Now a "fallen woman," legally declared dead, and without any immediate family to assist her or shield her from social judgment and sentencing, Grace must turn to other sources for her identity and her reputation (which was inextricably tied to a woman's identity).

To read Grace's racial passing through the family romance is to recognize the creation of two illegitimate familial relationships (first the sibling relationship between herself and her lover, and second the relationship between the father and the baby), which leave Grace completely bereft of a legal, legitimate identity. Having consumed and exhausted all the socially acceptable familial roles open for an Anglo American female, Grace assumes the asexual and racialized identity of Don José's daughter. Assuming the pious, nun-like qualities under the guise of Doña Dolores, as attested to by Father Felipe and Doña María Sepulvida, protects Grace's reputation.

The family romance's obsession with homogeneity, sameness, and legitimacy promotes a consumptive quality that not only compels self-replicating sameness, but also leads to its own demise through the consumption of the racial other. I mean to suggest that racial passing—which occurs in *Gabriel Conroy* through the character of Grace Conroy who assumes the identity of Doña Dolores Salvatierra, a *mestiza* (of indigenous and Spanish ancestry)—is a scaled-down version of metaphorical cannibalism, a symbolic version of the literal cannibalism of the Donner party to which the situation in *Gabriel Conroy* alludes. Cast out of all of the possible family positions that she could claim, Grace takes advantage of her only recourse—which is to dye her skin, learn Spanish, and assume the identity of Salvatierra's "half-breed" daughter. Instead of assuming the character of a socially white member of the *gente de razón*, a pure-blooded Spaniard, Grace usurps a mestiza identity, a racial identity that retains the stigma incurred for the birth of an illegitimate child. In other words, Grace retains her "fallen" character in her alias as Doña Dolores. Yet despite the "fallen" nature of her disguise, Grace indeed inherits more cultural capital as a mestiza in a Mexican society than she could ever hope for as an Anglo woman in the United States:

> At the beginning of the nineteenth century, the basic principle guiding American law was that a husband was the natural guardian of his wife's interests. . . . A married woman was prohibited from bringing legal suits or being sued, from making contracts, and from owning property individually. By the Civil War . . . many states . . . adopted married women's property acts, which permitted married women to control their own property and earnings. (Basch 62)[13]

By passing as Doña Dolores, Grace Conroy compromises the family romance, but gains social respectability and inherits one of the largest haciendas in California. And it is in a Spanish document, written up by José Hermenizildo Salvatierra, Grace's adoptive father, that her racial transformation is revealed: "Wishing to keep her secret from the world and prevent recognition by the *members of her own race and family*, by the assistance and advice of an Indian peon, Manuela, [Grace] consented that her face and hands should be daily washed by the juice of the Yokoto—whose effect is to change the skin to the color of bronze" (496). Just as a Spanish document initially left Grace bereft of her own identity, this second document restores to her new racial and familial identities. For Grace to assume an identity that would protect her from recognition by her own family, she must dye her skin and affect a different racial identity. The assumption of racial difference appears in *Gabriel Conroy* as the only escape from the family romance. Tellingly, the overly invasive legal system figures in the novel as the means to force one's way into a family.

Introducing people of color into the national imaginary, signified by interracial adoption, subverts the mechanisms for conferring identity and property. Harte's novel addresses the post-1848 turmoil in identity and property claims. At one point in the novel, as if to indicate the absurd degree to which this identity crisis had risen, the titular character appears on the witness stand and declares himself to be John Dumbledee, not Gabriel Conroy (460). The racial and familial identities of Harte's characters are challenged repeatedly, echoing the ambiguous position that Mexicans, Chinese, and Native Americans alike held in the nation after the War. In the assembly of foster families, identity is not the only claim at stake. Inheritance, legally expressed through wills and land grants, represents another facet of the family romance encroached upon in the war's aftermath. Family and national romances, two interdependent stratagems for conferring identity onto individuals, are challenged in the wake of the United States-Mexican War.

In the chaos that followed the Treaty's dismantling of the domestic apparatus as the stronghold of whiteness, residents of California, regardless of race, sought retribution and refuge in the United States judicial system. Individuals petitioned their claims to racial identities and property rights to judges in the belief that a legal decree would secure their rights and privileges, allow them to maintain their lands, and render them safe from vigilantes, squatters, and other criminal products of Manifest Destiny. Documents, wills, testimonials, and land grants—several of the legal methods for establishing and securing inheritance, both political and territorial—became the very targets of United States colonialism, which drafted legislation intended to reverse past promises to Mexicans and Californios (such as the Treaty of Guadalupe Hidalgo) and to regain territorial control. In 1851, California constructed the Land Commission as the legal apparatus for overturning Spanish and Mexican land grants. During his time in California, Harte witnessed first hand the devastating effects this legal act, coupled with the Pre-Emption Act, had on residents of the state.[14]

The Land Commission's impact on residents of California is registered through the questions of ownership over the mine and the abundance of land grants signed by Pío Pico: "In 1849, while still Army Secretary of the State, [Capt. Henry W.] Halleck had produced the first official report on California land matters, setting forth a negative interpretation. He believed that most California claims were inchoate and the Pico grants totally invalid, if not openly fraudulent" (Pitt 91–92). "Governor Pío Pico, it was rumored, had dreamed up some eighty new land grants *after* the American occupation and had doled them out to his '*worthless* cronies'; certainly [reasoned Captain Halleck] all such grants must be retracted at once," according to Pitt (87). Harte's Victor Ramirez, former Secretary under Governor Pico, forges false land grants on old official stationary bearing Pico's signature. Harte brings into sharper focus the methodologies for "legally" robbing Mexicans and Native Americans alike of their rightfully held lands. The abuse of legal methods to affect illegal gain, the novel argues, jeopardizes the very claims individuals make on their own identities. *Gabriel Conroy* reads like a detective story where readers and characters must sift through the multiple disguises and identities assumed by its characters.

Taken together, these two points—that the inclusion of racial difference removes one from the family romance and that the legal system can advocate inclusion into the family—reveal the very foundation of the family romance and the basis for the threat that Mexicans, Chinese, and Native Americans pose after the United States-Mexican War. In *Gabriel Conroy*, the Treaty of Guadalupe Hidalgo's guarantee of United States citizenship to Mexicans living in the newly annexed territory is explored through the family romance in the form of interracial adoption. Grace Conroy, a heroine who is socially and racially white is adopted into a Mexican family in a fictional reversal of the national narrative scripted for the post-1848 Southwest (particularly California). Whiteness, a social and racial category imagined to be the sole purview of the republican family, is jeopardized when Mexicans are granted United States citizenship. In the national family's desire socially to erase Mexicans' racial difference (noted by Mexicans' status in California as "socially white") and thus maintain a legacy of whiteness, the monomaniacal preoccupation with sameness raises the specter of incest.

Harte's novel does not conclude comically with the restoration of the family and national romances. Instead, he leaves his readers to contemplate an unvarnished portrait of the United States government and its imperialist agenda. The legal system and the family are both equally corrupt, so much so that characters easily manipulate both systems to their own ends. What prevails at the conclusion of *Gabriel Conroy* is not love or reconciliation played out on familial and national scales, but greed and a racist legacy of legislative acts intent on making Anglo Americans the sole inheritors of Manifest Destiny. The bodies that testify to this legacy are the corpse of Victor Ramirez and the silent Ah Fe.

Notes

1. As a sign of its obscurity, James Joyce based the protagonist's name in "The Dead" on the titular character from Harte's novel.

2. The Gadsden Purchase, ratified in December of 1853, but not enacted until the following year, secured areas in Southwestern New Mexico and southern Arizona from Mexico for the sum of $10 million. James Gadsden, United States Minister of Mexico, desired the land to create a southern railroad that would make California dependent upon the South rather than the North.

3. In *The American Woman's Home* (1869), Harriet Beecher Stowe and her sister, Catherine Beecher, argue that the work of housewives constituted the "sacred duties of the family state." Historian Ann Douglas Wood argues that women expressed a "complicated urge to make the front truly a home front, to replace the captain with the mother" ("The War within the War" 206). As early as 1778, John Adams asserted that the "foundation of national morality must be laid in private families" (*Diary* 4). Also see Sommer's *Foundational Fictions*.

4. As Tate argues, post-Reconstruction black women writers were keenly aware of the political currency of the family romance and, not surprisingly, employed the domestic as an indirect, but socially recognized maneuver for political capital (*Domestic Allegories*).

5. See Carby ("'On the Threshold'") for a critical and historical account of the logic of lynching laws and how the sanctity and preservation of the white female body became the very ideological grounds on which black males were killed.

6. Geographical proximity played such an influential role in the loyalty of Mexican citizens that a direct correlation existed between people living close to the capital fighting for Mexico during the Mexican War and those residing in Alta and Baja California who welcomed United States annexation. Sánchez (*Telling Identities*) notes that proto-nationalism in Alta California took the form of a nativist association with California in particular, not with Mexico. The closer subjects were to the capital in Mexico City, the stronger their ties with the nation.

7. Even when Mexico scaled back on its colonization plans, its Act of 1844 "forbidding foreigners from engaging in retail trade . . . contained a clause which exempted those foreigners who were naturalized citizens, those who were married to Mexicans, and those who were residents of Mexico with their families" (reported in Craver, *Impact of Intimacy* 29).

8. Colorado's state laws made exception expressly for "people living in that portion of [the state] acquired from Mexico [who] may marry according to the custom of that country" (Snyder, *Geography of Marriage* 202).

9. The term, Californio, describes a wealthy landowner born in California who boasts of pure Spanish ancestry. Mestizos, bi-racial people who have both Spanish and indigenous ancestors, make up the majority of Mexicans living in the United States and Mexico. Unlike the Californios who claimed and were granted access to citizenship and its rights and privileges on their basis of their shared European heritage with Anglo Americans, mestizos comprised the middle to lower classes in Mexican society and provided the labor required to operate haciendas for nearly 300 years.

10. Article V of the Gadsden Purchase guaranteed that "the eighth and ninth, sixteenth and seventeenth articles of the Treaty of Guadalupe Hidalgo shall apply to the territory ceded by the Mexican Republic in the first article of the present treaty. And to all the rights of persons and property, both civil and ecclesiastical, within the same, as fully and effectively as if the said articles were herein again recited and set forth" ("Boundaries" 102–4).

11. "Article II, Sec. 1. Every white male citizen of the United States, and

every white male citizen of Mexico, who shall have elected to become a citizen of the United States, under the treaty of peace exchanged and ratified at Queretaro, on the 30th day of May, 1848 of the age of twenty-one years, who shall have been a resident of the State six months next preceding the election, and the county or district in which he claims his vote thirty days, shall be entitled to vote at all elections which are now or hereafter may authorized by law: Provided, nothing herein contained, shall be construed to prevent the Legislature, by a two-thirds concurrent vote, from admitting to the right of suffrage, Indians or the descendants of Indians, in such special cases as such proportion of the legislative body may deem just and proper."

12. McClain quotes extensively from the Supreme Court decision on this point: "'From [Columbus's] time, down to a very recent period, the American Indians and the Mongolian, or Asiatic, were regarded as the same type of human species.' Scientists, the court continued, had until quite recently believed that Indians and Asians came from the same ethnic stock" ("Chinese Struggle" 549).

13. For additional information on married women's property rights, see Basch (*In the Eyes of the Law*).

14. Harte resided in California from 1854 to 1871; even after his return to the east coast, California, gold miners, and squatters were the primary subject matter of his prose. Stories like "The Story of a Mine" (1878) satirized lobbyists and federal bureaucrats involved in determining the legal status of a quicksilver mine (Scarnhorst, *Bret Harte* 63). See Pitt (*Decline*) for exact figures on land-holdings in post-war California.

Works Cited

Adams, John. *Diary of John Adams*. Ed. L. H. Butterfield, et al. Cambridge, MA: Harvard University Press, 1961.

Almaguer, Tomás. *Racial Fault Lines: The Historical Origins of White Supremacy in California*. Berkeley: University of California Press, 1994.

Bardaglio, Peter. "'An Outrage upon Nature': Incest and the Law in the Nineteenth-Century South." *Joy and Sorrow: Women, Family, and Marriage in the Victorian South, 1830–1900*. Ed. Carol Bleser. New York: Oxford University Press, 1991. 32–51.

Basch, Norma. *In the Eyes of the Law: Women, Marriage, and Property in Nineteenth-Century New York*. Ithaca, NY: Cornell University Press, 1982.

"Boundaries: Gadsen Treaty 1853." *Reference Library of Hispanic America*. Vol. 1. Farmington Hills, MI: Gale, 2003.

Carby, Hazel V. "'On the Threshold of Woman's Era': Lynching, Empire, and Sexuality in Black Feminist Theory." *"Race," Writing, and Difference.* Ed. Henry Louis Gates, Jr. Chicago: University of Chicago Press, 1986. 301–16.

Craver, Rebecca McDowell. *The Impact of Intimacy: Mexican-Anglo Intermarriage in New Mexico, 1821–1846.* El Paso: Texas Western Press, 1982.

Griswold del Castillo, Richard. *The Treaty of Guadalupe Hidalgo.* Norman: University of Oklahoma Press, 1990.

Harte, Bret. *Gabriel Conroy.* New York: Houghton Mifflin, 1876.

McClain, Charles J., Jr. "The Chinese Struggle for Civil Rights in Nineteenth Century America." *California Law Review* 72.4 (1984): 529–68.

Menchaca, Martha. "Chicano Indianism: A Historical Account of Racial Repression in the United States." *American Ethnologist* 20.3 (August 1993): 583–603.

People v. Hall 3C3 992 (92 Cal Rptr 304).

Pitt, Leonard. *The Decline of the Californios: A Social History of the Spanish-Speaking Californians, 1846–1890.* Berkeley: University of California Press, 1966.

Sánchez, Rosaura. *Telling Identities: The Californio Testimonios.* Minneapolis: University of Minneapolis Press, 1995.

Scharnhorst, Gary. *Bret Harte.* New York: Twayne, 1992.

Snyder, William. *The Geography of Marriage, or Legal Perplexities of Wedlock in the United States.* New York: Putnam, 1889.

Sommer, Doris. *Foundational Fictions.* Berkeley: University of California Press, 1991.

Stowe, Harriet and Catherine E. Beecher. *The American Woman's Home: Or, Principles of Domestic Science.* New York: Ford, 1869.

Tate, Claudia. *Domestic Allegories of Political Desire.* New York: Oxford University Press, 1996.

Thorpe, Francis Newton. *The Federal and State Constitutions, Colonial Charters, and Other Organic Laws of the States, Territories, and Colonies Heretofore Forming the United States of America.* Washington, D.C.: Government Printing Office, 1909.

Wood, Ann Douglas. "The War within the War: Women Nurses in the Union Army." *Civil War History* 18 (1972): 197–212.

3 The Color of Money in *The Autobiography of an Ex-Colored Man*

ARIEL BALTER

WHY DOES THE PROTAGONIST OF JAMES Weldon Johnson's *The Autobiography of an Ex-Colored Man,*[1] an intelligent, talented pianist of mixed race, sell himself to a white, capitalist culture, and why did Johnson, a prominent, educated poet, writer, lyricist, lawyer, diplomat, and Secretary of the NAACP, publish such a work anonymously? Although Johnson's text is, in part, an exposé of a black man's experience in turn-of-the-century America and an indictment of white racism, it also, to a degree, adopts the gaze of the dominant white culture and caters to a white audience. By using class and sexuality as analogs or veils for race, Johnson shows how race, class, and sexuality overlap, while he simultaneously obscures the controversial issues he's depicting. Since nothing is what it seems to be in *The Autobiography of an Ex-Colored Man*—nonfiction is fiction, white is black is white, and heterosexual may be homosexual—Johnson can critique without offending too much.

Because of the enigmatic nature of Johnson's text and his position in relation to the first-person narrator of his "autobiography," some critics assert that Johnson takes an ironic and critical view of his narrator, while others suggest that he shares many of the protagonist's attitudes

48

and experiences. For example, Joseph Skerrett contends that the narrator functions as an alter-ego and is based on one of Johnson's long-time friends.[2] In my view, however, although Johnson clearly shares some of the experiences and attitudes of the narrator, he is not the Ex-Colored Man and his work is not an autobiography, but a work of fiction. He uses the narrator, with whom he identifies at times, yet also critiques and distances himself from, as a means by which to criticize white America and its values. As Stephen Ross says, "Johnson attacks a hypothetical white audience; the narrator is unreliable not because he is obtuse or hypocritical, but because Johnson wants us to see him as betrayed by a white, upper-class value system he cannot escape" (Ross 199). Johnson takes on the perspective of his largely white and middle- and upper-class readers in such sections as his lengthy analysis of the "three classes" of blacks in Jacksonville, his patronizing critique of Atlanta's lower-class blacks, and his admiration of the colored upper-class doctor and his circle, while he ironizes the narrator's decision to be white and many of his personal and professional decisions and attitudes. Roger Rosenblatt nicely summarizes the position of Johnson's work: "In a sense, the novel, like its hero, passes for white, yet, also like its hero, it quietly indicts the white nation, North and South, by its existence" (178). Because Johnson shares some of the outlooks of middle-class whites and is keenly aware that he is writing primarily for a white audience (in 1912) but is deeply critical of white America, he deftly constructs his text so that it appeals to and reaches a white audience while also critiquing them.

Johnson's impressive education and careers perhaps reflected and contributed to his snobbish attitudes towards black people. Though he was strongly influenced by Booker T. Washington's *Up From Slavery*, his novel and his own career path more strongly reflect Du Bois's ideologies. Houston Baker asserts that "*The Autobiography of an Ex-Colored Man* is both the history and the confession of one of the 'talented tenth'" (Baker, "Forgotten Prototype" 439). Even Johnson's friend Zora Neale Hurston critically (perhaps jokingly) commented on his "whiteness": "Take James Weldon Johnson, for instance. There's a man white enough to suit Hitler, and he's been passing for colored for years. Now, don't get the idea that he is not welcome among us. He certainly is. He has more than paid his way. But he just is not a negro" (qtd. in Sundquist, *Hammers* 26). Eric Sundquist responds to Hurston's barb: "Quite possibly it was Johnson's cultivated, urbane manner, his easy travel in privileged circles, or even his comparatively light skin color and somewhat Hispanic features that sparked her comic remark. . . . Most likely, it was the decided aesthetic gulf between" them (*Hammers* 26). No doubt Johnson's work for the NAACP and his writings and support of black civil rights and culture were not the bases of Hurston's criticism. But their aesthetic differences are telling and important. For Johnson chose to write and gain power by using the aesthetic sensibilities of the middle class, and, in America, middle-class culture has been defined by whites who have held economic and political power, or, as Clyde Taylor asserts, the "dominant discourse" establishes "the frame of the dialogue (knowledge), according to the golden rule which says, 'them with the gold makes the rules'" (180). Consequently, middle-class culture has reflected white, European culture.[3]

In "The Dilemma of the Negro Author," Johnson acknowledges that black writers cannot afford to disregard "nine-tenths of the people of the United States," namely, whites (481). He maintains that "The Aframerican author faces a special problem which the plain American author knows nothing about—the problem of the double audience. It is more than a double audience; it is a divided audience, an audience made up of two elements with differing and often opposite and antagonistic points of view. His audience is always both white America and Black America" ("Dilemma" 477). Johnson's comment is reminiscent of Du Bois's assertion that the Negro is only allowed to "see himself through the revelation of the other world. It is a peculiar sensation, this double-consciousness, this sense of always looking at one's self through the eyes of others, of measuring one's soul by the tape of a world that looks on in amused contempt and pity" (214–15). Both Johnson's and Du Bois's statements suggest that blacks have to adopt a white gaze, distinct from a black conception of the self, and this white point of view, according to Jane Gaines, tended to reflect white, middle-class values which supported the stereotype of an "irredeemable Black underclass" (66). The content, genre, style, and publication of Johnson's work clearly reflect his need to cater to these two audiences. He masks his novel, a traditionally white genre, with an autobiography, a form associated with slave narratives, which were popular with white and black audiences.[4] Despite Johnson's clever marketing strategies and awareness of audience, the seemingly sellable, anonymous 1912 "autobiography" was not particularly successful, whereas the 1927 authored fiction was a critical and popular success, which was most probably connected to the Harlem Renaissance and the growth of the black middle class. Since Johnson's novel and hero, as Eugenia Collier says, are "middle class to the core" (373), it is no wonder that it appealed most to a middle-class audience—black and white. Benjamin Lawson adds that Carl Van Vechten's preface to the 1927 edition gave it the stamp of "the white intellectual" and thus the "approval of blacks and whites, and a new prominence in the culture of the 1920's" (98). Johnson's text also alludes to black folk culture and music, exposes white racism, and refers to Washington and Du Bois, thereby appealing to an African American audience as well as to liberal white readers (Goellnicht 19). However, Johnson tones down his "color" by having his protagonist convert folk music into Europeanized, classical music (which Johnson himself did in his own music career), and condescendingly commenting on unsophisticated lower-class blacks.[5] Most strongly, because he knew that power and voice were held by the white nine-tenths of the American population, he makes his text palatable to that audience perhaps by allying and masking the less marketable issue of race with those of class and sexuality.

Before Johnson published the novel, his brother suggested that he title it *The Chameleon* (Johnson, *Along This Way* 238), a title he considered and one that in some ways best reflects the way that he structures his work. A chameleon changes color in order to protect itself and adapt to its environment; one skin serves as a sort of mask for another. At the conclusion of the novel, the Ex-Colored Man, like a chameleon, certainly changes color so that he can succeed in a white bourgeois world. But the title also applies to Johnson who plays to different audiences and veils, in layer upon layer, the different themes of the novel. By initially publishing his book anonymously, Johnson transforms himself from a black novelist to a blank whose text and identity remain to be colored in.

Because the issues of race, class, and sexuality overlap so heavily in Johnson's text, I will analyze the novel chronologically rather than thematically, since it is impossible to distinguish a particular theme without discussing its analog. In *The Autobiography of an Ex-Colored Man* one subject stands in for, is akin to, or masks another. For instance, whiteness is equated with money, culture, and class; middle-class blacks are associated with access to money and culture and by extension a degree of "whiteness"; blackness and sexuality, particularly homosexuality, are linked; and sexuality is tied up with money, which circles back to class and skin color. In his own autobiography Johnson himself admits that "in the core of the heart of the American race problem the sex factor is rooted; rooted so deeply that it is not always recognized when it shows at the surface" (*Along This Way* 170). Throughout his novel he also illustrates how materialism and the class problem are deeply rooted alongside the "sex factor." Although Johnson gradually unfolds and then intertwines the various concerns of the text, their intersection with and subordination to one another create a pervasive undercurrent in the novel.

In the Preface to the Original Edition of 1912, Johnson, in the guise of "The Publishers," introduces and authenticates the "autobiography." He mimics the voice of the publishers much like he plays the ex-colored man. This false preface in fact presents what is to come in the novel though not entirely in the way it purports. By misleading the reader about the identity of the author and preface writer, Johnson intimates that other elements of the novel are not necessarily what they seem to be either. In the preface he asserts that the *Autobiography* is a "composite and proportionate presentation of the entire race, embracing all of its various groups and elements, showing their relations with each other and to the whites. . . . In these pages it is as though a veil had been drawn aside" (*Selected Writings* 2:273). While it is true that the novel depicts a "composite" portrait of the race, it does not really lift veils but lowers them. By obscuring its presentation of the race with allusions to homosexuality and dazzling pictures of middle-and upper-class society, the text illustrates, only indirectly, the composition of American blacks. Johnson concludes the preface by claiming that the autobiography brings the reader "upon an elevation where he can catch a bird's-eye view of the conflict which is being waged" (*Selected Writings* 2:274). Placing the narrator and reader outside and above the subject of the book elevates and distances Johnson, and this position thus affiliates him with a white or middle-class black audience who can critically analyze the black race without dirtying their hands too much. The narrator's perch also protects him from disclosing too much about his identity and alliances and consequently enables him to profit from the very group he discreetly critiques.

The first paragraph of the novel hints at how themes intertwine and calls into question the reliability of the narrator. Partially confessing his duplicity and linking his identity to his society or audience and to money and material goods, the Ex-Colored Man states: "I know that in writing the following pages I am divulging the great secret of my life, the secret which for some years I have guarded far more carefully than any of my earthly possessions. . . . I find a sort of savage and diabolical desire to gather up all the little tragedies of my life, and turn them into a practical joke on society" (*Autobiography* 393). Since the autobiography is not truly an autobiography, his confession is suspect. By confiding in the reader, the narrator tries to gain his or her trust, which he then undermines by admitting that he's playing a joke on society, which, in effect, warns his audience that he's untrustworthy. In a way, the novel is a form of revenge on white America; it seems as if the Ex-Colored Man is saying, "I sold out because of you and now you'll pay and I'll make money and have a good laugh at your expense." The joke also suggests that in *The Autobiography of an Ex-Colored Man* things aren't what they seem to be. In this opening statement, the narrator further alludes to his own complicity by linking his "great secret" to his "earthly possessions." By exchanging his black identity or color for power and money in a white consumer culture, he creates the "secret" of his life, which he then trades back in the form of his autobiography. He then uses this account of the "little tragedies" of his life as a slap in the face to the very society to which he sold out.

The narrator's account of his childhood as a young "white" boy also sets up his audience for what is to follow. Recollecting his father, the Ex-Colored Man connects, in a seemingly naïve voice, race and money or class. His "distinct mental image" of his white father consists of his shiny shoes and his watch and chain; for him, whiteness is equivalent to material goods. The narrator, who doesn't yet know that he is not legitimately white, appropriately and ironically plays the role of his father's houseboy for which he is given, "in return for this service," a coin. Before departing, the father drills a hole through a gold piece and ties it around his son's neck. This gesture labels the boy a slave who has been and will be bought and sold; he is literally enchained by money controlled and bestowed by a white man. The scene also emphasizes the ways in which money goes hand in hand with racial oppression. The narrator's response to his father's gift, "I have wished that some other way had been found of attaching it to me besides putting a hole through it," suggests that the narrator is more than willing to enter into the capitalist system of exchange, so long as he profits from it (*Autobiography* 394–95). If he is going to sell himself, he expects enormous returns, an attitude that foreshadows his final decision in the novel. However, his concluding comment, "On the day after the coin was put around my neck my mother and I started on what seemed to me an endless journey," implies that what he trades may not have a monetary equivalent and hints that he pays a high price to become white (*Autobiography* 395).

Not only does the narrator introduce, early on, the relationship between race and class, but he also obliquely points to how race, sexuality, and economics obfuscate one another. The Ex-Colored Man who is "shy of the girls, and remained so" develops a friendship with a fourteen-year-old boy whom he "bound" to himself "with hooks of steel" (*Autobiography* 397). He then goes on to describe his red-headed friend's physique and concludes that they were "mutually attracted" to one another because of the services they could perform for each other. Since he has already been inducted into the American capitalist ethos by his great white father, the narrator knows the exchange value of friendship. The economic basis of his camaraderie, that is, the Red Head's brawn traded for his brains, justifies his relationship and masks the Ex-Colored Man's homoerotic desire for the Red Head.

The Ex-Colored Man immediately follows his illustration of his white friend with a description of the African American boy, "Shiny," who "strongly attracted my attention from the first day I saw him. His face was as black as night, but shone as though it were polished; he had sparkling eyes, and when he opened his mouth, he displayed glistening white teeth. It struck me at once as appropriate to call him 'Shiny Face,' or 'Shiny Eyes,' or 'Shiny Teeth,' and I spoke of him often by one of these names to the other boys" (*Autobiography* 399). The narrator simultaneously objectifies and eroticizes Shiny as though he were a white man sizing up a black servant. He notes and admires Shiny's features, which suggest his strength, health, and virility, emphasizing his friend's sparkle and "Shine" as a type of commodity to the narrator. Like a strapping slave, Shiny is profitable and desirable. The narrator's initial description of Shiny precedes his own outing as a black boy, which accounts, in part, for his white overseer's view of his friend. But, his perspective also marks his own investment in the ideologies of white, American culture, both before and after he discovers his racial identity. His desire for Shiny mirrors his yearning to shine in a white capitalist society whose economy developed as a result of the labor of his friend's and his own ancestors.

When the narrator learns of his own blackness, he responds by gazing at himself narcissistically in the mirror. Roger Rosenblatt points out that "he realizes a duality in his life, the difference between himself as subject and object" (180). Itemizing and eroticizing his own features, much as he did Shiny's, the Ex-Colored Man emulates the gaze of the white man, even as his newfound identity bestows on him a "dual personality" or perspective (*Autobiography* 403). Johnson's reference to Du Bois points not only to the fact that African Americans hold two outlooks but also play to two different audiences. The narrator's admission of his doubleness is loaded, for it refers to his awareness of race as well as sexuality, and it reminds his dual audience of his duplicity. Although he has just disclosed his "secret" dark side, he still has not disclosed all and may be doubled over with laughter at his "practical joke on society." The Ex-Colored Man plays it both ways, or is honest in his dishonesty, when he himself admits, "It is strange how in some things honest people can be dishonest without the slightest compunction" (*Autobiography* 407).

The narrator's duplicity and double perspective on race mirror the ways in which he both conceals and reveals his own sexuality and worships and despises women. His relation to his first female love object is mixed up with his anxieties about his race and sexuality and is finally obliterated by the dazzle of the dollar. The Ex-Colored Man states that he loved "his first love . . . as only a boy loves. I dreamed of her, I built air castles for her, she was the incarnation of each beautiful heroine I knew" (*Autobiography* 408). Unlike his more sensual descriptions of Shiny and Red Head, the narrator's asexual construction of his first female love reflects the idealized fantasies of a boy, and he then confesses that his adoration of the girl "was in secret" because of his "dread that in some way she would find it out" (*Autobiography* 408). The vague pronoun, *it*, which lacks any referent in the paragraph, could refer to his race or his sexuality, and his conclusion about the girl suggests that his ambiguous assertion is quite deliberate. The narrator concludes, "It makes me laugh to think how successful I was in concealing it all," and when he realizes the futility of his affections, he exclaims, "the heartless jade, how she led me on!" (*Autobiography* 409). Though the narrator conceals "all" from the girl, he reveals perhaps more than he intends to us since his racial and sexual identities function as masks for one another; they are *it* and *all*. Accordingly, in what has become a jaded trope, the narrator turns his self-hatred and confusion onto the white female who signifies the unsettling of his racial and sexual orientations.

Fortunately, the narrator's aristocratic father and his entourage of goods overshadow his attention towards the girl. Once again, the Ex-Colored Man is saved or ensnared by his father's trappings, his derby hat and polished shoes, and symbolically by the white capitalist culture he believes will hide and redeem him. Material goods and the upward mobility they represent displace his first love a second time and erase her from the narrative. After playing a duet together, the narrator explains that the nameless, faceless girl "impulsively threw both her arms round me and kissed me, while I struggled to get away" (*Autobiography* 413). Evidently his escape is successful since we hear little of the girl again, but we do learn that shortly after this scene the Ex-Colored Man receives a gift from his father of an upright piano about which he feels disappointed that it was not a grand. In contrast to his revulsion from the desirous girlfriend, the narrator expresses great affection for the "beautiful" piano whose "full, mellow tone" was "ravishing" (*Autobiography* 413). Not only does the piano represent an expensive material surrogate for the narrator's desires, but it also allows him to acculturate into white, European society. Just as he is trained as a classical pianist and given the piano by his white father, so too can the Ex-Colored Man use the very same tool to become white and drown out his blackness and homosexuality.

The death of the narrator's mother marks yet another loss of a female love object who is replaced by money and success. Just as he fails to detail the nature of and demise of his relationship with his first girlfriend, so too does the narrator gloss over his adored and despised black mother's death. He writes, "I will not rake over this, one of the two sacred sorrows of my life: nor could I describe the feeling of unutterable loneliness that fell upon me" (*Autobiography* 419). Although he finds himself at a loss for words upon losing the person who brands him as black, he manages to describe, in detail, his "little estate" which consists of "a good supply of clothes, a piano, some books and trinkets . . . about two hundred dollars in cash" and of course the benefit concert for himself, which earns him an additional two hundred dollars (*Autobiography* 419–20). His mother's death and the convenient marriage of his first love to another are only the first of many loves and advantageous losses that the narrator experiences.

In order for the Ex-Colored Man to succeed in a white-run society, he must adopt the ideologies of his oppressors. In post-Civil War, turn-of-the-century America, authority entailed financial power that provided cultural mastery or the illusion of possessing taste and class. When the narrator goes to Atlanta, he must distinguish himself from the lower-class, provincial blacks so that he can continue to "act white," despite the fact that he has gone down to the South to study at a black university. His "repulsion" by the "unkempt appearance, the shambling gait and loud talk and laughter of *these* [my emphasis] people" (*Autobiography* 422) indicates that he separates himself from *them*. Eric Sundquist describes the narrator's position as one of a "European explorer in colonial Africa" on an "imperial exploration" (*Hammers* 12). As he sojourns deeper into the South, the Ex-Colored Man further distinguishes himself from poorer blacks by analyzing them as an anthropologist or economist and then allying himself only with "the best class of coloured people in Jacksonville" (*Autobiography* 433–36). Such an affiliation includes attending "dances and dinners and card parties, their musicals, and their literary societies. The women attend social affairs dressed in good taste, and the men in dress suits which they own; and the reader will make a mistake to confound these entertainments with the 'Bellman's Balls' . . . which the humorous press of the country illustrates 'Cullud Sassiety'" (*Autobiography* 438). The narrator's defensive analysis and fine distinctions serve to distinguish himself as colored rather than "cullud," and he "acts white" by displaying his ability to differentiate between high European/Anglo American culture and cheap imitation. His keen eye and fine taste elevate him to a higher class and, by extension, distance him from his "lower" race.

Unlike many blacks, including some of "the best class of coloured people," the narrator has the choice of living as a black man or passing for white. Despite his options, however, he seems to admire and advocate African American culture and promotes the education and fair treatment of blacks. At the same time, the Ex-Colored Man essentializes and universalizes the tenets of white, European culture without questioning what they signify and to whom they belong. In reference to the cakewalk and ragtime, admired in Europe as "American" art forms, the narrator asserts: "These are lower forms of art, but they give evidence of a power that will some day be applied to the higher forms. In this measure, at least, and aside from the number of prominent individuals the coloured people of the United States has produced, the race has been a world influence; and all of the Indians between Alaska and Patagonia haven't done as much" (*Autobiography* 441). Because he and other educated, "cultured" blacks have assimilated successfully and been accepted by white society, the narrator concludes that they must be truly cultured, unlike the Indians whose non-European ways mark them as uncultured and consequently outside society. Although, at this point, the narrator does not admit that the only way to attain power and culture in the United States is by being white, he does show that one's cultural values are strongly connected to race and that power lies in the hands of those who are wealthy, cultured, and white.

Aptly, after acknowledging his artistic and social biases, the Ex-Colored Man decides to move to New York, the city of high finance and culture, whose bay is "glistening gold" (*Autobiography* 441). In many ways New York functions as a synecdoche for the consumer culture and racism of turn-of-the-century America and further, within the novel, serves as a site or marker for the narrator's confusion about his race, sexuality, and social class. The narrator describes New York as

> an enchanted spot. New York City is the most fatally fascinating thing in America. She sits like a great witch at the gate of the country, showing her alluring white face and hiding her crooked hands and feet under the folds of her wide garments—constantly enticing thousands from far within, and tempting those who come from across the seas to go no farther. And all those become the victims of her caprice. Some she at once crushes beneath her cruel feet; others she condemns to a fate like that of galley-slaves; a few she favours and fondles, riding them high on the bubbles of fortune; then with a sudden breath she blows the bubbles out and laughs mockingly as she watches them fall. (*Autobiography* 442)

As narrator, he projects and conflates his own ambivalence about his race, social class, and sexuality onto a specific place. In the guise of a white femme fatale, New York seduces and destroys the masculinity and fortunes of those attracted to her white face and dazzling, bubbling riches. Clearly, the image also reflects the Ex-Colored Man's attraction to the white woman as a means of social advancement and his fear of and discomfort with her as a source of sexual interest and potential exposure and destruction of racial identity.

As an antidote to the fatal woman, New York, the narrator begins to frequent male social or gambling clubs, a milieu providing him with access to a "darker," less prestigious social class and a locus of male bonding. The Ex-Colored Man boasts that the poker players on the upper floor, to which he has been admitted, "were evidently the aristocrats of the place . . . frequently using the word 'gentlemen': in fact, they seemed to be practising a sort of Chesterfieldian politeness towards each other" (*Autobiography* 443). He is attracted to the attention and respect he earns from his gambling prowess and by the "brilliancy of the place, the display of diamond rings, scarf-pins, ear-rings, and breast-pins, the big rolls of money" (*Autobiography* 445–47). Attaining the status of an "habitue" of the "Club," as he comes to know it, the Ex-Colored Man joins what he fancies is a classy circle of white and coloured people in New York. He quickly learns "to fake a knowledge" of various celebrities and particular brands of wine and champagne and styles of clothing (*Autobiography* 451–52), since being in the know marks him as a member of the moneyed class. Johnson's Ex-Colored Man believes that through connoisseurship, he can gain power and move up the social ladder. Although the narrator naïvely falls for the tacky imitation of the social mores of the white middle class, which he ultimately enters, his apprenticeship at the Club serves as a learning experience and stepping stone to the whiter, more fiscally conservative and secure, finer things in life.

The Club is also reminiscent of the Victorian gentlemen's clubs to which respectable Englishmen belonged. Such clubs functioned as social communities in which heterosexual bachelors and married gentlemen could legitimately gather and escape from their wives and domestic obligations. The Club to which the Ex-Colored Man belongs exemplifies a site of homosocial bonding that promotes a male, heterosexual, capitalist power structure at the expense of women and homosexuals. Eve Sedgwick argues that "in any male-dominated society, there is a special relationship between male homosocial (*including* homosexual) desire and the structures for maintaining and transmitting patriarchal power" (25). By ensconcing himself in the exclusive, high roller world of the Club, the narrator can gain power, money, and prestige in a male world and successfully mask his homosexual proclivities in an established homosocial environment. The Club provides him with an alternate way to rise up the social ladder without the help of a woman, or so the Ex-Colored Man believes.

The social club that the Ex-Colored Man frequents may also refer to the Harlem basement cabarets and clubs of this period in which many well-known homosexuals mingled with other patrons (Chauncey 17). In this respect, then, homosexuality and blackness ally with one another either as analogs or tropes of otherness. Like these New York hangouts, the Club represents a "centre of coloured Bohemians and sports" whose "walls were literally covered with photographs or lithographs of every coloured man in America who had ever 'done anything'" (*Autobiography* 450). The narrator's emphasis on a Bohemian black male culture undermines the Club's similarity to its ostensibly heterosexual, white, British precursor. And yet, he reminds us that the Club is "well known to both white and coloured people of certain classes" (*Autobiography* 449). Once again, though the narrator pays lip service to various loci of black culture and even subtly alludes to homosexual hangouts, he quickly resituates himself in the seat of white male power.

The Ex-Colored Man's encounter with the wealthy, white "widow" and her black companion also highlights how "deviant" sexual behavior, race, and economics interconnect. As if acting on behalf of the narrator, the "widow's" black boyfriend, who is supported by the white woman and consequently is known as a "bad man," shoots her in a fit of jealous rage. Again, the text conveniently kills off the white woman who attempts to seduce the narrator with her charm and riches. This murder scene mirrors the Ex-Colored Man's own predicament: like the black companion, he too depends upon the patronage of wealthy whites and ends up succeeding, in part, by marrying a white woman. The companion's connection to the widow also signifies a sexually transgressive relationship reflecting the narrator's own illegitimate desires. Cheryl Clarke explains that "The 'oppressing social structures' of segregation and the patriarchal code of heterosexual monogamy are transgressed and disrupted in the Club by racial mixing and illicit sexuality, including interracial homosexuality and bisexuality. In the Club, Ex-Coloured Man . . . learns about the sexually illicit, though he withholds this information from the reader through an announced silence, . . . a gap that serves as a space of transgressive sexuality" (87). Although the white female "patron" and her black companion function as analogs to the narrator, they are presented as other, deviant, and separate from him. As merely a passive observer in the love triangle, he indirectly causes the widow's murder and is thereby extricated from the clutches of a white woman and the more sordid side of the Club.

However, fortune, this time with the face of a white man, an alternative to the widow, smiles upon the Ex-Colored Man when he meets his "millionaire friend" or patron whom he describes as "the means by which I escaped from this lower world" (*Autobiography* 456). The nameless patron, who is identified primarily by his financial relationship to the narrator, represents the most overt homosexual relationship that he develops, but this relationship seems legitimate because the patron's homosexuality is buffered by his wealth and whiteness. Because he is white, cultured, and very rich, the millionaire enables the narrator to move up and out of the black, less refined "lower" classes. Using eroticized and stereotypical descriptions of homosexuals, the narrator presents his patron as an object of his desire, writing that his benefactor is "a clean-cut, slender, but athletic-looking man, who may have been taken for a youth. . . . He was clean-shaven and had regular features, and all of his movements bore the indefinable but unmistakable stamp of culture. He spoke to no one, but sat languidly puffing cigarettes" (*Autobiography* 456). His extravagant dinner parties include "a girlish-looking youth" and the millionaire "seemed to take cynical delight in watching and studying others indulging in excess" (*Autobiography* 458). All of the homosexual allusions to the patron and his circle are peppered with references to money and signs of wealth. The narrator observes that he is in "the midst of elegance and luxury" and notices "a table which already looked like a big jewel" (*Autobiography* 457). Further, the entire premise behind the narrator-millionaire relationship is one of master and slave. The Ex-Colored Man performs and the patron rewards him with money, gifts, and trips. The benefactor, who frequently works the Ex-Colored

Man to the point of exhaustion, "made" him take a glass of wine, gave him money, and promised him lots of work, "his only stipulation being" that he play exclusively for him (*Autobiography* 459). Cheryl Clarke explains the Ex-Colored Man's contract with his "millionaire friend" serves as his "entree into a new kind of bondage, Mammonism. On the appointed evening, Ex-Coloured Man enters this new patriarchal and homosocial space much like a slave who is brought into the house of a new master. . . . The language Johnson chooses . . . can be read as a code for the homosexual dimension of male or female homosociability" (89). The narrator justifies and explains his loyalty to his "relentless tyrant" patron by saying that "he paid me so liberally I could forget much. There at length grew between us a familiar and warm relationship, and I am sure he had a decided personal liking for me. On my part, I looked upon him at that time as about all a man could wish to be" (*Autobiography* 460), all of which points to the ways in which race, sexuality, and economics play off of one another in the novel. As if competing with one another, for the narrator and within the narrative, money and status play off of or juxtapose blackness and homosexuality. However, despite all of the signs, the patron-narrator liaison remains ostensibly a heterosexual, business relationship. For just as homosexuality screens blackness, money and whiteness obscure homosexuality.

The work that the narrator performs for his patron deflects the homosexual undertones of their friendship and simultaneously highlights the fact that they do not maintain a partnership but an unequal relationship determined by race and economic status. The Ex-Colored Man is paid to play classical music and later transcribe classic to ragtime. Although this adaptation suggests that the narrator takes European culture and recreates it into an African American music form, it implies that the true foundation or pure form of music is classical. Also, the Ex-Colored Man is forced to play the role of the black entertainer who caters to the amusement of a white audience. Like a performer in a minstrel show, he mimics the black man as whites have constructed him.[6] Later, while in Europe, the Ex-Colored Man decides to convert ragtime into classical music, which makes him into an "American" commercial success and reflects Johnson's and the text's position that folk culture must be reconfigured into European forms in order to reach a higher level (Sundquist, *Hammers* 24). Johnson's narrator hints that performing for

his white patron may entail sex, entertainment at the expense of denigrating his own race, and labor in exchange for which the narrator moves
a step closer to the inner circle of wealthy whites.

Both in contrast to and as an extension of the United States, Europe,
the next destination of the Ex-Colored Man, functions as another site
in which his culture, sexuality, and race veil one another. In the novel
there is a pretense that Europe is color neutral.[7] Unlike America where
the one-drop rule designates one as black, Europe, in Johnson's portrayal,
does not define people by their color. For him, race is an American problem. However, the narrative's uncritical view of European culture also
suggests an acceptance of white, European standards as universal. In
America, the narrator could pass for white if only his biology or one drop
of "black blood" did not get in the way, whereas in Europe he can be a
man of the world or cultured by virtue of his mannerisms and savoir
faire. Paris, the first city on the Ex-Colored Man's grand tour, serves as
a cultural training ground for the narrator in his quest to become white.
The narrator explains that "Americans are immensely popular in Paris"
and Paris exemplifies all that is beautiful and artistic (*Autobiography*
467–48). His cultural grooming consists of learning to speak French,
accumulating a new wardrobe, frequenting cafes, and attending musical performances such as the opera *Faust*, where a scene prefigures the
narrator's final sale of his racial identity for economic and social power
much as Faust sells his soul for earthly pleasures and knowledge. Furthermore, while at the opera, the narrator quickly falls in love with a lovely
white girl who he discovers is the daughter of his white father, in other
words, his half sister. This attraction to his white other half emphasizes
how his sexual desire intersects with his wish to be white and to be accepted
by his Caucasian father. Yet, once again he is released from fulfilling or
following through on his desire for a woman since, after all, the girl is
his sister. He can then safely worship her whiteness and regret most of
all the "real tragedy" (*Autobiography* 467) that he cannot acknowledge his
other or whiter half as well as his resistance to heterosexuality.

England, in contrast to France and America, exemplifies a culture
far more ambivalent about consumerism and the acquisition of culture
and higher social status. The Ex-Colored Man observes that "The Lon-
doner seems to think that Americans are people whose only claim to be
classed as civilized is that they have money," implying that the English

possess "true" culture and civilization and their crass American cousins attempt, in vain, to acquire it (*Autobiography* 467). The narrator further notes that whereas Paris seems "hand-made, artificial, as though set up for the photographer's camera," the English city is "rugged, natural, and fresh" (*Autobiography* 468); but what unsettles the narrator is the inaccessibility of England. He can "whiten" himself in France by buying clothes and sipping wine in cafes, but he cannot purchase Anglo-Saxon culture since it is "natural" and inherent to the white English. In frustration and also ironically, in a clever money-making scheme inspired by his European experience, the Ex-Colored Man decides to return to America, to the heart of the South, to learn about ragtime. Since he cannot become English, and hasn't yet decided to become white, the Ex-Colored Man opts to succeed in the United States by mining the music of the American South and reaping profits by reconfiguring it into the gold of classical music. The Ex-Colored Man uses his worldly knowledge to earn money and move up the social ladder. Ironically, the Ex-Colored Man personifies the English view of the American; he exploits "natural" resources in the hope that his earnings will grant him culture.

When the narrator returns to the South, instead of immersing himself in folk culture and learning about ragtime, he distances himself from all blacks, other than those who are light skinned and upper class, and maintains an outsider's, observer's view of black people and culture. At first he proclaims that he "made up [his] mind to go back into the very heart of the South, to live among the people, and drink [his] inspiration firsthand" (*Autobiography* 471), learning from even as he also would help "his" people, but then he admits that he decides to return to the South "on purely selfish grounds, in accordance with my millionaire's philosophy" (*Autobiography* 474). When he arrives at the site of his musical and cultural education, the narrator, like an anthropologist studying an "uncivilized" culture, and also as a writer in the position of a white man, takes notes on the southern blacks he encounters: "All the while I was gathering material for work, jotting down in my note-book themes and melodies, and trying to catch the spirit of the Negro in his relatively primitive state. I began to feel the necessity of hurrying so that I might get back to some city like Nashville to begin my compositions and at the same time earn at least a living by teaching and performing before my funds gave out" (*Autobiography* 489). His comment indicates that his two options are not mutually exclusive since living among the people and making money off of them are a useful means of elevating himself socially, culturally, economically, and even racially. Donald Goellnicht comments on the narrator's mercenary fact-finding trip: "How completely he becomes absorbed into the role of white musician exploiting black music can be seen by the fact that he later seeks to earn a handsome profit from recording black music in the South, the very thievery he had been critical of white musicians for" (27). In effect, the Ex-Colored Man distances himself further from "his" people and exploits them more when he is living among them than when he lived apart from them. Although he returns to his "roots," he acts whiter than ever.

The Ex-Colored Man's relation to other blacks in the South and to the lynching he observes further illustrates that his perspective is Eurocentric and white and that he has, again, passively decided to profit from the culture that has exploited him. En route to the South, the narrator befriends upper-class American blacks who "were all people of education and culture and, apparently, of means," and he notes: "I could not help being struck by the great difference between them and the same class of coloured people in the South. In speech and thought they were genuine Yankees. . . . It is remarkable, after all, what an adaptable creature the Negro is. I have seen the black West Indian gentleman in London, and he is in speech and manners a perfect Englishman" (*Autobiography* 477). What he admires is essentially what he is in training to do, that is, to become a Yankee who is indistinguishable from those with a pure white bloodline. The narrator's observation also prefigures and highlights the ways that class and race overlap in America. In a Darwinian analysis of race and social class in the U.S., the Ex-Colored Man concludes that blacks of "stronger mental endowment" tend to marry people with lighter complexions than themselves. Like Darwin's theory of Natural Selection, marrying whiter, according to the narrator, is "natural" and "a tendency in accordance with what might be called an economic necessity" (*Autobiography* 478). The blacks who survive are the ones who become white and, by extension, financially fit.

The lynching, which one might assume would cause the Ex-Colored Man to identify and sympathize with other African Americans, instead provokes him to forsake his race and become white. Although he experiences shock and outrage at the lynching, his primary response is shame in his position, that of observer. The narrator explains, "I was fixed to the spot where I stood, powerless to take my eyes from what I did not want to see," and yet he describes, in methodical, journalistic detail, the scene of the lynching (*Autobiography* 497). He then confesses that he feels ashamed of being black and a citizen of a country that tortures its people, suggesting feelings of embarrassment and self-hatred in relation to his African American roots but also outrage against white racism. The narrator's response to the lynching is always two-sided. After witnessing this horrifying act, he concludes that "the Southern whites are in many respects a great people. . . . If one will put oneself in a romantic frame of mind, one can admire their notions of chivalry and bravery and justice," while a few lines later he asserts that "The Southern whites are not yet living in the present age; many of their general ideas hark back to a former century, some of them to the Dark Ages" (*Autobiography* 498–99).[8] The narrator's tone and distanced, third-person perspective position him as an outsider or white observer who cannot even register his feelings about what he sees. In analyzing the lynching scene, Eric Sundquist asserts that "the spectatorship that marks the protagonist's relation to his blackness throughout the book . . . rises to a wrenching height in this scene, where he stands both on and off stage, on both sides of the color line. . . . The unnamed lynching victim is the narrator's inverted double, his mirror image, for it is in the act of witnessing that he most becomes an 'ex-coloured man,' inadvertently as savage a spectator as the others who flock to the public ritual" (*Hammers* 43–44). As a sympathetic spectator, the narrator responds with a lengthy diatribe on white abuse of blacks, but also as one who can afford to distance himself from the object of persecution, he decides to become white. Jane Gaines points out that lynching, which was inflicted on blacks particularly during the period of Reconstruction, reflected a displacement of economic concerns onto the sexual and racial. She explains that "Whites' nightmare vision of Blacks voting and owning property" led to "punishing" blacks for "threatening" "symbolic property—White womanhood" ("Fire" 54, 60). Also, this suggests that not just in Johnson's novel, but in American culture, sexual and juridical concerns are often masked economic ones. Gaines's analysis of the implications of lynching makes the Ex-Colored Man's post-lynching conversion to whiteness even more apt. In response to a punishment for owning property and gaining power, he gives whites their just desserts by purchasing real estate and earning large sums of money. The narrator's conversion, however, is a passive, non-decision to live as he has been living up to this point. The lynching rationalizes or sparks the Ex-Colored Man's decision to live, dress, and act like a white businessman, and, as he protests, "let the world take me for what it would" (*Autobiography* 499). Without assuming responsibility for his actions, the Ex-Colored Man (in the passive voice) finds himself in New York again in the racial and economic position for which he has trained his whole life—a white businessman.

Although the Ex-Colored Man presents his career and color move as a path of least resistance, his quite calculated decision exemplifies passive-aggressive behavior. The narrator, who includes only the "impor-tant facts" of his time as a white man, details, as if he is compiling a resume, his financial and social ascent. In order to accommodate or mask his "Bohemian tastes," which may refer to homosexuality, the narrator enrolls in business school, saves money, and becomes a real estate mogul and slumlord. The "pleasure" that the narrator derives from his earn-ings compensates for the unnamed, costly pleasures he experienced in his first few days in the city and militates against his blackness. In this novel, money, used advantageously, solves the difficulties of a black or gay man (*Autobiography* 499–502). Once the narrator is a wealthy landowner, he enters the elite social circles of New York, signifying his full membership into the brotherhood of upper-class white men. The narrator comments on his success: "I laughed heartily over what struck me as the capital joke I was playing" (*Autobiography* 503). Even though, in one sense, he sticks it to white society by infiltrating their inner cir-cles and tainting them, socially, economically, and physically through his white wife and his children with his "black blood," in another way, he also plays a joke on blacks. As a slumlord he may be earning large profits from people living in his old tenement houses. In response to the narrator's sell out, Sundquist asserts that African Americans "could be lynched as well by those, like the Ex-Coloured man, who expunge their color and their history in a fantasia of whiteness" (*Hammers* 47). By forsaking his culture, the Ex-Colored Man undermines it and enables further discrimination against black people. Although Sundquist's analysis points to the gravity of the narrator's decision, it seems one-sided and blames the victim without critiquing the basis of his choice.

Sundquist's reading is also problematic in that it implies that the narrator's action has real-life consequences even though the narrative, though realist, is fictional. However, Sundquist's harsh assessment of the Ex-Colored Man also critiques one of the most troubling scenes in the novel in which the narrator, after witnessing a gruesome lynching that in many ways epitomizes white treatment of blacks in America, opts to join the oppressing group by becoming white. And yet, despite the equivocation, the bottom line in this novel and to Johnson seems to be white America's economic and social exploitation of blacks. While the Ex-Colored Man's sell out and revenge may not be admirable, they are fitting, for they respond in kind to the treatment of African Americans. The narrator gains power and success the same way white men do. By portraying the mercenary and soulless behavior of the Ex-Colored Man, Johnson, guardedly, shows us a "composite portrait" of America and its power brokers. Thus, in this respect, the narrator functions as a veil for Johnson. On the surface his actions point to the problems and hypocrisy of passing, while on a deeper level they reflect and critique the institutionalized racism of capitalist America.

In order to solidify his deal, the narrator must marry a white woman. Such a marriage will veil any vestige of blackness or homosexuality and ensure him a secure place in American society. Aptly, the Ex-Colored Man chooses the whitest woman he can find to negate his blackness and to straighten out his homosexuality, or "difference," and "whiten [his] sullied soul." He asserts, "She was as white as a lily, and she was dressed in white. Indeed, she seemed to me the most dazzlingly white thing I had ever seen" (*Autobiography* 503–5). The narrator's description of his bride anticipates Fanon's portrayal of the black man's desire for a white woman:

> Out of the blackest part of my soul, across the zebra striping of my mind, surges this desire to be suddenly *white*.
> I wish to be acknowledged not as *black* but as *white*.
> Now—and this is a form of recognition that Hegel had not envisaged—who but a white woman can do this for me? By loving me she proves that I am worthy of white love. I am loved like a white man.
> I am a white man.

Her love takes me onto the noble road that leads to total
realization. . . .
I marry white culture, white beauty, white whiteness.
When my restless hands caress those white breasts, they grasp
white civilization and dignity and make them mine. (63)

Through the white woman, not only does the Ex-Colored Man gain white
culture and, luckily for him, white children and therefore legitimacy
within a white patriarchal structure, but also he gains financial success.
The narrator refers to his unnamed wife by her color and, like his millionaire friend, in financial terms. He "wins" the "wealth of her love"
for which nothing "can be profitably exchanged," and suffers an "irrepara-
ble loss" when she dies (*Autobiography* 508–10). The narrator's marriage
and his wife's death merely figure into his social and economic plan;
she has served her function of granting him economic, racial, sexual,
and social legitimacy and so, like his blackness and homosexuality, can
be erased from the text.

In the final paragraph of his narrative, the Ex-Colored Man admits
that he has been a "spectator" of his life and has sold out: "I cannot repress
the thought that, after all, I have chosen the lesser part, that I have sold
my birthright for a mess of pottage" (*Autobiography* 511). No doubt, his
confession emphasizes his betrayal of his people for material goods.
Unlike Booker T. Washington and others, the Ex-Colored Man avows
that he sacrifices "making history and a race" for making money. The
separation of race, specifically the black race, from money, suggests that
in early-twentieth-century America whiteness connoted money and
power and blackness their absence. By extension, then, wealth could make
one culturally or figuratively white. The narrator's final statement also
begs comparison to Johnson's own position in relation to his narrator
and narrative. Johnson's tale clearly critiques white materialism and
exploitation of African Americans, yet Johnson was also aware that
money and culture were the routes to power. In *Black Manhattan* he
explains that at the opening of the twentieth century "The general spirit
of the race was one of hopelessness or acquiescence. The only way to
survival seemed along the road of sheer opportunism and of conformity to the triumphant materialism of the age" (128). Like his joking narrator, he plays both sides in that he veils his critique and benefits from

the audience he condemns. However, his use of the word "seemed" suggests a discomfort with the path to survival, and the cynical tone implied by such words as "sheer opportunism" and "conformity" reflects his disgust at the predicament of blacks in a triumphantly material age. Unlike the Ex-Colored Man, Johnson profited from those he censured without sacrificing his birthright. He sold less but gained more.

Notes

1. In this essay I use the 1912 edition of the novel rather than Knopf's 1927 reprint in which Johnson was identified as the author and the title was changed so that it used British spelling variants (Fleming, *James Weldon Johnson* 6–9). It seems apt to draw on the earlier edition since I will discuss the issue of publishing anonymously a pseudo-autobiography. Also, the British spellings were a marketing strategy on the part of Knopf, not Johnson, and Johnson's concerns about race in the novel are very much American, which he clearly distinguishes from issues of race in England.

2. See Faulkner ("James Weldon Johnson's Portrait"), Goellnicht ("Passing as Autobiography"), Pisiak ("Irony and Subversion"), Ross ("Audience and Irony"), Skerrett ("Irony and Symbolic Action"), and Levy (*James Weldon Johnson*) for detailed discussions about Johnson and the narrator of his novel.

3. In *Our America*, Walter Benn Michaels asserts that "racial authenticity becomes the principle of class distinction" and that membership in the middle class depends on imitating whites (87). Thus, according to this logic, blacks must "act white" in order to enter middle-class society, meaning that they imitate or appropriate the mores of America's white ruling class. In a related discussion about the Ex-Colored Man's renunciation of black culture, Sundquist states that Johnson was "caught" in terms of "how to balance the acquisition of white, European cultural forms against the preserved beliefs and cultural patterns of black America that had originated in slavery or in Africa" (*Hammers* 39). Sundquist's comment implies that Johnson believed that Anglo American aesthetics differed from African American culture. In his essay, "The Ironies of Palace-Subaltern Discourse," Clyde Taylor posits three modes of "other-representation:" the Ethiopic, the Cyclopean, and the Aesopian. In the Cyclopean, the "minority . . . identify so ardently with the values and forms of their colonizers that . . . they hold as valid expressions those that mimic the genres and traditions of their masters." Both the Ethiopian and Aesopian modes "rely on masking, the one miming the 'other,'

the second adopting masks in order to defend an unacknowledged self"
(184–85). See Taylor for an elaborate discussion about the ways in which
blacks have been represented and represent themselves in literature and film
and have evolved a "symbolic" black middle class that mediates between the
values of the white elite class and the black under class.

4. Stepto asserts that the autobiography is indebted to anti-slave writings
and slave narratives (96). Goellnicht discusses, in detail, how the black autobiography was used as a potential source of profit in the late nineteenth and
early twentieth centuries. He asserts that black autobiography had become
"immensely successful, gaining support for the abolition cause in particular
and sympathy for the plight of African Americans in general, making many
of the authors famous, and turning profit for the publishers" (18–19).

5. In the chapter, "These Old Slave Songs," Sundquist discusses, at length,
the history of black American music and its relation to Johnson's text (see
Hammers 14, 15, 20, 21, 26–31).

6. See Sundquist for an interesting discussion about minstrelsy by
African Americans and the implications of blacks imitating whites playing
blacks (*Hammers* 7–9).

7. Cheryl Clarke suggests that not only does the Ex-Colored Man run away
from his American racial identity, but also from his homosexuality. She
asserts that "Johnson banishes homosexuality, along with Ex-Colored Man
and his white benefactor, to Europe" (93).

8. Sundquist comments on the narrator's contradictory response: "The
narrator's characteristically double-edged prose, which allows him to ridicule
neo-Confederate traditions of masculine heroism while at the same time
himself luxuriating in detached, philosophical judgment, is the remark of
a white man, not a black man in the age of Jim Crow" (*Hammers* 45).

Works Cited

Baker, Houston A. "A Forgotten Prototype: *The Autobiography of an Ex-
Coloured Man* and *Invisible Man*." *The Virginia Quarterly Review* 49.1
(1973): 433–49.

Baker, Houston A., and Patricia Redmond, eds. *Afro-American Literary Study
in the 1990s*. Chicago: University of Chicago Press, 1989.

Bell, Bernard B. *The Afro-American Novel and Its Tradition*. Amherst: University of Massachusetts Press, 1987.

Butterfield, Stephen. *Black Autobiography in America*. Amherst: University of
Massachusetts Press, 1974.

Chauncey, George. "A Gay World, Vibrant and Forgotten." *New York Times* 26 June 1994: A17.

Clarke, Cheryl. "Race, Homosocial Desire, and 'Mammon' in *Autobiography of an Ex-Coloured Man.*" *Professions of Desire*. Ed. George E. Haggerty and Bonnie Zimmerman. New York: MLA, 1995. 84–97.

Collier, Eugenia. "The Endless Journey of an Ex-Coloured Man." *Phylon* 32 (1971): 365–73.

Diawara, Manthia, ed. *Black American Cinema*. New York: Routledge, 1993.

Du Bois, W. E. B. *The Souls of Black Folk. Three Negro Classics*. Introd. John Hope Franklin. New York: Avon, 1965. 207–390.

Fanon, Frantz. *Black Skin, White Masks*. Trans. Charles Lam Markmann. New York: Grove Press, 1967.

Faulkner, Howard. "James Weldon Johnson's Portrait of the Artist as Invisible Man." *Black American Literature Forum* 19 (1985): 147–51.

Fleming, Robert. "Irony as a Key to Johnson's *Autobiography of an Ex-Colored Man.*" *American Literature* 43 (1971): 83–96.

———. *James Weldon Johnson and Arna Wendell Bontemps: A Reference Guide*. Boston: G. K. Hall, 1978.

Gaines, Jane. "Fire and Desire: Race, Melodrama, and Oscar Micheaux." *Black American Cinema*. Ed. Manthia Diawara. New York: Routledge, 1993. 49–70.

Gates, Henry Louis, Jr. *The Signifying Monkey: A Theory of Afro-American Literary Criticism*. New York: Oxford University Press, 1988.

Goellnicht, Donald C. "Passing as Autobiogtraphy: James Weldon Johnson's *The Autobiography of an Ex-Coloured Man.*" *African American Review* 30.1 (1996): 17–33.

Japtok, Martin. "Between 'Race' as Construct and 'Race' as Essence: *The Autobiography of an Ex-Coloured Man.*" *The Southern Literary Journal* 28.2 (1996): 32–47.

Johnson, James Weldon. *Along This Way*. New York: Penguin, 1933.

———. *The Autobiography of an Ex-Colored Man. Three Negro Classics*. Introd. John Hope Franklin. New York: Avon, 1965. 391–512.

———. *Black Manhattan*. New York: Arno Press and New York Times, 1968.

———. "The Dilemma of the Negro Author." *American Mercury* 15 (1928): 477–81.

———. *The Selected Writings of James Weldon Johnson*. Ed. Sondra Kathryn Wilson. 2 vols. New York: Oxford University Press, 1995.

Lawson, Benjamin Sherwood. "Odysseus's Revenge: The Names on the Title

Page of *The Autobiography of an Ex-Coloured Man.*" *Southern Literary Journal* 21 (1989): 92–99.

Levy, Eugene. *James Weldon Johnson: Black Leader, Black Voice.* Chicago: University of Chicago Press, 1973.

Michaels, Walter Benn. *Our Amercia.* Durham: Duke University Press, 1995.

Pisiak, Roxanna. "Irony and Subversion in James Weldon Johnson's *The Autobiography of an Ex-Coloured Man.*" *Studies in American Fiction* 21.1 (1993): 83–96.

Rosenblatt, Roger. *Black Fiction.* Cambridge: Harvard University Press, 1974.

Ross, Stephen M. "Audience and Irony in Johnson's *The Autobiography of an Ex-Coloured Man.*" *CLA Journal* 18.2 (1974): 198–210.

Sedgwick, Eve Kosofsky. *Between Men: English Literature and Male Homosocial Desire.* New York: Columbia University Press, 1985.

Skerrett, Joseph T., Jr. "Irony and Symbolic Action in James Weldon Johnson's *The Autobiography of an Ex-Coloured Man.*" *American Quarterly* 32 (1980): 540–58.

Stepto, Robert B. *From Behind the Veil: A Study of Afro-American Narrative.* Urbana: University of Illinois Press, 1979.

Sundquist, Eric J., ed. *American Realism, New Essays.* Baltimore: Johns Hopkins University Press, 1982.

———. *The Hammers of Creation.* Athens: University of Georgia Press, 1992.

Taylor, Clyde. "The Ironies of Palace-Subaltern Discourse." *Black American Cinema.* Ed. Manthia Diawara. New York: Routledge, 1993. 177–99.

4 Passing as the "Tragic" Mulatto

Constructions of Hybridity in Toni Morrison's Novels

ANNAMARIE CHRISTIANSEN

It almost goes without saying that the nature of being human has a great deal to do with mimesis, adaptability, absorption, shapeshifting, souleating.
—REGINALD MCKNIGHT, *Confessions*

N HER ESSAY "UNSPEAKABLE THINGS UNSPOKEN,"
Toni Morrison says, "We are not, in fact, 'other.' We are choices." This comment provides the foundation for the way I am looking at the mixed-race characters in her novels. My argument here is that Toni Morrison is revising the stereotype of the tragic mulatto found in nineteenth-century American literature. While W. E. B. Du Bois famously argued that the color line is *the* problem of the twentieth century, Morrison displaces the limiting metaphor of the color line by envisioning a creative and autonomous space for mixed-race identity, which, in literature as in life, has usually been contained in some way. The mulatto subject in Morrison's work distends the dominant stereotype of the tragic mulatto as she re-imagines mixed-race identity, moving beyond the static representations in earlier American literary texts. To connect the tragic mulatto in Morrison's work to the body of literature that has limited the

74

figure previously, I will briefly survey the history and literary representations of the character. Morrison is not, of course, the first to challenge
this figure, and, in order to situate Morrison in a larger literary genealogy, I compare her more contemporary work with that of Pauline Hopkins,
whose last serially published novel, *Of One Blood* (1904), interestingly
prefigures aspects of Morrison's intervention. Morrison's own depiction
of the mixed race character is itself not static but rather subject to evolution over the course of her oeuvre, and thus her work revises the tragic
mulatto by gradually displacing the stereotype in favor of more complex representations.

To begin, in order to understand the ways in which Morrison begins
to imagine beyond the limiting metaphor of the "color line," it is important to examine W. E. B. Du Bois's notion of Negro double-consciousness, one that he defines as

> this sense of always looking at one's self through the eyes of others, of
> measuring one's soul by the tape of a world that looks on in amused
> contempt and pity. One ever feels his two-ness—an American, a Negro;
> two souls, two thoughts, two unreconciled strivings; two warring ideals
> in one dark body. (38)

Here, Du Bois articulates the New Negro ideas of the divided self and
the consequent lack of subjectivity that black Americans experience, the
inability to shape perceptions of self and community in a context in
which, Du Bois points out, the "problem of the twentieth century is the
problem of the color line" (54). Du Bois's comments, while psychological in nature, are useful to keep in mind when evaluating the cultural
dynamic of the color line at the end of the twentieth century.

It is valuable to examine Morrison's work in the context of Du Boisian
double-consciousness, since her work is the literal affirmation of the
black artistic movement he predicted. Yet instead of focusing on the
dynamic of being viewed and, ultimately, racially constructed as Du Bois
suggests, Morrison points out that "we are not, in fact, 'other.' We are
choices" ("Unspeakable Things" 9). In this way, Morrison suggests that
embedded within a revision of double-consciousness is the ability to
build realities, to crystallize perceptions of self or multiple selves. Further, she argues that "we are the subjects of our own narrative, witnesses

to and participants in our own experience, and . . . in the experience of those with whom we have come in contact" ("Unspeakable Things" 9). Morrison is privileging the multiple contexts in which the "Afro-American artistic presence" thrives ("Unspeakable Things" 9). Such a position is not limiting, but rather enabling for black subjectivity, suggesting agency and multiple identity. Her position embraces Africanism, which she defines as "an investigation into the ways in which a nonwhite, Africanlike (or Africanist) presence or persona was constructed in the United States, and the imaginative uses this fabricated presence served" (*Playing* 6–7). When we interrogate constructions of race, as Morrison suggests, we can begin to shape our own representations and displace dominant notions of color and culture. As Morrison constructs African-ist subjectivity as the point of departure in examining literary texts, the color line becomes a space of creativity in which new identity is formed from cultural fragmentation. Thus Morrison, in her constructions of her mulatto characters, displaces the color line Du Bois talked about and replaces it with an autonomous space for such figures. In this way she disrupts the stereotyped tragic figure in the works of canonical nine-teenth-century writers like Cable, Melville, Stowe, Howells, and Twain, among others.

My project in this essay is to analyze Morrison's overt constructions of mixed-race identity and how such representations displace the ear-lier literary stereotypes of the "tragic mulatto" in favor of hybrid or, ulti-mately, more complex interpretations of mulatto subjectivity. I am borrowing from Homi Bhabha who defines hybridity as the "articula-tion of ambivalent space where the rite of power is enacted on the site of desire, making its objects at once disciplinary and disseminatory . . . a negative transparency" (112). Bhabha points out that hybrid subjec-tivity reveals the dominant discourse as "something other than what its rules of recognition assert" (112). Thus, the hybrid subject position, a product of dominant discourse and its gaps, is problematic since it "rep-resent[s] the unpredictability of its presence" and "terrorizes authority with its ruse of recognition, its mimicry, its mockery" (114, 115). The hybrid subject, then, reflects instability even as dominant discourses attempt to contain her or him as either member or Other. Bhabha sug-gests in his discussion that the hybrid subject will always identify as both member and Other, yet never fully be one or the other. The representation of the tragic mulatto as it reflected the social value of its time, when reconceived through Bhabha's definition of hybridity and through Morrison's lens of Africanism, becomes a figure of power, with the ability to negotiate (mimic and mock), instead of a figure at the mercy of discourses containing her or him. Read in the spirit of Bhabha's notion of hybridity, Morrison's mixed-race characters are not tragic, they merely appear to be so because of how they occupy marginal spaces within her narratives. Their pivotal positions within her novels, however, suggest their abilities to shape their own identities and affect those around them in the process. Morrison's characters only pass as tragic mulattoes.

Within her canon, Morrison has only explicitly represented three characters as mixed-race subjects. These characters, Soaphead Church in *The Bluest Eye* (1970), Golden Gray in *Jazz* (1992), and Pat Best in *Paradise* (1998), occupy fairly minor yet pivotal roles in each work, all functioning as the characters who critique the racial dynamics within each narrative, even while they are enmeshed in them. Morrison's mixed-race characters are also significant because they each must re-imagine what hybrid identity means within each community before taking steps to define himself or herself. Thus Soaphead Church, Golden Gray, and Pat Best all experience identity crises based on their hybrid identities, taking cues from the dominant discourses about racial construction. But rather than play the role of the "tragic mulatto," the characters form their own versions of selfhood. They are autonomous figures who break from the past to determine their future.

In order to link the mulatto characters in Morrison's work to literary tradition, I want briefly to survey the "tragic mulatto." Although evidence exists that the term may have also been derived in part from the Arabic word *muwallad*, mestizo or mixed,[1] the *Oxford English Dictionary* cites the first printed reference to the term as appearing in 1595 in *Drake's Voyages*. The Oxford English Dictionary cites the word's etymology as Spanish and defines the mulatto as "one who is the offspring of a European and a Black; also used loosely for anyone of mixed race resembling a mulatto." In general, early references to the mulatto defined such a figure as one who is neither white nor black; a separate "species" altogether. Our contemporary definitions of the mulatto are more expansive. Jonathan Little indicates the term extends to any individual with a fraction of black blood (512), extending to, as E. B. Reuter points out, any person "with a visible admixture of white blood," including "all Negroes of mixed ancestry regardless of the degree of intermixture" (12). As Valerie Smith has observed in her discussion of narratives of racial passing, which feature characters who are legally black but pass as white, "the light-skinned black body . . . both invokes and transgresses the boundaries between the races. . . . It indicates a contradiction between appearance and 'essential' racial identity within a system of racial distinctions based upon differences presumed to be visible" (45). Historically, then, the mulatto was scientifically, socially, and culturally determined as an outsider whose difference voided any ability he/she had to identify fully with one group or another. This dilemma for the mulatto character in nineteenth-century American literature usually led to tragedy.

Yet the "tragic mulatto," stereotyped as a solitary anomaly, is a complicated figure who suggests more about the union of races than their separation. In nineteenth-century American literature, the mulatto character is usually a product of a master and slave relationship; if female, she is in danger of suffering the same sexual imprisonment that produced her. But even as blacks were considered less than human for the purpose of their continuing subjugation, the mulatto as a product of white/black union suggested otherwise.

In nineteenth-century representations of the "tragic mulatto," the character's fate is predictable—the vulnerability of color usually results in death, often suicide, or at the very least, being sold down the river. The mulatto's dilemma, as conceived by white American writers, is rooted in the issue of eugenics. If a person, or his/her descendants, had one drop of black blood, then the mulatto character was black and entitled to all of the oppression of blackness in the nineteenth century. Houston A. Baker, Jr., perhaps best defines the mulatto in white American literature as a "sign of the legitimacy and power of white male patriarchy: an economically, politically, and socially maintained authority" (36). Baker suggests that the figure most often functioned as a representation of the hegemonic patriarchal order. Literary works of the nineteenth century generally strove either to fix the mulatto's identity as black or to point out the problems of hybrid identity and survival when society imposes the one-drop rule upon an individual. Significantly, Suzanne Bost points out that biracial figures have always possessed "decentered identities forced upon them by the historical circumstances, politics, and racial dynamics of their times" (675). The mulatto characters in Morrison's contemporary novels are weighted with these literary and "everyday" traditions of the "tragic mulatto." However, whether in a conscious response to the "tragic mulatto" trope or not, Morrison configures a new space of autonomy and creativity for mixed-race identity.

It would be far too simple, though, to assume that Morrison is the first to reconfigure the tragic mulatto. Henry Louis Gates, Jr., suggests that "repetition and revision are fundamental to black artistic forms" (xxiv). Gates's notion of "Signifyin'," of repetition with a difference, implies that intertextuality is crucial when examining literature; not only black texts but "all texts Signify upon other texts, in motivated and unmotivated ways" (xxiv). In this way, the black tradition is "double-voiced" (xxv) and can repeat a specific trope, or theme, while at the same time revising it. However, Morrison is not the first to Signify on the "tragic mulatto." Pauline Hopkins, writing at the turn of the twentieth century, was much more explicitly concerned than Morrison with articulating a new mulatto presence in her work.

As a postscript to nineteenth-century representations of the "tragic mulatto" and a precursor to Morrison's mixed-race characters, Pauline Hopkins's serialized novels about mulatto characters focus not on the tragedy of their circumstances but on how they can create new spaces of cultural and psychological autonomy. Thomas Otten points out that, for Hopkins, "racial difference becomes something that lies *inside* [Ottens's emphasis] an individual. . . . [If] race can be seen as a pathologically hidden side of the self, then it can also be therapeutically brought to the surface and refigured . . . [and] racial difference can be acknowledged and its threatening qualities diffused" (229). If, for Hopkins, racial identity was self-imposed, than it could certainly be self-managed and/or reconfigured. For Hopkins, the tragic mulatto was no longer a tragic figure, as the possibilities for negotiating identity came from within rather than from without. It is particularly crucial to examine Hopkins's work since Morrison has made it a point to study and discuss both white American writers as well as black (see her "Unspeakable Things Unspoken" and *Playing in the Dark*). Because of this, and keeping in mind Gates's theory of tropological repetition with a difference, Hopkins's work can inform how we look at Morrison's canon. Such a literary genealogy calls into question exactly how Morrison's mulatto characters align with and depart from both the nineteenth-century mainstream literary representations of the "tragic mulatto" and the more complex representations of these characters in Hopkins's work.

From 1900 to 1904, Hopkins published her fiction in *The Colored American Magazine*, a periodical for which she was literary editor for a time. In her last serially-published novel, *Of One Blood*, Hopkins suggests that the double-consciousness of mixed-race identity cannot be resolved within the physical boundaries of the United States. Instead, it must be negotiated within Africa where blackness is celebrated rather than denigrated. Otten points out that Hopkins's project "render[ed] identity itself problematic as a way of countering both racist structurings and black-authored displacements of black identity . . . attempt[ing] to undermine and obliquely to reorganize structures of identity" (234). Rather than presenting the mulatto's isolation between two worlds, Hopkins supports the mixed-race figure's alignment with the African American community. By envisioning the mulatto's return to the African community as a site of strength and empowerment, Hopkins reinscribes the tragedy of the mulatto. But the mulatto's position in the African American community is not without problems. Judith Berzon points out that the mulatto bifurcated not only American white communities but also the black community, where a caste system of color also existed (4). Hopkins's work, particularly *Of One Blood*, highlights the complicated nature of mixed-race identity.

Prior to the novel-of-passing genre that grew out of the Harlem Renaissance, Hopkins deployed the mulatto character as a strategy for examining the psychological location of hybrid ethnicity. Hazel Carby points out that if racism was historically socialized through disenfranchisement, lynching, and the institution of Jim Crow, it was displaced by Hopkins's narrative about close blood ties between the races caused by master/slave miscegenating practices (*Reconstructing Womanhood* 128). Hopkins subverted the racist discourse, which emphasized difference and separateness, by replacing it with one suggesting genetic and cultural sameness or, at the very least, closeness. If, as Hopkins argues in *Of One Blood*, the races are interconnected, then the mulatto actually destabilizes the distance between whites and blacks rather than emphasizes it. Further, Otten suggests that in *Of One Blood* an "unknowable 'mystery' takes the place of deeply concealed degeneracy; the story counters the 'already-read text' of stereotyped black identity by making that text nearly unreadable" (236). It is in this displacement of the tragic mulatto that Hopkins offers a solution to Du Bois's problem of the color line. The divided self must look to African origins to subvert the mulatto stereotype. The revision of the African American self "owes to Africa its powerful gifts" (Otten 244).

Within *Of One Blood*, the question of post-Civil War African American identity for mulatto subjects seems to hinge on African origins. The three main characters, Reuel Briggs, Dianthe Lusk, and Aubrey Livingston, all negotiate their mixed-race origins in different ways. By the end of the book, what began as a love triangle becomes a coincidental web of incest as the three realize they are brothers and sister, descended from a royal Ethiopian family. For the three mulatto characters, their American lives are rife with the intrigues and psychological burdens of hidden identity. Hazel Carby notes that "the movement of the novel takes the reader away from the American consequences of secret histories and toward an Africa that embodies both the history and future possibilities of black people" ("Introduction" xliii). Carby suggests that Hopkins's solution to the dilemma of American mulatto identity cannot be resolved within the boundaries of the United States ("Introduction" xlvii). Hopkins's preoccupation with Pan-Africanism, like Du Bois's, replaces the discourse of genetic mulatto inferiority in favor of one that interrogates the cultural and spiritual origins of hybrid ethnicity. When we apply Bhabha's theory of hybridity to Hopkins's work, we can see the ways in which her characters recognize, mimic, and mock American racial constructions. Dianthe dies soon after she learns of her origins, as does Aubrey. Reuel, the one character who has consciously passed for white, returns to African origins in which mixed-race subjectivity is considered a sign of the unification of races. Thus he cites the biblical reference: "Of one blood I have made all races of men" (Hopkins 590). In the novel, the mulatto subject's denial of an African American identity parallels the denial of an African heritage. The mulatto, then, in Hopkins' work, representing the past as well as the future, is reconfigured as a powerful figure instead of a tragic one, having both the potential of the past in Africa and the possibilities of the future located in the United States.

Curiously, although many of Morrison's characters seem to be of mixed-race origins, only three are constructed as such with explicit reference to their origins of birth.² Unlike Reuel Briggs in Hopkins's *Of One Blood*, Morrison's mulatto characters do not travel to Africa to affirm their Africanness. Instead, they find themselves having to create spaces for mixed-race identity within their own communities.³ For Pauline Hopkins, collective cultural memory reaches beyond black history in the Americas to a literal return to Africa. For Morrison, the voyage is figurative, although no less important. To argue the hybrid subjectivity of the tragic mulatto is to suggest that it functions to mimic and mock the dominant discourse that attempts to shape it. I want to suggest that the hybridity of the tragic mulatto character not only transforms the color line into an autonomous space, but also creates a cultural autonomy for mixed-race identity, innovations clearest in Morrison's *The Bluest Eye, Jazz,* and *Paradise.*

The Bluest Eye

Toni Morrison's first novel, *The Bluest Eye,* published in 1970 but set in 1939, focuses on the rape of eleven-year-old Pecola Breedlove and on how both the local community of Lorain, Ohio, and the more broadly national societal standards of beauty are implicated in what leads to the rape. Through the various narrators, as well as the Dick and Jane primer excerpts punctuating each chapter, we understand how Pecola is constantly compared to a white aesthetic of beauty until she regards herself as ugly. While staying with the McTeers (a consequence of her father having set fire to their house and sent her family "out of doors"), Pecola drinks more than her share of the family's milk because, as Claudia McTeer says, "she was fond of the Shirley Temple cup and took every opportunity to drink milk out of it just to handle and see sweet Shirley's face" (22). Kimberly G. Hébert argues that Pecola enacts Franz Fanon's idea of whiteness as desire. Such a position "depends on the erasure of visible signifiers of blackness, requir[ing] . . . the erasure of oneself" (193–94). But white desire isn't purely Pecola's idea—both her parents re-see themselves and their own worth in comparison to whiteness, the unspoken measure of beauty and power. Pauline, the girl's mother, notices "white men taking such good care of they women, and they all dressed up in big clean houses with the bathtubs right in the same room with the toilet. Them pictures gave me a lot of pleasure but it made coming home hard, and looking at Cholly hard" (97). Cholly, Pecola's father, goaded by white men as they witness his first sexual encounter, is haunted forever by their gaze, which makes him despise his own blackness: "they were big, white, armed men. He was small, black, helpless" (119). Cholly, raging at the victims of white desire rather than the oppressor, rapes his daughter in an act of both love and hate. The weight of her parents' judgment, in various ways, rests heavily upon Pecola until, pregnant by her father and shunned by the black community, she turns to Soaphead Church, "Reader, Advisor, and Interpreter of Dreams" (130). Twelve years old and pregnant, Pecola believes Church has the power to give her blue eyes.

Soaphead Church, "a cinnamon-eyed West Indian with lightly browned skin" (132), chooses his profession because it gives him "numerous opportunities to witness human stupidity without sharing it or being compromised by it" (131). He fetishizes young girls because they are innocent, clean, and do not require a sustained erection from him. Raised in a family that "married 'up'" by "lightening the family complexion and thinning out the family features" (133), Church assumes that his family's prominence is based on their mixed blood (132). It is this kind of person who thinks Pecola's request for blue eyes is a reasonable one because "God had done a poor job. . . . It was in fact a pity that the Maker had not sought [Church's] counsel" (136). Because he falsely practices spirituality and molests children, Church becomes the worst example of how hybrid identity can shape an individual. In the character, alternative space for the tragic mulatto is cleared, even as Morrison inscribes a different kind of tragedy within the character.

When asking what constructs Church as one who molests little girls and practices false workings of the spirit, critics often focus on the effects such a character has within the text instead of examining the causes. In other words, critics overlook his racial in-betweenness. As John Duvall points out, Church functions "as a significant early figure in [Morrison's] attempt to fashion a usable racialized authorial identity" (28). Such a character, others note, lacks the ability of self-definition. Morrison herself suggests this when she points out that Church is "someone who 'would be wholly convinced that if black people were more like white people they would be better off'" (qtd. in Duvall 30). Morrison's Soaphead Church never achieves any sort of self-definition, assuming what Cheryl Wall calls a "false identit[y] that ensure[s] social survival but result[s] in psychological suicide" (89). But it is this false sense of identity that allows him to sympathize with the little girl and concoct a pseudo-charm to give her blue eyes. What becomes ironic is that Church hearkens back to the art of conjuring, a specifically African American practice, to advance a Western aesthetic of beauty.

Conjure, religious and medicinal power with African origins, is Church's blatant vehicle to position himself within the black community of Lorain, Ohio. Within an American context, conjure may get labeled as a specifically African belief system. However, N. N. Puckett suggests that conjure is a product of West African tribal beliefs and European, English, and American ideologies passed down from master to slave (79). Morrison's use of conjure, a mixed system of belief, suggests that Church privileges a culturally hybrid practice to grant Pecola's request. In this way, Morrison suggests that the mixed-race subject, Church, favors a mixed space of creativity, even as this creativity is used, ironically, to reproduce an aesthetic that denigrates mixing.

Conjure, for Soaphead Church, transforms his mixed-race heritage into power, a negative power that pushes Pecola over the edge of madness but, in the process, Morrison constructs a text about the agency of the mulatto figure. Because of his disinterest in "normal" sexual relations, female members of the community decide that Church is "supernatural rather than unnatural" (135), suggesting their willingness to contain him as a spiritualist. Through Church's willingness to wield power through conjure, we find Morrison suggesting that the character's mixed cultural background allows him to shuttle, as necessary, between racialized identities. He values the white/mixed pedigree of his family but does not cut himself off from the African American community or the practice of conjure. With Soaphead Church, Morrison reveals that identity is not an all-or-nothing project. It is a process and for Church to value whiteness yet use conjure to falsely grant a white aesthetic of beauty to Pecola is to suggest that the mulatto character does, in Church's twisted fashion, bridge the gap between the white and black communities in the novel. In this way, Morrison's mulatto character in *The Bluest Eye* espouses the close ties between races, as Pauline Hopkins does in *Of One Blood*.

Admittedly, Soaphead's use of conjure, as a means of granting Pecola's wish for blue eyes, is artificial. Morrison writes: "His practice was to do what he was bid—not to suggest to a party that perhaps the request was unfair, mean, or hopeless" (136). Although he values the physical attributes of whiteness and ascribes his own worth to it, it is in the practice of conjure that he finds the power to challenge God and thus constructs a place for himself within the black community of Lorain, Ohio. This dynamic is both reified and complicated when Church wishes for the authentic power to grant Pecola blue eyes, one of the traditional genetic markings of whiteness. Morrison points out in an interview with Robert Stepto that Church's function in *The Bluest Eye* is to understand Pecola's longing for blue eyes: "there had to be . . . that kind of figure . . . who would believe that she was right, that it was preferable to her to have blue eyes. . . . Someone who would never question the request in the first place. That kind of black" (388–89). Church's white racist ideology is what spurs him to fulfill Pecola's wish within the explicitly African-American context of conjure.

Secondly, Morrison's construction of Soaphead Church uses the historical reading of the "tragic mulatto" as an inverse example because Church's flaws of character seem to be a result of miscegenation in the biological sense rather than the psychological hardships of racial construction.[4] Morrison further inverts the traditional interpretation of the "tragic mulatto," when she points out that the flaws in character can be blamed on his white ancestry, "the original genes of the decaying lord" (133), rather than his blackness. Solidarity of race is promoted within the mulatto subtext of *The Bluest Eye*, but ironically it is not the mulatto character who consciously espouses it. The reader simultaneously experiences the horror of being inside the mind of a pedophile and of witnessing Church's desire to grant Pecola the white aesthetic of blue eyes. Church is thoroughly aberrant. Through Morrison's characterization of Church, readers are implicated in the text of race loyalty and resistance to a white aesthetic, especially since the character is constructed as a dishonest predator. Such a cultural location, situated within the African American community, is not a desirable one, and the mulatto figure is once again constructed as racial and psychological outsider. Thus Morrison at once challenges and recapitulates the literary tradition of the "tragic mulatto," "Signifying" on the theme.

Jazz

First published in 1992, and following the critical success of Morrison's fourth novel, *Beloved* (1987), *Jazz* spans the 1850s post-slavery South to the Harlem of 1926 where the narrator insists that New York is a city better than perfect, one "that makes me dream tall and feel in on things" (7). The main plot of the novel handles Joe Trace's tragic desire for the light-skinned Dorcas, "his necessary thing for three months of nights" (28), who comes between him and Violet, his wife. Within *Jazz*, the subplot of the mulatto character, Golden Gray, functions as Violet's unspoken desire—her childhood is punctuated by the stories that True Belle tells about him. In fact, Violet suggests that Joe is a stand-in for Gray: "Standing in the cane, [Joe] was trying to catch a girl he was yet to see, but his heart knew all about, and me, holding on to him but wishing he was the golden boy I never saw either. Which means from the very beginning I was a substitute and so was he" (97). Angels Carabi suggests that the Golden Gray narrative in *Jazz* is "a deliberately designed imitation of a nineteenth-century American romance tale . . . but as is typical in Morrison's work, the Golden Gray story also uses mythic and literary containers to master and distance its disturbing racial—and emotional—content" (175).

Termed by Roberta Rubenstein "the most cryptic figure of *Jazz*"(157), the mulatto character of Golden Gray distinctly differs from Soaphead Church in *The Bluest Eye* in that he actively searches for his black identity. Once again, Morrison skews the typical mulatto identity (historicized as deriving from the male master/female slave relationship) this time through her characterization of Golden Gray. Because he is a product of a white mother and black father, the stereotypical mulatto origin is inverted in several ways. Further, the narrator suggests that Gray's father may even be half brother to his mother, the daughter of Colonel Gray: "realizing the terrible thing that had happened to his daughter made [Colonel Gray] sweat, for there were seven mulatto children on his land" (141). The Colonel's response to his daughter's pregnancy is to disown her and send her away with a large gift of money. Only later, when Golden Gray is a grown man, does his mother tell him about his origins and he travels south from Baltimore to find his father.

Yet, Golden Gray doesn't search for his father intent on joyful reunion. His pursuit is characterized by emotional detachment as he examines Wild, the black pregnant woman he encounters on the road: "the picture he does imagine is walking away from her . . . climbing into his carriage and leaving her . . . he is uneasy with this picture of himself, and does not want to spend any part of the time to come remembering having done that" (145). When Henry LesTroy discovers who Golden Gray is, he does not welcome him with open arms: "What you want? . . . Want to stay here? You welcome. Want to chastise me? . . . A son ain't what a woman say. A son is what a man do. You want to act like mine, then do it, else get the devil out my house" (172). Thus, the mulatto's search for his black origins does not result in a happy family reunion. The problem of the color line, Morrison indicates, cannot be solved by siding with one community or the other. The problems of mixed-race identity are not that easily resolved.

Further, as the unnamed narrator reveals Gray's story, she outlines his quest for African American heritage: "How could I have imagined him so poorly? Not noticed the hurt that was not linked to the color of his skin, or the blood that beat beneath it. But to some other thing that longed for authenticity, for a right to be in this place, effortlessly without need to acquire a false face, a laughless grin, a talking posture" (160). In discussing the narrator's reassessment of Gray, Doreatha Drummond Mbalia argues that only pages earlier the narrator had painted him as a "cold-hearted, racist individual, seeing to his horse, his trunk, and Wild—in that order" (637). What I want to suggest about the narrator's doubling back to retell and revise Gray's search for his father is that such a distention of the narrative illustrates Du Bois's notion of double-consciousness as constructed by the narrator, one who creates identity through corporeal presence and then again by interrogating the psychology of the character. Further, the narrator's double-consciousness in *Jazz* suggests that she is discovering and understanding the events and characters in the novel just as she is talking about them. Thus, the narrator's double commentary constructs Golden Gray as well as the other characters as complex, multifaceted beings.

The double-voiced narration, an example of Gates's tropological revision, is yet another way that Morrison resists the tragic mulatto stereotype. First, we see Gray as both the arrogant young white man, who exists on the surface of the narrative, and also as the divided mulatto subject, who circulates within Gray's mind. Thus readers have access to the "two souls, two thoughts, two unreconciled strivings" of Gray. The binary readings exist not as evidence of eugenic theory or as efforts to contain hybridity but rather as a way to understand and negotiate the binary position of the tragic mulatto. Further, Bouson suggests that "by focusing on Golden Gray's mixed racial origins, the narrative questions the social logic of received racial categories" (177).

Morrison's narrative strategy in *Jazz* underscores how the reader/observer/narrator is implicit in assembling a coherent mulatto identity, whether it is a stereotype or a revisioning of one. The narrator moves from her first opinion of Gray to another in much the same way an individual's first impression shifts from one idea to another upon meeting someone for the first time. In this way, Morrison is actually shifting the responsibility of meaning-making from author to reader. While it may be easy to dismiss this dynamic in *Jazz*, attentive readers will notice that the narrator only does this in reference to Gray. This suggests a conscious effort, on Morrison's part, to revise the mulatto stereotype, not only in all of the ways mentioned thus far, but with a concerted effort to modify a stereotype and to make the reader complicit in the shift of perception.

Morrison also constructs the absence of the father for Gray as the absence of a limb, suggesting the very necessity of origin: "Only now . . . that I know I have a father, do I feel his absence: the place where he should have been and was not. . . . I thought everybody was one-armed, like me. . . . I don't need the arm. But I do need to know what it could have been like to have had it" (158). It is as he searches for his father, Henry LesTroy, that he encounters Wild, a pregnant woman who seems to represent the black essence free from taint of Negro identity in the South. Described as "his own dark purpose" (146) and the "liquid black woman" (149), Wild is the fluid representation of blackness without slavery.

Wild[5] hovers around Vienna, touches the men out in the fields and runs away, reminding them of the possibility of boundless existence. While Morrison does not detail how or specifically why Golden Gray removes himself from both the white and African American communities, the narrator suggests such a resolution for him as LesTroy sees "the young man's head of yellow hair as long as dog's tail next to her skein of black wool" (167), and Joe notes all of Golden Gray's belong-ings in the clearing where he believes Wild lives (184). Bouson points out that "by showing how the black-fathered Golden Gray finds himself sexually attracted to Wild and her unfathomable black skin despite his initial attempts to preserve the coherence of his white identity by keep-ing Wild distanced and contained, *Jazz* subverts and also rewrites the classic script of nineteenth-century American literature" (177). In choos-ing to be with Wild, Gray dismisses both the white and black commu-nities that threaten to contain him. Morrison, in the Gray storyline, also displaces the traditional narrative of the tragic mulatto.

Gray's isolation from the two communities can be read as another way that Du Bois's double-consciousness is personified as Gray desires to "merge his double self into a better and truer self" (39). Double-consciousness aligns with the notion of authenticity that Golden Gray appears to be in search of. Since his birth, he has perceived himself as white. When his mother divulges the identity of his black father, he searches for Henry LesTroy in anger and then he altogether removes himself from society. Such a departure from a culture that constructs binary identity echoes Hopkin's theme in *Of One Blood*. Morrison is sug-gesting that the problem of the mulattoes' spiritual and cultural hybrid-ity cannot be resolved within the traditional boundaries of the United States, where the double bind of mixed-race ethnicity consists of pass-ing or not passing for white. Through Golden Gray's retreat with Wild in *Jazz*, Morrison suggests that the alternate construction of mixed-race identity has to evolve apart from both the black and white communities and, canonically, away from the American literary tradition of the tragic mulatto.

Thus, Golden Gray is Morrison's second revision of the "tragic mulatto" (perhaps even an evolution of the disturbing figure of Soap-head Church), a character who challenges the stereotype by represent-ing a solution to the problem of hybrid identity that veers away from the two communities seeking to contain him. Like Hopkins's Reuel Briggs, Golden Gray discards the discourse of eugenics in favor of a nar-rative that does not place slavery and miscegenation at its center. It is within such a discourse that African origins of African Americanness are privileged and the "tragic mulatto" is no longer tragic. Gray does not suffer the mental degeneration of the hybrid subject as Soaphead

Church does. Instead Golden Gray, like Briggs in *Of One Blood*, removes himself from society, joining with Wild, the signifier of a stable identity that is possible when contact with both black and white communities is deferred. Golden Gray represents the instability of hybrid subjectivity. Because Golden Gray will never be fully white or black, he steps outside of such racial/cultural constructions when he joins Wild. To do so is to avert the stereotypical demise of the tragic mulatto.

Paradise

Published in 1998, *Paradise* brutally opens with the men in the black settlement of Ruby attacking the women of the nearby Convent. Ruby, Oklahoma, has survived for decades on the town Fathers' narrative of race solidarity. When the men of the town note changes around them, they blame the Convent women and plot an attack on them. Carried out in the early morning, the attack involves the Ruby men storming the place and killing, they think, six women total: one white woman and five black ones. When they go to check on the bodies, however, all of the women are gone.

In *Paradise*, the past and present, the black and white, the supernatural and everyday all collide as the town Fathers resist change. They even try to outrun it in 1949 by moving their families from Haven, Oklahoma, to Ruby to escape the encroachment of the "impure" and the whites. Pat Best, the mulatto character, says that the town Fathers come from "8–rock blood." The term defines "blue-black people, tall and graceful, whose clear, wide eyes gave no sign of what they really felt about those who weren't 8–rock like them" (193). The 8–rocks succeed at destroying the Convent women but in doing so they also destroy themselves. Morrison writes about them: "They think they have outfoxed the white-man when in fact they imitate him. They think they are protecting their wives and children, when in fact they are maiming them" (306).

Paradise offers a more contemporary examination (both in terms of the setting as well as the time of publication) of the problem of mulatto identity in a community where distinctly black bloodlines are valued above all else. John Duvall notes that in *Paradise* "race matters but in an upside down, through-the-looking-glass kind of way. The racially pure black community of Ruby emerges out of the doubled insult of class and colorism" (144). Ana Maria Fraile-Marcos suggests that "the adoption of the Puritan foundational paradigms on the part of the people of Ruby seems to corroborate Homi Bhabha's view of mimicry as a site of resistance since the citizens of Ruby are able to reverse the racist discriminatory practices they suffer by appropriating the ideas which oppressed and excluded them from mainstream America" (4). Indeed, the town Fathers, in valuing 8–rock bloodlines, reify the color line sociocultural dynamic that had previously excluded them. This is a paradox that escapes their attention but heightens the dramatic irony of the story for readers. Through this kind of mimicry, Morrison is emphasizing the constructedness of race.

In this novel, one in which Morrison has publicly admitted to blurring racial distinctions of some of the female characters in order to make readers question how they construct racial identity,[6] Pat Best is one of the few female characters overtly described in the novel as mixed-race. Invoking Bhabha's theories on hybridity when discussing Best is useful as her position in the community is distinctly separate from others in Ruby. In fact, her perspective mirrors Bhabha's notion of the Third Space of enunciation which "constitutes the discursive conditions of enunciation that ensure that the meaning and symbols of culture have no primordial unity or fixity; that even the same signs can be appropriated, translated, rehistoricized and read anew" (37). It is Pat Best who acknowledges the 8–rock reality of Ruby and who rejects it as she burns the town history. To begin with, she seems, initially, to follow the type of mulatto heroine that Jean Fagan Yellin describes: a woman who "embraces her black identity, lives in a black community, and chooses a black man" (198). However, as a product of an 8–rock Ruby native and the "hazel-eyed girl with light brown hair who'd had his child during the war" (201), Best recognizes the insidious ways she and her family are left out of the major town events and blames their outsider status on her father's marriage.

After marrying 8–rock Billy Cato "partly (mostly?) because he had the midnight skin of the Catos and the Blackhorses" (198), Pat Best takes her "lightish but not whiteish baby" (199) after his death and moves back to her father's house where she reverts back to her maiden name of Best, not through choice but rather through the community's fixed perception of her. Further, she reflects upon her own desire to attack her daughter as an urge to "smash the girl that lived in the minds of the 8–rocks, not the girl her daughter was" (204). Best's part of the narrative suggests that she recognizes her own double-consciousness. She sees herself as she is but she also knows how the 8–rocks see her and her daughter. This shuttling between truth and perception separates Best from the rest of Ruby and allows her to see what others cannot about the town, that the narrative of race loyalty has become hopelessly twisted. Indeed, Best exists in Bhabha's "Third Space" as an agent who sees and rehistoricizes the race solidarity narrative of Ruby, Oklahoma.

In *Paradise*, Du Bois's problem of the color line becomes complicated as the "Fathers" of Ruby struggle to keep outside influences from polluting both their literal and figurative 8–rock purity. For the Fathers, threatening outsiders assume several forms: Reverend Meisner who espouses the civil rights movement ideologies of the '60s; the Convent women who do not conform psychologically, culturally, or racially to the founders' ideas of propriety; and Pat Best, whose light skin reminds them of her mother, one of the first outsiders in Ruby. It is because of her mixed-race identity that Best functions as the outsider within the community of Ruby; she is, however, the one "best" able to read their race solidarity as well as understand the problems caused by it. Duvall cites her as one of the artistic voices in *Paradise*, even comparing her to Morrison herself in that, as the keeper of the history project, Best is the one best fit to "name and narrate" (144) the effort of the town Fathers to keep their 8–rock bloodlines pure. Within her isolation, Best can interpret and re-read the town's narrative of racial purity.

Instead of someone like Soaphead Church, constructed as deviant because of his white ancestry, or like Golden Gray, who abandons the communities that can only see him through the tainted lens of miscegenation, with Pat Best, Morrison develops a character who recognizes the racism within the isolated community of Ruby. Best understands how racism circulates in the town, how a paradise free of prejudice against blacks (whether from white outsiders or other freedmen) is built on exclusion: "They hate us because she [her mother] looked like a cracker and was bound to have cracker-looking children like me, and although I married . . . an 8–rock like you . . . I passed the skin on to my daughter . . . we were the first visible glitch" (196). Further, by making the textual interloper a mulatta, oppressed by gender as well as her racial admixture,

Morrison seems to be commenting on the coercion of patriarchy as well as race imposed by the men of Ruby. The very name of the town, Ruby, as an example of metonymy and metaphor suggests that the men equate the value of their town with the value of their women (Duvall 142). Best understands that the taint from outside must involve reproduction since "everything that worries them comes from women" (217) and, as a product of Ruby insider/outsider relations, she herself is a threat to the town. The Convent women also appear threatening to the men of Ruby as they provide an alternative model for sexuality, one that does not involve 8–rock patriarchy. At the end of the novel, Best evaluates why the Ruby men attacked the Convent: "nine 8–rocks murdered five harmless women (a) because the women were impure (not 8–rock); (b) because the women were unholy (fornicators at the least, abortionists at most); and (c) because they *could*—which was what being an 8–rock meant to them" (297).

It is Pat Best, both an outsider and an insider in Ruby, who understands what motivates the men of the town to lead an attack on the Convent. Further, while Soaphead Church and Golden Gray function as characters who represent the intercultural/interracial problems of mulatto identity, Pat Best's mixed-race origins circulate as value or nonvalue within an exclusively black community. This, she knows, is the pretext to shut her out of everything except "the obvious, the superficial" (216). As an act symbolizing her conscious separation from the town of Ruby, Best burns her history and in doing so effectively symbolizes a future of change. Best occupies the kind of space Bhabha describes as "the 'inter'—the cutting edge of translation and negotiation, the inbetween space—that carries the burden of meaning of culture" (38–39). In destroying the history of the town, Best is in effect rejecting the 8–rock privileging of race.

Like the mulatto figures in Hopkins's work, Best functions as the signifier between new and old notions of African American identity— although Morrison's notions of old and new are different. Instead of delineating between Africa and African America as Pauline Hopkins does in *Of One Blood*, Morrison indicates that old ideas of race solidarity (as represented in the bootstrap narrative of the Fathers), no matter which culture espouses it, are indeed damaging and, for the women of the Convent, downright dangerous. New and hopeful notions of black identity involve interaction with the African American community at large as represented by Reverend Meisner's discourse on civil disobedience. Du Bois's color line is indeed blurred through signifiers like Pat Best as well as through the positive exchanges between the 8–rock citizens of Ruby and the women of the Convent who are not racially coded throughout the novel.

With this last representation of the mulatto in *Paradise*, Morrison seems to be asking, much like Hopkins did at the turn of the century, how can Paradise exist in racial isolation. Indeed, all three of the mulatto characters in Morrison's novels function as subjects who create alternative space for hybridity in contexts where others seek to keep them static. Morrison's mulatto characters are textual ruptures in the overall weave of her novels. The characters of Soaphead Church in *The Bluest Eye* and Golden Gray in *Jazz* solve the problems of border identity through a return to African origins—Soaphead Church through conjure and Golden Gray through his retreat to his refuge with Wild. With these two characters, Morrison is revising the idea of the "tragic mulatto" with an emphasis on African American tradition in which the dilemma of the American Negro—that of double-consciousness—is resolved. Further, the white gaze can no longer fragment black identity or create a dual perception of self if it is displaced or mediated as Morrison shows us.

In *Paradise*, Pat Best is the physical signifier of Du Bois's double-consciousness as she shuttles back and forth between her own racialized perceptions of self and the views of a community determined to dislocate the physical signifiers and psychological violence of white supremacy. In the end, both in the novel *Paradise* specifically and Toni Morrison's canon more generally, Pat Best functions as a visionary who has the power to re-vision the class, color, and gender politics of the Edenic town of Ruby, supposedly free from the problems of race because it is a black community isolated from and independent of white supremacy. It is this isolation, "nothing inside or out rots the all-black town worth the pain" (5), that drives the Convent shooting. The evolution of mixed-race characters in Morrison's works suggest an evolution in her conception of them so that Pat Best is not inherently flawed (like Soaphead Church in *The Bluest Eye*) even as Best recognizes that the community thinks she is. Morrison has moved from representing the mulatto as a complicated subject position, as in *The Bluest Eye*, to advancing Pat Best's position as the only one able to understand the racism of Ruby. Morrison is, indeed, challenging the old stereotypes of the tragic mulatto.

While redefining the figure is not Morrison's main project in her novels, it is a part of her ongoing efforts to envision a complex and vibrant African American community. We can see this will to refashion master narratives about African American life, including mulatto identity, as one of Morrison's major projects in her novels. Paul Gilroy notes that "Morrison [is] drawing upon and reconstructing the resources supplied to [her] by earlier generations of black writers who allowed the confluence of racism, rationality, and systematic terror to configure both their disenchantment with modernity and their aspirations for its fulfillment" (222). Morrison revises the history of the tragic mulatto, and, in her hands, such a figure of despair evolves into one of hope and change.

Notes

1. Werner Sollors suggests that "the zoological analogy with mules may thus not have been the word's original or exclusive source, but the term 'mulatto' certainly did become intertwined with the animal that was a cross between two *species* [Sollors's emphasis]; and numerous texts have explicated, or alluded to that etymology" (127–28).

2. Several of Morrison's other characters seem to be light skinned (Jadine in *Tar Baby*, Dorcas in *Jazz*, to name a few) but she divulges each of the three characters' histories in *The Bluest Eye*, *Jazz*, and *Paradise*, indicating that such information is important in each text.

3. In *Oxherding Tale*, Charles Johnson creates a mulatto character, Andrew Hawkins, who by the end of the novel has discovered an alternative location for mixed-race identity but it is not within the African American community. Hawkins's journey out of slavery ends with satisfaction in his marriage to a white woman, although he does acknowledge his past by buying out of servitude the slave seamstress he once loved. Unlike Johnson, Morrison situates the possibilities for mulatto identity within the African American community.

4. Naomi Zack cites Morrison's depiction of the mulatto in *The Bluest Eye* as "malevolently destructive to the well-being of black people," reflecting "some of the worst racist fears of miscegenation from a black point of view" (138). Morrison's interpretation of such a character, Zack argues, indicates a "racial bias against such individuals" and "perpetuates the tragedy of genocidal images of mixed race" (139, 140). I disagree and, again, point to Church's

complicated identity politics to indicate that Morrison is doing much more than what Zack suggests.

5. Critics have pointed out that Wild bears a striking resemblance in appearance and character to Beloved in Morrison's novel of that name. Morrison herself has suggested this in an interview: "Wild is a kind of Beloved. . . . You see a pregnant black woman naked at the end of *Beloved* . . . at the same time . . . in the Golden Gray section of *Jazz*, there is a crazy woman out in the woods. . . . [She] could be Sethe's daughter, Beloved . . . who runs away, ending up in Virginia, which is right next to Ohio" (qtd. in Carabi 43). Bouson points out that "through the cryptic character of Wild, who comes to represent the stigmatized racial and sexual Otherness of black female identity, *Jazz* extends and makes an intertextual commentary on the story of the ghostly Beloved . . . depicting Wild as a naked pregnant girl running in the woods, which is the reader's final image of Beloved" (166).

6. Morrison also erases the markers of skin color in the only short story she has written to date, "Recitatif," where the two female characters never divulge their own or each other's racial identities through the course of the story. Her comments about how she purposely blurred the racial identities of the Convent women can be found in Gray, "Paradise Found." The literary buzz about Morrison's resistance of racial coding in both "Recitatif" and *Paradise* is ironic since a white author never has to code characters who are white, only those who are black.

Works Cited

Baker, Houston A. *Workings of the Spirit: The Poetics of Afro-American Women's Writing*. Chicago: University of Chicago Press, 1991.

Berzon, Judith. *Neither White nor Black: The Mulatto Character in American Fiction*. New York: New York University Press, 1978.

Bhabha, Homi K. *The Location of Culture*. New York: Routledge, 1994.

Bost, Suzanne. "Fluidity without Postmodernism: Michelle Cliff and the 'Tragic Mulatta' Tradition." *African American Review* 32.4 (Winter 1998): 673–690.

Bouson, J. Brooks. *Quiet as It's Kept: Shame, Trauma, and Race in the Novels of Toni Morrison*. Albany: SUNY Press, 2000.

Carabi, Angels. "Toni Morrison." (Interview) *Belles Lettres: A Review of Books by Women* 10.2 (Spring 1995): 40–43.

Carby, Hazel V. "Introduction." *The Magazine Novels of Pauline Hopkins*. By Pauline Hopkins. New York: Oxford University Press, 1988. xxix-1.

————. *Reconstructing Womanhood: The Emergence of the Afro-American Woman Novelist*. New York: Oxford University Press, 1987.

Du Bois, W. E. B. *The Souls of Black Folk*. Boston: Bedford, 1997.

Duvall, John N. *The Identifying Fictions of Toni Morrison: Modernist Authenticity and Postmodern Blackness*. New York: Palgrave, 2000.

Fraile-Marcos, Ana Maria. "Hybridizing the 'City upon a Hill' in Toni Morrison's *Paradise*." *MELUS* 28.4 (Winter 2003): 3–33.

Gates, Henry Louis, Jr. *The Signifying Monkey: A Theory of Afro-American Literary Criticism*. New York: Oxford University Press, 1988.

Gilroy, Paul. *The Black Atlantic: Modernity and Double Consciousness*. Cambridge, MA: Harvard University Press, 1993.

Gray, Paul. "Paradise Found." *Time* 151.2 (19 Jan. 1998): 62+.

Hébert, Kimberly G. "Acting the Nigger: Topsy, Shirley Temple, and Toni Morrison's Pecola." *Approaches to Teaching Stowe's* Uncle Tom's Cabin. Ed. Elizabeth Ammons and Susan Belasco. New York: MLA, 2000. 184–98.

Hopkins, Pauline. *The Magazine Novels of Pauline Hopkins*. New York: Oxford University Press, 1988.

Johnson, Charles. *Oxherding Tale*. New York: Plume, 1995.

Little, Jonathan D. "Mulatto." *The Oxford Companion to African American Literature*. Ed. William L. Andrews, Frances Smith Foster, and Trudier Harris. New York: Oxford University Press, 1997. 512–13.

Mbalia, Doreatha Drummond. "Women Who Run with Wild: The Need for Sisterhoods in *Jazz*." *Modern Fiction Studies* 39.3–4 (Fall/Winter 1993): 623–46.

McKnight, Reginald. "Confessions of a Wannabe Negro." *Lure and Loathing: Essays on Race, Identity, and the Ambivalence of Assimilation*. Ed. Gerald Early. New York: Penguin, 1993.

Morrison, Toni. *Beloved*. New York: Knopf, 1987.

————. *The Bluest Eye*. New York: Washington Square Press, 1970.

————. *Jazz*. New York: Plume, 1992.

————. *Paradise*. New York: Knopf, 1998.

————. *Playing in the Dark: Whiteness and the Literary Imagination*. Cambridge, MA: Harvard University Press, 1992.

————. "Recitatif." *Call and Response: The Riverside Anthology of the African American Tradition*. Ed. Bernard W. Bell, Trudier Harris, William J. Harris, R. Baxter Miller, Sandra O'Neale, and Horace Potter. Boston: Houghton Mifflin, 1998. 1776–86.

————. "Unspeakable Things Unspoken: The Afro-American Presence in American Literature." *Michigan Quarterly Review* (Winter 1988): 1–34.

"Mulatto." *The Oxford English Dictionary*. Second Edition. Prepared by J. A. Simpson and E. S. C. Weiner. Oxford: Clarendon, 1989.

Otten, Thomas J. "Pauline Hopkins and the Hidden Self of Race." *ELH* 59.1 (Spring 1992): 227–256.

Puckett, N. N. *Folk Beliefs of the Southern Negro*. Chapel Hill: University of North Carolina Press, 1926.

Reuter, E. B. *The Mulatto in the United States: Including a Study of the Role of Mixed-Blood Races throughout the World*. Boston: Richard G. Badger, 1918.

Rubenstein, Roberta. "Pariahs and Community." *Toni Morrison: Critical Perspectives Past and Present*. Ed. Henry Louis Gates, Jr., and K. A. Appiah. New York: Amistad, 1993. 126–58.

Smith, Valerie. "Reading the Intersection of Race and Gender in Narratives of Passing." *Diacritics* 24.2/3 (Summer 1994): 43–57.

Sollors, Werner. *Neither Black Nor White Yet Both: Thematic Explorations of Interracial Literature*. Cambridge, MA: Harvard University Press, 1997.

Stepto, Robert. "'Intimate Things in Place': A Conversation with Toni Morrison." *Toni Morrison: Critical Perspectives Past and Present*. Ed. Henry Louis Gates, Jr., and K. A. Appiah. New York: Amistad, 1993. 378–95.

Twagilimana, Aimable. *Race and Gender in the Making of an African American Literary Tradition*. New York: Garland, 1997.

Wall, Cheryl A. "Nella Larsen: Passing for What?" *Women of the Harlem Renaissance*. Ed. Cheryl A. Wall. Bloomington: Indiana University Press, 1995. 85–138.

Wood, Michael. "Sensations of Loss." *The Aesthetics of Toni Morrison: Speaking the Unspeakable*. Ed. Marc C. Conner. Jackson: University Press of Mississippi, 2000. 113–124.

Yellin, Jean Fagan. *Women and Sisters: The Antislavery Feminists in American Culture*. New Haven, CT: Yale University Press, 1989.

Zack, Naomi. *Race and Mixed Race*. Philadelphia: Temple University Press, 1993.

5 Re-Viewing the Literary Chinatown

Hybridity in Gish Jen's Mona in the Promised Land

JEFFREY F. L. PARTRIDGE

I

WHAT SEPARATES A GOOD MARKETING
strategy from the rest is its ability to anticipate, feed,
and sometimes even produce taste. Identifying the consumer's tastes, or the possibility for certain tastes to develop,
is critical to selling the product. Consider, for example, this advertisement for a product (Patricia Chao's *Monkey King*) as it appeared in Harper-
Flamingo's February 1998 book catalogue: "A critically acclaimed first
novel that transports readers into the vibrant and sometimes harrowing world of a Chinese-American family as a young woman explores
the past in order to come to terms with her hidden demons." "Critical
acclaim" comes first for obvious reasons: readers have a taste for novels
that are already validated by those who are supposed to have good taste,
i.e., professional reviewers. But the rest of the advertisement sells more
than a good book: it sells an experience. The advertisement promises
the readers a voyeuristic journey into another "world." Readers will be
transported into a new place—an unfamiliar place, a dangerous and
restricted place: "the vibrant and sometimes harrowing world of a Chinese-American family." The reader will witness the unleashing of the
young woman's "hidden demons" by going back to their source: the Chi-

nese American family's past. What the advertisement anticipates, feeds, and perhaps even produces, therefore, is the reader's taste for ethno-graphic adventure—the opportunity to explore another world as an arm-chair social scientist, to move in the safety of virtuality from outside to inside.[1]

I begin with this brief dissection of an advertisement in order to sug-gest some ways in which Chinese American ethnicity continues to be perceived and portrayed in America at the turn of the twenty-first cen-tury. For in order to discuss the ways Chinese American ethnicity is being re-viewed through literature, it is essential to offer a description of how Chinese American ethnicity is presently viewed. To figure the reception of Chinese American literature, I postulate the notion of a literary Chi-natown as a means of describing the ways in which publishers, readers, and sometimes even Chinese American writers themselves tend to pri-vatize and compartmentalize (or, to put it negatively, to ghettoize) Chi-nese American ethnicity in literature.[2] The HarperFlamingo advertisement is an example of the literary Chinatown phenomenon. Its fetishization of Chinese Americans as objects of exploration and ethnographic intrigue reifies notions of difference based on a special ethnic aura. Not only are the "demons" of Chinese American families unique to Chinese Amer-icans, but they are expunged only through the interrogation of family history and familial relations. The advertisement suggests that, through the novel, non-Chinese Americans sit as privileged witnesses, or as con-sultant pathologists, to the resolving of internal and incestuous conflicts,[3] not as participants.

Since the 1970s, "claiming America" has been the most consistent counterattack against the ghettoization of Asian American literature and discourse. According to Sau-Ling C. Wong, claiming America refers to "establishing the Asian American presence in the context of the United States' national cultural legacy and contemporary cultural production" ("Denationalization" 16). This strategy has consistently placed the expe-riences of Asian Americans squarely on American soil, actively writing the histories of Asian immigrants back into the history books from which they were excluded.[4] Nonetheless, the strength of a Euro-American prej-udice in the defining of true Americanness has proven formidable.[5] The tendency, especially for Euro-Americans, to view Chinese American lit-erature as "their" experience or "their" community-building project, rather than integral to "our" American experience relates directly to the misconception that Asians are "inassimilable," or that their ability to assimilate is obstructed by the starkness of their difference. As Shirley Lim says, "the reified signifiers of Kipling's 'East is East and West is West, and never the twain shall meet,' are . . . still potent with divisive force" (xxii). At its foundation, this bias boils down to physical difference: a European immigrant, for example, might blend into American life within one generation, whereas fourth-, fifth-, and sixth-generation Chinese Americans will continue to face the question, "Where are you from—originally?" But it also relates to a problematic emanating from the European immigration model of assimilation that was adopted by social scientists in the early and mid-twentieth century. The European immigration analogy, according to Michael Omi and Howard Winant, "suggested that racial minorities could be incorporated into American life in the same way that white ethnic groups had been" (12). This analogy fostered the expectation that non-European immigrant groups would assimilate into United States society following the four-fold cycle developed by Robert E. Park—contact, conflict, accommodation, and assimilation—and based on his observations of European immigrants. In Omi and Winant's view, this analogy ignored "what was in many cases a qualitatively different historical experience—one which included slavery, colonization, racially based exclusion and, in the case of Native Americans, virtual extirpation. In addition, it has been argued, the paradigm tends to 'blame the victims' for their plight and thus to deflect attention away from the ubiquity of racial meanings and dynamics" (21). Thus, rather than acknowledge the racist barriers that excluded the Chinese from full assimilation, people tended to view their failure as "the irrational products of individual pathologies" (Omi and Winant 10).

The notion of the inassimilable Asian also relates to assumptions about the personal aspirations of Chinese immigrants themselves. The prevalence of Chinatowns and sprawling Asian communities like Monterey Park, California, seems to support an assumption that Chinese Americans do not wish to belong to America. In the preface to Gwen Kinkead's 1992 ethnographic foray into New York's Chinatown, tellingly subtitled "A Portrait of a Closed Society," the author concludes that "Americans" can learn much from the "Chinese," but what the Chinese of Chinatown need to learn is that "they can't have it both ways—they cannot charge mistreatment and racism and, at the same time, refuse to talk to outsiders, or vote, or lend a cup of sugar to their neighbor" (x). Kinkead's work, portions of which were featured in *The New Yorker* prior to her book's publication, repeats the long-held view of the insular and clannish Chinese in a way that makes difference, rather than the dialectical relationship between racist exclusion laws and the Chinese struggle for survival in the formation of Chinatowns, central. In short, the Euro-American view of Chinese American ethnicity as, to use K. Scott Wong's phrase, "forever foreign," or at least always tinged with an irreconcilable foreignness, remains central to Euro-American assumptions.

These binary perceptions of outside/inside, ours/theirs, American/ Chinese color the ways non-Chinese Americans read Chinese American literature and, in fact, are sometimes reinforced in the literature itself in the ways conflicts, tensions, and resolutions are portrayed. Lisa Lowe's well-known argument against the homogenizing effects of the nativist/assimilationist preoccupation effectively explains the way Asian American literature often participates in the literary Chinatown phenomenon. According to Lowe, readers tend to view Asian Americans and their fictional representations from a nativist/assimilationist dialectic that interprets the experiences of Asian Americans according to "the question of the loss or transmission of the 'original' culture" (26). This topos is commonly figured in literature as the trope of "generational conflict and familial relation" (Lowe 26). The nativist/assimilationist preoccupation, in Lowe's opinion, masks the heterogeneity and multiplicity of Asian American culture and blurs "inter-community differences" (26). Important to my argument is the tendency for the nativist/assimilationist dialectic to privatize Chinese American literature. To view Asian American culture simply in terms of native culture and assimilation is to compartmentalize the literature and experiences of Asian Americans into a minority sphere—a literary Chinatown—from which other Americans can too easily divorce themselves. "This is a book by a minority writer," Gish Jen said in an interview in parody of such assumptions, "that must mean this is a book about preserving her heritage" (qtd. in Hart 26). On the positive side, the proliferation of Chinese American works that explore the difficulties faced by families may raise awareness of prejudice and increase acceptance of Chinese Americans. On the negative side, such literature may encourage the perception of the Chinese

American experience as a communal, privatized, internal affair divorced from the experiences of other Americans by focusing the tension of fictional works on familial relations, by positing the shaping of personhood on the clash of cultures within generations of a family.

The novel explored in this essay, *Mona in the Promised Land* (1996), confronts and destabilizes the literary Chinatown. By bringing her Chinese American protagonist and other characters to self-realization through a multicultural, pan-ethnic experiment known in the novel as "Camp Gugelstein," Gish Jen valorizes choice, change, and creolization as phenomena that are part of the American experience. In this way, Jen radically de-privatizes the Chinese American novel and significantly re-views all race and ethnicity in America as interdependent, dialogic, and hybrid. Yet, as I will discuss below, Jen's fictional solution to ethnicity's "Chinatown" problem unleashes its own practical and theoretical difficulties.

II

Mona, whose surname, Chang, is one vowel shy of the word *change*, becomes the prototypical subject of hybridity in Gish Jen's *Mona in the Promised Land* when she converts to Judaism and becomes known among her temple-friends as "Changowitz." As the centrality of Mona's transformation suggests, *Promised Land* is a "book of changes." The novel's world is a heteroglossia, which, according to Mikhail Bakhtin's definition, "permits a multiplicity of social voices and a wide variety of their links and interrelationships" (263). Set in the heteroglot arena of Mona's high school years during America's tumultuous 1960s, *Promised Land* allows the interplay of myriad "voices": Judaism, existential philosophy, concepts of America and China, Zen Buddhism, sexuality, black power, social action, and pubescent expressions of popularity and fashion. As Bakhtin asserts, "consciousness awakens to independent ideological life precisely in a world of alien discourses surrounding it" (345). As Mona and her friends negotiate a multicultural field of disparate voices and "alien discourses," what emerges is not a sense of fixed and static identities, but identities that are interstitial, contingent, and ever in the process of becoming. The consciousness that awakens is a multicultural, or as we will see by the end of this essay, a "polycultural" hybrid.

What characterizes Americanness in the novel is not what one becomes, but the very act of becoming. In other words, "becoming," the novel suggests, is the hallmark of being American. Each self in the heteroglossia of Gish Jen's America is, to borrow Alberto Melucci's description, "more of a field than an essence . . . , a dynamic system defined by recognizable opportunities and constraints" (64). However, Jen does not offer this view in a simplistic vacuum, sealed off from the racialized forces of society at large. In her youthful emphasis on the "opportunities" rather than the "constraints," Mona presents this simplistic definition: "American means being whatever you want" (49). But the events of the novel, primarily the breakup of Camp Gugelstein discussed below, reveal Mona's hopeful statement about America to be nothing short of naïve. What Mona has not learned at this point, but will later learn through her friendship with Alfred, the black American cook in her father's restaurant, is how persistent and pervasive racialized categories are in American society.

In their description of the dynamics that allow this continued insistence on race and racial hierarchy in the United States, Omi and Winant make a distinction between micro-level social relations and macro-level social relations. At the micro-level "race is a matter of individuality, or the formation of identity," whereas at the macro-level "race is a matter of collectivity, of the formation of social structures: economic, political and cultural/ideological" (66–67). In Omi and Winant's view, "the racial order is organized and enforced by the continuity and reciprocity between these two 'levels' of social relations" (67). Mona's concept that "American means being whatever you want" is naïve because it assumes micro-level social relations trump macro-level social relations. It assumes, in other words, that individual identity formation is self-determined and works independently from the rest of society. Mona's childish philosophy is the "American dream" in its most uncritical and unrealistic manifestation.

However, Mona does learn her lesson. Her attempts to help Alfred while hiding her actions from adults and neighbors reveals her budding awareness that promoting color-blind social relations puts one at odds with the rest of society. Her visit to the Rhode Island resort where her sister is working for the summer opens her eyes to her own place as a Chinese American in the social hierarchy of the United States. Most significantly, the breakup of the color-blind experiment called "Camp Gugelstein" shakes her world to the core and teaches her that a trite statement like "American means being whatever you want" is no match for the ubiquity of racialized thinking in the United States. The novel does show, as we will see below, that while Mona's early formulation of the American dream is unrealistic and impotent, her continued belief in the power of individual choice and the ideal of racial equality allows her in the end to come to a more mature and viable expression of this idea.

Jen most distinctly renders this hybridity in the "Camp Gugelstein" segment of the novel, a segment that at once glitters with the hope of a new racial order and fades with the disappointment of the old racial chaos. Mona and her Jewish American friends, Seth Mandel and Barbara Gugelstein, decide to promote minority solidarity by inviting Alfred, the African American cook in the Changs' pancake house, to stay in Barbara's home, which she and her cousin Evie occupy alone while Barbara's parents are away for the summer. Afraid that Evie will inform Barbara's parents that she is harboring a black man in their house, Barbara, Mona, and Seth arrange for Alfred to sneak into the house via a tunnel to the basement and to take up a quiet residence in the empty servant's quarters. They call the tunnel the "underground railway," a phrase that becomes increasingly ironic as Alfred's "freedom" in the Gugelstein home begins to look more like imprisonment as time goes by.

The irony of their brand of social action is soon exposed. The three friends have been willing to act on behalf of another minority to the point of inconvenience, but not to the point of endangering their own privileged position. Through their inability to allow Alfred hospitality as an equal, Jen exposes a serious impediment to pan-ethnic alliances: while Chinese Americans, Jewish Americans, and African Americans may share a common position as minorities in a hegemonic political and social environment, their minority status is not equally conceived. Alfred even goes to the extent of lumping Mona, Seth, and Barbara together under the signifier "white." He says to them,

> You white folk look at the calendar, and at the end of the year comes Christmastime, and at the beginning of the year comes a whole new year, maybe the year you pack your white ass off to college, maybe the year you go off traveling somewhere nice. Me, I look at that calendar,

and at the end of the year there's flapjacks, and at the beginning of the
year there's flapjacks, and when I die, man, they're going to cover me
with flapjacks, and put the butter and the syrup on top. (154)

From Alfred's perspective, Jewish and Chinese Americans may be
much closer to the white majority position than blacks. Alfred defines
their "whiteness" according to their social position and economic
empowerment, not by the precise color of their skin. "Whiteness," as
Gwendolyn Audrey Foster asserts in her book, *Performing Whiteness*, "does
not exist at the biological level. It is a cultural construct" (2). The culturally constructed line drawn between Chinese Americans and Jewish
Americans is, from Alfred's perspective, completely erased. This perception is reinforced in the novel by the apparent ease with which Mona
is able to identify with Jewish Americans in contrast to her perception
that one cannot become black (118).

The point of *Promised Land*, and one would assume its central "joke,"
is that Mona becomes Jewish. She does not simply identify with Jews
or recognize similarities—she switches. She converts not only to the Jewish religion, but she also adopts the speech patterns, attitudes, and
lifestyles of her Jewish American friends. In terms of the physical or
blood heritage often associated with race, Mona's switch would be an
impossibility, as Alfred has in mind when he denies Mona's Jewishness
on account of her not "growing a nose" (137). Even Barbara's nose job,
which her mother hopes will make her look less Jewish, does not seem
to erase the "fact" of Barbara's race. The question of racial predestina-
tion versus free will is debated during a "temple rap-session" in relation
to Eloise Ingle's discovery of her Jewish heritage (56). Is it "blood" or
"diet" that define race, the group wonders, or can Eloise simply "be what
she wants to be"? (56). The answer they seem to settle on is the latter,
individual preference, and they point to Mona, "The Changowitz" (56),
as living proof.

Mona insists to her parents, however, that she can become Jewish,
but she and her family cannot become black, so they need not worry.
Mona's distinction here confuses physical and cultural constructs of both
Jewishness and blackness: Mona sees Jewishness as a belief, while blackness is determined by physical features and skin color. One wonders,
therefore, whether within Mona's logic is an aesthetic preference for Jew-

ishness over blackness. Perhaps what makes Mona's conversion acceptable (to her and eventually to her parents[6]) is the perception that she is
moving forward, from what in the 1960s was not yet considered a "model
minority" to what was at least considered a "better" minority, a move
that brings her one step closer to whiteness.

This problematic, which is implicit in Mona's characterization, is
explicit in the character of Helen, Mona's mother. Helen fears turning
black, by which she means being perceived as socially and economically
on par with blacks. When an African American social activist asks her
to sign a petition on creating a subsidized family-planning clinic, Helen
is insulted at the woman's implication that Chinese Americans would
be united with African Americans in what the woman calls a "common
cause." "We live in Scarshill," says Helen. "You should see our tax bracket"
(119). Helen clearly perceives the racial category "black" as a social and
economic position and believes her social status to be markedly higher
than that of blacks because of her own economic position. "We are not
Negroes," she says to Mona. "You hear me? Why should we work so
hard—so people can talk to us about birth control for free" (119). In relation to this issue as a barrier to cross-ethnic solidarity, Vijay Prashad
asks, "since blackness is reviled in the United States, why would an immigrant, of whatever skin color, want to associate with those who are racially
oppressed, particularly when the transit into the United States promises the dream of gold and glory?" Prashad goes on to explain, "the immigrant seeks a form of vertical assimilation, to climb from the lowest,
darkest echelon on the stepladder of tyranny into the bright whiteness.
In U.S. history the Irish, Italians, Jews, and—in small steps with some
hesitations on the part of white America—Asians and Latinos have all
tried to barter their varied cultural worlds for the privileges of whiteness" (*Everybody* x).

Despite sharing with African Americans a minority position in society, Mona and her friends are unable to breach the line drawn between
them and Alfred. Instead, the line is breached for them: returning to
Barbara Gugelstein's house one day, the three friends find Alfred and
his African American friends partying in the living room with Evie sit-
ting on Alfred's lap. This marks the birth of Camp Gugelstein, an experiment in cross-ethnic integration and solidarity. Every evening for the
rest of the summer, Luther the Race Man, Big Benson, Ray, Professor

Estimator, Alfred and Evie, and Seth, Barbara, and Mona hang out together at the Gugelstein mansion. They smoke dope, drink, talk, dance, practice yoga, sit cross-legged in a circle, and rap heart-to-heart. They listen to Soul Train, dance the funky chicken, and play mah-jongg, chess, and Chinese checkers. Camp Gugelstein becomes for each of them a symbol of interracial communication and alliance. In Professor Estimator's opinion, "Agape, meaning love of all humanity . . . redemptive love is still alive here, at Camp Gugelstein, but he thinks elsewhere it is on the wane" (201). The culture of agape in Camp Gugelstein allows the participants to engage in a dialogic interplay of various social languages and ideologies: these include Martin Luther King's liberation theology, Malcolm X's black power, materialism, humanism and free will, Protestantism, Judaism, integration versus Jim Crow separatism, and transcendental meditation. From this multiplicity is born a rich polycultural hybridity where difference is embraced and the common bond of humanity is extolled. This sense of oneness is represented in Mona's experience while touching hands during yoga: "There are warm palms and cool palms, firm grips, loose; and attached to them such an amazing array of humanity" (202).

Hybridity in the Camp Gugelstein episode is not merely emotional or ideological; Jen's description of the African Americans as ranging in skin color from "gingerbread" and "cream" to "papaya" and "the color of old iron" (197–98) suggests a complex biological hybridization that is altogether ignored in the term "black." "Black" is thus revealed as an inaccurate description of physical difference, and shown, rather, to be a signifier of difference in racialized constructions that refuse hybridity. Alfred says to Mona, "White is white, man. Everything else is black. Half and half is black" (155). In the context of their discussion, Alfred is clearly not expressing solidarity with Chinese Americans; rather, he is articulating the way racist constructions of race tend to homogenize what is actually diverse. Similarly, the "paper-bag" color of another African American character is explained in this way: "if she were a cabinet door or a shade of hair dye, people would have a name for her exact shade. But as she is only a person, she is called black" (170). Again, the description of difference is not a physical reality but an ideological construction, a way of conceptualizing the foreign in a way that marks and retains its alterity vis-à-vis whiteness. The fact that the various shades of color represented in these characters is the result of biological hybridizations that include white blood is ignored by the generic term "black."[7]

On the other hand, the same label that the majority uses as a distancing mechanism can become the marker of solidarity for the minority group. Stuart Hall makes this observation in relation to the term "black" in his essay, "Old and New Identities, Old and New Ethnicities." In the 1960s, says Hall, "black" was divested of its racist connotations when black people, regardless of color shade and national origin, adopted it as a unifying description that defined their community. The term "black" as a signifier of solidarity and community is what connects Alfred and his African American friends despite their various skin colors, class backgrounds, opinions, and education levels. Thus, while on the one hand "black" is an unfair homogenization of a diverse community, it is paradoxically the same term that unifies African Americans and provides the basis for political and social action.[8] In fact, it is in this ethnic and racial unification that multiculturalism has come under attack in the 1990s. While racial tension exposed by such events as the O. J. Simpson trial, the Rodney King beating, and Hurricane Katrina reveal that there is a great need for increased interracial and interethnic communication in American society today, multiculturalism, its critics assert, seems to be dividing and reifying ethnic groups into privatized, parochial enclaves.[9] The demise of Camp Gugelstein can be seen as reinforcing this criticism, but, as will be discussed below, the novel's moral vision is recovered by a polycultural engagement with race.

Camp Gugelstein—the utopian, "world-without-borders" experiment (208)—splinters and dissolves as quickly as it had formed. When Barbara finds an expensive flask missing, she, Mona, and Seth question their black guests, and the three accusers are then accused of racism. In an expression of black solidarity, all the African Americans, including Alfred, leave in outrage. The lines between ethnic groups, which seemed to have disappeared under the Camp Gugelstein banner, reappear with a vengeance.

The failure of Camp Gugelstein illustrates the precariousness of panethnic efforts and the tenacity of racist attitudes. The event that precipitates the black exodus is the questioning of the black men regarding the missing flask. This assumption is racist: in the face of a crime, it is the black man who is immediately suspected of committing it. However, while clearly exposing the latent racism beneath Camp Gugelstein's veneer, the novel is strangely silent about the expression of black solidarity and the role it plays in the closure of dialogue. Mona, Seth, and Barbara express an acute sense of angst and guilt over their actions, but they never question whether the black walk-out was justifiable. They assume, apparently, that their own expression of racism, unintended as it was, provided a sufficient defense for the black group's reaction. In this, *Promised Land* may be seen as excusing a gross overreaction by the black members of Camp Gugelstein and placing the blame on the three non-black members. Black separatism is thus exonerated and white guilt preserved. This patronizing representation of the black man as a simple "victim" widens the gap between the black and non-black characters, thereby re-enforcing Alfred's view that Mona, Seth, and Barbara are white in comparison to blacks. To extend this reading, we could argue that Camp Gugelstein, the utopian ideal, may be less a literary experiment in pan-ethnicity than a fantasy for a market motivated by the dynamics of white guilt.[10]

Nevertheless, viewed from the notion of multicultural hybridity, the pan-ethnic vision of Camp Gugelstein is not entirely lost. In fact, we might see it as the impetus for the deeper transformations in the lives of its participants. As discussed previously, Omi and Winant argue that the "racial order is organized and enforced by the continuity and reciprocity between" the micro-level and macro-level social relations. But the micro-level experiments of individual identity formation in Camp Gugelstein eventually work to challenge and subvert the macro-level social relations signified by racial relations in Ralph's restaurant and the underlying social pressures that force Mona, Seth, and Barbara to hide Alfred in the Gugelstein home. Read in the Gramscian terminology of Omi and Winant's argument, the Camp Gugelstein gathering may be considered a "war of maneuver," which describes "a situation in which subordinate groups seek to preserve and extend a definite territory, to ward off violent assault, and to develop an internal society as an alternative to the repressive social system they confront" (Omi and Winant 74). The breakup of Camp Gugelstein forces the members of the group who are truly committed to the cause into a direct political struggle with the racialized hierarchies of society, an oppositional program Gramsci calls a "war of position."

The contact between these individuals of different ethnic backgrounds was not, the novel attests, without its impact. For Mona and Seth the breakup of Camp Gugelstein marks a coming of age in their own development, one that ultimately makes them more dedicated to the cause of interracial dialogue and social action (see 207, for example). Moreover, when they visit Alfred to apologize for the flask incident, there is a real sense of solidarity and friendship between them, a sense of healing and restoration that suggests barriers had indeed been broken down (290–92). This development in the relationship between the novel's black and non-black characters is signified by the reuniting of Alfred and Evie, who eventually marry and have three babies. Alfred and Evie become staunch activists for social change—"Mr. and Mrs. Community Organization" (297).

I I I

Camp Gugelstein's pan-ethnic interaction and its resultant multicultural hybridity reflect a significant new direction in Chinese American literature. The hybridity of *Promised Land* subverts the literary Chinatown discussed in Part One by displacing notions of ethnic essence and cultural stasis. A popular Asian American novel such as *The Joy Luck Club* may raise awareness among a largely white, middle-class readership of the lives of Asian Americans and their particular struggles. Unfortunately, *The Joy Luck Club*'s focus on Chinese American relationships and familial problems reinforces for many readers the impression that Chinese Americans suffer from Chinese American problems.[11] On the other hand, *Promised Land* suggests that Chinese American ethnicity is not forged through the clash of two monolithic cultures, but, as Bakhtin describes all human consciousness, is continually evolving in a heteroglot "multiplicity of social voices" and their "interrelationships." *Promised Land* significantly de-privatizes the Chinese American novel by re-viewing American identity, not just one ethnic group's identity, as an individualized process characterized by the "internal variation" (Wicker 37) of hybridity. This, I suggest, moves beyond "claiming America" to an important process of "transforming America."

Gish Jen's concern is, in her words, to push "the limits and expand . . . the notion of America's view of itself . . . to create a new notion of what it means to be American" (qtd. in Snell 58–59). But *Promised Land*'s "new notion" of America, if we are to accept my reading of hybridity's triumph over separatism, does in fact present serious problems for multicultur-alists. Although we might see the failure of Camp Gugelstein as the nec-essary impetus for a "war of position," we should also note that the "positions" taken in the post-Gugelstein era are almost entirely individual positions. The group that comprised Camp Gugelstein never reunites. One difficulty here is that an articulation of cultural identity as amor-phous and fluid threatens, in Sau-Ling Wong's words, to leave "certain segments of the . . . population . . . without a viable discursive space" ("Denationalization"16). Moreover, in the political realities of represen-tational government, a system that necessitates a unified articulation of need, hybrid identities seem powerless and pointless. The Jane Auste-nesque epilogue to *Promised Land*, which describes the radically different identities achieved by various characters, seems to fail in precisely this area. The only characteristic that unites the disparate identities at the end of the novel is the experience of transformation itself. How, one might rightly ask, can economically disadvantaged individuals and oppressed groups make themselves heard as political constituents when all that unites them is an experience of change?[12]

The political sterility of the cultural hybridity model implied in these objections thus lies in cultural hybridity's inability as a postmodern the-ory to accommodate cultural objectification. According to some articu-lations of postmodernism, all forms of essentialization are to be questioned and condemned. In a kind of twisted logic, as Pnina Werb-ner explains, "citizenship rights and multiculturalist agendas are as much dependent on collective objectification as are racist murders and ethnic cleansing." However, she continues, "it is critical to establish clearly the difference between modes of objectification and modes of reification" (229). "Reification is representation which distorts and silences" in order to manipulate those of another racial or ethnic community (Werbner 229). The violence enacted upon that community is situated funda-mentally in the power to name, to define, to essentialize from a posi-tion outside that group. Thus, the assumption that a black man stole the flask in Camp Gugelstein stems from a racialized, essentialist definition—a reification—of blacks. However, the kind of essentializ-ing Werbner points to, and what San Juan in a similar context calls "a

positional articulation of identity and difference" (150), is an "objectification" that is rightfully performed by a person of ethnicity as a means
of social and political identification, as, for example, in the term "black"
discussed above—and, significantly, in the naming of the short-lived
pan-ethnic community "Camp Gugelstein." "In their performative rhetoric," Werbner says, people of ethnicity "essentialise their imagined communities in order to mobilise for action. . . . In this regard, the politics
of ethnicity are a positive politics: they serve to construct moral and aesthetic communities imaginatively" (230). The difference here is that the
objectification of the ethnic community is established by the power to
name itself rather than the powerlessness necessary to being named.[13]

I agree with Werbner's argument, but I would also argue that internal objectification introduces its own difficulties. My critique of Camp
Gugelstein's breakup implies that a group's freedom in defining itself
does not guarantee racial harmony and fairness. The African American
group's objectification of itself in the breakup of Camp Gugelstein did
not happen in a vacuum, but performed a kind of violence on the community that all of them—African American, Jewish American, and Chinese American—were trying to build. Thus, in an adjustment to
Werbner's thesis, I would suggest that within the right of an ethnic community to name and define itself is a responsibility to anticipate and
preserve alliances with other communities.

In *Promised Land*, it is the pan-ethnic interaction and its resultant
cultural hybridity, produced through the Camp Gugelstein experience,
not Camp Gugelstein itself, that provide a provocative re-visioning of
race and ethnicity. The linkages forged between these otherwise distinct
cultural groups is an example of what Vijay Prashad calls "polyculturalism" in his book *Everybody was Kung Fu Fighting*. As with hybridity
theory, polyculturalism questions our culture's insistent belief in primordial, static, and pure cultures, but it furthermore seeks actively to
engage oppressed peoples and white "allies" in forging anti-racist communities. We can conceive of polyculturalism as a term that rejects the
notion of discrete and contained cultures. Prashad explains, "even
though people form what appear to be relatively discrete groups (South
Asians, African Americans, Latino Americans), most of us live with the
knowledge that the boundaries of our communities are fairly porous
and that we do not think of all those within our 'group' as of a cohesive

piece" (*Everybody* 66). This may sound like hybridity in another name, and in some respects it is. Polyculturalism, as a term, evades the British Imperial connotations of "hybridity" and what Cyrus Patell calls hybridity's "philological baggage" (qtd. in Prashad, *Everybody* 173). But I would argue for a more important distinction: hybridity connotes a passive reception of multiple cultural lineages, whereas polyculturalism connotes an active and strategic accumulation of lineages. According to Prashad, polyculturalism "draws from the idea of polyrhythms—many different rhythms operating together to produce a whole song, rather than different drummers doing their thing" (*Everybody* 66). The image of "different drummers doing their thing" represents multiculturalism's emphasis on discrete cultures, which has more popularly been represented by the mosaic or salad bowl. Where the melting pot analogy envisioned a monocultural America, and the salad bowl a multicultural America, we might conceive of polyculturalism as a pluralistic society made up of pluralistic people—people who are continually in the process of (often intentionally) combining the rhythms in an ongoing and ever-changing song. Prashad quotes hip-hop MC Q-Unique as an example of the type of linkages and combining that are characteristic of polyculturalism: "You study everybody's techniques and you strip away what you don't find necessary and use what is necessary and modify it" (*Everybody* 148). This marks one difference between hybridity theory and Prashad's polyculturalism—the former emphasizes the development of the individual as the result of various cultural linkages and is more-or-less passive, whereas the latter emphasizes the individual's active construction of identity, the choosing and rejecting of lineages. In other words, hybridity is received, while polyculturalism is achieved. Mona "Changowitz" is a supreme fictional example of the polycultural idea.

Here, too, I believe polyculturalism sidesteps the postmodern tendency to view race as a disappearing marker, or as a socially constructed marker that, if we could just successfully deconstruct, we would understand "that we are all one" (Palumbo-Liu 393). Polyculturalism's "painful embrace of the skin and all its contradictions" (Prashad, *Everybody* xii) recognizes that race will not "cease to be a negative and destructive element of identification" (Palumbo-Liu 393) by simply our choosing to see ourselves as hybrid. Polyculturalism is based on hybridity's theory that our identities are constructed out of a matrix of cultural influences, but it retains a pragmatic comprehension of the realities of racial inequality in today's society. Multiculturalism served as a "defensive tactic" that has allowed people of color to embrace their lineage and regain pride in the face of racism, but polyculturalism offers a "strategy for freedom" that wrenches the good intentions of multiculturalism from the grasp of racists and hegemonic order (Prashad, *Everybody* 147–48).

Although it falls short of a true "war of position," Camp Gugelstein's radical and active cultural hybridity—its polycultural experiment— emerges as a "new notion of America," and Mona might be seen as its poster girl. In the final pages of the novel, Mona discusses with Aunt Theresa the possibility of changing her name when she marries Seth Mandel: "'To Mandel?' says Theresa, surprised. 'No more women's lib?' . . . 'No, no. To Changowitz,' says Mona. 'I was thinking that Seth would change his name too'" (303).

In choosing the name Changowitz, a name that was established early in the novel as a marker of hybridity, Mona exerts the power to name herself, to define who she is. In suggesting that Seth change his name as well, Mona is establishing a community signified by the hybrid name Changowitz. Thus the heroine of *Mona in the Promised Land* steps boldly and decisively out of the literary Chinatown and into the pan-ethnic, antiracist world of the polycultural.

Notes

1. The virtuality of the reading experience and the desire to "escape" or "explore" without leaving one's chair is not confined to the reading of Chinese American texts. In a sense, all reading involves leaving "our world" and entering "another world" in a virtual way. What I mean to emphasize here is not that the advertisement presents a unique purpose for reading, but rather that it presents a fetishized, exoticized image of that "other world." In other words, I am interested in the advertisement's *view* of Chinese Americans.

2. A fuller articulation of this "literary Chinatown" phenomenon can be found in my book *Beyond Literary Chinatown* (2007).

3. The novel in question, *Monkey King*, is, in fact, about incest.

4. For example, Maxine Hong Kingston's *China Men* (1980), Shawn Wong's

Homebase (1979), Gish Jen's *Typical American* (1992), Frank Chin's *Donald Duk* (1991), Elaine Kim's *Asian American Literature* (1982), and Ronald Takaki's *Strangers from a Different Shore* (1990).

5. Walter Benn Michaels's discussion of "nativist modernism" in *Our America* traces the threads of this kind of exclusion to the modernist literature and discourse of the 1920s. In that era, Michaels argues, the criterion of exclusion from the "family of America" shifted from the specific concept of racial inferiority to the general concept of racial difference. Foreignness, thus, was no longer a matter of not fitting in, or not contributing to the strengthening of the nation, but a matter of plain and simply not belonging.

6. Mona's parents even go so far as to say, "better to turn Jewish than Asian American" out of their prejudice toward Japanese, Koreans, and South Asians (*Promised Land* 302).

7. In *Colonial Desire: Hybridity in Theory, Culture and Race*, Robert J. C. Young explains that hybridity found its earliest and most prominent articulations in the racialized debates of nineteenth-century colonialism. Hybridity, the biological mixing of the races, was constructed as a threat to the white colonialist's mandate and responsibility as member of the "superior race" to rule the world. The dissemination of the white man's seed among the "inferior races" would lead to the disintegration of civilization, an idea that was most poignantly expressed in the trope of the hybrid's supposed sexual impotency. For many theorists of today, the notion of cultural hybridity is a positive formulation, a "radical inversion" (Papastergiadis 257) of racist constructs. Even so, Young cautions against an uninformed acceptance of the language of hybridity in today's Cultural Studies, a language he claims utilizes "the vocabulary of the Victorian extreme right" (10).

8. Such reversals are common in the discourse and literary traditions of ethnic minority groups. Henry Louis Gates, Jr., for instance, argues that the well-known trope of the "signifying monkey" in African American literature is "the ironic reversal of a received racist image in the Western imagination" (236). The positive use of the formerly negative image turns the power of racist language on its head. "Queer" as a unifying term for the homosexual community provides a recent example, as do "Hybridity," discussed in the previous note, and "Changowitz," discussed at the conclusion of this essay.

9. Walter Benn Michaels potently attacks multiculturalism's pluralist foundation in his claim that the essentialist criterion for identity that pluralism seeks to destroy is actually reinforced in pluralism's insistence on the primacy of the group over the whole. Pluralism's claim to locate identity in performative terms ("what we do") rather than essentialist terms ("who we

are") is contradicted, Michaels argues, by the legitimization of the local over and against the universal, in which case "performance" can only be validated by "essence" (14–15). The breakup of Camp Gugelstein underscores this inherent flaw in multiculturalism in its reification of group boundaries, but, as I argue in this chapter, cultural hybridity (like Mona's) recognizes a responsibility toward larger alliances. See also Prashad's *The Karma of Brown Folk*, San Juan's *Racism and Cultural Studies: Critiques of Mulitculturalist Ideology and the Politics of Difference*, and Eduarto M. Duarte and Stacy Smith's *Foundational Perspectives in Multicultural Education*.

10. I am indebted to John Whalen-Bridge for this observation in particular, and for his critical comments on earlier drafts. I would also like to acknowledge the guidance of Barnard Turner, whose many helpful comments helped to shape my overall argument.

11. In other words, it pathologizes Asian American lives. David Palumbo-Liu, in his discussion of "model minority discourse and the course of healing," argues that, for many white middle-class readers, Asian American literature invokes "the expected themes of subject-split, cultural alienation and confusion, and coming-to-terms that fit the stereotypical image of the model minority" (410). Palumbo-Liu goes on to explain the problem with this view: "the perpetuation of the marketing of Asian American literature as the literature of an assimilated group now at peace after a 'phase' of adjustment is dangerous in its powerful closing-off of a multiplicity of real, lived, social contradictions and complexities that stand outside (or at least significantly complicate) the formula of the highly individuated 'identity crisis'" (410). Furthermore, according to Christopher Douglas, this "ethnographic gaze" that pathologizes the Asian American serves to indulge the white reader's sense of his/her own coherence: "By reading Chinese American fiction ethnographically, contemporary white American readers are rediscovering themselves and their own cultural-psychic coherence—that is, against the supposed cultural confusion experienced by Tan's young Chinese American heroines, they discover their own unproblematic place within American society" (119). See, also, "Sugar Sisterhood" by Sau-Ling C. Wong, and chapters on *The Joy Luck Club* in David Leiwei Li's *Imagining the Nation* and Patricia P. Chu's *Assimilating Asians*.

12. Other objections to the hybridity model center on its tainted linguistic genealogy, its literal botanic reference to the mixing of two essences, and its euphoric and utopian promise to eradicate essentialism. Anne Anlin Cheng, for instance, asks whether the hybridity model sets up "an illusory opposition . . . between hybridity and essentialism, as though the former cures the

latter, as though differences of class, gender, and nationality eliminate essentialist positions when clearly those different positions are themselves each effecting their own brands of allegiances, each demanding 'an' identity" (26). Vijay Prashad claims that the problem with the hybridity metaphor is its literal definition that "retains within it ideas of purity and origins (two things melded together)" ("Bruce Lee" 54). Added to this is the problem of hybridity's historic origins in the racial theories of the Victorian era highlighted in note 7.

13. Prashad makes a similar argument about strategic deployments of cultural essence and primordialism: "Minority groups may mobilize around the notion of an origin to make resource claims, to show that despite the denigration of the power elite, the group can lay claim to an aspect of civilization and the cultural currency attached to it. Furthermore, to demarcate oneself from the repressive stereotypes, the oppressed frequently turn to their 'roots' to suggest to their children that they have a lineage that is worthy despite racism's cruelty. These are important social explanations for the way we use both origins and authenticity (to protect our traditional forms from appropriation by the power elite)" (*Everybody* 147). But he goes on to claim that these are tactics for defense that must eventually be transcended by "a strategy for freedom" (*Everybody* 148).

Works Cited

Bakhtin, M. M. *The Dialogic Imagination.* Ed. Michael Holquist. Trans. Caryl Emerson and Michael Holquist. 1981. Austin: University of Texas Press, 1987.

Bloom, Harold. *Asian American Women Writers.* Philadelphia: Chelsea House, 1997.

Chao, Patricia. *Monkey King.* 1997. New York: HarperFlamingo, 1998.

Cheng, Anne Anlin. *The Melancholy of Race.* New York: Oxford University Press, 2001.

Chu, Patricia P. *Assimilating Asians: Gendered Strategies of Authorship in Asian America.* Durham, NC: Duke University Press, 2000.

Douglas, Christopher. "Reading Ethnography: The Cold War Social Science of Jade Snow Wong's *Fifth Chinese Daughter* and *Brown v. Board of Education.*" *Form and Transformation in Asian American Literature.* Ed. Zhou Xiaojing and Samina Najmi. Seattle: University of Washington Press, 2005. 101–24.

Duarte, Eduarto M. and Stacy Smith, eds. *Foundational Perspectives in Multicultural Education*. New York: Longman, 2000.

Foster, Gwendolyn Audrey. *Performing Whiteness: Postmodern Re/Constructions in the Cinema*. Albany: State University of New York Press, 2003.

Gates, Henry Louis, Jr. *Figures in Black: Words, Signs, and the "Racial" Self*. New York: Oxford University Press, 1987.

Hall, Stuart. "Old and New Identities, Old and New Ethnicities." *Culture, Globalization and the World System*. Ed. Anthony D. King. New York: Macmillan, 1991. 41–68.

Hart, Denise. "Gish Jen." *Poets and Writers Magazine* (Nov./Dec. 1993): 20–27.

Jen, Gish. *Mona in the Promised Land*. 1996. New York: Vintage, 1997.

Kinkead, Gwen. *Chinatown: A Portrait of a Closed Society*. New York: HarperCollins, 1992.

Li, David Leiwei. *Imagining the Nation: Asian American Literature and Cultural Consent*. Stanford, CA: Stanford University Press, 1998.

Lim, Shirley. Introduction. *The Frontiers of Love*. By Diana Chang. 1956. Seattle: University of Washington Press, 1994. v–xxiii.

Lowe, Lisa. "Heterogeneity, Hybridity, Multiplicity: Marking Asian American Differences." *Diaspora* 1.1 (1991): 24–44.

Melucci, Alberto. "Identity and Difference in a Globalized World." *Debating Cultural Hybridity*. Ed. Pnina Werbner and Tariq Modood. London: Zed, 1997. 58–69.

Michaels, Walter Benn. *Our America: Nativism, Modernism, and Pluralism*. Durham, NC: Duke University Press, 1995.

Omi, Michael and Howard Winant. *Racial Formation in the United States: From the 1960s to the 1980s*. New York: Routledge, 1986.

Palumbo-Liu, David. *Asian/American: Historical Crossings of a Racial Frontier*. Stanford, CA: Stanford University Press, 1999.

Papastergiadis, Nikos. "Tracing Hybridity in Theory." *Debating Cultural Hybridity*. Ed. Pnina Werbner and Tariq Modood. London: Zed, 1997. 257–81.

Partridge, Jeffrey F. L. "*Mona in the Promised Land*." *American Writers Classics*. Ed. Jay Parini. Vol. 2. New York: Thomson Gale, 2003. 215–32.

———. *Beyond Literary Chinatown*. Seattle: University of Washington Press, 2007.

Prashad, Vijay. "Bruce Lee and the Anti-imperialism of Kung Fu: A Polycultural Adventure." *Positions* 11.1 (Spring 2003): 52–91.

——. *Everybody was Kung Fu Fighting: Afro-Asian Connections and the Myth of Cultural Purity*. Boston: Beacon, 2001.

——. *The Karma of Brown Folk*. Minneapolis: University of Minnesota Press, 2000.

San Juan, E., Jr. *Racism and Cultural Studies: Critiques of Multiculturalist Ideology and the Politics of Difference*. Durham, NC: Duke University Press, 2002.

Snell, Marilyn Berlin. "The Intimate Outsider." *NPQ* (Summer 1991): 56–60.

Werbner, Pnina. "Essentialising Essentialism, Essentialising Silence: Ambivalence and Multiplicity in the Constructions of Racism and Ethnicity." *Debating Cultural Hybridity*. Ed. Pnina Werbner and Tariq Modood. London: Zed, 1997. 226–54.

Wicker, Hans-Rudolf. "From Complex Culture to Cultural Complex." *Debating Cultural Hybridity*. Ed. Pnina Werbner and Tariq Modood. London: Zed, 1997. 29–45.

Wong, K. Scott. "Chinatown: Conflicting Images, Contested Terrain." *MELUS* 20 (Spring 1995): 3–16.

Wong, Sau-Ling C. "Denationalization Reconsidered: Asian American Cultural Criticism at a Theoretical Crossroads." *Amerasia Journal* 21.1–2 (1995): 1–27.

——. "'Sugar Sisterhood': Situating the Amy Tan Phenomenon." *The Ethnic Canon: Histories, Institutions, and Interventions*. Ed. David Palumbo-Liu. Minneapolis: University of Minnesota Press, 1995. 174–210.

Young, Robert J. C. *Colonial Desire: Hybridity in Theory, Culture and Race*. London: Routledge, 1995.

6 Reading *The Turner Diaries*

Jewish Blackness, Judaized Blacks, and Head-Body Race Paradigms

JOE LOCKARD

HE TURNER DIARIES, WILLIAM PIERCE'S futuristic and white supremacist race-war novel—made famous as Timothy McVeigh's favorite inspirational reading— is usually condemned with opprobrium. The novel, first published in 1978, is not one that invites prolonged contemplation on issues of critical undecidability. Morris Dees and the Southern Poverty Law Center, the American Jewish Committee, the Simon Wiesenthal Center, and others joined forces in 1996 to denounce Lyle Stuart, the publisher of Barricade Books, for issuing the book in a new edition, one that included a denunciatory forward by the publisher. According to Morris Dees, "We've come across *The Turner Diaries* in almost every single case that we've had against white supremacy, neo-Nazi, Ku Klux Klan-type activity that resulted in violence that caused deaths and injuries to many innocent people" (qtd. in Olson).

Responding to criticism of his publishing decision, the notably independent and now-deceased Lyle Stuart stated, "I felt it was important the average American see how sick these minds are and how dreadful and perverted their thinking process is" (qtd. in Olson). Stuart and his opponents—who circulated a call to major book chains asking them to refuse to handle the book—essentially disagreed on the means of social prophylaxis.[1] Whereas Stuart advocated the liberalism of First Amendment absolutism to achieve this end, the book's opposition relied upon an appeal to consumer sensitivity and an implicit end run around the certainty of First Amendment protection for the text. Both sides of the argument joined together in a fundamental belief that the novel represented a perverse worldview.

While the "sick minds" that Lyle Stuart sought to expose through publication are clearly repulsive, they are far from unique or especially diseased; indeed, they operate only within an exaggerated scale of social normality, one that has a clear history. The novel's hierarchical racialism[2] has an entirely classical formation and a contemporary reader's sense of shock comes from a barely mediated encounter with fundamental precepts of "race." The ideology that governs the *Diaries* can be specifically located within the European Enlightenment and its naturalized classifications of racial characteristics. After briefly historicizing this race classicism within twentieth-century American racial discourse, I shall elaborate on the respective characterizations of Jewishness, blackness, and their narrative interdependency within the *Diaries*.[3]

One of the deeper constructs informing the social ideology of "race" is a division of humanity into "head" and "body." The body represents labor capacity divorced from cognitive ability; the head represents cognitive ability in need of a laboring body to direct. This racial paradigm came to the fore in the eighteenth century as an entrained logic of European imperialism's economic expansion, and the human bifurcation it expresses found its first scientific rationalizations during the Enlightenment.[4] Head/body, as both economic paradigm and social trope, was a common form of description for a racial order to the world during the nineteenth century and well into the twentieth, albeit with declining respectability. The language and practices of racialism begin with the body and seek to extrapolate an irreducible and primary character across select physiognomic commonalities. In this pursuit of broad human characterization, the body substitutes for the head; the body becomes an unalterable sign of the head and possible mentalities. The trope establishes an order of rank, and questions of intelligence, whether alleged greater or lesser, attach themselves to racial characterizations in parallel alignment.

Various Enlightenment intellectuals, in their efforts to construct a naturalistic and rationalist description of global human geography, relied upon this head-and-body hierarchy by positing a cerebral and advanced (white) portion of humanity, as opposed to a brutish (non-white) portion doomed to physicality without the resplendent intellectualism that constituted true civilization. Thus David Hume could write in "Of National Characters" that "I am apt to suspect the negroes and all other species of men (for there are four or five different kinds) to be naturally inferior to the whites. There was never any civilized nation of any other complexion than white" (Hume 1: 521, note M).[5] With specific reference to Hume, Kant in his *Observations of the Feeling of the Beautiful and Sublime* (1764) posits that "the Negroes of Africa have no feeling that rises above the trifling. . . . So fundamental is the difference between these two races of man [referring to European whiteness as an opposite], and it appears to be as great in regard to mental capacities as in color" (110). Similar sentiments can be traced through Herder, de Buffon, and Jefferson in his Linnean moments, a historical exercise that has been performed sufficiently often. Each of these writers performs the identical narrative act of first making copious observations on physical appearance, contours, and limbs, and then proceeding to deduce mental attributes that identify black inferiority. A more apt observation might concern the contradiction of professed rationalism embedded in this illogical transit, but the purpose here lies in specifying this history of observational dualism between body and head, and its consolidation in European natural philosophy of the eighteenth century.

It was against precisely this discursive tradition on racial intelligence that early nineteenth-century African American writer David Walker spoke in exasperated anger concerning its foremost American proponent: "Has Mr. Jefferson declared to the world, that we are inferior to the whites, both in the endowments of our bodies and our minds?" (Walker 20; see also 38–39). Walker scorned these terms of Jeffersonian debate as demeaning and dishonorable, and as no more than a search for a means of black suppression through the fraudulent objectivity of white supremacist anthropological sciences. In a manifesto such as Walker's *Appeal* we can locate early resistance to the European frame for racialist discussion; from this perspective Walker may be understood as an enlightened counter-Enlightenment thinker who contended with the dominant discourse of racialism that the Enlightenment sought to legitimate. Rejec-tions of the Enlightenment's bifurcation of head and body, of intelligence and labor, such as that voiced by Walker, were ignored throughout the nineteenth century as effeminate emotionalism, sentimental philo-Negroism, or were claimed to be subject to scientific proof of racial inequal-ity. The prevailing voices were those such as Henry Hughes, a pro-slavery ideologue and arguably the first United States sociologist, who asserted in his *Treatise on Sociology* (1854), "The sovereignty of one race, and the subsovereignty of the other, are morally commanded. . . . All of one race, are thinkers. This by their vocation. They are mentalists" (286).[6] The rationalizations of America race slavery lay most centrally in these asser-tions of a superior destiny arising from the white mind's prowess.

The same basic head-body paradigm and hierarchical principle attained throughout a steady and consistent body of racialist literature, emerging in the early twentieth century as "race science" and eugenics. During the 1920s American racialism achieved a coherent public intel-lectual constellation for perhaps the first time since prior to the Civil War. Figures like Madison Grant, Theodore Lothrop Stoddard, Earnest Sevier Cox, and Charles Conant Josey published copiously and to great public attention on the global sociology of "race," and Madison Grant was central in drafting the Johnson Act of 1924 that barred most immi-gration. As nativists, Grant and his supporters felt that the color line and alien immigration represented the same lesson of racial preserva-tion, or in Grant's words, "It has taken us fifty years to learn that speak-ing English, wearing good clothes, and going to school and to church, does not transform a negro into a white man. . . . Americans will have a similar experience with the Polish Jew, whose dwarf stature, peculiar mentality, and ruthless concentration on self-interest are being engrafted upon the stock of the nation" (16). As an ostensibly modern group, they represented a socially respectable school of thought—Josey was a pro-fessor of psychology at Dartmouth, no less—and all were declared white supremacists. When European colonialism encountered growing anti-colonial nationalism throughout Africa and Asia after the First World War, the divisionary and classificational lexicons of Kant's continent-sized anthropologies and Hegel's *History of Philosophy* (1840) become visible in the racialist reaction of Grant's *The Passing of the Great Race* (1916), Stoddard's *The Rising Tide of Colour* (1924), and Josey's *Race and National*

Solidarity (1923). The civilizational erasures so evident in Hume translate into Stoddard's assertions that "the black peoples have no historic
pasts" (Stoddard 91), and Kant's ranking of geo-racial cultures and mentalities (see "Of National Characters" 194–210) provides a foundation
for Josey's claim that "the race which makes the most rapid progress of
a creative, as opposed to an imitative sort, should be regarded as possessing superior abilities for creativeness" (151). The instrumental racialization of cognition within this school derived its philosophical authority
from Hegel, who viewed intellectual progress as deriving from the passage of ideas from one race to the next, a progression that had found its
supposed summit in the nonreferential abstractions of pure philosophy
in Protestant Europe.[7] While these American ideologues were far less
complex than their sources, their simplifications drew on underlying
tropes of racial abilities and inabilities that derived intellectual legitimization from European natural philosophy.

By the 1920s, modern supremacist American intellectuals faced the
reverse of questions that David Walker asked when observing a strong
and numerically superior black community in his native North Carolina:
why did white masters prevail? For believers in white supremacy watching European colonialism falter visibly against new nationalisms in Asia
and Africa, the question became: why weren't the white masters prevailing? The failure, Grant, Stoddard, Josey, and others agreed, was a
crisis of the racial spirit: the subordinate body no longer obeyed its natural head because of an alienated spirit, and that alienation arrived
through a variety of modern causes. For such racialist thought, too, there
was a parallel question of how a supposedly inferior corporate racial persona could find the intelligence to challenge a natural hierarchy.

One canonical writer of race theory, the late Victorian and Britain-
to-Bayreuth cross-cultural figure of Houston Stewart Chamberlain, had
already supplied a helpful Wagnerian obsession: the Jew. According to
Chamberlain, whose *Foundations of the Nineteenth Century* treated Jewish craniology as one of the major topics necessary for a cultural understanding of that century,[8] the Semite was a controlling and conspiratorial
social element:

> Like a blind power of nature—for the will is blind—he hurled himself
> upon other races; he disappeared in them, they took him in; it was

obvious what these races had given him, not what he had given them; for what he gave possessed no physiognomy, no form, it was only will; an increased energy which often impelled to great achievements, an excitability difficult to control, and an unquenchable thirst after posses- sion which often led to destruction, in short, a definite direction of will; wherever he settled, the Semite had, to begin with, only adopted and assimilated what he found, but he had changed the character of the people. (*Foundations* 408)

Chamberlain's anti-Semitic vision of Jewishness attributed to it a pas- sion for race survival, one that put a full reserve of collective mental resources at the service of that overriding racial project. Relying explic- itly and heavily upon Herder for his racial characterization, Chamber- lain describes *homo judæus* as a philosophically incapable alien, one whose monotheism "arises not from the idea of the Infinite but from the poverty of ideas of a poor, hungry, greedy man whose range for thought hardly rises above the conception that possession and power would be the high- est bliss" (*Foundations* 427).

The Semitic intelligence, according to Chamberlain, must eventu- ally fail because Jews are incapable of founding a state, inasmuch as "everyone always endeavoured to grasp all power for himself, thus show- ing that their capabilities were limited to despotism and anarchy, the two opposites of freedom" (*Foundations* 543). As a leading exegete of Kant, Chamberlain derived a Kantian tradition of address to "pure reason" into a parallel obsession with racial purity and European ideological hygiene. Thus in his magnum opus study of Kant, Chamberlain concluded that "we must therefore begin by once [and] for all getting rid of the heavy burthen of inherited and indoctrinated Jewish conceptions. Kant's doc- trine of religion . . . is a true fountain of youth: out of it we may emerge washed and purified from Semitic delusions after millenniums, able to adopt as our own that most modern form of primeval Aryan religiosity" (Chamberlain, *Immanuel Kant* 2: 390)—which is the result of transcen- dent idealism and best fitted to the preservation of racialized conscious- ness in the face of modernity. In this philosophico-racial scheme, the Jew represented the power of an antagonistic will, an intense capac- ity to infiltrate and direct European society—and, by implication, Euro- American society—towards collective Jewish ends through the appeal of ideas. The force counterposed to Jewishness was, for Chamberlain and his ideological descendants of the Third Reich, a heroic Teutonic calling towards future glory as realized through a race-protective *Uberstaat*. Racial purity would be protected against the colored body and Jewish mind, which were joined in their greedy desires for self-gratification, and, indeed, Jewish body and black mind were barely distinguishable in their quintessential non-whiteness.

Having traced the distinctions of head and body through Enlightenment and modernist theorizations of race with necessary brevity, let us now look at their instantiation in William Pierce's *The Turner Diaries*, published under the Celtic pseudonym of Andrew Macdonald. Beneath a fairly crude narrative surface, *Diaries* relies on an unsophisticated but accurate assimilation of Kant's contempt for non-European intellect, Herder's characterization of blacks as unbounded sensualists, and Chamberlain's preoccupation with Jews as an infiltrating and civilizationally enfeebling intelligence. The novel borrows its central narrative device—a manuscript discovered and published with annotations by a future historian—together with its underground political themes and scenes of apocalyptic violence from Jack London's 1907 novel of class revolution, *The Iron Heel*.[9]

The novel, commencing in 1989, traces two years in the life Earl Turner, an underground American revolutionary. At that point, the United States has come under the control of "the System," roughly corresponding with what far-right literature terms the "Zionist Occupation Government," while Turner is an activist in the white resistance, "the Organization." Pierce traces out a stark political binarism of oppressors (based roughly on London's "Oligarchy" and *Iron Heel*) versus a well-motivated and righteous underground resistance ("the Cause" in *Iron Heel*).

The opening scene captures Pierce's vision of an abject America suffering beneath racial oppression. His underground hero, Turner, is woken from his sleep by "four Negroes" armed with kitchen knives and a baseball bat who are "'special deputies' for the Northern Virginia Human Relations Council" searching for firearms, which have been banned by the recent Cohen Act (2). Although they find nothing, their leader Mr. Tepper, "a Caucasian, though of an unusually dark complexion," easily ferrets out a handgun Turner has concealed in the wall and arrests him as a serious felon (10). After a quick release, in a rob-

bery committed to finance their underground cell, Turner and a part-
ner rob "Berman's Liquor" and club down a black clerk, then walk down
to "Berman's Deli" where they gratuitously slit Mr. Berman's fat throat,
knock down Mrs. Berman with a well-aimed jar of kosher pickles, and
empty the cash register. An unconsciously self-parodic voice inhabits
Pierce's efforts to mock his targets for racial violence. From the beginning, Pierce describes a social system where the quasi-official muscle-
men, police and petty subordinates are blacks, and where mercantile
Jews exercise neighborhood, national, and international command-
and-control. The Jewish community and their invention for black
pacification—para-statist human relations councils—are interlinked in
a powerful network that serves as the System's ideological intelligence,
and that compliant media echo.

In this dystopia, the white race has been reduced to slavery, having
been betrayed by liberal believers in racial equality, race-mixers, and well-
paid government *shabbos goys*. Passages throughout the novel repeat a
theme of white racial slavery, one that is mental rather than truly physical. White racial slavery, for Pierce, is the culmination of a cunning
process of gradual measures introduced through liberalism, feminism,
and egalitarian arguments of a wide variety. Pierce identifies the rise of
mass society and loss of individualism as responsible for white deraci-
nation and a submission to tyranny. "Our average White American,"
Pierce argues, "hasn't an idea in his head that wasn't put there by his
TV set" and has become "a mass-man; a member of the great, brain-
washed proletariat; a herd animal; a true democrat" (101). This somno-
lent condition of racial passivity derives from an induced loss of spiritual
grandeur, from a whiteness that has lost touch with its history and accom-
plishments. That condition, more than any other, creates the simultaneous necessity and difficulty for racial revolution: "The plain, horrible
truth is that we have been trying to evoke a heroic spirit of idealism which
just isn't there any more. It has been washed right out of 99 per cent
of our people by the flood of Jewish-materialist propaganda in which
they have been submerged practically all their lives" (101). Whereas David
Walker was asking in the early nineteenth century why systematized white
racial oppression was so successful, in the later twentieth century
William Pierce asks and conjectures why white racial domination has
been gradually failing. In contrast to Walker's emancipatory position

against the naturalisms of "race," Pierce cannot escape the conceptual economy of slavery and remains trapped by an avowal of the Enlightenment's anthropological codifications of "race," or the same profound representational limitation against which Walker had rebelled a century and a half previous.

If whiteness has lost knowledge of the power inherent in its own whiteness, then there must be culpable agents. "We have allowed a diabolically clever, alien minority to put chains on our souls and our minds," writes Turner, "These spiritual chains are a truer mark of slavery than the iron chains which are yet to come" (33-34). He concludes his meditation on white abjection with a call for self-liberation by eliminating its source: "Why didn't we roast them over bonfires at every street corner in America? Why didn't we make a final end to this obnoxious and eternally pushy clan, this pestilence from the sewers of the East, instead of meekly allowing ourselves to be disarmed?" (78). Taking advantage of white identity erosion, increment by ideological increment, the inherently unequal human elements of the Great Chain of Being attempt to cast off their subordination and assume an unnatural superiority to their natural masters: the body attempts to control the head. The prerequisite for this strategy is an alien and alienated pseudo-white caste—the Jews—who manifest a preternatural capacity for social manipulation and trouble-making among the inferior racial classes. In essence, Turner advances a claim of colonization directed against white identity and casts the "White American" as a colonized subject, one who retains a repressed consciousness but who has been deprived of a holistic integration of head and body.

The Jews, who possess perverse mental capacities although they lack substantial bodies (for other than sensuousness), operate through "local Toms" who preach black equality and cooperate with the System's masters to enforce white racial subordination. Jews and blacks merge in the novel's descriptions of both physiognomy and social interests. At a Chicago rally, for instance,

the skilled agitators of the Human Relations Council worked various sections of the crowd up into a real brotherhood frenzy. These swarthy, kinky-haired little Jewboys with transistorized megaphones really knew their business. They had the mob screaming with real blood lust for any "White racist" who might be unfortunate enough to fall into their hands. . . . Shoppers, workers and businessmen on the sidewalks were ordered by the Black "deputies" to join the march. Anyone who refused was beaten without mercy. (84–85)

This is a world of government-mandated race-mixing and one where, according to Turner, "Life is uglier and uglier these days, more and more Jewish" (65). This is a world created because "We have allowed a diabolically clever, alien minority to put chains on our souls and our minds" (33). Between manipulative Jewish mouths and black enforcement muscle, the white racial body politic has been enslaved to the point that it cannot recognize either its own interests or self-consciousness. The Organization's response comes in acts such as the assassination of a Jewish community spokesman, where one of its underground fighters approached him and then "pulled a hatchet from under his coat, cleaved the good Jew's head from crown to shoulder blades, then disappeared in the rush-hour crowd" (17). A *Washington Post* editor, a Jew whose "words dripped with Talmudic hatred" (48), provides editorial defenses for black thugs and rapists, and receives his due reward from a shotgun blast. Pierce makes clear his belief that Jewish physiognomy reflects black origins. For example, a Jew directing black deputies in a search of Turner's apartment for weapons, enforcing a Cohen Act that bans private gun ownership, is "a Caucasian, though with an unusually dark complexion" (2). A black-Jewish alliance emerges not only as fulfillment of a head-body race paradigm, but also because of a common familial origin.

Pierce reiterates this concept of collaborative black-Jewish racial subversion and oppression in explicitly sexual terms. One subplot turns on white slavery in the form of the kidnapping and sale of young women to the gangster "Kappy the Kike" for enforced prostitution, a business towards which the System turns a blind eye (84ff). Jerry Siegelbaum, a Jewish union agent with a taste for pornographic photos of himself with blonde Gentile women, black women, and young boys, ends up executed in the hallway of his Los Angeles luxury apartment (138). White women are harassed, stopped, and brought to "field headquarters" of human relations councils, where black deputies rape them repeatedly (68). Sexual assault of white women, repeated throughout the novel, is the most egregious form of racial assault. Formulated as a discrete corporate racial whole subject to sexual overlordship, Euro-American whiteness has become subject to unaccustomed injury and captivity. Pierce's dystopic vision re-racializes the terms of oppression that blacks suffered under slavery and lynch mobs, and conceives of a de-privileged whiteness as the ultimate human victimization that must be countered through revolutionary opposition and the Organization.

That underground activity gets Earl Turner caught once again after he inadvertently reveals himself through a display of chivalric sensitivity to Elsa, a young white woman whom he prevents from being kidnapped, and Turner encounters the System in its full brutality. When Turner awakes from unconsciousness on a cell floor after a preliminary interrogation and torture session at the hands of FBI agents, he meets his true adversary. A group including FBI agents and "large, muscular-looking Negroes" enters the cell, but their leader is a stooped, white-haired old man with "a thick Hebrew accent and a disarmingly mild, professorial manner," who introduces himself as Colonel Saul Rubin of Israeli military intelligence (90–91). With the acquiescence of the FBI agents, the colonel—who recites his experience extracting information from Germans and Arabs—proceeds to interrogate his captive in preparation for an international tribunal that will try Turner for his racist activities. When Turner resists, Rubin's two black assistants seize the prisoner. "Under Rubin's instructions, they proceeded to give me a vicious, thorough, and scientific beating. When they finished my whole body was a throbbing, searing mass of pain, and I was writhing on the floor, whimpering" (91). With repeated torture sessions, including anal rape with a blunt rod, the Israeli/African American team overcomes Turner's resistance and he provides them with detailed information on the Organization.[10]

The head/body paradigm of racial function thus extends beyond the organization of black-Jewish political power; Pierce conceives of their combination as the originating site of a vicious, cruel, and primordial evil. The "muscular" African American blackness and the aged Yiddish *Kopf* operate in tandem not only within a dysfunctional social neuropathology, but further because each recognizes and appreciates the evil intrinsic to the other's self-construction. Jews are "white niggers," blacks are cognitively colonized and Judaized, and they fulfill each other's insatiable drives. In Pierce's imagination, blacks and Jews have been joined as a recombinant monster whose purposes are located in racial imperialism and the degradation of an intrinsic white heroism. Yet their communal interests are ultimately divergent and irreconcilable, as by mid-novel blacks come to resent their colonization, leading to political and street conflicts where "Izzy and Sambo are really at one another's throats, tooth and nail, and it is a joy to behold" (122).

The novel locates the organizing nexus of a collective Jewish intelligence in Israel and its expropriative illegitimacy, exhibiting a conspicuous preoccupation with transnational Israeli action against "race criminals" and their unlawful abduction. Pursuing similarly violent anti-white activities, a murder squad operates out of the Israeli embassy until over three hundred die when "we struck with heavy mortars while the Israelis were throwing a cocktail party for their obedient servants in the U.S. Senate" (118). When, late in the novel, the Organization commands the nuclear missiles of Vandenberg Air Force base in "liberated" and Aryan-ruled southern California, it precipitates the System's slow collapse by nuclear strikes against New York and Israel, "two of world Jewry's principal nerve centers" (191). Within a day, "hundreds of thousands of Arabs were swarming across the borders of occupied Palestine, . . . across mine fields, through Jewish machine-gun fire, and into the radioactive chaos of burning cities, their single thought being to slay the people who had stolen their land, killed their fathers, and humiliated them for two generations. Within a week the throat of the last Jewish survivor in the last kibbutz and in the last, smoking ruin in Tel Aviv had been cut" (198). A worldwide series of pogroms breaks out and the final major refuge for the Jews is Toronto, but as Turner informs his readers, "We'll go to the uttermost ends of the earth to hunt down the last of Satan's spawn" (199). The head of the hydra has been eliminated, but its elements and the possibility of regeneration still live.

This omnicidal animosity towards Jews emerges from Pierce's passionate investment in the idea of a "prevailing race," a race that can maintain its blood cohesion through the tribulations of divisive modernity. The Manichean polarity Pierce invests in separating a primary and positive raciality—whiteness—from secondary, defective and negative racialities of color emerges into a moral commandment to kill the embodiment of evil, to kill the Jew, the black, and the Asiatic. Just as good must prevail against evil, so too for Pierce there can only be one prevailing race.

Purity is the key to survival in this edge-of-the-apocalypse scenario. The System is doomed because "it has become so corrupt and so mongrelized that only the Jews feel at home in it, and no one feels any loyalty toward it" (136). Corruption and racial mongrelization nest within each other, inseparable phenomena. The racial war that Earl Turner witnesses—having escaped from captivity and assumed a responsible position in the Organization's offensive in southern California—emerges from a postlapsarian modernism where social dissolution must be attributed to a singular figure: "If the White nations of the world had not allowed themselves to become subject to the Jew, to Jewish ideas, to the Jewish spirit, this war would not be necessary" (195), Turner writes in a sentence that would resonate for Chamberlain,[11] Stoddard, or Grant. Like each of these writers, Pierce employs a redemptive voice that directs readers towards a new consciousness of the degradation of purity, of the evil inhering in race-mixing. Pierce devotes chapter 23 to a description of the Day of the Rope in the now-conquered Los Angeles, where triumphant race purifiers hang thousands of white women who married Jews or blacks, each with "race defiler" placards, together with politicians, liberal Hollywood actors, and real estate agents who sold homes to blacks in white neighborhoods.

Purification requires racial and ethnic cleansing, which means the deportation of blacks and Hispanics into the California desert. The "dysgenic breeding" (Pierce 209)[12] that has created mixed-race people represents the rotten fruit of liberalism, an old order that is now only a "shell with only a surface semblance of strength" (209) that revolutionary white supremacism is sweeping aside. The inherent weakness of political liberalism, mixed-race society, and "race traitors" leads to their collective collapse in short order. The fate of Los Angeles demonstrates that history can be reversed, that there are means to restore racial power regimes.

As the novel comes to an end, Earl Turner flies off on a suicide mission to nuke the System's last great stronghold—the Pentagon—and achieve race immortality. The true moment of spiritual glory for Earl Turner comes just prior to his self-sacrificial death, when he is inducted into the secret governing order of the Organization and achieves full fraternity in their sacred racial project. Standing with his comrades in their hooded robes, Turner realizes that "these were real men, White men, men who were now one with me in spirit and consciousness as well as in blood" (203). What neither blacks nor Jews could attain, a holistic singularity that reunifies masculinity and fully realized race consciousness, has been achieved, and Turner dies to guarantee the perpetuation of this millennial achievement.

An epilogue and explanatory notes explain how Asia was sterilized of Asians through chemical, biological, and nuclear means; how black Africans died out in Africa; how "mongrel" Puerto Ricans were exterminated and the island resettled by white refugees; how *gastarbeiter* met their bloody end throughout Europe; and how "undesirable elements" were eliminated from the white race itself (205–11). A global race purification has been achieved: the world is safe for whiteness. Although Hispanics and Asians appear occasionally within the novel, their presence remains largely peripheral until the epilogue, when their concluding extermination arrives as a police action of revolutionary whiteness.

In terms of representation, Pierce's racial ideology is severely restricted and dualistic; it cannot accommodate more than a basic black-white binarism, with Jews posited as an incorporative middle point between blackness and whiteness. At the same time, that binarism struggles to rearrange a complex and diverse humanity into simple, easily-segregated parts. When, in the last days of his life, Earl Turner participates in the Organization's conquest of Los Angeles, he writes that the problem of achieving racial separation is that "the process of mongrelization has gone so far in this country and there are so many swarthy, frizzy-haired characters of all sizes and shapes running around that one doesn't know where to draw the line" (153). If the Organization's solution is to send columns of blacks and Hispanics towards enemy lines to the east in order to increase pressure through refugee flows, there is a different fate awaiting those who fall between the sharp racial lines that Pierce wants to define. In the Los Angeles mountains, Turner encounters another miles-long column of marchers:

> As we drove slowly past, I observed the prisoners closely, trying to decide what they were. They didn't appear to be Blacks or Chicanos, and yet only a few of them appeared to be Whites. Many of the faces were distinctly Jewish, while others had features or hair suggesting a Negroid taint. (157)

Racial un-identifiability in this new order constitutes an immediate death sentence: these marchers will be executed in a canyon. The existence of a multiracial or non-racial world strains and outrages Pierce's imaginative limitations, so his response is to imagine the genocidal obliteration of humanity that does not fit neat racial typologies.

Although *The Turner Diaries* might well be credited with instigating the Oklahoma City attack that caused massive loss of life, Pierce's racist ravings are self-discrediting and crude. William Pierce relies on a backward ideological traditionalism cobbled together with blood-washed prose. In this imitative imagination, Pierce was less a political oddity than he was an ideological extrovert, a violent racist who saluted the flag of "race" in public and unashamedly. As unappealing as Pierce appears, what is far more threatening is ideological introversion on issues of race, or those discussions where the unstated controls stated positions. There is a common willingness to believe—especially in academic discussions— that crude racialism has disappeared into richly-deserved obsolescence. When Tzvetan Todorov argues that "the period of classical racism seems definitely behind us" (157), and posits the ascension of a modernized "racialism as culturalism" that replaces physical race with linguistic, historical, or psychological race, his argument operates at the level of textual tradition. Yet if that textual tradition of racial physicality is now marginal, as Pierce's political isolation during his lifetime would suggest, the classical legacy of head-body discourses on race still flows powerfully beneath current United States debates pertaining to race.

It is no accident that one of the most vigorous and heated current debates involving racialism focuses on access to higher education, the economic transition point between manual and mental labor, or between body and head. The features of "classic racism" have only been submerged beneath new rhetorical formations that seek to deny that every human has a mind for education, not just a body for exploitation. "Race" has been a historic denial of that simple truth.

Notes

1. For reactions, see Caravajal, "Group"; Oder and Hill, "Should Bookstores"; "Mein Culpa"; and Allon, "Seller."
2. I am employing here the distinctions between racism and racialism

elaborated by Todorov in *On Human Diversity*. Briefly, "racism" refers to prejudicial behaviors based on group difference, and "racialism" refers to ideologies of racial difference.

3. The *Diaries* were published in 1978 and became a right-wing underground classic, with perhaps only a dozen or two of the first eighty thousand copies sold through bookshops. Approximately two hundred thousand copies were sold in the book's first twenty years in print, and translations have appeared in several languages. Its author William Pierce died in 2002. *The Turner Diaries* constituted a critical near-void for many years and was treated as untouchable by the English profession, not a profession known for its taboos. The first treatment appeared on the twentieth anniversary of the novel's publication. See Brodie, "The Aryan New Era." Subsequent critiques included Baringer, *Metanarrative*; Perkinson, "Color"; Cullick, "Literary Offenses"; and Zimmerman, *Disarming*. For critiques of Pierce's theology, see Whitsel, "*The Turner Diaries*" and Gallagher, "Goad and Country."

4. For an excellent discussion, see Jordan, *White Man's Burden*, esp. 165–93.

5. Prior to his death in 1776, Hume revised his original 1754 essay to include this statement after comment from his critic, James Beattie, who argued against innate racial characteristics. Pierce's attribution of racial characteristics is very similar to that of Hume's "Of National Characters" essay (*Essays* 201–17).

6. Frederickson traces the growing influence of Count Gobineau on Hughes (*Black Image* 69–70).

7. As Hegel phrased this development, "One form, one stage in the Idea comes to consciousness in one particular race, so that this race and this time expresses only this particular form, within which it constructs its universe and works out its conditions. The higher stage, on the other hand, centuries later reveals itself in another race of people" (*Lectures* 1: 33). Hegel begins consideration of philosophy proper in ancient Greece, and eliminates Indian, Oriental, and Egyptian thought as religious speculation on existence and death, and as such "they are not to be taken as being proper philosophical utterances" (*Lectures* 1: 90). Hegel treats "Oriental Philosophy" (117ff.) as pre-philosophy, as a product of the "Eastern mind" whose product is "a dry, dead understanding, which cannot take up the speculative Notion into itself" (*Lectures* 119). Thus in relevance to present purposes, racial hierarchialism in the Hegelian tradition exerts itself from within a claim that non-Europeans lack a capacity to derive abstractions from abstractions.

8. See Chamberlain (*Foundations* 1: 356–411), for an extended discussion

that links Semitic physiologies with "national souls" in order to theorize the debilitating effects of the Jewish "race" in then-contemporary Europe. In *The Turner Diaries*, Pierce echoes Chamberlain's call for a contest against "Jewish materialism" in order to achieve civilizational rejuvenation, stating that "it is because our new civilization will be based on an entirely different world view than the present one that it can only replace the other in a revolutionary manner. There is no way a society based on Aryan values and an Aryan outlook can evolve peacefully from a society which has succumbed to Jewish spiritual corruption" (111).

9. Pierce owes such major imaginative, narrative, and plot device debts to *The Iron Heel* that the *Diaries* might be called a racialist re-write of London's novel. It is quite possible that London's well-known racialism attracted Pierce's attention in plotting this novel. Alternatively, it is possible that cultural knowledge of an available and useful plot typology characterized Pierce's borrowing in the same manner as Margaret Mitchell's *Gone With The Wind* borrowed its plot structure and action, apparently without direct reference, from William Makepeace Thackeray's *Vanity Fair*. There are other ideological commonalities between London and Pierce. For example, both *The Turner Diaries* and *The Iron Heel* rely on clear conventions of masculinism and plots featuring male-admiring women drawn into supportive roles in an underground struggle. London's near-futurist story of class revolution and Pierce's vision of race revolution bear significant comparability in their descriptions of gender relations. However, while London and Pierce can be compared in their endorsements of white racial and male supremacy, Pierce remains uninterested in the issues of social class that preoccupy London. For Pierce, race is the only relevant factor for theories of naturalism, and gender issues are a System-created divisive diversion from race issues (see Pierce, *Turner Diaries* 45). Such obsessive focus on race distinguishes Pierce from London.

10. It is disturbing to realize that the neo-Nazi Pierce condemns the kidnapping, trial, and execution of Adolf Eichman in similar tones, albeit with much different logic, in asserting an absence of jurisdiction and the incompetence of the trial court, as found in Max Horkheimer's 1960 essay, "The Arrest of Eichman." Whereas Pierce suggests that Eichman's abduction constituted a racial injustice and a propaganda exercise to gain world sympathy (*Turner Diaries* 92), Horkheimer argues that this was an act that abused state authority and served no achievable justice. Despite their differences, both arguments make sanctuary available to racial genocidists and predicate demonstrative revenge as the primary motivation for state action. This motive of retribution, which Pierce deploys throughout the novel as an explanation

of Jewish racial character, appears in Horkheimer's essay (122–23) as an anti-trait of traditional Jewishness that understands worldly suffering and eschews punishment as a redundancy. From politically disparate positions, both writers identify a putative racial characteristic of vengeance to define their understandings of the Eichman case and an alleged Jewish cultural concept of punishment.

11. For several years, the National Alliance website at http://www.natall .com/index.html enabled Internet visitors to purchase the organization's reprint of Chamberlain's *Foundations of the Nineteenth Century* and other Chamberlain texts.

12. For comparison of this concern for "racial bastardization," one that locates Pierce's racial lexicon as appearing simultaneously within both pre-World War II United States and Europe, see Grill and Jenkins, "The Nazis" 671–75.

Works Cited

Allon, Janet. "Seller of Incendiary Books Takes a Few Direct Hits." *New York Times* 26 May 1996. Sec.13: 7.

Baringer, Sandra Kay. *The Metanarrative of Suspicion: Surveillance and Control in Late Twentieth Century America.* Ph.D. diss. University of California, Riverside, 1999.

Brodie, Renee. "The Aryan New Era: Apocaplyptic Realizations in The Turner Diaries." *Journal of American Culture* 21.3 (Fall 1998): 13–22.

Caravajal, Doreen. "Group Tries to Halt Selling of Racist Novel." *New York Times* 20 April 1996. 8.

Chamberlain, Houston Stuart. *Foundations of the Nineteenth Century.* Trans. John Lees. New York: John Lane, 1912.

———. *Immanuel Kant.* 2 vols. Trans. Lord Redesdale. London: Bodley Head, 1914.

Cullick, Jonathan S. "The Literary Offenses of a Neo-Nazi." *Studies in Popular Culture* 24.3 (April 2002): 87–99.

Frederickson, George. *The Black Image in the White Mind.* Hanover, NH: Wesleyan University Press, 1971.

Gallagher, Eugene V. "Goad and Country: Revolution as Religious Imperative on the Radical Right." *Terrorism and Political Violence* 9.3 (Autumn 1997): 63–80.

Grant, Madison. *The Passing of the Great Race, Or the Basis of European History.* New York: Scribner's, 1916.

Grill, JonPeter Horst, and Robert L. Jenkins. "The Nazis and the American South in the 1930s: A Mirror Image?" *Journal of Southern History* 58.4 (Nov. 1992): 667–94.

Hegel, G. W. F. *Lectures on the History of Philosophy.* 3 vols. Trans. E. S. Haldane. London: Kegan Paul, 1892.

Horkheimer, Max. "The Arrest of Eichman." *Critique of Instrumental Reason.* New York: Continuum, 1996. 119–23.

Hughes, Henry. "A Treatise on Sociology, Practical and Theoretical." 1854. *Slavery Defended: The Views of the Old South.* Ed. Eric L. McKitrick. Englewood Cliffs, NJ: Prentice-Hall, 1963.

Hume, David. *Essays and Treatises on Several Subjects.* 2 vols. Edinburgh: James Walker, 1825.

Jordan, Winthrop D. *The White Man's Burden: Historical Origins of Racism in the United States.* New York: Oxford University Press, 1974.

Josey, Charles Conant. *Race and National Solidarity.* New York: Scribner's, 1923.

"Mein Culpa." *New York* 29.19 (13 May 1996): 15.

Oder, Norman, and Sean Hill. "Should Bookstores Sell Hate Book?" *Publishers Weekly* 243.18 (29 Apr. 1996): 23.

Olson, Rochelle. "Turner Diaries Author Urges Supremacist Stand." Associated Press (7 May 1996).

Perkinson, Jim. "The Color of the Enemy in the New Millennium." *Crosscurrents* 50.3 (Fall 2000): 349–58.

Pierce, William. *The Turner Diaries.* 1978. New York: Barricade Books, 1996.

Stoddard, Theodore Lothrop. *The Rising Tide of Colour Against Our White World-Supremacy.* London: Chapman and Hall, 1924.

Todorov, Tzvetan. *On Human Diversity: Nationalism, Racism and Exoticism in French Thought.* Cambridge, MA: Harvard University Press, 1993.

Walker, David. *Walker's Appeal, With a Brief Sketch of His Life by Henry Highland Garnet and Also Garnet's Address to the Slaves of the United States of America.* 1848. New York: J. H. Tobbit, 1994.

Whitsel, Brad. "*The Turner Diaries* and Cosmotheism: William Pierce's Theology of Revolution." *Nova Religio* 1.2 (Apr. 1998): 183–97.

Zimmerman, Lynn D. *Disarming Militia Discourse: Analyzing The Turner Diaries.* Ph.D. diss., Kent State University, 2003.

II

Re-Contextualizing Race and Ethnicity:
Texts in Historical and Political Perspective

7 Smallpox, Opium, and Invasion

Chinese Invasion, White Guilt, and Native American Displacement in Late Nineteenth- and Early Twentieth-Century American Fiction

EDWIN J. MCALLISTER

THE COVER ILLUSTRATION ON A FEBRUARY 1879 *Harper's Weekly* shows a well-dressed Chinese man and a Native American man looking over a poster featuring Irish-American labor leader Dennis Kearney's anti-immigration slogan: "The Chinese Must Go!" The Native American observes to the Chinese man, "Pale face 'fraid you crowd him out, as he did me" (Tchen 205) (fig. 7.1). The poster's immediate political frame of reference was the public debate surrounding Chinese immigration that ultimately resulted in the passage of the 1882 Chinese Exclusion Act. However, in its juxtaposition of Native American as past victim and Chinese immigrant as potential future victimizer of white Americans, the cartoon points toward a more tenacious representational tradition connecting these ethnic groups, a connection arising from the historical process through which white Europeans displaced Native Americans in the American West, a process nearly complete by 1879.

The ethnic connections suggested by the cartoon are, I will argue, borne out by a surprising number of novels and magazine short stories published at the turn of the century. In these works, the Chinese are figured as the potential agents of a terrible reversal of white America's

Fig. 7.1. *Cover of* Harper's Weekly *(February 1879)*.

displacement of Native American tribes in the West. This fiction exposes anxieties among white middle-class Americans that a *new* wave of soldiers and settlers would come, not west to east in the classic American pattern of settlement, but from east to west in a disruption of the mythic narrative of America's westward expansion (Lee 9), pouring across the Pacific from China into California, over the Rockies, into the Great Plains, and finally into the American heartland. These Chinese invaders bring with them diseases and drugs to wipe out whatever Anglos the armies do not kill first, leaving the entire continent under Chinese control. This fiction thus expresses a deep-seated white fear that the Chinese would act as the agents of a providential vengeance on Euro-Americans for their displacement of the Native Americans; the connections of this fear to white guilt regarding the displacement of Native Americans are clarified by the fact that the invaders in these works of fiction accomplish their nefarious designs using the same means through which white Europeans had decimated Native American populations: a huge, unstoppable migration, military superiority, drugs, and disease.

That such a deeply ingrained sense of white guilt even existed by the late nineteenth century is a matter of some scholarly debate. For example, in *Hard Fact: Setting and Form in the American Novel* (1985), Philip Fisher suggests that by the time American realist and naturalist fiction became popular, historical novels like James Fenimore Cooper's Leatherstocking tales had already made "morally tolerable the ethical complexities of settlement and the superseding of the Indians" (6). Yet a substantial body of American realist fiction produced long after Cooper's novels suggests that white guilt over the settlement of the West had not been as smoothly managed out of existence as Fisher suggests. I will argue here that this guilt evidences itself in late nineteenth-century American fiction via a process of displacement whereby the destructive energies and practices of white settlement are projected onto a convenient set of outsiders—Chinese immigrants.

American realist fiction from the late nineteenth century makes visible this process of displacement; the guilt Americans might have experienced for their complicity in the destruction of Native Americans is shifted onto the Chinese, who in this fiction occupy the position of aggressors with white Europeans as their innocent victims. And the "tools" of these aggressors sound all too familiar against the backdrop of Euro-

American displacement of Native Americans: smallpox-tainted hand-kerchiefs spreading disease from mainland China to the western United States, whites addicted to opium and enslaved to those who can provide it, mass heathen migrations displacing European Christian settlers, huge armies of Chinese soldiers invading the United States or taking it over from within, were all seen as potential threats of Chinese immigration. Fears like these, often spelled out prior to the appearance of this fiction in anti-immigrant propaganda and sensationalist journalism, resulted in the passage of a series of "Exclusion Acts," beginning in 1882, that singled out Chinese immigrants as unassimilable. Thus, the use of this fiction, in its historical context, was both to manage white guilt over the genocidal destruction of Native Americans and to galvanize public opinion against Chinese immigration.

Western fear of Chinese invasion has a long historical pedigree, dating to the thirteenth century when Genghis Khan's Mongol armies swept across eastern Europe, defeating every European army that opposed them. Their advance finally halted when the tribesmen were forced to return to Mongolia to take part in a succession squabble after Genghis Khan died. The Europeans did not know what had saved them, but the fear of a second Mongol onslaught remained for centuries and may have contributed to the paranoia regarding Chinese invasion that manifested itself in America during the late nineteenth century. The west coast of the United States was, after all, the first cultural space shared by large numbers of Europeans and East Asians anywhere in the world; small numbers of Asians had lived in European and American cities prior to this, as small numbers of Europeans had lived in Asian cities, but large populations from both ethnic groups were rubbing shoulders in California for perhaps the first time since the Mongolian invasion.

Of course, one need not look so far into the past to discover why white Americans feared a violent clash of cultures with the Chinese that might be similar to the one they had had with Native Americans. Chinese immigrants were, aside from the Native Americans, the first free, non-white non-Europeans to live in close contact with white Americans in any large numbers. Their language, culture, religion, and appearance made assimilation a far more difficult challenge than it was for European immigrants. Chinese arrivals in California in the nineteenth century almost certainly seemed no stranger to white Americans than the Europeans themselves had seemed to the Native Americans when Europeans began arriving on American shores; the fact that so many creative artists imagined subsequent chapters of that contact taking on the same shape as European contacts with Native Americans should not be surprising.

Despite their immense cultural differences, however, Chinese immigrants were at first welcomed, or at least tolerated, while jobs and economic opportunities were plentiful. Cheap labor was needed on the railroads, in the mines, and in the goldfields—a need prompted largely by white American territorial expansion and the expropriation of Native American land. The specter of Chinese invasion only appears after those jobs dried up in the late 1860s and 1870s with the completion of the transcontinental railway and the collapse of the silver mining industry in Nevada. Suddenly European immigrants found themselves competing with Chinese workers for scarce, low-paying jobs; the arrival of Chinese immigrants in California began to look more like the Mongol invasion.

A body of literature began to appear in the late nineteenth century that raised the specter of Chinese domination of the American West, and then of the North American continent itself. Three of the major means through which these creative (but extremely paranoid) artists imagined this invasion taking place were: (1) military invasion, either from within or without; (2) smallpox and other infectious diseases; and (3) addiction to opium. The links to the history of the Anglo European conquest of Native Americans should be apparent, for these were the decisive factors in the struggle for the American West. White Americans in the late nineteenth century began to imagine the same kind of racial holocaust happening to them, the sins of the fathers being visited on the sons, Manifest Destiny shifting into reverse as "yellow hordes" of Chinese poured across the Pacific into California and eastward across the United States, spreading disease and addiction in their path, decimating, enslaving, and reducing to desperate poverty the white populations that stood in their way.

When fiction writers began to explore the dangers of a smallpox epidemic in the United States started by Chinese immigrants, they drew on a climate of hysteria regarding the health threat of Chinese immigration fueled by books like prominent physician Arthur B. Stout's *Chinese Immigration and the Physiological Causes of the Decay of a Nation* (1862). Stout, cataloging the various susceptibilities of the Chinese to

diseases in general and skin diseases like smallpox and leprosy in particular, insisted that the introduction of the Chinese into North America would be "a cancer" in "the biological, social, religious, and political
systems" (qtd. in Miller 162). In a report to the California Board of Health
published nine years later, Stout raises the specter of Genghis Khan and
the Mongolian invasions of the thirteenth century as a figurative parallel for the effects of Chinese immigration to the United States:

> Better it would be for our country that the hordes of Genghis Khan
> should overflow the land, and with armed hostility devastate our valleys
> with the sabre and the firebrand than that these more pernicious hosts
> in the garb of friends, should insidiously poison the well-springs of life,
> and spreading far and wide, gradually undermine and corrode the vitals
> of our strength and prosperity. In the former instance, we might oppose
> the invasion with sword and rifled cannon, but this destructive intru-
> sion enters by invisible approaches. (qtd. in Miller 163)

In 1870, Chinese prostitutes in San Francisco were identified as the
racially distinct carriers of more virulent and deadly strains of vene-
real disease (Lee 90). When the Chinese took over the cigar-rolling trade
in New York, stories circulated about whites contracting leprosy from
Chinese-rolled cigars.

Fiction writers responded to these fears by producing their own
images of China as a source of disease and of the Chinese as the carriers of disease to America. A representative short story in this tradition
is entitled "The Canton Shawl" and appeared in 1914 in *Overland
Monthly Magazine*. It concerns a white American named John Sargent
who has a brief, platonic flirtation with a Chinese courtesan he meets
during a visit to Canton. As he leaves the port, she gives him a shawl
on which a bit of her rouge has been smeared. Sargent forgets about
the Chinese woman and returns to San Francisco, where he meets and
falls in love with a Spanish woman named Dolores de Valle. He gives
the shawl to her as a gift. However, when Sargent returns from his next
voyage, he finds the yellow flag of smallpox flying over Dolores's home.
In this case, even the briefest contact of a westerner with the Chinese
is thought to spread the contagion.

The connection of the threat of smallpox to Chinese immigration is made far more explicit in Atwell Whitney's *Almond Eyed, or, the Great Agitator; A Story of the Day* (1878). Whitney sets his tale in a fictional California small town named Yarbtown, which has recently been overrun by Chinese immigrants coming to work in its starch factory. Protagonist Job Stearns, an upright working man, opposes employing the Chinese on moral grounds. He is overruled by Deacon Spud, the wealthy owner of the factory where the Chinese have come to work. Spud justifies his decision by arguing that the white citizens of Yarbtown have a responsibility to Christianize the heathen Chinese who have come among them. The missionary do-gooder gets his just comeuppance when he contracts smallpox in the Chinese slum and dies unattended—save for Job Stearns. The smallpox quickly spreads through the town, carrying off legions of good white citizens. The town doctor, seeking the source of the disease, traces it to the new immigrants, whose guilt, it appears, is double, for not only had they brought and spread the disease among the whites, but they had neglected to report its presence to anyone: "It had been existing in the China dens for over a month. No report had ever come, to that effect, from those honorable heathen; they had harbored the dread visitor in their crowded houses, giving neither sign nor warning to others" (Whitney 74). Weakened by the disease, the whites of Yarbtown find themselves strangely passive in the face of the next plague that the Chinese bring along with them: opium.

The connection of the danger of an opium-addicted American public with Chinese immigration is made evident by the interesting fact that on the same day American lawmakers were passing into law the notorious Chinese Exclusion Act of 1882, which prohibited almost any immigration from China, they were also signing a commercial treaty with China prohibiting the importation of opium into the United States. The immigration and the opium were, as far as Americans were concerned, part of the same problem. Of course, the mental association obscures the historical origins of the Chinese opium problem: the British, under the banner of "Free Trade," fought two wars with the Chinese earlier in the century to force the Chinese government to permit British importation of opium. American merchants took advantage of the concessions won by the British at gunpoint. American trading firms made fortunes selling Turkish and Indian opium in China in spite of the objections of the Chinese government.

In the late nineteenth century, many Westerners, including some physicians, believed that the Chinese were immune to the effects of opium and could smoke it for years without apparent harm or addiction. Whites, on the other hand, particularly white women, were thought to be highly susceptible to the drug, and could be led through their addiction into prostitution and virtual slavery to Chinese immigrants—who were overwhelmingly male. A representative article in *The New York Times* in 1873, for example, reported to its shocked readers the presence of white women in Chinatown opium dens. To the reporter's inquiry about "a handsome but squalidly dressed young white girl" present in the opium den, the owner "replied with a horrible lear [*sic*], 'Oh, hard time in New York. Young girl hungry. Plenty come here. Chinaman always have something to eat, and he like young white girl, He! He!'" (qtd. in Miller 184). In this case, the reporter implies, the "something to eat" has become far less important to the "young white girl" than the opium to which she has evidently become addicted. Her addiction is, of course, shocking in itself, but is made more disturbing by the implied sexual predation by the Chinese man, who, as he says, "like young white girl."

How the Other Half Lives (1890), Jacob Riis's study of urban poverty in the ethnic ghettos of New York City, paints a portrait of the Chinese heavily dependent on early beliefs regarding the immunity of the Chinese to opium and their propensity to use the drug to enslave white women. Published in 1890, *How the Other Half Lives* includes a chapter on the Chinese that reports that "the Chinaman smokes opium as Caucasians smoke tobacco, and apparently with little worse effect upon himself," but adds an apocalyptic warning to curious whites: "Woe unto the white victim upon which [the Chinaman's] drug gets its grip!" (Riis 122). The tenements are, according to Riis, filled not with Chinese women, for there are almost none in the United States, but are rather populated by "white slaves of their infernal drug . . . hapless victims of a passion which, once acquired, demands the sacrifice of every instinct of decency to its insatiate desire" (122). Riis describes the "conventional households of the Chinese quarter" as consisting of "the men worshippers of Joss; the women, all white, girls hardly yet grown to womanhood, worshipping nothing save the pipe that has enslaved them body and soul" (122). Riis is careful to answer those who claim that it is only adults who choose this state of moral degradation by pointing to what was commonly assumed to be a characteristic of Chinese men: their unnatural attraction to underage girls.

> The frequent assertions of the authorities that at least no girls under age are wrecked on this Chinese shoal, are disproved by the observation of those who go frequently among these dens. . . . Even while I am writing, the morning returns from one of the precincts that pass through my hands report the arrest of a Chinaman for "inveigling little girls into his laundry," one of the hundred outposts of Chinatown that are scattered all over the city, as the outer threads of the spider's web that holds its prey fast. (123)

Clearly, the fear of Chinese using opium to seduce and destroy whites was fed by reports such as these. Thus, American fears regarding the immigrant drug menace helped to displace white guilt over the sale of alcohol to Native Americans.

Atwell Whitney's novel *Almond-Eyed* plays on these same fears. After smallpox ravages the town, the survivors notice that the town's children seem "uncommonly drowsy and stupid" in school. The town doctor is again sent for, and in the company of the Rev. Smudgins, he again makes his way to Yarbtown's Chinese slum, where the astonished pair discover many of the town's schoolchildren sleeping off an opium binge in a basement den.

> The two professionals stood in silence and looked at the sleeping group. There, scattered promiscuously on the wide couch, with heads and feet intermingling, were young men, boys, and even girls, with also one or two aged men. They were lying in stupid intoxication, disheveled and in disorder. (Whitney 129)

The disorderliness of the scene with young and old lying together, "scattered promiscuously on the wide couch," suggests strongly that the danger posed by the Chinese is not only in their provision of opium to whites, but the moral decay that will result from that.

Short story writer William Norr's collection *Stories of Chinatown: Sketches from Life in the Chinese Colony of Mott, Pell, and Doyers Street*

(1892), contains six stories that deal with the relationships of white women with Chinese men. Norr claims in his introduction to be puzzled regarding the mystery of "how young and comely women cast their lot with the repulsive Chinese" (4). Despite his puzzlement, he solves the riddle clearly enough in the stories themselves; in each, opium addiction plays a major part in how his white female protagonists, most of them Irish immigrants living in or near New York's Chinatown, become yoked to their Chinese partners.

In the short story "Mrs. Morrissey's Present," a young Irish girl named Mamie Morrissey has become the kept woman of wealthy Chinese gambler Lee Hing. While smoking opium in a Chinese-owned opium den, Mamie has a vision of her mother. She rouses herself and returns to Lee Hing's apartment to fetch a letter she has already written to her mother proposing Mamie's return to work as a seamstress to support her mother. When Mamie arrives at Lee Hing's apartment in the company of a local Irish prizefighter named Chuck Connors, Lee Hing scolds her for spending the night at Sam Sing's opium den: "'What for you no stay here? You got pipe here. I cook you pill. What for you go way?'" (Norr 20). Hing threatens to throw her out for good. Later, Connors attempts to deliver the letter for Mamie, only to discover that Mamie's mother died the night before. By the end of the story, it is clear that Mamie will remain with Lee Hing because there is nowhere else for her to go; but the ubiquitous presence of opium in the story (and in all of Norr's stories about the European women living in Chinatown) makes clear the nature of Lee Hing's power over Mamie.

The most dramatic evidence of white fears regarding Chinese invasion is found in the novels and short stories that represent this threat literally. The images of Chinese invasion presented in these novels are literal reworkings of rhetorical figures used in anti-immigrant discourse, which long had warned of a figurative "invasion" of the Chinese in the form of a mass migration to America. For example, in 1869, four months prior to the completion of the transcontinental railroad, labor activist Andrew C. Cameron wrote:

We warn working men that a new and dangerous foe looms up in the far west. Already our brothers of the Pacific have to meet it, and just as soon as the Pacific railroad is completed, and trade and travel begins [*sic*] to flow from the east across our continent, these Chinamen will begin to swarm through the rocky mountains, like devouring locusts and spread out over the country this side. . . . In the name of the working-men of our common country, we demand that our government . . . forbid another Chinaman to set foot upon our shores. (qtd. in Tchen 171)

In the same year, Horace Greeley, editor of *The Tribune*, the foremost Republican journal in the United States, and, prior to the 1880s, one of the most staunchly "Pro-Chinese" publications in America (Tchen 278), would use flood images to suggest the same dangers:

But what has hitherto been a rivulet may at an early day become a Niagara, hurling millions instead of thousands upon us from the vast overcrowded hives of China and India, to cover not only our Pacific slope but the Great Basin, and pour in torrents through the gorges of the Rocky Mountains into the vast, inviting valley of the Mississippi. (qtd. in Tchen 194)

Chinese American scholar William Wu, in his study *The Yellow Peril: Chinese Americans in American Fiction, 1850–1940*, identifies three early novels of Chinese invasion as representatives of a larger fictional tradition. The first of these, Robert Woltor's *A Short and Truthful History of the Taking of California and Oregon by the Chinese in the Year A.D. 1899*, was published in 1882, the year of the first Chinese Exclusion Act. The narrator begins by lamenting the failure of San Francisco to move its Chinese immigrants to Goat Island as a sanitary measure against "the hydra of contagion always fermenting in the embryo of the pools and dirt of Chinatown, and ever awaiting a favorable chance to be delivered from its filthy and inactive womb" (Woltor 23). Thus the novel begins by invoking familiar fears of disease and (as a missed opportunity) the displacement of Chinese immigrants to their own "reservation" on Goat Island. Having neglected to treat the Chinese with the same iron fist used against Native Americans—and to move them to the last point West before the Pacific—white Americans have put the means of their own destruction into the hands of the enemy.

Woltor's long title more or less sums up the plot. A huge Chinese army, led by Prince Tsa Fungyan, launches a successful naval attack on

San Francisco, then proceeds to take over the West Coast. Introducing a fictional theme that will appear frequently in representations of the Chinese in American literature, the Chinese act as one large organism, "the drones of the Oriental hive" (Woltor 30). Their single object is conquest and their most prominent traits are mindless, puppet-like obedience. The novel ends with the Chinese poised in the West to sweep across the rest of the United States. The narrator finally draws an even more direct connection between a Chinese invasion and the displacement of Native Americans by white Europeans:

> The Europeans displaced the red Indians by driving them first to the west of America, thence back to a point midway between the Atlantic and Pacific oceans, and, at last, to the corner of their fate—extermination. Just such a fate seems to await the Caucasian race in America at the hands of the alien Mongolian, now irredeemably engrafted on her shores. (Wolter 79)

The narrator ends by suggesting that the success of the Chinese invasion is indeed a providential vengeance on America by connecting the Chinese with the angel of death described in the first chapter of Revelation.

The conquest of the United States is far more thorough in the second novel of invasion identified by Wu, Pierton W. Dooner's *The Last Days of the Republic* (1880). Chinese immigration is again seen as part of a sinister plot toward the eventual conquest of the United States. Unlike in the sudden invasion of Woltor's *Short and Truthful History*, the Chinese in Dooner's novel enter the United States at first as peaceful citizens, quietly infiltrating the country, intermarrying, then controlling elections in the West, and finally attempting to win the presidency. White citizens, awaking to their danger, begin to resist, only to find that it is too late. The Chinese have been planning their conquest all along, and they meld suddenly together into a huge, disciplined army, again obeying orders without any thought of personal danger. By the end of the novel, the Chinese have taken over the entire United States with the exception of Washington, D.C. Euro-American military forces, battered and demoralized by a succession of defeats at the hands of the Chinese, are pushed eastward across the continent they had only so recently won from the Native Americans. By the end of the novel, they are surrounded and clearly doomed.

One of the more bizarre of these novels of invasion is Oto Mundo's *The Recovered Continent: A Tale of the Chinese Invasion* (1898). A boys' adventure tale much like an H. Rider Haggard novel, Mundo's narrative involves no Chinese individuals at all. It is instead the tale of Toto Topheavy; initially an idiot, through experimental brain surgery Topheavy is converted to an evil supergenius. Feeling unappreciated at home, Topheavy takes his show on the road, organizing and leading the Chinese in a successful military strike first against Europe, repeating the geographic movement of the Mongol invasion. After Europe is thoroughly conquered, the Chinese move on to the United States.

Such narratives are, of course, specific to their times, and the explicit xenophobia they represent is, in many ways, a thing of the past. However, if the novel or short story of Chinese invasion has become relatively rare in our time, the underlying fear of the Chinese certainly remains, and colors our contemporary journalism and scholarship. Books like *The Coming Conflict with China* (1998), by Richard Bernstein and Ross H. Munro, and *China Wakes* (1995), by Nicholas D. Kristof and Sheryl WuDunn, continue to raise the specter of China, the sleeping giant, soon to awake and dominate the world.

Works Cited

Bernstein, Richard, and Ross H. Munro. *The Coming Conflict with China.* New York: Vintage, 1998.

Dooner, Pierton W. *The Last Days of the Republic.* San Francisco: Alta, California, Publishing House, 1880.

Fisher, Philip. *Hard Facts: Setting and Form in the American Novel.* New York: Oxford University Press, 1985.

Havermale, Hazel H. "The Canton Shawl." *Overland Monthly,* 2nd series. 64 (Sept. 1914): 269–72.

Kristof, Nicholas D., and Sheryl WuDunn. *China Wakes: The Struggle for the Soul of a Rising Power.* New York: Vintage, 1995.

Lee, Robert G. *Orientals: Asian-Americans in Popular Culture.* Philadelphia: Temple University Press, 1999.

Miller, Stuart Creighton. *The Unwelcome Immigrant: The American Image of the Chinese, 1785–1882.* Berkeley: University of California Press, 1969.

Mundo, Oto. *The Recovered Continent: A Tale of the Chinese Invasion.* Columbus, OH: Harper-Osgood, 1898.

Norr, William. *Stories of Chinatown: Sketches from Life in the Chinese Colony of Mott, Pell, and Doyers Street.* New York: William Norr, 1892.

Riis, Jacob A. *How the Other Half Lives.* 1890. Ed. David Leviatin. New York: Bedford, 1996.

Stout, Arthur B. *Chinese Immigration and the Physiological Causes of the Decay of a Nation.* San Francisco: Agnew and Deffebach, 1862.

Tchen, John Kuo Wei. *New York Before Chinatown: Orientalism and the Shaping of American Culture, 1776–1882.* Baltimore: Johns Hopkins University Press, 1999.

Whitney, Atwell. *Almond-Eyed, or, The Great Agitator: A Story of the Day.* San Francisco: A. L. Bancroft, 1878.

Woltor, Robert. *A Short and Truthful History of the Taking of California and Oregon by the Chinese in the Year A.D. 1899.* San Francisco: A. L. Bancroft, 1882.

Wu, William F. *The Yellow Peril: Chinese Americans in American Fiction, 1850–1940.* Hamden, CT: Archon Books, 1982.

8 Visualizing Race in American
Immigrant Autobiography

GEORGINA DODGE

"THE UNITED STATES IS A NATION OF immigrants." For many Americans, this cliché evokes a vague notion of ancestry that originates with the Pilgrims and culminates in waves of immigration from Europe during the late nineteenth and early twentieth centuries. These images and mythologies of the immigrant experience have created an archetypal emigrant who flees his or her European homeland because of religious persecution or economic depression, conditions that allow for the retelling of heroic Mayflower and rags-to-riches narratives, which have become the basis of an American ethos and identity.

As an extension of this Eurocentric concept of Americanness, Ellis Island is seen as the seminal site of modern America's origin, a view further sanctioned by the United States government. The National Park Service co-sponsored the American Family Immigration History Museum at Ellis Island, which opened in April 2001.[1] In addition to the museum, a newly-launched website allows the approximately forty percent of Americans whose ancestors passed through Ellis Island to check the passenger lists of incoming ships, almost all of which departed from Europe or Canada. The name of the museum and website helps to further the idea that *the* American family is European in origin. Although concepts of the American immigrant have been influenced by the influx of Cuban asylum-seekers and East Asian refugees in the 1970s, the recent focus on illegal immigration through Mexico and Canada has reinforced, to some extent, the image of the "true" immigrant as one that is not "alien"—in all senses of the word. While the largest percentage of America's turn-of-the-century immigrants entered the country through Ellis Island, many nineteenth- and twentieth-century non-European immigrants were processed through Angel Island in California, Nogales in southern Arizona, Florida's coastal peninsula, or one of the nation's other entry points.[2] Like their European counterparts, several of these "nontraditional" immigrants have written about their experiences, but their stories have been subsumed within a master narrative of immigration that does not adequately consider how race complicates the assimilation plot within the autobiographies of non-European immigrants.

This essay explores the significance of race within the narrative of the immigrant of color through considerations of visual racialization, distinctions between race and ethnicity, and concepts of Americanness. By way of example, I refer to two immigrant autobiographies published in the twentieth century: *A Daughter of the Samurai* (1925), by Japanese writer Etsu Sugimoto; and *Barrio Boy* (1971), by Chicano activist Ernesto Galarza. Scenes from these two texts enable me to illustrate some of the general observations I make about the function of visualized race in the American immigrant narrative. By focusing upon autobiographies written by immigrants of non-European descent whose visible difference from the dominant Euro-American population—a difference marked upon the body that we identify as raced—makes complete assimilation impossible, I show that rather than a narrative of eventual assimilation, the story of becoming American is one of negotiating individual and community identities within racist culture.

By invoking race, I refer to visible features, particularly skin color but other physical aspects as well, to differentiate my approach from methods of categorization such as ethnicity or religion, which have traditionally been the vantage points for considerations of immigration. My approach is not a naïve return to essentialist definitions of race as being simply constituted by physical characteristics; in fact, the theory of the social construction of race in America is central to this analysis of immigrant autobiography because changing concepts of race have led to shifting categorizations of racial and ethnic groups.³ The fluidity of racial classifications enabled ethnic Europeans who were initially racialized when they arrived in the United States to become recognized as white, in part due to their difference from African Americans and other non-white groups. According to Matthew Frye Jacobson, "The European immigrants' experience was decisively shaped by their entering an arena where Europeanness—that is to say, whiteness—was among the most important possession one could lay claim to. It was their *whiteness*, not any kind of New World magnanimity, that opened the Golden Door" (8, emphasis in original).

Both historically and currently, to be seen as white denotes privileges that can make whiteness desirable, and those who possess the requisite features can choose to pass as white. The naturalization (in both senses of the word) of whiteness in the United States positions anything other than white as forever alien, making the assimilation plot that characterizes the immigrant narrative insufficient for immigrant writers of color whose degree of assimilation is limited due to nonwhite status. According to literary critic Patricia McKee, America's visual culture operates in the service of whiteness and maintains the status quo of white privilege (10–11). The "invisibility" of whiteness, which situates anything-other-than-white as the object in view, makes complete assimilation impossible for the immigrant writer of color, who sees his or her image always reflected in and through the eyes of the dominant gaze. Of course, seeing is a two-way affair; objects do indeed stare back, and writers of color respond to America's visual culture through their autobiographical envisionings of themselves and America. By gaining recognition through the autobiographical act, immigrant writers of color assert subjectivities that draw attention to those on the margins of society, forcing a reconsideration of what constitutes an American and helping to displace whiteness as the sole category for citizenship. Although the autobiographical American identities constructed by immigrants of color must be read through the lens and the disciplinary power of the visual, their voices decenter whiteness and create spaces for racialized bodies.

Because people of color are not always seen—or treated—as "real" Americans, they must constantly (re)assert an American identity. Of course, the success of their attempts depends upon audience reception and, interestingly, sometimes those who do not seek to become American are in fact considered so. Etsu Sugimoto, a Japanese woman who did not pursue U.S. citizenship and eventually returned to Japan, never claims a specifically American identity in her 1925 autobiography, *A Daughter of the Samurai*; yet she has been heralded as a "loyal citizen of America" (Gilbert 128). Today, critics dismiss her autobiography as an assimilated immigrant's homage to the U.S. While the text ostensibly follows the pattern of the immigrant narrative of assimilation, it also deconstructs western stereotypes of the passive Asian woman through Sugimoto's subversion of both gendered and racialized identities. Her ceremonial style of writing conceals the play of words that undermines the feminine Japanese American identity she seemingly celebrates. She refuses assimilation by subtly critiquing the United States, an act that allows Sugimoto to assert the superiority of the racialized body through a Japanese nationalist narrative embedded in her immigrant story. Rather than the tribute of a loyal citizen, her autobiography should be seen as a celebration of traditional Japanese morals and values.

Much like Sugimoto's autobiography, Ernesto Galarza's 1971 *Barrio Boy* is usually read as a story of successful immigration, but the text's protagonist resists assimilation through the manipulation of nationality and race. The creation of a Latino or Hispanic "race" in the United States is based upon a political conflation of language, national origin, and physical appearance that was fueled by the Chicano Movement of the 1960s. Although Galarza's autobiography focuses upon his family's immigration from Mexico to California during the Mexican Revolution of 1910, sociocultural events that occur between the time of his narrative's setting and his autobiography's publication, particularly the Chicano Movement, impact the textual community of the barrio that Galarza constructs. Through autobiographical retrospective he imposes the political manifesto of the Chicano Movement upon the earlier narrative of immigration, thus giving a politicized identity to the racialized body and the immigrant community. The concept of *la raza* that was central to the Chicano Movement provides the basis for Galarza's barrio community, and his childhood is framed within a political discourse of racial struggle. Like the autobiographical writings of Mexican Americans who faced annexation by the victorious United States after the U.S.-Mexican War of 1846–1848, Galarza's narrative resists the erasure of a distinct Mexican identity. The strength of family and community identity results in the idealization of the racialized body within the barrio that provides an ideological barrier against racism encountered without.

Although both Galarza's and Sugimoto's autobiographies are seen as immigrant success stories, neither text's protagonist is presented as an assimilated immigrant. In fact, Galarza makes it a point to talk about his "acculturation" rather than his "assimilation." Sugimoto's permanent return to Japan prior to World War Two, as well as the theme of Japanese sovereignty within her final novel, *Grandmother O Kyo* (1940), suggest that if she ever considered herself to be an American, her national affiliation was temporary. Although both authors follow established patterns of the immigrant narrative in their texts, their life stories imply that certain elements of that narrative are not available to the immigrant writer of color. Because race cannot be "left behind" during the assimilation process, the non-European immigrant's narrative of Americanization is disrupted by a racialized identity that is imposed upon the immigrant by society, assumed and asserted (often with great pride) by the immigrant, and always visible. In other words, a racial identity based upon appearance is not only the product of a prejudiced society, it is also a central feature of autobiographical self-representation that is simultaneously suppressed and foregrounded throughout the text. While some form of difference is a salient feature within all immigrant autobiographies (difference that European protagonists outmaneuver to become American), the manipulation of race by the immigrant autobiographer of color that ostensibly challenges racial categories in America also reinscribes racial difference and maintains the inassimilability of race. That this is a self-conscious act within the autobiography suggests that the narrative of Americanization is seen as always already unavailable to the immigrant of color.

Seen as unresolvably different, the autobiographer of color must make race a salient feature of self-presentation, particularly if the goal is to produce a realistic—and marketable—product. The result is that race provides the visual lens through which the protagonist is viewed by the reading audience. Strikingly, however, there are no descriptions of the autobiographer's physical body within either Sugimoto's or Galarza's narratives, even though it is the visible body upon which racial categorization is imposed. The authors provide few details concerning their appearance, effectively e-race-ing the visible body from the text while simultaneously foregrounding race. Once race has been established as central to the identity of the author, descriptions of other physical characteristics become unnecessary; in other words, the reader has been told all s/he needs to know to identify the protagonist as either a male or female member of a particular racialized group. Thus narrative subjectivity is itself predicated upon a stereotypical racialized identity, so the protagonist's provisional Americanness is based first and foremost upon difference that will not dissolve in the melting pot. By simply acknowledging possession of a racialized body, the immigrant writer of color invokes an already existing image within the mind's eye of the dominant culture and any further description is not considered necessary.

Acts of presumptive categorization based on appearance render the individual transparent, subsumed within a larger visual field of color or race. Sugimoto is told by a European American neighbor that she is an exotic addition to their neighborhood, the "'only Japanese woman that I ever saw—except at the exposition'" (*Daughter* 202). Thus, the racialized body is perpetually on display, and the bi-directional look exchanged between the immigrant of color and the white New World inhabitant is diverted by race, and this deflection is mirrored in the act of assimilation. As a two-way process, assimilation is complete only when society embraces the immigrant's assimilation, and how the immigrant is seen, and sees, has a major impact upon the degree of assimilation permitted and undertaken. Of course, various immigrant groups have been accorded different degrees of welcome throughout history, and race itself is an ever-changing concept in America, as evidenced by nineteenth-century classifications of Irish and Italian immigrants as "black" (Jacobson 48, 57). But throughout the twentieth century, the persistence within popular culture of categorizing people primarily by markings of race rather than ethnicity suggests that the visible elements of race make it an easily identifiable basis for differentiation.

In American visual economy, the most dominant manifestation of racial identity is skin color. While skin color itself is certainly not the reason for racism and not even a reliable indicator of race, it provides an important basis by which people are categorized within public culture by all members of society.[4] The persistence of basing insider/outsider relations upon skin color or other distinguishing features, such as gender markers, is pervasive within contemporary society and provides one indication of the crucial role that vision plays in human interactions. According to sociologist James Vander Zanden, "In order for a dominant-minority situation to exist, it is essential that there be some visible and conspicuous feature or features present by which the members of the two groups can be differentiated" (15). This is not to imply that discrimination on the basis of racial appearance is an a priori condition in the West. Cultural historians have shown that ideas of race based on skin color are a fairly recent phenomenon.[5]

The visible body is, of course, marked by numerous features other than racial, and physical characteristics that are not necessarily indicative of race are often considered to be so. For example, the appearance of the brown-skinned mestizo/a of native Indian and Spanish ancestry has caused the term "Latino" to become racially connotative although there is no officially recognized Latino race. Similarly, the term "Hispanic," which refers to language, has also been used to indicate race. To claim that Latino or Hispanic refers to national origin or native language has limited applicability within the visual culture of America's racial hierarchy. For example, a black Cuban who comes to the United States is considered African American while a lighter skinned Cuban remains Latino.[6] Just as racial categories can be created and reconfigured within public culture, they can also be reinscribed over national or cultural origin.

The distinction between race and ethnicity is important to discussions about the assimilation of peoples and texts because an ethnic identity is often fluid while the ability to affirm or deny a racial identity is not always an available option for immigrant populations of color. The concepts of consent and descent, central to Werner Sollors's 1986 *Beyond Ethnicity*, do not apply as readily to the circumstances of people of color as they do to European immigrants. Sollors defines consent as the choices that ethnic subjects make as "free agents" and descent as "our hereditary qualities, liabilities, and entitlements" (6). While consent is a democratic ideal, it is, however, overshadowed by descent for people of color, who are primarily defined by dominant society according to factors such as the perceived liability of a darker skin hue and all of the stereotypes attached to color. Subsuming race under the category of ethnicity allows us to avoid exploring the complex interplay between race and ethnicity. Race cannot and should not be considered merely one element of ethnicity because it is a "heavily charged term" that has assumed different meanings throughout American history (Sollors 39). As Sollors himself points out, the meaning of ethnicity has also changed over the years, making it an equally unstable concept (39). The instabilities of both ethnicity and race make it prudent to recognize their differences while attending to their complex interactions.

Rather than regarding race as an unwieldy concept, confronting its various definitions and manifestations in different eras enables us better to understand the larger framework of assimilation in which shifting definitions of race—and ethnicity—have been situated. As Michael Omi and Howard Winant argue, race is a fluid concept based upon "an unstable and 'decentered' complex of social meanings constantly being transformed by political struggle" (55).[7] Contemporary concepts of race as simply a "myth" must be situated within that struggle. Toni Morrison rightfully sees recent efforts to dismiss race as suspect: "Suddenly (for our purposes, suddenly), 'race' does not exist. . . . It always seemed to me that the people who invented the hierarchy of 'race' when it was convenient for them ought not to be the ones to explain it away, now that it does not suit their purposes for it to exist" (3). Morrison identifies a tendency within intellectual circles to deny the existence of race, thereby (suddenly) clearing the slate of historical and current injustices enacted upon bodies that remain racialized within popular culture— no matter how hard academics and politicians seek to change the terms of discourse. As Omi and Winant note, we cannot "do without" race, for it "continues to play a fundamental role in structuring and representing the world" (55).

My distinction between race and ethnicity is not meant to minimize the horrifying ordeals faced by immigrants of European heritage, particularly the Irish, Italians, and Jews, who were (and in some cases still are) confronted by bigotry and conflicting societal expectations. Scenes of ethnic and religious oppression are all too common in European immigrant narratives from the first half of the twentieth century and earlier, but the continued experiences of European immigrants have not followed the same trajectory as have those of immigrants and migrants of color.[8] Simply put: A visibly black person cannot choose to be white, but various European immigrant groups can and have been allowed to claim the privileges that the visual field of whiteness provides, although it has often taken one or more generations to achieve that goal.⁹ Recent titles, such as Karen Brodkin's *How Jews Became White Folks* (1998) and Noel Ignatiev's *How the Irish Became White* (1995), illustrate the changing status of European ethnic groups. Ignatiev's study of Irish immigration and assimilation focuses upon the relationship between Irish immigrants and African Americans during the nineteenth century to show how the Irish achieved social mobility, in part, by adopting mainstream America's racism towards blacks.

The ability of certain "out-groups" to assimilate through the adoption of "in-group" prejudices is based upon established racial ideologies within a society that often become manifest in language. The labels that the dominant population uses to describe particular immigrant groups reflect the potential—and lack of potential—for assimilation. Early Irish immigrants were often called "niggers turned inside out" (Ignatiev 41),¹⁰ while Italians were referred to as the "Chinese of Europe" and deemed "just as bad as the Negroes" (Dinnerstein and Reimers 48). The use of racialized metaphors and similes to define Irish and Italians also impacts the perceived status of Negroes and Chinese. As the vehicle or metaphorical term, "Negroes" and "Chinese" provide the grounds for the metaphor while "Irish" and "Italians" occupy the position of subject or tenor to which the metaphor is applied. Thus, European immigrants were provided linguistic subjectivity that permitted them to change applied definitions while people of color were placed within an unalterable category as the basis for the definition.¹¹ For example, in Abraham Cahan's 1896 novelette *Yekl: A Tale of the New York Ghetto*, the newly arrived Gitl, a Russian Jewish immigrant, made dark by her days at sea, resembles a "squaw" (34). But by the end of the text, "a suggestion of that peculiar air of self-confidence with which a few months' life in America is sure to stamp the looks and bearing of every immigrant," coupled with "her general Americanized make-up" indicates that Gitl has transformed from racialized foreigner to American, something that the "squaw" cannot do (83, 84).

Of course, racial classifications applied to people of color also undergo change over time. For example, Asian Americans, who, in the nineteenth century, were feared as the "yellow peril," are now referred to as the "model minority."¹² However, this change in terminology does not provide Asian Americans with the same cultural capital enjoyed by whites but simply creates a hierarchy among minorities and reinforces cultural stereotypes. As Neil Gotanda argues, the model minority is contrasted to the stereotype of African Americans as violent and criminal, which results in the African American minority being "monitored" by the Asian American minority. In other words, the "model minority" becomes the basis against which African Americans are the "monitored minority." According to Gotanda, "Implicit also is the idea that 'monitored' and 'model' racial minorities are subordinate to an 'invisible majority.' That invisible majority is, I believe, the White majority and its position of White racial privilege" (240). To be white is to be race-free, while belonging to a minority group implies the possession of a racialized identity with its attendant stereotypes. Although the labels applied to visible race may shift (e.g., Negro to black to African American), racial classifications remain the same and continue to be used in order to separate, distance, and subordinate groups of people. Visible features that allow for visual differentiation provide the basis for this categorization.

A direct effect of racial categorization is that whether or not early immigrant writers of color considered themselves to be representative of their races, they were assigned that position by their audience. The idea that autobiographies by people of color should be representative was promoted within a literary community whose own assumptions of what constituted immigrant autobiography tended to downplay individual differences in favor of a synthesizing immigrant experience. By accepting only those works that met their specifications, publishers established models for immigrant autobiographies and effectively defined the canon. For example, during the early part of the twentieth century, Asian American autobiographies were almost exclusively written by women who, like Sugimoto, had converted to Christianity.[13] The universalizing effect of a common religion led reviewers to praise *A Daughter of the Samurai* because it "asked no vexing questions" but focused instead upon "tell[ing] a tale with delicacy and taste."[14] By the time Ernesto Galarza published *Barrio Boy* in 1971, models of representation within immigrant autobiography were well established, and in the introduction that begins his text, Galarza writes, "In many ways the experiences of a multitude of boys like myself, migrating from countless villages like Jalcocotán and starting life anew in *barrios* like the one in Sacramento, must have been similar" (1). While Galarza's autobiography fits within the paradigm of the "up-from-the-ghetto" narrative that characterizes much of American immigrant literature (Ferraro 7), Sugimoto's narrative reflects her background of wealth and social privilege. The lack of interaction with an immigrant community situates Sugimoto's text as an individualistic endeavor that is not representative of an essentialist immigrant experience, regardless of whether or not the she presents herself as somehow typical. However, the bilateral nature of racial stereotypes—that the characteristics of a race are possessed by all individuals of that race and each individual serves as a microcosm of the race—meant that in the eyes of mainstream readers, as a racialized author, Sugimoto created not only an image of her self within her text but one of the entire race, whether or not such a communal act was intentional.

The fallacy of such racial classification is made evident in Sugimoto's autobiography when she applies the standards of racial categorization to the population of the United States from a Japanese perspective. Her autobiography follows the pattern of arrival, confusion, and eventual acculturation characteristic of the European immigrant narrative that flourished during the early years of the twentieth century and was meant to identify its author as a newly formed American. And much like white European immigrants, Sugimoto quickly discovers that the social hierarchy of visible race in America can be used to help establish her own position as not-so-foreign as the black Other. Shortly after the birth of Sugimoto's first daughter, the family laundress, an African American woman named Minty, visits the baby and asks the nurse to display the infant's feet. Minty expresses surprise that the baby has five toes; washing the two-toed slipper socks, or *tabi*, that Sugimoto traditionally wore, Minty assumed that the Japanese possessed only two toes. In relating this scene, Sugimoto displays a disturbing understanding of the discourse of racial positioning in turn-of-the-century America. Minty the laundress speaks in a caricature of black southern dialect (the only appearance of dialect of any sort in the entire text), which serves to highlight her class status, particularly when compared to Sugimoto's flawless English. Sugimoto's main point, of course, is how little is known, much less understood, about the Japanese people. She uses Minty's ignorance to show that at least in regards to one biological characteristic—the feet—the Japanese are just like Americans. While her obvious intent is to show that the Japanese are not so physically different from Americans, positioning an African American woman in the role of uninformed inter-locutor seems to imply that such ignorance is characteristic among blacks, a racial group even more stigmatized than the Japanese. Her presenta-tion of Minty as a comic, almost minstrel-like character reflects portrayals publicized by a white patriarchy and enables her to assert her superi-ority over the "other" race that she encounters during her stay in Amer-ica. She positions herself, and by extension all Japanese, as being more similar to whites, both biologically and intellectually, than blacks are.

While the incident with Minty seems indicative of Sugimoto's under-standing of American racial discourse, the scene that follows provides a specifically Japanese perspective on racial classification in the United States:

> When the nurse told my husband he shouted with merriment and finally said, "Well, Minty has struck back for the whole European race and got even with Japan."
>
> The nurse was puzzled, but I knew very well what he meant. When I was a child it was a general belief among the common people of Japan that Europeans had feet like horses' hoofs, because they wore leather bags on their feet instead of sandals. That is why one of our old-fashioned names for foreigners was "one-toed fellows." (*Daughter* 223)

Ironically, Sugimoto situates Minty as a champion for the European race, making the African American woman representative of European America. Minty's ignorance reflects that of mainstream America about the Japanese, who were once (but are no longer) similarly in the dark concerning Westerners. By positioning her own "foreignness" against Minty's, and then strategically placing Minty in the role of representa-tive European, Sugimoto thus positions the Japanese against all West-erners. Her attitude reflects the traditional tendency (still prevalent today) of the Japanese to classify all foreigners as *gaijins*, or simply not Japa-nese, regardless of racial origins.

This is not to imply that the Japanese have no understanding of West-ern racial hierarchies. According to Yukiko Koshiro, the modern Japa-nese imitated the West in adopting current concepts of racial prejudice based on skin color. Their reason for doing so was to elevate their sta-tus in the eyes of the West, much in the same way that European immigrants assumed racist behavior towards African Americans in order to solidify their own social positions in America (Koshiro 56, 166). Sugimoto herself seems well aware of the difference between the racialized physical differences between the Japanese and European Americans. When her second daughter is born, her first daughter, five-year-old Hana, is dismayed by the baby: "'I wanted a baby with yellow hair like Susan's sister'" (*Daughter* 239). This poignant scene marks the child's awakening to her physical difference from her playmates and provides a much-too-brief reflection on internalized racism.

Through events such as this, Sugimoto continues to highlight differences, defining herself as Japanese and situating herself as an outsider studying American culture rather than as an assimilated immigrant. Throughout her autobiography, her attitude towards the United States remains that of a tourist, "shopping" for cultural exports that can benefit Japan. She continually compares American customs with those of her homeland, and, while Japanese traditions are usually given precedence, she occasionally finds New World traits to admire. She is particularly pleased by the autonomy that American women enjoy, especially in marriage, where they are not expected to consume only foods that their husbands enjoy nor to sleep only when their husbands do. The ability of individuals to step outside narrowly defined social boundaries pleases Sugimoto. She generally praises her new home and its inhabitants, but she does critique Americans, whom she finds "a great people . . . both admirable *and faulty* in a giant way" (*Daughter* 155–56, emphasis mine).

Like Sugimoto, Ernesto Galarza also (re)constructs race within his autobiography in order to create a particular image of the racialized body. In *Barrio Boy*, Galarza writes that during the early years of the twentieth century, "*chicano*" was "the name by which we called an unskilled worker born in Mexico and just arrived in the United States" (200). The Chicanos contrasted themselves with the *pochos:*

Mexicans who had grown up in California, probably had even been born in the United States. They had learned to speak English of sorts and could still speak Spanish, also of sorts. They knew much more about the Americans than we did, and much less about us. The *chicanos* and the *pochos* had certain feelings about one another. Concerning the *pochos,* the *chicanos* suspected that they considered themselves too good for the *barrio* but were not, for some reason, good enough for the Americans. Towards the *chicanos*, the *pochos* acted superior, amused at our confusions and not especially interested in explaining them to us. In our family when I forgot my manners, my mother would ask me if I was turning *pochito*. (Galarza 207)

The recently arrived immigrants feel disdain towards the pochos who have not maintained cultural links with their Mexican heritage, even though "turning *pocho* was a half-step toward turning American" (Galarza 207). Becoming American is not considered a primary goal of the Chicanos, who seek to preserve aspects of a specifically Mexican identity even though they adopt some elements of white American culture.

In his 1971 autobiography, Galarza looks back upon his childhood communities in Mexico and the United States in order to trace the preservation of values and traditions that characterize the Mexican American community. Because *Barrio Boy* was written several decades after the events related in it, the sensibilities Galarza develops during the years between the experiences and the descriptions of them have a distinct impact on his narrative. In particular, the Chicano Movement of the 1960s provides the basis for the political discourse that subtly characterizes the autobiography. By placing the language of politics upon the template of the immigrant narrative, Galarza writes a manifesto for Chicano identity that refutes the value of assimilation. Through autobiographical retrospective, he superimposes political principles of the Chicano Movement upon the narrative of immigration, allowing him to illustrate through example that success in the U.S. does not require the full-scale adoption of European American culture.

The resistance to European American values in *Barrio Boy* is itself an inherited aspect of Mexican American culture, as shown by Genaro Padilla's analysis of early Mexican American autobiographical writing that appeared after the United States annexed much of northern Mexico in 1848. According to Padilla, "Mexican American autobiography came into formation as a personal and communitarian response to the threat of erasure" (x). As a site of preservation, the Mexican American autobiographical text sustains and enhances cultural memory, providing Mexican Americans an avenue through which better to understand their heritage in America. Galarza's autobiography focuses on the heritage that the Chicano Movement sought to recapture, which was based upon both an ancient and more recent past. By the late 1960s, a generation of Mexican Americans who had been born in the United States began to question the relevance of declaring loyalty to a country that would not allow them to progress economically or socially beyond the level of the working underclass. Chicanos called for a more active role in the governance of institutions such as schools and the Catholic Church, but rather than accept the token memberships offered as concessions by European American society to "acceptable" community members, they resisted assimilation and sought to incorporate Mexican culture into a distinct American lifestyle (Alvarez 939–42).[15] One of the most important symbols of the movement, and a symbol through which the past and present merged, was the concept of Aztlán, a mythical region portrayed as an earthly paradise. According to legend, the Aztec tribe had left Aztlán around the tenth century A.D. at the command of their god Huitzilopochtli to search for the promised land, the present site of Mexico City, where they established their empire (Pina 18). Although the existence or geographical location of Aztlán has never been established outside of mythology, Aztlán is a symbol for the American Southwest that became part of the United States upon the signing of the Treaty of Guadalupe Hidalgo and also symbolized the spiritual unity that bound all Chicanos regardless of geographical location (Leal 5–9). The use of the designation "Chicano" also served as a unifying symbol that Galarza explains is a term of sympathy used among working-class peoples (Galarza 269). As a designation that originated within the Mexican American community rather than one imposed by European America, the use of "Chicano," rather than "Mexican American" or "Spanish American," paralleled the ideological implications found behind the use of "black" instead of "Negro" that characterized the Black Power Movement (Penalosa 24).

This investiture was racialized through the concept of "La Raza," which unified the diverse mestizo racial heritage of Mexican Americans through the ideological creation of a Chicano race. In *El Plan Espiritual de Aztlán*," which was written at the First Chicano National Conference held in Denver, Colorado in 1969 and which provided the ideological framework for the Chicano Movement, the term La Raza is used to invoke a common political cause for peoples of Mexican heritage. Within that manifesto, the identities of Chicano and La Raza are closely linked from the very first sentence of the program: "*El Plan Espiritual de Aztlán* sets the theme that the Chicanos (*La Raza de Bronze*) must use their nationalism as the key or common denominator for mass mobilization and organization." Chicanos are called upon to affiliate with a common political party, "*La Familia de la Raza*."[16] The already existing tendency of European America to racialize peoples of Latino heritage was appropriated and used for political expediency during the Chicano Movement.[17]

In *Barrio Boy*, Galarza uses the racialized language of the Chicano Movement to distinguish between Mexicans and Americans on the basis of visualized race, marking the differences between bodies as indicators of identity. During their migration northward, the Galarza family lives for a short period near Mazatlán, where his uncles work for the railroad. The superintendent and other railroad officials are white Americans who provide Galarza with his first exposure to racialized differences and allow him to formulate an antiassimilationist theory based upon appearance: "Two remarkable things about the American *bilillos* were the way their necks turned red with sunburn, and their freckles, both good reasons why no Mexican could ever become an American, or would want to" (Galarza 125).[18] By making the physical aspect of an "American" unappealing, Galarza elevates the brown bodies of *La Raza de Bronze*, bodies that are usually the object of white disdain.

The tenacity of racial categorization that exists within the visual realm of human interaction extends to a variety of other arenas, including the literary. It is the concept of race that prevents either Sugimoto or Galarza from receiving recognition for writing *the* American immigrant autobiography. Galarza may be lauded for his rendition of the *Mexican* immigrant's narrative, and Sugimoto may receive acknowledgment for portraying *Asian* immigrant perspectives, but neither of these authors is recognized for presenting *the* American story. The categorization of texts is an extension of the classification of people, and because people of color are seen as perpetually foreign Others, their works are not received as representative of the American experience. When noted social historian Oscar Handlin writes that he "discovered that the immigrants *were* American history," he is not referring to peoples of Asian or Mexican descent (*Uprooted* 3, emphasis in original). Because the American is perceived as white, the American immigrant autobiography must therefore reflect that whiteness. The narratives of European immigrants, like the autobiographies of white founding fathers such as Benjamin Franklin, are seen as universal texts that speak to the sensibilities of all Americans.

In contrast, autobiographies by immigrants of color are typically analyzed according to the authors' racially identified groups rather than as part of the larger canon of American immigrant narratives. Asian American immigrant autobiographies, for instance, with the exception of popular successes like Maxine Hong Kingston's *The Woman Warrior*, are considered in the context of the Asian American canon; Latina/o immigrant narratives are taught in courses focused on Latina/o literatures; and so on. The primary exception to these categorizations are courses or anthologies specifically designated as multicultural, in which culture, rather than race, provides a framework that allows for the inclusion of immigrant narratives written by members of European ethnic groups, such as the Irish, Italians, and Jews, as well as racialized groups, such as Asian and Latina/o Americans.

For many marginalized Americans, and particularly for writers of color, autobiography provided possibly the only means for declaring subjective agency. But even though their texts were an assertion of individual existence, their narratives were often seen simply as records of social conditions and historical events. Caught between history and literature, the autobiographies of visibly racialized writers were (and are) often read solely as social documents rather than as literary products. Rather than consider this a negative reflection on the texts, I believe that the double nature of culturally-situated narratives results in an increased value of the texts both as literary works and social documents. The challenge of situating the self among historical events results in an imaginative series of cause-and-effect moments that subsequently anchor the entire text. Immigrant authors position their narratives against the social and historical backgrounds of their homelands as well as the "mainstream" of United States culture, providing a multifaceted perspective on world history that incorporates personal responses to significant global events. Sugimoto writes about the restoration of the Japanese emperor and Galarza observes the Mexican Revolution. These international occurrences yield insights into the effects of American policies both at home and abroad, while also providing different perspectives from which to appraise the formation of an American identity.

Notes

1. Jointly supported by the Church of Jesus Christ of Latter-day Saints, the National Park Service, and the Statue of Liberty-Ellis Island Foundation, the American Family Immigration History Center and website at http://www.ellis islandrecords.org lists the names of more than twenty-two million passengers who arrived at the Port of New York between 1892 and 1924.

2. I use the term "non-European" to refer to immigrants who do not possess European racial ancestry. Thus, immigrants from Australia whose ancestors came from Europe would not be included in this categorization, while immigrants of color who come to the United States from England would. According to Daniels, of the approximately 16,900,000 immigrants who legally entered the United States between 1900 and 1924, around 85 percent came from Europe and were processed through Ellis Island (122–24).

3. Several important texts that contribute to our understanding of how race is socially constructed within the United States and its literatures include: Gossett, *Race*; Corcos, The *Myth of Human Races*; Wiegman, *American Anatomies*; Omi and Winant, *Racial Formation in the United States*; and Hannaford, *Race*.

4. The continued primacy of skin color became all too obvious to Roslyn Jones in April 2001 during rioting by African Americans in Cincinnati— violence that had been sparked by a white police officer shooting and killing an unarmed black man. Driving home to her apartment in Over-the-Rhine, the African American neighborhood where the shooting and much of the subsequent rioting occurred, Jones, who is an albino black woman, was attacked and beaten by the mob until someone shouted, "She's black!" She was taken to a hospital where she was treated for severe bruises and cuts, including a head wound from a brick. Although the medical prognosis was that she would be fine, a deeper injury was inflicted. "It hurts," she told a reporter, noting that her "own people" failed to recognize her, adding, "They didn't even look long enough to see. The first piece of white skin they saw, they hit it" (Horn B1).

5. Following the lead of Michel Foucault, Ivan Hannaford argues that erroneous readings of Plato and Aristotle by biometrist Francis Galton and

others have mistakenly traced current concepts of race back to the Greeks. Hannaford sees twentieth-century ideas of race beginning to take shape in fourteenth-century Europe, with the culmination of "scientific" understandings of race in the late nineteenth century (41–128). Wiegman also notes that human difference based upon color did not become a primary means of racial classification until the seventeenth century, but that in the West, it is difficult to see beyond such categorizations due to the cultural primacy of the body, which makes it impossible to dismiss the role of the visual (23–24).

6. Best friends in Cuba, Joel Ruiz and Achmed Valdés played soccer and spent special occasions like birthdays together. Upon coming to America, the sharp racial divide in Miami resulted in Ruiz, who is black, living in a black neighborhood where he now plays basketball with other African Americans. Valdes lives in a white Cuban neighborhood and the two men seldom see each other (Ojito A1+).

7. Omi and Winant define race as "a concept which signifies and symbolizes social conflicts and interests by referring to different types of human bodies," and note that while the "concept of race invokes biologically based human characteristics (so-called 'phenotypes'), selection of these particular human features for purposes of racial signification is always and necessarily a social and historical process" (55).

8. And yet, incredibly, there are those who seem to think that somehow, someday, they will. The title of a recent book by Michael Barone, *The New Americans: How the Melting Pot Can Work Again*, seems to say it all. Barone argues that similarities between certain groups (he pairs Irish and blacks, Italians and Latinos, and Jews and Asians) implies that the successful assimilation of the European part of the equation means that the corresponding racialized group will assimilate in similar ways. Barone seems to have failed to notice that blacks have been in this country much longer than the Irish and their assimilation is possibly the least likely to occur in any imaginable near future. Barone's ultimate project is to blame the American elite, particularly those with university training, for destroying the "basic goodness and decency of American institutions and the American people" (279). That "basic decency" is challenged in African American writer Richard Wright's photojournalistic text, *12 Million Black Voices: A Folk History of the Negro in the United States* (first published in 1941). In that book, Wright notes the ability of recent European immigrants to achieve greater social and economic success than African Americans whose ancestors lived in the United States for several generations. It was not uncommon for black residents of the slums to read the newspaper and learn of the social achievements of white immi-

grants. The American institutions that Barone feels will somehow restoke the melting pot are the very ones that Wright accuses of racist discrimination (Wright 102–03).

9. Classic sources for the conditions confronted by European immigrants include the writings of Oscar Handlin, particularly *The Uprooted* and *Race and Nationality in American Life*. Studies that focus primarily upon the literature of European immigrants include Marcus Klein, *Foreigners*; Ferraro, *Ethnic Passages*; and Boelhower, *Immigrant Autobiography in the United States*.

10. According to Ignatiev, this was not fully a one-sided definition as Negroes were sometimes referred to as "smoked Irish" due to the limited forced integration that occurred between the early Irish immigrants and the black population (41). However, the preponderance of metaphors that were more commonly used situates Negroes as the basis for comparison.

11. This distinction is also significant in comparing the status of African Americans who migrated from South to North during the first half of the twentieth century and the "Okies," white migrant farm workers who sought work in California during the Great Depression. My colleague Chadwick Allen, a native of Oklahoma, recalls his uncle telling him that the Oklahoma migrants were disparagingly referred to as "white-ass niggers."

12. It is important to note that any one stereotype can (and often does) co-exist with other stereotypes. In addition to the label of "model minority," Asian Americans are also subjected to multiple stereotypes of, for example, the geisha girl and the inscrutable Oriental.

13. This tendency is noted in Brian Niiya's discussion of early Asian American autobiography (41–45).

14. Elaine Kim attributes this praise to the *New York Tribune* 22 Nov. 1925, p. 10 (27, 286).

15. Particularly since World War II, much of the organizing efforts on the part of Chicanos have focused upon the issue of education. Seen as a means through which successive generations can gain full participation in American society, education was and continues to be a political rallying point for the entire Mexican American population as evidenced by the ongoing debates concerning bilingual education and the institution of Chicano/a or Latino/a Studies programs at major American universities.

16. The copy of *"El Plan Espiritual de Aztlán"* consulted here is from Anaya and Lomeli, eds., *Aztlán*.

17. To this day, the term "Latino," or the affiliated "Hispanic," is used to refer to race within both popular culture and intellectual circles. For example, in Hogue, *Race, Modernity, Postmodernity*, the "four major non-white racial

groups" in the United States are listed as "Asian Americans, African Americans, Hispanics, and Native Americans" (6).

18. According to Galarza, the name *bilillo* "came from the fact that most Americans preferred, instead of tortillas, the small baker's loaves with a nipple on each end and a curl of crust between" (125).

Works Cited

Alvarez, Rodolfo. "The Psycho-Historical and Socioeconomic Development of the Chicano Community in the United States." *Social Science Quarterly* 53.4 (March 1973): 920–42.

Anaya, Rudolfo A., and Francisco Lomeli, eds. *Aztlán: Essays on the Chicano Homeland.* Albuquerque: University of New Mexico Press, 1991.

Barone, Michael. *The New Americans: How the Melting Pot Can Work Again.* Washington, D.C.: Regnery, 2001.

Boelhower, William. *Immigrant Autobiography in the United States: Four Versions of the Italian American Self.* Verona, Italy: Essedue Edizioni, 1982.

Brodkin, Karen. *How Jews Became White Folks: And What That Says about Race in America.* New Brunswick, NJ: Rutgers University Press, 1998.

Cahan, Abraham. *Yekl and the Imported Bridegroom and Other Stories of Yiddish New York.* 1896. New York: Dover, 1970.

Corcos, Alain. *The Myth of Human Races.* East Lansing: Michigan State University Press, 1997.

Daniels, Roger. *Coming to America: A History of Immigration and Ethnicity in American Life.* New York: HarperCollins, 1990.

Dinnerstein, Leonard, and David M. Reimers. *Ethnic Americans: A History of Immigration.* 3rd ed. New York: HarperCollins, 1988.

Ferraro, Thomas J. *Ethnic Passages: Literary Immigrants in Twentieth-Century America.* Chicago: University of Chicago Press, 1993.

Galarza, Ernesto. *Barrio Boy.* Notre Dame, IN: University of Notre Dame Press, 1971.

Gilbert, George Henry. *Pioneers in Self-Government: Informal Studies in the Natural Philosophy of Self-Government.* Segreganset, MA: Builders of America, 1948.

Gossett, Thomas F. *Race: The History of an Idea in America.* 1963. New York: Oxford University Press, 1997.

Gotanda, Neil. "Multiculturalism and Racial Stratification." *Mapping Multiculturalism.* Ed. Avery F. Gordon and Christopher Newfield. Minneapolis: University of Minnesota Press, 1996. 238–52.

Handlin, Oscar. *Race and Nationality in American Life*. Boston: Little, Brown, 1948.

——. *The Uprooted*. 2nd ed. Boston: Little, Brown, 1973.

Hannaford, Ivan. *Race: The History of an Idea in the West*. Washington: Woodrow Wilson Center Press; Baltimore: Johns Hopkins University Press, 1996.

Hogue, W. Laurence. *Race, Modernity, Postmodernity: A Look at the History and the Literatures of People of Color Since the 1960s*. Albany: State University of New York Press, 1996.

Horn, Dan. "Civility Turned to Anarchy: How It Happened." *Cincinnati Enquirer* 16 Apr. 2001: B1.

Ignatiev, Noel. *How the Irish Became White*. New York: Routledge, 1995.

Jacobson, Matthew Frye. *Whiteness of a Different Color: European Immigrants and the Alchemy of Race*. Cambridge: Harvard University Press, 1998.

Kim, Elaine H. *Asian American Literature: An Introduction to the Writings and Their Social Context*. Philadelphia: Temple University Press, 1982.

Klein, Marcus. *Foreigners: The Making of American Literature, 1900–1940*. Chicago: University of Chicago Press, 1981.

Koshiro, Yukiko. *Trans-Pacific Racisms and the U.S. Occupation of Japan*. New York: Columbia University Press, 1999.

Leal, Luis. "In Search of Aztlán." *Aztlán: Essays on the Chicano Homeland*. Ed. Rudolfo Anaya and Francisco Lomeli. Albuquerque: El Norte, 1989. 6–13.

McKee, Patricia. *Producing American Races: Henry James, William Faulkner, Toni Morrison*. Durham, NC: Duke University Press, 1999.

Morrison, Toni. "Unspeakable Things Unspoken: The Afro-American Presence in American Literature." *Michigan Quarterly Review* 28.1 (Winter 1989): 1–34.

Niiya, Brian T. "Open-Minded Conservatives: A Survey of Autobiographies by Asian Americans." Master's Thesis. University of California, Los Angeles, 1990.

Ojito, Mirta. "Best of Friends, Worlds Apart." *New York Times* 5 June 2000, late ed.: A1+; part 2 of a series, "How Race is Lived in America," begun 4 June 2000.

Omi, Michael, and Howard Winant. *Racial Formation in the United States: From the 1960s to the 1990s*. New York: Routledge, 1994.

Padilla, Genaro. *My History, Not Yours: The Formation of Mexican American Autobiography*. Madison, WI: University of Wisconsin Press, 1993.

Penalosa, Fernando. "Recent Changes Among the Chicanos." *Sociology and Social Research* 55.1 (Oct. 1970): 47–52.

Pina, Michael. "The Archaic, Historical and Mythicized Dimensions of Aztlán." *Aztlán: Essays on the Chicano Homeland*. Ed. Rudolfo Anaya and Francisco Lomeli. Albuquerque: El Norte, 1989. 14–45.

Sollors, Werner. *Beyond Ethnicity: Consent and Descent in American Culture.* New York: Oxford University Press, 1986.

Sugimoto, Etsu Inagaki. *A Daughter of the Samurai.* 1925. Rutland, VT: Charles E. Tuttle, 1966.

———. *Grandmother O Kyo.* New York: Doubleday, 1940.

Vander Zanden, James. *American Minority Relations: The Sociology of Race and Ethnic Groups.* 2nd ed. New York: Ronald, 1966.

Wiegman, Robyn. *American Anatomies: Theorizing Race and Gender.* Durham, NC: Duke University Press, 1995.

Wright, Richard. *12 Million Black Voices: A Folk History of the Negro in the United States.* 1941. New York: Arno, 1969.

9 *Maud Martha* Versus *I Love Lucy*

Taking on the Postwar Consumer Fantasy

TRACY FLOREANI

O N   T H E   D A Y   T H A T   I   B E G A N   R E A D I N G
Gwendolyn Brooks's only novel, *Maud Martha* (1953), I
had finished the graphic scene of Maud's daughter's
birth in a tenement apartment when I decided to break for
lunch. That day, I watched syndicated 1950s sitcoms while eating, as is my
habit when working at home. The broadcast was the *I Love Lucy* episode
in which Lucy enters the hospital to give birth ("Lucy Goes to the Hospital," 19 January 1953). I was struck by the difference between these two
birth scenes created within the same year, Maud Martha's a graphic blood-
and-wailing nod to literary naturalism, Lucy's an ultra-sterilized birth—
to the extent that Lucy disappears completely from the episode once she
enters the hospital. (The remainder of the episode occurs mostly in the
waiting room, to which the discussion will return later.)

Witnessing these two birth scenes back-to-back served as a catalyst
for helping me see how *Maud Martha* and *I Love Lucy* represent enlightening reverse narratives of 1950s womanhood through the ways in which
they play out divergent relationships with gendered consumerism and
cultural production.[1] The births themselves function as complementary
events within larger narratives about the positioning of female identi-

ties within a consumer fantasy. Threaded throughout both the novel and the television program, the specter of consumer desire evolves in fascinating ways according to the politics of representation and participation determined by race, ethnicity, gender, and socioeconomic class in the American 1950s.

Gwendolyn Brooks' short novel *Maud Martha* was published at the same historical moment in which the *I Love Lucy* show was establishing the popularity of the television situation comedy. In the lyrical style of Brook's poetry, the novel presents a series of vignettes and interior monologues that comprise the life of Maud Martha from her early childhood to the advent of her second pregnancy at the end of World War II. While the ongoing narrative of *I Love Lucy*'s seven-year run was one of increasing consumer desire and participation within the middle-class mainstream, *Maud Martha* offers a reverse narrative that begins with the protagonist sharing a desire for "the good life" similar to Lucy Ricardo's, but that slowly unfolds into a debunking of that fantasy. Race and ethnic identity will have everything to do with that debunking. While these two texts cannot represent all of the complexities and varieties of 1950s female experience, they operate within the same cultural field to provide very different visions of—and important insights into—the construction of American women's identity along racialized lines in this era.

My intention here is not to argue that Gwendolyn Brooks meant her novel to be a reaction to what she saw on television. While studies of this novel have aptly placed it within various literary traditions, my goal in expanding its critical contexts and pairing it with a popular culture text is to allow for further investigation of the specific cultural context in which the book appeared, and, consequently, provide for a new perspective on the novel's cultural significance. By reading this novel and television show together, by recognizing their interplay within a shared national context in which the notion of a unified national identity was consistently promoted, I examine the ways in which their positions and functions within that context necessarily inform one another. As John Fiske argues, cultural texts constantly work together in a variety of ways; "any one text is necessarily read in relationship to others and . . . a range of textual knowledges is brought to bear upon it" (108). He argues that the "space *between* texts" is as important as the texts themselves, and the meanings of any given text are found when cultural texts are read in dialogue with one another.

As the economy progressed after the war, and consumer culture became an identifying trait of the nation, the ideological investment in consumerism played out clearly in the mass media and was vividly and powerfully brought to life upon the television screen. As television increasingly occupied the domestic space, it played an ever more influential role in identity formation. Utilizing an important text from this medium and forcing it into "conversation" with the novel (a work governed by a much different set of formal principles), I intend to bring to light both the inherent complications of mass-mediated practices of identity construction and the simultaneous counter-cultural role of literary narrative in what has been doggedly portrayed as an age of consensus.

Television Culture

Arriving in American homes shortly after World War II, the television quickly began to change the ways in which Americans saw the world—and themselves. As an object, it literally changed the domestic space; changes in architecture, furnishings, accessories, family dining habits, and even clothing helped the television assume its place as the central apparatus in most American households.[2] Its programs and commercials provided at-home entertainment, displacing the radio in the majority of homes and introducing many new and influential cultural narratives into the private space of the home. The television became an increasingly important presence in the lives of most American families, and, thus, a powerful ideological apparatus. Extensive arguments have been made regarding the ideological functions of television, but for the purposes of this analysis, I want to focus on its specific role in shaping consumer identities. As George Lipsitz has argued in *Time Passages*, programmers, advertisers, writers, producers, and policy makers quite deliberately made use of television as a tool within the consumer economy. Not only did it make goods visible to viewers, "it also provided a relentless flow of information and persuasion that placed acts of consumption at the core of everyday life" (47). Lipsitz asserts that television's commercial lifeblood was so powerful as to influence actively the reformulation of "American ethnic, class, and family identities into consumer identities" (47). Through various popular visual media—especially through television—performative whiteness and consumerism became normative signifiers of "American." Moreover, purchasing power became an important component of national belonging in that "consumerism provided a means for assimilation into the American way of life: classless, homogenous, and family centered" (May 172). Television became the ideal vehicle for disseminating and making habitual these new, consumer-driven cultural practices, itself a purchased product through which other buying began.

As many theorists of mass media rightly point out, however, we should not regard television's cultural function one-sidedly, envisioning mass media as a kind of sprinkler system that bathes the unwitting public with conservative ideological messages. Lynn Spigel, for instance, notes that there were a variety of active discourses regarding the role that television was to play in the U.S., and that cultural commentators and ordinary citizens were well aware of its potential to alter daily life in possibly negative ways. Rather than simply viewing television as a "consciousness industry" for maintaining the status quo, Spigel argues, we should recognize the various possibilities for meanings and "contradictory ideas and values" within this medium that inherently "absorb[s] the discourses of social institutions" (*Make Room* 8).[3] Despite overt criticisms of the new medium, the rapid expansion of the television industry and successful sales of television sets reveal that its arrival was mostly welcomed as wholesome at-home entertainment and innovative technology. Television was new and modern, designed for leisure time—characteristics embraced by the average, upwardly mobile postwar American family. Civil Rights groups also viewed television's arrival with optimism, hoping that it would be "the answer to a variety of social problems," and believing that it "had the potential to reverse centuries of unjust ridicule and misinformation" for the African-American population (MacDonald xiv-xv).

While television became an increasing presence in American life, though, its programming offered an increasingly homogenous picture of America. As more Americans moved to the suburbs and gained (or worked toward, through credit purchasing) middle-class status, the ethnic and class identifiers that were once the "crucible of personal identity" within the cities slowly became diluted (Lipsitz 55). Television programs with working-class or ethnic characters, such as *The Goldbergs* and *Life with Luigi*, waned in popularity and left the airwaves by mid-decade. And because television, like U.S. society, was racially segregated, it was susceptible to the same racial politics. Consequently, programs hosted by or featuring African Americans became fewer as the decade progressed, and the escalating racial conflicts in the South complicated politics within the representational media.[4]

In his book *Selling Culture*, Richard Ohmann provides an excellent model for examining the effects a widely distributed and consumed cultural form can have on identity construction. He delineates the "charting of social space" by turn-of-the-century "home" magazines that simultaneously reflected and helped to construct the values of the newly forming professional-managerial class—especially through their advertising pages. "They taught readers a symbolism of commodities and social life," Ohmann argues, "they flattered a new class for its values while elaborating and clarifying those values" (219). I would argue that television takes on this same function approximately fifty years later. With new postwar lending practices, the boom in suburban housing construction, and the creation of new white-collar jobs contributing to the construction of a new "social space" for the young families of the post-war generation, television became integral to this process as an "instrument of legitimation for transformations in values initiated by the new economic imperatives of postwar America" (Lipsitz 44). In this sense, television operated the way home magazines did decades earlier, solidifying "a large group of people into an audience" (Ohmann 219). However, African American families were inherently excluded from much of this process on the basis of race.

Because so much identity construction took place within the domestic space, most of the consumer imperative was aimed at women. While they were not often the sole bread-winners, women's roles in the family's consuming practices were clearly defined in both advertising and programming. One can identify patterns in commercials from the postwar era that persist today: products marketed solely to women and children, regardless of who actually finances a household's purchases or uses the products. Of course, women of the 1950s were pictured enjoying the conveniences of the modern kitchen, but even automotive advertising frequently placed a well dressed *woman* within a fantasy world of space-age automobile technology, more prized for its design and convenience than its performance. In programming, domestic comedies played out the now stereotypical marital conflicts over spending, and good behavior within the fictional family space often resulted in material rewards for wives and children.

Star Power and the Consumer Ethos

Considering these sociohistorical circumstances enables us to interrogate gender dynamics, consumer practices, and cultural capital more closely within the domestic spaces of *Maud Martha* and *I Love Lucy*, where the physical signifiers of race play into the levels of cultural citizenship afforded or inhibited. The importance of *I Love Lucy* must be emphasized here, as it was almost instantly one of the most popular shows in early television and was number one in the television ratings for most of its initial seven-year run. Its popularity expanded and changed the star industry, as Lucille Ball's personal life merged with the plot of the show in a way that captivated the public and served simultaneously to make television stars seem more like "real people" that audience members could know. In the case of the Ricardos, the actors were married in real life, photo spreads of their real home were featured in reviews of the program, and early in the same year of *Maud Martha*'s publication, Lucille Ball and her character Lucy Ricardo gave birth to, essentially, the same baby boy (Desi Arnaz Jr./Ricky Ricardo Jr.). Television histories never fail to note this monumental event, as it found some fourteen million viewers tuning in to share in the happy occasion, winning an audience larger than that of the first-ever televised presidential inauguration (Eisenhower's) the next morning.[5] All of these factors, these lines blurred between the real actors and their fictional characters' lives, allowed for what Lori Landay calls the "bizarre public fantasy" of the ideal marriage. In tracing our culture's intimate psychological connections to the characters on television—and our tendency to conflate those characters with the people who portray them—the *I Love Lucy* show clearly plays into the construction of such television viewing practices.

Most feminist readings of the *I Love Lucy* show center around questions of where Lucy, as a character, positions herself within the domestic ideology of the 1950s. Some understandably read her life as one of containment, as she is often literally confined to the urban apartment, preparing meals for Ricky, with no financial independence apart from the housekeeping allowance he gives her. In such a scenario, her antics in show business and the workplace can be read as attempts (almost always unsuccessful) to liberate herself from the domestic sphere and gain some financial independence. Other feminist interpretations, especially Lori Landay's study "Liminal Lucy: Covert Power, Television, and Postwar Domestic Ideology," convincingly posit these very antics as progressive moves away from the domestic. Because of the ways in which Lucy breaks gender boundaries by, for example, cross-dressing or being generally "unlady-like" in her physical humor, her performances may be read as transgressive of the feminine-domestic ideals of the day.

Unspoken within such studies is the assumption that the feminist possibilities or impossibilities of such popular icons mattered only to those women who looked like Lucy: white and middle class (that is, women with the potential for upward mobility). Such is implied when, for example, Landay interprets producer Jess Oppenheimer's belief that *I Love Lucy* "held up a mirror" to the everyday life of Americans, and notes that "because of television's place in the home and the domestic subject of the series, *I Love Lucy* speaks in and to the homelife of its viewers" (179). Reading the implications within these phrases, the image of this homelife and of these viewers comes directly from the popular culture of the 1950s. In short, we envision middle-class white housewives who looked something like Lucy. In popular nostalgia we are not encouraged to associate the period's consumers of television to look like Brooks's protagonist Maud Martha, a young struggling mother in Chicago's Southside, who, in fact, would not have been one of these consumers, for she would not have been able to afford a television set. There was little attempt to represent such an individual in the commercialized medium that enabled the circulation of our "various memories, myths, histories, traditions, and practices" in the postmodern era (Gray 4). Unlike the recording industry of previous decades, which, though segregated, did recognize and market to African American audiences, the television industry offered little space for African American producer or consumer agency.

The written narrative, however, readily affords a space for representing and offering some level of cultural power for this type of marginalized identity. Indeed, the postwar period saw a "proliferation" of new voices in the popular literary scene, picking up where writers of the Harlem Renaissance and the Works Progress Administration had left off before the war (Lhamon 7). *Maud Martha* is related, in some ways, to the traditions established within those movements, most notably to the genre that Michael Denning calls the "ghetto pastoral." Brooks was involved with Left-oriented writers' groups in earlier years, but *Maud Martha*, though set during the 1930s and '40s, possesses a rather different cultural function than the social protest ghetto novels of the Depression, such as Michael Gold's *Jews without Money* (1930) or Richard Wright's *Native Son* (1940). *Maud Martha* takes the ghetto pastoral beyond the familiar documentary tone and offers a narrative that is much less overtly politicized than its predecessors.

The novel offers an ambivalent, exploratory, and imagistic representation of a non-mainstream American identity. As I will demonstrate, the consumer fantasy turned upside down within this novel does result in a politicized narrative that, at the very least, demands that the black female subject be positioned differently than she is within other contemporaneous narratives. After all, *Maud Martha* examines the workings of an identity not represented in the popular media at the time, that of an individualized black female character. Black women did appear occasionally on television in the postwar period, but usually as familiar stereotypes—such as the eponymous character on *Beulah*, an always-happy domestic worker for a white family, or the domineering, money-grubbing Sapphire on *Amos 'n' Andy*—or as high-class, glamorous entertainers on variety shows (e.g., Lena Horne, Ella Fitzgerald). *Maud Martha* engages representational politics within this context, and, as a book, complicates status quo narratives in ways not usually possible for women of color on television.

It is the kind of mainstream consumer fantasy represented in the *I Love Lucy* show against which we can effectively read a narrative like *Maud Martha*'s in context. Because a large portion of Lucy's and Ricky's marital struggles center on the accumulation of commodities, the issues of consumption and economics become central to the narrative of the show. At the show's outset, Lucille Ball intentionally reworked her own star image to portray Lucy Ricardo as an ordinary housewife.[6] As Landay notes, the commercial success of the show relied upon the image of Lucy as "just a typical housewife":

> Because television was broadcast into people's homes at a time when domesticity was a central tenet of the dominant value system, the more the Ricardos mirrored ordinary people (and Ball and Arnaz were represented as typical, not glamorous stars), the more appealing they were. (177)

Ironically, though, Lucy Ricardo registers as a woman who is anything but content to be just a housewife, as every episode centers on her attempts to break out of the daily routine (Landay 168). The instigator of conflicts within the home (or, sometimes, between the Ricardos and the Mertzes) is almost always a consumer product: a new hat, the latest designer dress, a new appliance, new furniture. The program maintains its narrative momentum by keeping Lucy fixated on constant desire for, and acquisition of, perpetually obsolescent consumer products.

As the show's narrative progresses, so does Ricky's career, and, consequently, Lucy's consumer appetite. Her requests evolve from housework-reducing conveniences, like a modern washing machine and dryer, to more luxury items, such as minks and French haute couture. Likewise, the family's shared acquisitions fall into line with those desired and experienced by the growing middle class over the course of the decade, as the Ricardos contribute to the Baby Boom, leave the urban center for the suburbs of Connecticut, buy a car, and become increasingly mobile—both literally and socially. Lucy's activities while in the suburbs shift and re-center around the pursuit of social acceptance and "keeping up with the Joneses." For example, she wants new furniture for the new house (partly motivated by envy of a wealthier neighbor), and she joins the garden club and the country club. The Ricardos' travels also increase, and they make every imaginable type of voyage, from taking trains to Hollywood to live in full-service hotels while Ricky pursues his career, to going on cruises, to flying to Europe with Ricky's band. Traveling increases the Ricardos' consumer options, but more important, the travel episodes enable Lucy to do what no "typical housewife" was able to, such as to interact frequently with the likes of John Wayne,

Maurice Chevalier, Alan Ladd, and Milton Berle. On the surface, the appeal is one of letting everyday people enjoy vicariously the sensation of "a typical housewife" meeting a star. Over the course of the series, the line between the actors and the characters becomes further obscured as the frequency of celebrity appearances increases, making it obvious that these are Ball's and Arnaz's real-life friends. This crumbling away of the "everyday" veneer of Ball and Arnaz serves an additional market-oriented function in the overall narrative. While the U.S. economy took off and the average American family acquired more material goods, the show did indeed "hold up the mirror," with Lucy and Ricky sharing in the same postwar prosperity. What would keep people watching, though, would be the continued promise of more material gain; as the Ricardos started to look more like Mr. and Mrs. Suburban American, they had to keep the audience's desire alive by staying one step ahead of the "real Joneses," keeping always slightly ahead of the limitations of a real family. In other words, the program itself made the desires of its contemporary viewers continually obsolete by offering more fantasies of consumer and celebrity encounter to which the average family had no access.

Moreover, consumer desire not only functioned as a prime motivator within the narrative, but also became a driving force in maintaining the upward mobility of the show-as-product. Even as Lucy's performances transgress the behavioral boundaries of the ideal feminine, Landay notes, the program reinserts her performances within a commercially motivated (and consequently status quo) space:

> The series seems to offer consumption as the solution to Lucy's dissatisfaction, an example of the consumerist-therapeutic ethos that presented private solutions to public problems. Week after week, I Love Lucy endorsed the processes of mass consumer culture. From Lucille Ball and Desi Arnaz clothing, furniture, and nursery items to Lucy and Ricky dolls, record albums, and comic books, I Love Lucy spawned a widening circle of commodification. (176)

Lucille Ball also engaged in overt endorsements on the show when smoking the cigarettes of the show's sponsor, Philip Morris, and driving the 1955 Pontiac that was a product-placement deal with General Motors. What then results from the television series is a complicated set of identities; the lines between the public and private are blurred, but both are identified by a common role in constantly reproducing consumer desire.

What does it mean, then, that the monetary provider for this consumer fantasy is not a conventional Anglo-Saxon television father? An anomaly in domestic comedy programming, Arnaz's character on the show constantly shifts among several representative identities: the good husband (according to Middle American standards), the clown, and the exotic. In his more "serious" role as husband, Ricky enacts a patriarchal rule that serves to contain Lucy's urges to be other than a housewife. His role is to counteract her ventures outward by attempting to enforce her obedience within the domestic space. This is even more apparent after she becomes a mother, when Ricky often comments that he thinks she should be content with a baby and should no longer desire fame.[7] What makes Ricky a "good American husband," though, is not just his patriarchal rule, but the material goods with which he rewards or forgives Lucy. By the end of most episodes, Ricky relents and buys her the fur stole or the new washing machine she has been wanting. In this sense, he functions as an ideal material provider, rewarding Lucy each time she reinserts herself into the domestic space.

Ricky's ethnicity is many times rendered of secondary importance to his role as a good husband. When, however, ethnic identity is particularly emphasized in the script, he literally *performs* ethnicity in isolated moments of an episode, either as the exotic (a romantic Latin balladeer at his fashionable nightclub, Don Juan on a Hollywood movie set); or as a clown, when Lucy's antics push his temper to the point that he is only able to roll his eyes and scream in seemingly incoherent Spanish. These moments are often his most comedic, his native language a joke to both audience and cast members. Ironically, these stereotypical moments also reveal the marketability of Ricky's ethnicity, because his character is unique within the television landscape. Karen Christian describes Desi Arnaz's career as a type of "media invention" that allowed Americans to view Cubans as racially white and disregard the varieties of ethnicity and race in Cuba. Arnaz's popularity in the United States, Christian continues, "is evidence of the commodification of the exotic, of the ethnic Other," and with this commodification grew Americans' appetite for the "spectacle" of ethnicity performed in easily identifiable excesses (*Show and Tell* 60).

That Ricky Ricardo's episodes of anger are usually played out in a language other than English is telling, as this behavior undermines that of the level-headed father figure embodied in such television icons as Ward Cleaver (*Leave It to Beaver*) and Jim Anderson (*Father Knows Best*). In the end, though, the influence of Ricky's gender certainly outweighs the influence of his ethnicity within the home. After all, Lucy is never expected to "learn" the other culture in the household, but rather learns to tolerate Ricky's Cuban-ness as one would learn to overlook a spouse's idiosyncrasies. The issue of language exemplifies this, as Lucy never learns one word of Spanish in their years of marriage, while often mimicking his accent and mocking his temperament for comic effect. For example, in "Lucy's Mother-in-Law," she convinces a Spanish speaker to feed her lines through a transmitter while conversing with Ricky's mother because Lucy has not learned Spanish before the visit (11 Nov. 1954). Of course, the plan falls apart, and Lucy ends up bumbling through the visit with made-up Spanish and pantomime. While Lucy looks the fool in this episode, the comedy derives from mocking her husband's native language. Conversely, "Lucy Hires an English Tutor" centers on an elocution expert to tutor Ricky so that his imperfect English will not be a "bad influence" on their expected baby, an act that essentially asserts American whiteness in the household and ignores the mixed ethnicities of the child (12 Dec. 1952). In much the same way that Herman Gray describes black representation on television working within "boundaries of middle-class patriarchal discourse about 'whiteness'" (9), Ricky's Cuban-ness basically serves as an entertaining tangent in a narrative that is ultimately about the rise and entrenchment of the white, middle-class American family.

The Politics of Window Shopping

If we were to take the product-filled, always happy image of the *I Love Lucy* series back to the lab where it was processed and doctored, we might find a photo negative on the floor, one that possesses only the vaguest resemblance to what appears on television. That vague impression translates elsewhere into the dream of eighteen-year-old Maud Martha, about to head out on her own in the world carrying a symbol of what she wants to pursue:

Maud Martha loved it when her magazines said "New York," described "good" objects there, recalled fine talk, the bristling or the creamy or the tactfully shimmering ways of life. They showed pictures of rooms with wood paneling, softly glowing. . . . There were ferns in these rooms, and Chinese boxes; bits of dreamlike crystal; a taste of leather. . . . Her whole body became a hunger, she would pore over these pages. (48)

In these magazine-inspired daydreams, she defines her entry into adulthood by the acquisition of luxurious material goods. The desire for these objects—this lifestyle—is termed "a hunger," implying not only the desire to possess, but a desire that, if fulfilled, could sustain one completely.

This desire for living high culture is one shared by the pre-suburban Lucy of the show's early years, as she occasionally attempts to emulate the WASP echelon of New York society by, for example, taking etiquette lessons ("Charm School," 25 Jan. 1954). Richard Polenberg notes that the rhetoric of upward mobility, touted as an innate characteristic of democracy, permeated the social fabric of postwar America. Books like *Social Class in America* (1949) and magazine essays on the issue argued that, while class did exist in America, the categories were not static. Unlike in communist Russia's classless society, these texts argued, Americans were always afforded the opportunity to fulfill their dreams, redefine their lives, and climb the social ladder (Polenberg 103). What these optimistic views overlooked, of course, was that the social forces surrounding race, ethnicity, and gender had a lot to do with the enactment of that "climb," despite one's personal goals and formal training. While Lucy's trajectory does slowly fulfill that goal of social climbing, Maud Martha's experiences run the opposite direction, both by her own doing and for reasons determined by her socioeconomic class—as determined by her husband's lack of career opportunities.

If there is an avoidance of issues of race and ethnicity in the apparent upward mobility of the Ricardos, there is a focused attention on such issues in the limitations for upward mobility faced by Brooks's protagonists. Maud Martha and her husband Paul begin their marriage optimistically, finding a kitchenette apartment that is supposed to be temporary until they save some money. He continues to struggle in the low-paying service industry, however, and the family's prospects worsen until Maud Martha is finally forced to seek employment as a domestic worker:

> There is a pear in my icebox, and one end of rye bread. Except for three Irish potatoes and a cup of flour and the empty Christmas boxes, there is absolutely nothing on my shelf. My husband is laid off. There is newspaper on my kitchen table instead of oilcloth. I can't find a job filing in a hurry. I'll smile at Mrs. Burns-Cooper and hate her just some. (159)

In having to play the stereotypical role, she feels she has reached bottom, not just because of her poverty, but because of her economically motivated subservience to a white woman who represents the very lifestyle to which Maud Martha once aspired. These circumstances make up just one component of the larger narrative in which Maud's fantasies are forcefully challenged by progressively negative encounters with various white women who represent aspects of the upwardly mobile lifestyle.

The first of these encounters occurs well before her employment with Mrs. Burns-Cooper. It involves a cosmetics saleswoman who stops at Maud's neighborhood beauty parlor to sell "Black Beauty" lipstick. While looking through an old *Vogue* magazine, Maud Martha overhears the conversation between the white saleswoman (Miss Ingram) and Sonia Johnson, the shop's African American proprietor. Miss Ingram, wearing a new fur, chats with Sonia after making her sale, candidly remarking, "People think this is a snap job. It ain't. I work like a nigger to make a few pennies" (139). Maud Martha quickly decides she has imagined the derogatory phrase. Later, when she discovers that Miss Ingram had in fact used the expression "work like a nigger," she is as offended by the white woman's racism as she is by Sonia's silence. Critics always note the effect that this obviously racist encounter has upon Maud.[8] More than just hearing the word "nigger" used so lightly, though, the insult cuts deeply precisely because of what the woman represents to her at this stage in the novel: a glamorous example of feminine beauty that Maud Martha is in the process of trying to emulate.

Not coincidentally, the narrative later posits Maud Martha in another site of female economy especially significant to the postwar period: the millinery. In an odd perspectival shift, the narrative in this scene utilizes the shop manager's perspective. On this particular day, the white shopkeeper cannot bring herself to flatter customers, as she is preoccupied with her family crisis, and is thinking about "her daughter . . . gallivanting about with a Greek—a Greek!—not even a Jew, which, though revolting enough, was at least becoming fashionable" (154). She is especially annoyed to have to wait on Maud, who, she imagines, will leave hair oil on all the hats she tries on. As the episode culminates, Maud Martha finally haggles the annoyed manager into lowering the price of a hat, then calmly states that she has decided not to buy it. As Maud Martha exits, leaving the shopkeeper in a rage, one cannot help but see this moment as a small triumph for the protagonist. This triumph, though, is not a simple one, as the contemporary social significance of women's hats complicates the reading of this chapter. Karal Ann Marling notes that, in the early years of the decade, when Mamie Eisenhower was the barometer for mid-American fashion sense, "the hat was the ultimate mark of feminine empowerment" (23). The fashionable hat was a mark of status, since it served no practical function: "too small and delicate to shield the head from the elements, but visually obtrusive and subject to radical seasonal change." It also became a sign of willing participation in "America's vibrant new consumer culture" after the war because the possession of a hat signified participation within a market that offered an increased number of seemingly high-fashion items through the technology of mass production (Marling 21).[9]

In such a context, where hats signify social standing and a willingness to participate in a unified consumerist notion of the feminine, what does Maud Martha's decision to *not* buy the hat mean? Is her small triumph displaced by the fact that she is ultimately hatless and, therefore, "disempowered"? Her behavior has allowed the milliner to embrace and enhance her own racist assumptions about "these nigger women who [try] on every hat" (155). On the other hand, Maud Martha's choosing not to buy serves as a direct critique of conspicuous consumption. This scene marks a turning point in the narrative because it signals Maud Martha's willing abandonment of her previous fantasy of "the creamy or tactfully shimmering" life achievable through the acquisition of unnecessary goods. Moreover, in a world where "a woman becomes what her hat means to the world and to herself,"¹⁰ Maud Martha is deliberately denying this mark of "femininity" as one that can signify what she "means to the world and to herself."

The small awakenings that occur for Maud Martha in the previous encounters are what allow her to spend no more than one day as a well-paid employee of Mrs. Burns-Cooper, for whose lifestyle she has lost all admiration. This is evident in the narrative, when, to prove that she is "not a snob," Mrs. Burns-Cooper chats "at" Maud Martha while she works. The passage appears not as a dialogue, but as a litany of signifiers of wealth:

> In my college days. At the time of my debut. The imported lace on my lingerie. My brother's rich wife's Stradivarius. When I was in Madrid. The charm of the Nile. Cost fifty dollars. Cost one hundred dollars. Cost one thousand dollars. (161)

In the face of this inventory, Maud Martha realizes how useless it would be to try to explain to Mrs. Burns-Cooper the significance of "[her] own social triumphs, [her] own education, [her] travels to Gary and Milwaukee and Columbus, Ohio" (161), because they are not the kinds of mobility (like Lucy's) validated within mainstream culture. Moreover, she seems to realize that her being the employee allows Mrs. Burns-Cooper to use Maud Martha as a signifier of her own social status. Her interaction with the white woman forces Maud Martha to acknowledge the ideological accessories and classist attitudes that almost always accompany such ownership. While embracing these attitudes, for Lucy, would signify an improvement in social status, Maud Martha realizes that to do so would further devalue her own existence. She can own some of the signifiers of status, but can never occupy the status itself because she lacks the white privilege into which Mrs. Burns-Cooper and Lucy were born. Racial signifiers keep Maud Martha from occupying the arena in which such status symbols are assigned their value.

Maud Martha knows there is no point in trying to explain her quitting to the employer; the only way she can articulate it to herself is as a metaphor of escape from execution:

> One walked out from that almost perfect wall, spitting at the firing squad. What difference did it make whether the firing squad under-

stood or did not understand the manner of one's retaliation or why one had to retaliate? Why, one was a human being. One wore clean night-gowns. One loved one's baby. One drank cocoa by the fire—or the gas range—come the evening in wintertime. (163)

In her small social triumphs, always interiorized, it is important to note that Maud Martha does not speak out her anger or her pride. Though some critics have expressed disappointment in the character's silence, Mary Helen Washington defends it: "That disappointment ignores the novel's insistence that we read Maud's life in tone, in images, and in ges-tures" ("'Taming'" 465). Similarly, Maud Martha's rationale for quitting her job could be seen as "disappointing" not only because it remains interior, but because she does not use the pronoun "I," weakening the self-empowerment of her decision by not stating "*I* am a human being." Yet, if we read the "gestures" in her rationale, she places the insistence for humanity beyond just her own process of discovery. Maud Martha's semantic weight could translate into something like, "Why, a black woman is a human being. A black woman loves her own baby—more than she loves the babies of the white woman she works for." In the expansiveness of her rationale lies a potential for a larger reading of the novel to see beyond the exterior of any seemingly two-dimensional "Beu-lah" figure.

It is Maud Martha's love for her child that finally does cause her to speak out against an act of racism toward the end of the book. Where she may have remained silent for herself, "taming her anger down," she cannot do so when she sees her daughter being conditioned for self-hatred. Notably, the scene occurs at Macy's before Christmas, the famous temple of consumerism at the most consumer-frenzied time of year. While the department store Santa Claus delights in the white chil-dren, "push[ing] out plump ho-ho-ho's!" and patting their cheeks, Maud Martha's daughter Paulette elicits an obviously different response: "At her appearance, Santa Claus rubbed his palms together and looked vaguely out across the Toy Department. He was unable to see either mother or child" (173). When he does not acknowledge Paulette's requests for toys, Maud Martha calmly speaks out, "'Mister . . . my lit-tle girl is talking to you'" (173). She then forces him to go through with the routine, if only minimally. Of course, the damage has been done, and Paulette is convinced that Santa does not like her. Maud Martha finds herself wanting "to jerk trimming scissors from purse and jab jab jab that evading eye" (175). This desire for violent retribution functions as the climax to the various racist confrontations in a culture that has been revealed as validating consumer identities while simultaneously denigrating differences among consumers.

The episodes that comprise the gradual debunking of Maud Martha's consumer fantasy, and her coming into self awareness, make up the backbone of the narrative. In the novel's closing scene, we find Maud Martha on a spring day, outside with her daughter after learning of the end of World War II and of her second pregnancy. She is newly free of her anger after sloughing off her previous desires. As she takes in the landscape and activities of her neighborhood, she finds the same satisfaction in the mundane that she had as a child, when she thought dandelions were the best flowers to be found, "their demure prettiness second only to their everydayness; for in that latter quality she thought she saw a picture of herself, and it was comforting to find that what was common could also be a flower" (92). Here, she does allow an object to signify her, because, unlike with the hat, to do so requires no purchase—nothing but validation of the self.

Here, too, Maud Martha for the first time overtly acknowledges the current events outside of her own domestic space and unfulfilled desires: wars, lynchings, divorces, evictions, and taxes. She seems to find an odd satisfaction in acknowledging these unhappy events, as they make up the real texture of human experience. In the everyday world she finds perhaps what Cornel West defines as real "joy," that which encompasses "those non-market values—love, care, kindness, service, solidarity, the struggle for justice" (86). The last line of the novel, "The weather was bidding her bon voyage," indicates that the end of the book is the real beginning of her life, as, like the protagonist of *Invisible Man* getting ready to come out of hibernation in the novel's epilogue, she has understood the costs of performing mainstream cultural citizenship and will now opt to live by her own codes.[11] The "bon voyage" signals a metaphorical journey, one that is no longer defined by her previous desires; it is a voyage that is non-physical, non-commercial, non-exploitative.

While this ghetto pastoral does not end with a small people's revolution or a political manifesto, as do some of its Depression-era forebears, *Maud Martha* is no less political than its 1930s counterparts. As John Fiske argues about television narratives, the "interiority" of a narrative does not necessarily render it powerless. Instead, "fantasy" can become a realm of agency for those who are not able to engage in active public resistance (318). In the case of a novel, the lyrical use of language and narrative contemplations serve the same purpose as subversive fantasy. Never an overtly political character, Maud Martha decides at a very early age that her great contribution to the world is simply herself: "What she wanted was to donate to the world a good Maud Martha. That was the offering, the bit of art, that could not come from any other" (22). She cannot understand the desire for public attention, which causes people to "exhibit their precious private identities; shake themselves about; be very foolish for a thousand eyes" (21). What she realizes is that, on a smaller level, engaging in the cultural citizenship defined within the consumer context is a kind of forfeit of her "precious private identity." The narrative, then, portrays Maud in the process of "polishing and honing" herself in a very private way. The actual book allows that private process to become public before a contemporaneous audience that, like the Macy's Santa, might be "unable to see either mother or child."

Displaying private identities was exactly what the public medium of television was all about in the 1950s. By making private family identities public fodder, the public personae contributed to the reshaping of private lives of millions of viewers according to newly emerging values. And while novels of all types do offer private lives to the public, they do so in a way that arguably encourages more introspection on the part of the audience. Lucille Ball and Desi Arnaz certainly did "shake themselves about" for money. Despite the value systems *I Love Lucy* endorsed, however, the history of the series does reveal progressive elements for the representations of postwar women. Most notably, Lucille Ball was the one of the most powerful women in Hollywood, the co-owner of Desi-Lu productions, and she was the first woman ever to appear pregnant on television— after a good deal of controversy and threatened censorship.

Despite the potential for scandal, the Ricardo baby's birth is represented in a way that celebrates Lucy's "production" within the postwar feminine economy. Unfortunately, to do so, "Lucy Goes to the Hospital" employs a problematic representation of race in order to deflect from the "impropriety" that would have been going on in the delivery room. Indeed, the scandalous suggestion of a woman's labor is figuratively censored by racist play within the hospital waiting room while Lucy is hidden from sight. Ricky, in the middle of a "voodoo"-themed show for his nightclub, rushes back to the hospital dressed as a witch doctor. He is, essentially, in blackface, with huge barred teeth painted across his mouth, wearing a grass skirt and a fright wig. What proceeds is a comedy of errors in which Ricky scares the nurse, who calls the police, and so on. The uproar keeps Ricky in trouble and at the center of attention to distract the audience from the idea of birth that is occurring somewhere out of scene. On another level, this clowning within the spectacle of another ethnicity also serves to deflect Ricky's own ethnicity and, perhaps, the mixed ethnicity of the baby. Eventually, Ricky's identity is verified for the police by the Mertzes, and the episode ends with Ricky gazing at the baby through the nursery window. What one remembers of this episode, though, is less the joy of birth or the progressive act of representing a birth on television, but mostly the dominating image of Ricky in freakish blackface. The racist play contributes to the sense of uproarious joy accompanying the birth of Little Ricky/Desi Jr., resulting, essentially, in a sort of celebration of racism and a validation of the ethnically homogenizing forces at work within the Ricardo/Arnaz family.

Unlike Ricky's prime-time moment, Maud Martha's husband Paul meets his newborn child with a fear that the child is stillborn—the antithesis of the "coo" from an adoring audience. When he first sees the newborn child, it appears "gray and greasy," and the first words out of his mouth are, "It's dead, isn't it?" (97). Almost simultaneous to Lucy's sanitized birth appear the grim details of Maud Martha's labor:

> Presently she felt as though her whole body were having a bowel movement. The head came. Then, with a little difficulty, the wide shoulders. Then, easily, with a soft and slippery smoothness, out slipped the rest of the body and the baby was born. (96)

This graphic, naturalistically represented birth occurs within the tenement building, where "gray" pervades the imagery, where Maud Martha's "bloodcurdling scream[s]" are heard throughout the building and on the street below. The scene is stressful, chaotic, and Maud Martha's own mother is nauseated by the episode. In the act of birth, Maud Martha's and Lucy's bodies become the sites of cultural reproduction, and each body works as a signifier of womanhood and how womanhood is being deployed within the larger American culture. As Lauren Berlant argues, the body functions as the most basic vehicle or obstacle within the social order, and how the body is raced and gendered has everything to do with one's "cultural legitimacy" (114). While the production of Lucy's child instigates celebration, Maud's labor goes uncelebrated. Maud's labor—the production of a black child into the postwar cultural economy—seems truly devalued by anyone but herself.

But what does it mean that during birth Lucy's body is rendered invisible, while Maud Martha's stays firmly in frame? Perhaps, in the end, Maud Martha's presence, her conscious labor without medical intervention, provides her some measure of agency within her cultural production. While Lucy is off-screen, Maud Martha asserts herself and her labor through her screams and a birth that seeks to hide nothing from the witnesses present; while other characters dominate the narrative of Lucy's labor, Maud Martha's perspective dominates her own labor. Such elements within these contemporaneous birth scenes highlight how they function as the pivots around which the larger questions of female identity and cultural participation are explored within the two texts. Ultimately, the coexistence of these narratives complicates our reading of each, and *I Love Lucy*'s nostalgic veneer and the iconic notions it represents are successfully smudged by the presence of *Maud Martha*.

Notes

1. I am reading the *I Love Lucy* series as a cohesive narrative rather than as a set of unrelated episodes. The series ran from 1951 to 1957.

2. For an in-depth discussion of the television's impact upon the physical domestic space, see Spigel, "Installing the Television Set."

3. Spigel's work asserts agency where more extreme Marxist theories, such as those of Max Horkheimer and Theodor Adorno ("The Culture Industry"), do not.

4. Programming that featured African Americans in either starring or incidental roles was increasingly governed by the politics of consumerism, as was the case with the cancellation of *The Nat King Cole Show*, the produc-

ers of which were unable to keep a national commercial sponsor because of consumer complaints from southern states. See MacDonald, "The Promise Denied," in *Blacks and White TV*, 1–64; Riggs, *Color Adjustment*; and Dates and Barlow, *Split Image*.

5. The viewer number is that given by the series producer, Jess Oppenheimer (*Laughs, Luck . . . and Lucy* 3).

6. For a detailed account of Lucille Ball's repackaging for television, see Doty, "The Cabinet of Lucy Ricardo."

7. This proves true while she is pregnant, as in "Lucy's Show Biz Swan Song" (22 December 1952), and after the baby's birth. See Landay's analysis of "The Indian Show," in which Lucy incorporates motherhood into an Indian-with-papoose act ("Liminal Lucy" 190).

8. Noteworthy criticism includes: Lattin and Lattin's study of the novel within the African American canon ("Dual Vision"); Christian's examination of the novel within the context of African American women's writing ("Nuance and Novella"); and Washington's study of the book in the *bildungsroman* tradition ("Plain, Black").

9. Indeed, more than one episode of *I Love Lucy* centers on the social functions of hats. Ricky often ridicules Lucy's new hats, or scolds her for spending more money on hats when she already has dozens. Her defense is always that her other hats are old and "out of style." For example, "Ricky Loses his Temper" (22 Feb. 1954) centers on a bet to see whether Lucy can go longer without buying a hat than Ricky can go without losing his temper. If she wins, she gets the hat, so she spends the next days purposely trying to make Ricky angry by throwing the domestic routine into chaos. Of course, she gets the hat by the end of the episode.

10. Sally Victor, a mid-century milliner (qtd. in Marling 32).

11. "I'm shaking off the old skin and I'll leave it here in the hole. I'm coming out, no less invisible without it, but coming out nevertheless. And I suppose it's damn well time. Even hibernations can be overdone, come to think of it. Perhaps that's my greatest social crime. I've overstayed my hibernation, since there's a possibility that even an invisible man has a socially responsible role to play" (Ellison, *Invisible Man* 581).

Works Cited

Berlant, Lauren. "National Brands/National Body: *Imitation of Life*." *Comparative American Identities: Race, Sex, and Nationality in the Modern Text*. Ed. Hortense Spillers. New York: Routledge, 1991. 110–40.

Brooks, Gwendolyn. *Maud Martha*. New York: Harper, 1953.

Christian, Barbara. "Nuance and Novella: A Study of Gwendoyln Brooks's *Maud Martha*." *A Life Distilled: Gwendolyn Brooks, Her Poetry and Fiction*. Ed. Maria K. Mootry and Gary Smith. Urbana: University Illinois Press, 1987. 239–53.

Christian, Karen. *Show and Tell: Identity as Performance in U.S. Latino/a Fiction*. Albuquerque: University of New Mexico Press, 1997.

Dates, Jannette L., and William Barlow, eds. *Split Image: African Americans in the Mass Media*, 2nd ed. Washington, D.C.: Howard University Press, 1993.

Denning, Michael. "'The Tenement Thinking': Ghetto Pastorals." *The Cultural Front: The Laboring of American Culture in the Twentieth Century*. New York: Verso, 1996. 230–53.

Doty, Alexander. "The Cabinet of Lucy Ricardo: Lucille Ball's Star Image." *Cinema Journal* 29 (1990): 3–22.

Ellison, Ralph. *Invisible Man*. 1947. New York: Vintage, 1995.

Fiske, John. *Television Culture*. New York: Methuen, 1987.

Gray, Herman. *Watching Race: Television and the Struggle for "Blackness."* Minneapolis: University of Minnesota Press, 1995.

Horkheimer, Max, and Theodor Adorno. "The Culture Industry: Enlightenment as Mass Deception." *Dialectic of Enlightenment*. 1944. Trans. John Cumming. New York: Herder and Herder, 1972. 120–67.

Landay, Lori. "Liminal Lucy: Covert Power, Television, and Postwar Domestic Ideology." *Madcaps, Screwballs, and Con Women: The Female Trickster in American Culture*. Philadelphia: University of Pennsylvania Press, 1998. 155–96.

Lattin, Patricia H., and Vernon E. Lattin. "Dual Vision in Gwendolyn Brooks's *Maud Martha*." *Critique* 25.4 (1984): 180–88.

Lhamon, W. T., Jr. *Deliberate Speed: The Origins of a Cultural Style in the American 1950s*. Washington, D.C.: Smithsonian, 1990.

Lipsitz, George. "The Meaning of Memory: Family, Class, and Ethnicity in Early Network Television." *Time Passages: Collective Memory and the American Popular Culture*. Minneapolis: University of Minnesota Press, 1990. 39–75.

MacDonald, J. Fred. *Blacks and White TV: Afro-Americans in Television Since 1948*. Chicago: Nelson-Hall, 1983.

Marling, Karal Ann. "Mamie Eisenhower's New Look." *As Seen on Television: The Visual Culture of Everyday Life in the 1950s*. Cambridge, MA: Harvard University Press, 1994. 8–49.

May, Elaine Tyler. *Homeward Bound: American Families in the Cold War Era.* New York: Basic Books, 1988.

Ohmann, Richard. "Charting Social Space." *Selling Culture: Magazines, Markets, and Class at the Turn of the Century.* New York: Verso, 1996. 219–286.

Oppenheimer, Jess, and Gregg Oppenheimer. *Laughs, Luck . . . and Lucy: How I Came to Create the Most Popular Sitcom of All Time.* Syracuse, NY: Syracuse University Press, 1996.

Polenberg, Richard. *One Nation Divisible: Class, Race, and Ethnicity in the United States Since 1938.* New York: Viking, 1980.

Riggs, Marlon T., dir. *Color Adjustment.* Signifyin' Works, 1991.

Spigel, Lynn. "Installing the Television Set: Popular Discourses on Television and Domestic Space, 1948–1955." *Private Screenings: Television and the Female Consumer.* Ed. Lynn Spigel and Denise Mann. Minneapolis: University Minnesota Press, 1992. 3–38.

———. *Make Room for TV: Television and the Family Ideal in Postwar America.* Chicago: University of Chicago Press, 1992.

Washington, Mary Helen. "Plain, Black, and Decently Wild: The Heroic Possibilities of *Maud Martha.*" *The Voyage In: Fictions of Female Development.* Ed. Elizabeth Abel, et al. Hanover, NH: University Press New England, 1983. 270–86.

———. "'Taming All That Anger Down': Rage and Silence in Gwendolyn Brooks's *Maud Martha.*" *Massachusetts Review* 24.2 (1983): 453–66.

West, Cornel. "Discussion." *Black Popular Culture.* Ed. Michele Wallace and Gina Dent. New York: New Press, 1998. 85–91.

III

Re-Considering Race and Ethnicity:
Meta-Issues in Theory and Criticism

10 Some Do, Some Don't

Whiteness Theory and the Treatment of Race in African American Drama

WILLIAM OVER

ECENT ATTEMPTS WITHIN ACADEME TO DECEN-
ter whiteness have most often enlisted ontological language
and categories of identity for the purpose of implicating those
cultural pathologies that have sustained white power and ideology. A common extension of whiteness discourse involves the critique of
universalizing classifications that marginalize and oppose otherness and
imply oppositional arrangements. Such expositions, especially prominent in what has come to be identified as "first generation" or "first wave"
whiteness writing, typically posited European identity as the earliest, that
is, the primary human identity.[1] The result has been an essentialized
whiteness placed uncomfortably within a historically developed view of
hegemony. Hence, the underpinnings of white culture that must be
exposed to critique—presumably in order to change them—are nevertheless unalterable by virtue of their totalizing and monolithic nature.
Exposing the hegemonic agendas of whiteness becomes a pointless task,
since whiteness is defined in absolutist and universal terms.

In this vein, theorists of whiteness often reify the white person as
"offering a discourse of hegemony," wherein the unintended consequence always remains one of the maintenance of power and the cen-

tering of white cultural and political structures (for example, Craft, Clark, and Rowe). By contrast, the representation of white characters in African American drama is by no means so monolithic, nor its discourse so monotonic. The stereotyping of racial identities by black American playwrights was frequently exaggerated by critics and reviewers during the 1960s and 1970s, when attempts were made to dismiss African American political voices by focusing on the tendentious messages of these plays. However, playwrights such as James Baldwin, Lorraine Hansberry, Alice Childress, and Charles Fuller—and filmmaker Spike Lee, more recently—sought to present well-rounded white characters in realistic circumstances without sacrificing political statement and social relevance. Such writers recognized, perhaps better than anyone either at the time or through subsequent decades of racial theorizing, that the reified division of racial identities must give way to a genuinely historical and dialectical approach to the representation of race. They knew that racial groupings in American culture shared identities on different levels and, more importantly, were culturally and economically interdependent, not hermetically divided. Blacks and whites demonstrated an interrelatedness that typically maintained hierarchical arrangements, but they also occasionally sought to move beyond such oppositional stances. These and other African American playwrights left open opportunities for progressive change beyond unalterable, monolithic views of race. Such realistic, more developed character portraits effectively serve the end of political transformation, while the use of stereotypes common in other texts remain polemical and uphold traditionally divisive categorizations.

These depictions of race are of particular importance today, in a context in which "difference" is often prized over universality. Postcolonial and postmodern theorists have looked more closely at racial signifiers to attempt a nuanced understanding of the dynamics of racial categorizations, social identities, and power relations. In *The Location of Culture* (1994), for example, Homi Bhabha speaks of the inherent ambivalences of the colonialist perspective, which derive from the basic ambiguity of the colonizing project (85–92). Fredric Jameson observes that, in the context of "late capitalism," the "tolerance of difference" today is merely the result of a greater homogenization and "a new and more fundamental identity" (341, 357). Brought about by the increasing globalization of capital and culture, this new power arrangement may use difference for its own ends while ignoring the universality underlying twentieth-century human rights agendas.

Whiteness theory, although purporting to decenter whiteness in cultural discourse, often recenters whiteness through its use of absolutist notions of white intentionality. Placing white intentionality at the center always keeps the center white. But again, African American drama, reaching as far back as Brown's New York African Theatre in 1821, has consistently demonstrated a willingness to engage in interracial themes and settings that by no means assume historically determined outcomes or fixed modes of discourse. Besides oppositional racial positions, its playwrights have often sought an integrative interracial dialogue that holds the promise of positive social change. Contemporary theories of whiteness need to approach definitional frameworks from a similar pragmatic perspective, one that enables progressive social change rather than maintains overgeneralized categories of race and power. Regardless of the motivations of their theorists, theories of whiteness tend toward overdetermined, hierarchical arrangements that do not envision productive change through interracial and cross-cultural engagement, and thus resonate uncomfortably with racial stereotyping that film and theatre have practiced down to the present.

I will discuss plays by well-known African American playwrights that depict open-ended interracial possibilities rather than singular white perspectives, and that demonstrate the complexities of black/white relationships where the maintenance of power remains only one possibility. First, however, I wish to explore more fully the direction of whiteness discourse to better understand in social context both its present limitations and its possible enlistment for the project of cultural inclusiveness.

Recent Turns in Whiteness Theory

Perceiving the totalizing effects of much whiteness theory of the late 1980s to the mid-1990s, Henry A. Giroux has called for a rearticulation of the definition of whiteness within the movement to which he remains dedicated; this would involve a deeper sensitivity to the pedagogical effects of such discourse as it inspires political agency. Often enclosing the noun whiteness in quotation marks, Giroux remains skeptical about the pragmatic value of defining whiteness in negative terms. His notion that whiteness discourse needs to distinguish between positive "antiracist" and negative "racist" aspects of whiteness in order to establish a ground for political agency and cooperation with other groups is in part derived from Ruth Frankenberg (7). By recognizing types of whiteness, Giroux begins to break down this monolithic category. However, one could take the next positive step and suggest that whiteness discourse needs to avoid deterministic or essentialist definitional language altogether, a direction that would encourage white people to seek antiracist solutions without demanding the rejection of their own social and cultural identities for the sake of a deterministic understanding of white hegemony.

Whiteness studies scholars might profitably draw on Stuart Hall's anti-essentialist model of racial identity, for Hall places "ethnicity" within a historical, and therefore developmental, context and thereby avoids determinist, transhistorical definitions of race. Termed "the new ethnicity," this model understands "the place of history, language, and culture in the construction of subjectivity and identity, as well as the fact that all discourse is placed, positioned, situated, and all knowledge is contextual" (29). As such, the new ethnicity perceives racial identities as complex instead of one-dimensional and changeless, as permeable instead of hermetically sealed.

The historicizing of whiteness keeps open the possibility of a diachronic change over time within racial identities, while at the same time allowing for a synchronic understanding of levels of identity within the individual. In the latter sense, white individuals can perceive their identities as multifaceted, comprised of positive aspects that may be enlisted to overcome dominant structures of thought and practice within Western culture. Such openness was not usually apparent to first-wave whiteness theorists, who utilized the abstraction "whiteness" in part as a replacement for "white racism," a phrase possessing too much emotional resonance in American culture to withstand the new levels of discourse hoped for by the incipient movement. While "first-wave" whiteness theorists were certainly concerned with theorizing racism, they also hoped to theorize other aspects of white identity, and did not want to close down debate by using too potentially inflamatory a phrase. A similar move has characterized conversations about race outside of the academy. We have only to note, for instance, the substitution of "racial events" for "racism" among prominent officials and speech writers of

the Clinton Administration to find confirmation of this judgment. However, as we have seen, the choice "whiteness" has come with baggage of
its own, not so much emotional as reifying and totalizing.

Definitions of whiteness have usually centered on social and political formulas that present a rhetorical position. Thus whiteness is short
for "the discourse of whiteness," which is perceived in terms of the perpetuation of power. Daniel Bernardi's definition is drawn from recent
scholarship: "The discourse of whiteness refers to the persistence of racial
hierarchies that, in the United States, have systematically privileged those
who count as white—generally European Americans—at the expense
of those who do not count as white—generally non-European Americans" (104). In this passage, whiteness seems to be for Bernardi a sustained, transhistorical position of dominance within society. In the
same article, however, his definition shifts to accomodate a more flexi-
ble historical version of whiteness: "a representational and narrative
construction with identifiable properties and a specific history" (107).
Bernardi's shifting definition of whiteness is typical of its nonspecific
usage in current theory, an ambiguity that creates problems when such
a floating term is applied to actual human beings. Fred Pfeil laments
the recent equation of the hegemonic goal of whiteness with white people,
citing examples by journalists after the Oklahoma City bombing, which,
according to *Washington Post* writer Juan Williams, was committed by
"white men in their natural state" (qtd. in Pfeil 22). To this, Pfeil replies,
"such a broad-brush portrait of American white men, or, for that matter, of any gender and/or racial-coded group, is bound to occlude more
than it reveals" (22).

Pfeil rejects the reductive equations of whiteness with white people
as a group, finding instead a wider ground upon which white men in
particular can begin to construct new modes of relationality beyond exclusivity. Such perspectives seek to redefine universal definitions of the
human so as not to exclude any group: a "universal extention of the universal, a universal without a remainder, without an outside," as Warren
Montag has put it (289). These new openings may prevent once and for
all attempts to exclude any group from the human, while appreciating
the commonality of human rights standards and social justice issues
around the world. Culture is here seen as primarily educational and progressive, not static and determined, much the way Matthew Arnold envi-

sioned it in *Culture and Anarchy* (1869). For Arnold, culture remained an exploratory tool for progressive change, not an ontology defining particular originative peoples. A similar outlook appears in African American drama, where black and white characters probe pragmatic rather than definitional views of race. Though these plays describe an earlier cultural and historical moment in the U.S., their message remains current today, providing a particularly useful supplement to studies of whiteness.

White Possibilities in African American Drama

Given her background of political activism, Lorraine Hansberry recognized the potential of drama for political statement. Her father, Carl A. Hansberry, had been chief counsel for the landmark fair housing case before the U.S. Supreme Court, *Hansberry vs. Lee*, in 1943. *A Raisin in the Sun* (1959), her major play, dealt specifically with the problem of housing discrimination in American cities, but her characters were compelling portraits of individuals struggling to maintain dignity and to preserve their family integrity. In the early 1950s, Hansberry developed a political view that emphasized the determining factor of class as much as race. Her choice of a working-class rather than a middle-class African American family for *Raisin* was motivated by the conviction that the working class struggle is "more pertinnent, more relevant, more significant . . . more decisive in our political history and our political future" (Terkel and Hansberry 7–8).

The only white character in *A Raisin in the Sun*, the lawyer Karl Lindner, represented a white protectionist organization, ironically called the Clybourne Park Improvement Association, that sought to exclude the Younger family from its neighborhood. Lindner's motives fit current definitions of whiteness: the maintenance of power structures and economic exclusivity. The play's ending, however, keeps open the possibilities for change as the Younger family members unite to face the certain resistence of the white community. As Walter Younger tells Lindner, "We don't want to make no trouble for nobody or fight no causes, and we will try to be good neighbors" (148). Hansberry leaves the ending deliberately open-ended, not so much unresolved—as some critics at the time charged—as affirming, an outlook that implies the possible change of heart of the white community in Clybourne Park.

Hansberry's other work also depicts complex white characters, capable of emotional and political change. *The Sign in Sidney Brustein's Window* (1964) centers on a white protagonist who, unlike the working class members of Clybourne Park, possesses political awareness but also a cynicism that has prevented him from renewing the social struggle. Sidney Brustein's "whiteness," that is, his willingness to maintain exclusive power, or at least his refusal to fight against it, is, at the beginning of the play, a moral lassitude that has driven him to callous selfishness and a kind of bohemian snobbery in his life-long residency in Greenwich Village.

By the end of the play, however, Sidney's involvement in a local political campaign has rekindled his sense of social justice, and his passive cynicism gives way to a renewed commitment. Pondering the dilemma of radical change in American society—"how does one confront these thousand nameless faceless vapors that are the evil of our time?" (296)—he affirms a Whitmanesque optimism for social and spiritual transformation. He is, in fact, "[a] fool who believes that death is waste and love is sweet and that the earth turns and men change every day and that rivers run and that people wanna be better than they are and that flowers smell good and that I hurt terribly today, and that hurt is desperation and desperation is—energy and energy can—things" (339–40). But Hansberry is careful not to render her white protagonist too naïve for the disillusioning struggle that cannot be easily won: "some of us will be back out in those streets today. Only this time—thanks to you—we shall be more seasoned, more cynical, tougher, harder to fool— and therefore, less likely to quit" (338).

Hansberry's inclusive sense of the struggle for structural change within Western society grounded her view of whiteness. At the important July 1964 forum at Town Hall in New York, "The Black Revolution and the White Backlash," Hansberry expressed what was at the time an unpopular view among many African American activists. Pointing out that many who died in the civil rights struggle were white men, she commented, "I don't think we can decide ultimately on the basis of color. The passion that we express should be understood . . . in that context. We want total identification. It's not a question of reading anybody out; it's a merger . . . but it has to be a merger on the basis of true and genuine equality" (qtd. in Nemiroff 17). Hansberry's concept of merger paralleled her view that drama was a particularized expression of a universal struggle, a movement that was by necessity beyond what has since been termed identity politics. For Hansberry, this commonality gave all races the same mandate: "only . . . when the white liberal becomes an American radical will he be prepared to come to grips with . . . the basic fabric of our society" (qtd. in Nemiroff 24).

Sidney Brustein includes several white characters who are at different stages of political awareness and race consciousness, ranging from the unthinkingly narrow-minded (Mavis) to one (Gloria) who loves a black man (Alton) and hopes he will marry her. Gloria is rejected by Alton when he learns that she has been a street prostitute. She has felt the pain of social disdain and knows its racial signification in American culture: "Do you know what some of the other girls do? They go off and sleep with a colored boy—and I mean—colored boy so long as he is black—because they figure that is the one bastard who can't look down on them five seconds after it's over!" (326). In a long disclosure, Alton confesses to Sidney that he cannot marry a former prostitute because his family never took anything second hand from white people. "I don't want white man's leavings, Sidney. I couldn't *marry* her" (303). Alton, however, is not another version of George Murchison, the black bourgeois character in *Raisin* who thinks only of status and assimilation. Rather, Alton's rejection of Gloria follows from a family pride and political sensibility that rigidifies in the face of interracial commitment. In this, the politically committed Alton shows his hypocrisy, something that he is aware of intellectually but cannot bring himself to overcome. After Gloria's subsequent suicide, Sidney realizes more fully the dangers of compliance with society's structural evils, lamenting, "The slogans of capitulation can *kill!* Every time we say 'live and let live'—death triumphs!" (338). Sidney's choice is to fight a long-time friend who has become part of the New York political machine.

While *Sidney Brustein*'s depiction of a white liberal who learns the wisdom of organized commitment and interracial cooperation as the only means to progressive change received some measure of success in the New York theatre (101 performances at the Longacre Theatre), Hansberry perceived *Les Blancs* as a statement of global commitment and interracial cooperation. The play—its title an ironic reference to Jean Genet's *The Blacks*, which had received much critical attention in early

1960s New York—once again focused upon the exceptions to whiteness as a definition of power equated to white people. As in *Sidney Brustein*, a range of white characters are represented. In *Les Blancs*, however, the races dispute with one another (intra- and interracially) in dramatic dialogue that resurrects the discursive style of Bernard Shaw. Hansberry's most astute dialectic is saved for the conversation between Charlie Morris, a white liberal journalist, and Tshembe Matoseh, an African returned to his homeland after a period of assimilation and interracial marriage in England. Their debate is resumed throughout the play, continuing the tendency of the white and black characters in *Sidney Brustein* (and Shaw) to comment on political agendas without acting upon them.

Charlie is a certain type of white liberal who easily dismisses race as a reality and wants Tshembe to accept him without the barriers of race. Tshembe, however, knows that race, though only a perception, a consequence of colonialist ideology, has nonetheless become a reality that cannot be dismissed, even in relationships of individual intimacy. Charlie can only be educated by another white man, Dr. Willy DeKoven, who has spent years at the African medical mission and learned the truth of white attitudes towards the colonial subject. "Mr. Morris, the struggle here has not been to push the African into the Twentieth Century—but at all costs to keep him *away* from it! We do not look down on the black because we really think he is lazy, we look down on him because he is wise enough to resent working for us" (152).[2] DeKoven's years in Africa have radicalized him so that he supports the local uprisings that are resuming in earnest. He tells Charlie, "I came here twelve years ago believing that I could—it seems so incredible now—help alleviate suffering by participating actively in the very institutions that help sustain it" (153).

Another European who has rejected the power base of whiteness is Madame Neilsen, wife of the chief missionary doctor, who has long realized that the patronizing approach of her husband (an unseen character that Hansberry may have based on Albert Schweitzer) did not help Africans but instead reinforced the white power structure of colonialism. She encourages Tshembe, whom she helped raise from a small boy, to join the anti-colonial forces of his country, despite her knowledge that the same warriors just killed her husband and other white enforcers. In a particularly lyrical scene, she tells Tshembe, who hesitates choosing between his European and African worlds, "I once taught you that a line goes on into infinity unless it is bisected. Our country needs *warriors*, Tschembe Matoseh. Africa needs warriors. Like your father" (169). Her advice is taken, and she soon dies in crossfire between soldiers and the warriors now led by Tshembe, dressed in his father's robe. As she dies in his arms, Tshembe gives a deep cry of mourning. Earlier, when asked by Madame if he hates whites, his response is a succinct statement of the cooperative pluralism that grounded Hansberry's understanding that racial identity is not static and deterministic, but instead dynamic, offering the promise of change: "Madame, I have seen your mountains. Europe— in spite of all her crimes—has been a great and glorious star in the night. Other stars shone before it—and will again with it. The heavens, as *you* taught me, are broad and can afford a galaxy" (168). Another gesture of interracial promise beyond whiteness is the moment Charlie and Tshembe reach a plateau of agreement and even solidarity as the government helicopters sweep down. Tshembe then takes Charlie's hand and lifts their clasped hands "towards the sky" as the helicopter circles above (164). This theatrical image is powerful in the context of the struggle between the boundary-breaking solidarity of interracial understanding, on the one hand, and the forces of oppression and divisionism, represented by the white Major George Rice, on the other.

For the "merger on the basis of true and genuine equality" that Hansberry urged during the last year of her life at the New York Town Hall forum, white people—as represented by Charlie Morris, Willy Dekoven, and Madame Neilsen—need to begin a journey of understanding and self-critical exploration. Their goal, however, cannot be black and white separatism, which Hansberry recognized to be compliant with the current culture of domiance, but rather the breaking of boundaries that confirm racial identity. While Hansberry's sympathetic reviewers at the time defended her challenge to American and global racism, they ignored her efforts to transcend determinist definitions of race. Tshembe, becoming the play's *raisonneur*, explains to Charlie that, while race is an illusion, it is a fantasy the horrible consequences of which cannot be ignored.

If Lorraine Hansberry depicted the complexities of race and class in America, her contemporary, Alice Childress, similarly pioneered a drama of social realism that exposed the forbidden in American culture. She won critical acclaim for *Trouble in Mind* (1955 Obie Award), but per-

haps her most complex and moving drama was *Wedding Band* (eventually produced for television in 1973). The latter's depiction of an interracial relationship was ahead of its time in the expression of intimacy
and the interpenetration of cultural forces. Herman and Julia live in the
black section of a Southern city where Herman is tolerated as a white
but looked upon with suspicion. Julia is the subject of gossip by her neighbors and resentment by the men of the community, but she struggles
for dignity in the face of black suspicion, on the one side, and white ran-
cor and hypocrisy on the other. Childress's depiction of strong individuals who successfully overcome social opprobrium and isolation
promotes the themes of nonconformity and boundary-crossing. Herman becomes ill and this forces his family members to confront the interracial relationship. His sister's shock gives way to hostility, even though
she herself wants to leave with a white sailor whom her family has looked
down upon. Childress's paralleling of classism and racism expands the
theme of boundary crossing, but the representation of her white characters breaks new ground in American literature. While Herman's mother
responds contemptuously to his domestic arrangement, she knows
instinctively to cover over the relationship, announcing to Julia's black
landlady, Fanny, that her son was delivering baked goods when his ill-
ness struck. Fanny also knows instinctively to agree without comment,
and the complicity of both women demonstrates the cooperative
nature of cultural segregation. Their mutual hypocrisy succeeds in the
coverup, but Herman dies with Julia at his bedside in a final scene of
social isolation.

The poignancy of Julia and Herman's last moments together remains
a unique expression of interracial bonding in American, and world, literature. The playwright describes Julia's final rejection of the pillars of
her African American community, Fanny and Lula, in a revealing stage
direction: "She is going through that rising process wherein she must
reject them as the molders and dictators of her life" (Wilkerson 132).[3]
The "rising process" of the play brings about a final reconciliation between
the interracial partners, since, unknown to the outside world of black
and white, they themselves have undergone a struggle for acceptance
and understanding within the relationship. As Herman dies, Julia
offers him a compelling image of escape from the narrow limits of their
society, which has harmed each of them profoundly. Her image of their

departure on a passenger oceanliner bound for New York presents the realization of their freedom to love without limits, a freedom that has been prevented as much by their own struggle to love across racial lines as by the prejudices of their society: "out to sea . . . on our way . . . yes . . . yes . . . yes" (133). Julia's painful endeavor to accept Herman's unconscious prejudices throughout the years of their relationship eventually leads to Herman's realization that he has internalized the very cultural values that have destroyed his freedom to love.

As the communities of black and white threaten to force their way into their house—Herman's family through the police power that they control, and Fanny by her right as the owner of their house—Julia seeks a final closeness with her beloved by pressing the issue of Herman's contradictory allegiances. His father was a member of a KKK organization, but Herman has been unable to acknowledge the false values his father affirmed:

HERMAN: He never hurt anybody.
JULIA: He hurts me. There's no room for you to love him and me too . . . it can't be done. (129)

Julia then presses Herman to admit that he never condemned white oppression after hearing news of lynchings and discrimination. His response, that he was not personally responsible, was not the point for Julia: "Whenever somebody was lynched . . . you 'n me would eat a very silent supper. It hurt me not to talk . . . what you don't say you swallow down." Herman's response, "I was just glad to close the door 'gainst what's out there. You did all the givin' . . . I failed you in every way" (130), reveals his longstanding denial of the fact that their relationship could not exclude social reality, no matter how much their love revealed the basic lie of that reality. Before Herman dies, both achieve a newfound closeness as Herman confronts the false values of his upbringing, a realization that allows him to accept Julia's love unconditionally.

Representing the intimacy of an interracial relation, where power is more evenly based and discourse between the partners more negotiable than in the social sphere, allows Childress to explore white perspectives in an alternative space. Significantly, Annabelle, Herman's sister, secretly listens from the outside window during the deathbed conversation

between Julia and Herman. Her curiosity over interracial intimacy perhaps foreshadows the enlistment of great numbers of whites into the
civil rights movement of the late 1950s and 1960s. Annabelle is struggling to break free from social propriety herself, represented by her
mother's refusal to allow her to marry outside their social sphere. The
possibility remains for the sister to follow the brother's path of crossing
boundaries of power, an activity she is somewhat envious of, despite her
initial shock at his refusal to obey racial codes.

Childress presents a white family in various stages of moral and political awareness, but, more importantly, one that is challenged by a situation that demands the surrender of long held presumptions of power
and status. Herman's realization that his own tribal allegiances have hurt
the person he loves the most parallels Charlie Morris's understanding
that race is an illusion that nonetheless matters. His acceptance of the
inevitability of Tshembe's struggle allows both men to begin a friendship
they sought but could heretofore not achieve. Herman's full acceptance
of Julia comes only when their relationship is revealed to his family, a
circumstance that forces a choice between the ethic of white power and
his own urge toward inclusiveness.

In their work Hansberry and Childress wished to explore territories
of race beyond the stereotypical, which they regarded as overly determined and counterproductive for the new turn that civil rights activism
was prepared to take as the new era of desegregation began. Hansberry
was immediately aware of the limitations of *Raisin* soon after its New
York opening. For her, the play, though powerful and popular, relied too
much upon conventional representations of race to brings its audiences
into a new era of social consciousness. Ben Keppel has observed that
what Hansberry called her audience's "prior attitudes" were not overcome by the play: "In seeing through these screens, uncomfortable audiences could ignore representations too far afield from well-worn
stereotypes, and instead fasten onto a superficially familiar theme or plot
device, elevating it to the play's center" (181). In the early 1960s, Hansberry was ready for a more focused exploration beyond socially coded
racial identities. Accordingly, her later plays focused more on white identities and the dialectic between black and white, as she realized that
whites themselves must change their preconceptions—and hence
their identities—for the new era of social transformation.

By the early 1960s, Hansberry may have been familiar with Brecht's Epic Theatre technique, but whether or not she was familiar with his work, her disappointment with *Raisin's* reception mirrored Brecht's own disappointment with the popular theatre of his day. Brecht in his own way wished to overcome Hansberry's dilemma, the "prior attitudes" of the audience. For Brecht, only drama that could "make strange" through an "alienation effect" (*verfremdungseffekt*) would force the audience to look at overly determined social codes in a new light, exposing the invisible of collective denial. Although Brecht had class consciousness foremost in mind, his theatre technique applies most penetratingly to racial categories in twentieth-century America. Only by presenting the unmentionable, the denied, the covered, in a new way—a strange way—could audiences critique their most basic problems. For Hansberry and Childress, that meant above all racial identity. Whites need to be shown how their own identities prevent progressive change, but, even more importantly, both playwrights assume that such racial identities have the capacity to be changed from within.

This dual process of recognition and transformation also characterizes the work of James Baldwin. For Baldwin, whites must first be confronted with the inconsistencies and pathologies of their own racial identities before such identities can be changed. But Baldwin's devastating drama, *Blues for Mister Charlie* (1964), also presents a model (however flawed) for white consciousness in the central character of Parnell.

Baldwin's agenda for racial consciousness in the 1960s was to push back deterministic categories of race for the sake of an activist and transformative outlook. Hence, he shared a similar political optimism with Hansberry and perhaps Childress. In Baldwin's notes for *Blues*, a holistic view of human development is presented, an inclusive understanding of race, which, while hardly denying the tremendously negative effects of racial divisionism in American culture, speaks from a commonality of commitment to transcending race identities: "But if it is true, and I believe it is, that all men are brothers, then we have the duty to try to understand this wretched man; and while we probably cannot hope to liberate him, begin working toward the liberation of his children" (*Blues* 243). Baldwin's ironic language is surprising when considering the often pathological treatment of the play's characters and dialogue. More startling still is his suggestion of a shared responsibility—but not collective guilt—for the ethos of the "white man." As with Hansberry and Childress, white identity for Baldwin is not fixated on power in an irrevocable way, but rather is subject to historical development.

Baldwin's white character Parnell provides the clearest example of this potentially mutable notion of whiteness. Juanita, the black friend of Richard, a young black man who was murdered by Lyle, a white store owner, describes Parnell as a dragon slayer in their town. Son of a wealthy businessman, Parnell works for a newspaper that is progressive, nonconformist, and takes risks for causes. He is aware of the compromising position he holds in a community where his peers are white and his friends are black. He tells Juanita, who challenges him on his recent success prosecuting Lyle, "I am not a good man, but I have my little ways" (Baldwin 247). As events unfold, however, he becomes less sure of his ability to keep his promise to bring justice for Richard's murder. To Meridian, Richard's father and the chief black minister in town, Parnell confesses the ambivalence of being white with a conscience: "Please try to understand that it is not so easy to leap over fences, to give things up— all right, to surrender privilege! But if you were among the privileged you would know what I mean. It's not a matter of trying to hold on; the things, the privilege—are part of you, are who you are. It's in the *gut*" (267). Faced with Lyle's assertions of innocence, and pressure from the white community, Parnell begins to retreat from his modest sense of having "his little ways" around the boundaries of black and white. He turns away from his personal standards of nonconformity to associate his identity at least in part with "whiteness." When, during the climactic trial scene, Parnell, on the stand, becomes less certain about the guilt of his boyhood friend Lyle, choosing instead to stress the doubt of circumstances, the Blacktown court audience reacts with dismay. Suspicions are confirmed that all whites in the end close ranks around the maintenance of power.

Baldwin's categorization of Parnell is not so simple, however. Parnell has been capable of deep love for black people. He remains a victim of racial segregation as he laments the unfulfilled love for a local black woman years before. Parnell's soliloquy explores more deeply than ever before the ambivalence of white people toward the racial divisions they have created. For Parnell this perplexity combines the complex ratiocination of an intellectual with overwhelming libidinal imagery: "All your life you've been made sick, stunned, dizzy, oh, Lord! driven half mad by blackness. Blackness in front of your eyes. Boys and girls, men and women—you've bowed down in front of them all! And then hated yourself. Hated yourself for debasing yourself?" (304). Parnell's personal attempts to probe the deeper feelings of race leave him confused and despairing.

After the trial scene, Parnell is given another chance to recover the healing side of his identity when, in the closing dialogue of the play, he approaches Juanita to be included in the organized protest. In response Juanita becomes the reconciler in the play, taking up Parnell's job of civil protest after he seemingly failed the cause of justice in his court testimony. Her willingness to trust her white friend once again—there is an indication in their dialogue that they once had an incipient romantic relationship—parallels Baldwin's own inclusive language in the "Notes For *Blues.*" While whites have failed once again to bring justice and abolish divisionism, their misgivings qualify them for a second chance. Here whiteness is not monolithic reaction, but a determined willingness to continue the struggle despite its (here Parnell's) own failures. By joining the march of protest against the court ruling in the murder case, Parnell reaffirms his commitment to the cause of racial justice, a position incompatible with white power.

Fixing and Unfixing Race

Richard Dyer's seminal analysis of whiteness found that "white power secures its dominance by seeming not to be anything in particular" (44; see also Giroux 15, and Nakayama and Krizek 292–94). Accordng to this trajectory whiteness most often appears as invisible, entailing universalizing notions to which other cultures and races are negatively compared. Whiteness has functioned as a kind of white noise of unnoticed background, which whiteness studies has sought to identify in order to interrogate. However, the increased emphasis on whiteness and other racialized identities in critical theory and in much of applied discourse has once again fixed racial identity, giving support to deterministic notions of human development and relationality. AnnLouise Keating has expressed grave "misgivings" about such tendencies, and she places the noun whiteness in quotation marks (913). She finds that recent definitions

of whiteness that "attempt to deconstruct 'race' often inadvertently reconstruct it by reinforcing the belief in permanent, separate racial categories"
(902). Other theorists have emphasized the impermanence of racial identity, also pointing out the dangers of essentializing characteristics of race:
"Whatever 'whiteness' really means is constituted only through the rhetoric of whiteness. There is no 'true essence' to 'whiteness'; there are only
historically contingent constructions of that social location" (Nakayama
and Krizek 293). Hence, whiteness can only be understood as particular historically determined "discursive strategies that map the field of
whiteness" (303). Keating points out the ease with which her students
conflate "whiteness" with "white" people, some unable to see beyond
highly negative explorations of the latter (908).

In a special issue of *American Quarterly*, George Lipsitz calls for more
commensurate articulations of human identity that overcome the essentialization of whiteness and other racial categories. But Henry Louis Taylor's response to Lipsitz's prescription is a reminder of the power basis
of whiteness: "Unity across the color line has foundered. This happens
because the ideology of whites derives from racial exploitation and
oppression" (404). His solution, however, is not to retreat to the simplistic
binary oppositions into which Keating's students so quickly fall. Rather,
interracial cooperation and black/white unity lies in social planning, which
"promotes the interests of both blacks and whites. This will require stim-
ulating public discourse on the 'real' economic, social, and political issues
affecting blacks, whites, and the entire nation" (404–5). Taylor returns to
the bottom line of all race theory, which is the power base as revealed in
social structures, but affirms the capability of white people to move beyond
the current pathology of whiteness articulated in whiteness theory.

African American literature, represented by the playwrights discussed
here, has not remained content with unchanging binary oppositions;
instead, it has posited the commensurability of interracial relations and
the commonality of black and white identities within the political realities of oppression and exclusivity. Perhaps it is time for whiteness
theory to look back to this earlier work to learn new ways of viewing
whiteness. George C. Wolfe's stage critique of racial stereotypes, *The Colored Museum* (1988), opened the door, if only tentatively, for new conceptions of racial identity. His satire calls for new levels of understanding
in American culture, and criticizes many of the pioneers of the Black

Arts Movement and their predecessors for the unproductive reification of racial categories. However, the 1990s American theatre has not
moved beyond a hermetic monologue that does not question fixations
on race and all-encompassing definitions. In the 1960s and 1970s, Amiri
Baraka's "revolutionary" stagecraft enlisted broad-brushed character
stereotypes (often shocking theatrically but not overtly questioned) in
an attempt to define persistent cultural and institutional attitudes that
perpetuate racial and class power structures. The result often reinforced
traditional racial demarcations without encouraging positive political
alliances. In contrast, other African American dramatists and essayists,
foremost those mentioned here, conceived a project of interracial cooperation by presenting the malleability of racial identities for the realization
of cooperative change. An engaging politicized theatre freed from traditional negativities and dominant racial definitions offers the possibility
of new political alliances and strategies. This undertaking can build upon
the perceptions of earlier African American playwrights as they have
sought to engage white and black characters in deeper understandings
of themselves. The American theatre needs to pick up at the point where
Lorraine Hansberry's *Les Blancs* left her characters—with raised hands
of unity attempting greater understanding and intimacy towards cooperative efforts. And whiteness theorists, those whose work centers on
"les blancs," might learn from this scene as well.

Notes

1. The distinctions "first wave" and "second wave" whiteness theory are
developed by Mike Hill (*Whiteness* 1–18), who explores the critical stance of
the later movement towards previous theoretical categories. He acknowledges
that the points of contention within the movement are at present unresolved.
    2. All references to *Les Blancs* are taken from the Robert Nemiroff edition
(1972).
    3. All references to *Wedding Band* are taken from Wilkerson.

Works Cited

Baldwin, James. "*Blues for Mister Charlie.*" *Contemporary Black Drama*. Ed.
    Clinton F. Oliver and Stephanie Sills. New York: Scribner's, 1971.

Barnes, Clive. "Theatre: *Les Blancs.*" *The New York Times,* 16 Nov. 1970: D28.

Bernardi, Daniel. "Introduction: Race and the Emergence of U.S. Cinema." *The Birth of Whiteness: Race and Emergence of U.S. Cinema.* New Brunswick, NJ: Rutgers University Press, 1996.

Bhabha, Homi. *The Location of Culture.* London and New York: Routledge, 1994.

Childress, Alice. "*Wedding Band.*" *Nine Plays by Black Women.* Ed. Margaret B. Wilkerson. New York: New American Library, 1986.

Craft, Philip A., Rebecca Clark, and Aimee Rowe. "Performing Whiteness . . . Critiquing Identities." National Communication Association Convention. New York, 21 Nov. 1998.

Dyer, Richard. *The Matter of Images: Essays on Representations.* New York: Routledge, 1993.

Frankenberg, Ruth. *The Social Construction of Whiteness.* Minneapolis: University of Minnesota Press, 1993.

Giroux, Henry A. "Post-Colonial Ruptures and Democratic Possibilities: Multiculturalism as Anti-Racist Pedagogy." *Cultural Critique* 21 (1992): 5–39.

———. "Racial Politics and the Pedagogy of Whiteness." *Whiteness: A Critical Reader.* Ed. Mike Hall. New York: New York University Press, 1997. 294–315.

Hall, Stuart. "New Ethnicities." *Stuart Hall: Critical Dialogues in Cultural Studies.* Ed. David Morley and Kuan-Hsing Chen. New York: Routledge, 1996. 19–36.

Hansberry, Lorraine. *A Raisin in the Sun and The Sign in Sidney Brustein's Window.* Intro. and ed. Robert Nemiroff. New York: Vintage, 1995.

———. "Village Intellect Revealed." *The New York Times,* 11 Oct. 1964, Sec. 2: 1, 3.

Hill, Mike, ed. *Whiteness: A Critical Reader.* New York: New York University Press, 1997.

Jackson, Ronald L. "White Space, White Privilege: Mapping Discursive Inquiry into the Self." *Quarterly Journal of Speech* 85 (Feb. 1999): 38–54.

Jameson, Fredric. *Postmodernism, Or, The Cultural Logic of Late Capitalism.* Durham, NC: Duke University Press, 1991.

Keating, AnnLouise. "Interrogating 'Whiteness': (De)Constructing 'Race.'" *College English* (1995): 901–18.

Keppel, Ben. *The Work of Democracy: Ralph Bunche, Kenneth B. Clark, Lorraine Hansberry, and the Cultural Politics of Race.* Cambridge, MA: Harvard University Press, 1995.

Lipsitz, George. "The Possessive Investment in Whiteness: Racialized Social

Democracy and the 'White' Problem in American Studies." *American Quarterly* 47 (Sept. 1995): 369–87.

Montag, Morton. "The Universalization of Whiteness: Racism and Enlightenment." *Whiteness: A Critical Reader.* Ed. Mike Hill. New York: New York University Press, 1997.

Nakayama, Thomas K., and Robert L. Krizek. "Whiteness: A Strategic Rhetoric." *Quarterly Journal of Speech* 81 (1995): 201–309.

Nemiroff, Robert, ed. *Les Blancs: The Collected Last Plays of Lorraine Hansberry.* Intro. Julius Lester. New York: Random House, 1972.

———. "The 101 'Final Performances' of *Sidney Brustein." A Raisin in the Sun and The Sign in Sidney Brustein's Window.* Ed. Robert Nemiroff. New York: Vintage, 1995. 159–203.

Pfeil, Fred. "Sympathy for the Devils: Notes on Some White Guys in the Ridiculous Class War." *Whiteness: A Critical Reader.* Ed. Mike Hill. New York: New York University Press, 1997. 21–34.

Taylor, Henry Louis, Jr. "The Hidden Face of Racism." *American Quarterly* 47 (Sept. 1995): 395–408.

Terkel, Studs, and Lorraine Hansberry. "Make New Sounds: Studs Terkel Interviews Lorraine Hansberry." *American Theatre* (Nov. 1984): 7–15.

Watts, Richard. "Grim Fruits of Colonialism." *The New York Post,* 16 Nov. 1970: 32.

Wilkerson, Margaret B., ed. *Nine Plays by Black Women.* New York: Mentor Books, 1986.

11 Traumatic Legacy in Darryl Pinckney's *High Cotton*

ALEXANDRA W. SCHULTHEIS

To know where you were going, you had to know where you'd come from,
though the claims the past had on you were like cold hands in the dark.
—PINCKNEY, *HIGH COTTON*

THE ANONYMOUS PROTAGONIST OF DARRYL
Pinckney's novel, *High Cotton* (1992), begins enigmatically:
"No one sat me down and told me I was a Negro. That was
something I figured out on the sly" (3). The ostensible con-
fidence of that declaration unravels as we follow Pinckney's autobiographical narrator from his middle-class, midwestern upbringing in
the 1960s and '70s through travels abroad and an Ivy League education
to adult life in Manhattan. Negotiating his own maturation against the
nominative and historical changes from Negro to black to African American, the narrator presents less a conventional *Bildungsroman*, than a serious parody of one. Rather than follow a protagonist whose innate
sensitivity propels his loss of innocence and burgeoning awareness of
the larger world, we find one who, at every juncture, wants to "hurry
home, to sink back into that state where good news for modern Negroes

couldn't find me" (25). He is continually torn between his Grandfather Eustace's desire to inculcate him into a black elite and the identities presented by the predominantly white communities the narrator inhabits. Trying desperately to escape the former and embrace the latter, he initially seeks recognition at the expense of his corporeal self, a manifestly doomed endeavor. If, in Judith Butler's words, one "'exists' not only by virtue of being recognized, but, in a prior sense, by being *recognizable*," then Pinckney asks how we can conceive of a subject who refuses to see himself in the terms in which others see him (Butler 17). If identity itself is difficult to define, both in terms of names and what they signify, this is not only because identity is a process rather than fact, but also because of the inadequacies of the models of subjectivity used to frame it. In the novel, the difficulties are twofold: the protagonist continually confronts the racist history of psychoanalytic models of subjectivity as well as the traumatic legacy of slavery. *High Cotton* exposes the inadequacies of psychoanalytic theory in addressing racialized historical trauma even as it embraces some of that theory's potentially liberatory insights into rethinking subjectivity.

Pinckney challenges the centrality of naming, the oppositional relationship of self and Other, and the ideology of the white, patriarchal nation-as-family as foundational to coherent subjectivity. This challenge reiterates the question posed by Kimberly W. Benston, in her essay "'I Yam What I Yam': The Topos of (Un)Naming in Afro-American Literature," of "how [to] envision and name a people whose very existence was predicated upon expropriation of land, culture, and the binding imperatives and designations of what Ellison terms the 'familial past'" (152). In *High Cotton*, the narrator refuses to call himself by terms that bear with them a history of social negation; he strives instead to interrupt the binary oppositions of positive versus negative, white versus black, which underscore dominant American understandings of racial identity. The narrator reminds us that genealogy and full citizenship have been historically denied African Americans, and thus constitute suspect foundations for African American subjectivity. One potential response would be for the narrator to see himself as always and inevitably lacking these foundations, thereby reinforcing the fixity of this model of subjectivity. Instead, he strives to re-signify his relationship to those markers that form ideological bridges through time and across identifications based on race, gender, and class. The relationship balances on a fulcrum of historical specificity, such that the narrator strives to understand his own and his family's historical contexts through markers that elide them.

In *Male Subjectivity at the Margins*, Kaja Silverman has formulated a model of inessential subjectivity (defined by lack) that similarly recognizes the interplay of ideology and psychoanalysis and the need to read subjectivity within history. In order to work against the privileging of white and masculine identities, Silverman insists that we divorce psychoanalysis from paternal law as ontological foundation of the subject. According to Silverman, our dominant fiction is a Freudian one, based upon the Oedipus complex and its image of the paternal family. As the constitutive bond between subject and society, the dominant fiction maintains its hold by setting the terms for the articulation of concomitant ideologies of race and class. Ideological continuity is maintained by the expression of social groups, such as community or nation, in the language of the paternal family. In her analysis of the effects of the ideological process of identification, Silverman turns to Frantz Fanon: "*Black Skin, White Masks* helps us to understand, first of all, that our identifications must always be socially ratified. It also teaches us that only certain subjects have access to a flattering image of self, and that others have imposed upon them an image so deidealizing that no one would willingly identify with it" (*Threshold* 29). Social power then accrues to those subjects who can readily identify with dominant images of masculinity and whiteness. Fanon's thesis in *Black Skin, White Masks* is that ideology renders blackness the negative of whiteness, such that the black subject is most often predetermined as socially powerless.

For Fanon, the black subject's fantasy is ultimately an (unconscious) desire for whiteness, a desire negotiated in relation to the national metaphor of the patriarchal family. That the metaphor of the dominant fiction is coded first by sexual difference and then by race again restricts potential avenues of subversive agency.[1] As Jean Walton writes in another context, "restoring to black men the patriarchal power that had been historically denied them" defines such power as "essential to masculine subjectivity" (783). Since accommodation to the dominant fiction, through the bar between what is speakable and unspeakable, determines subjectivity in (post) Lacanian psychoanalysis, that process of accommodation necessarily constrains agency without predetermining it. The ongoing process of interpellation, the "hailing" of subjects that Louis Althusser describes, through which the dominant fiction maintains its power, repeatedly constitutes a subject capable of response. The *contesting* subject would need to rewrite the metaphor of the family in both gendered and racial terms. Asking the subject, reader, or text to subvert or re-signify its relationship to the same dominant fiction that structures subject formation and our sense of "reality" is undoubtedly asking too much. Nevertheless, Silverman and Fanon suggest the possibility of withdrawing from—by becoming conscious of—the workings of the dominant fiction in ways that hold potential for alternative significations of subjectivity. Without imagining that we can step out of the gendered division that underlies our own realities, we might learn to look again at its various manifestations within the signifying economy of the paternal family. It is in the conscious work of looking again, as Silverman stresses in *The Threshold of the Visible World*, that we can locate an ethics of subjectivity.

According to Silverman, one potential site of opposition to the dominant fiction, for recognizing the variability of its metaphors, is historical trauma, which she defines as "any historical event, whether socially engineered or of natural occurrence, which brings a large group of male subjects into such an intimate relation with lack that they are at least for the moment unable to sustain an imaginary relation with the phallus, and so withdraw their belief from the dominant fiction" (*Male Subjectivity* 55). As "a force capable of unbinding the male ego, and exposing the abyss that it conceals" (121), historical trauma reveals the structuring of ideological belief on the level of the psyche. In order to address contemporary African American subjectivities, we need to expand Silverman's concept to account for the current legacies of past historical events. Whereas she uses historical trauma to describe events the subject experiences directly,[2] we need to be able to read the contemporary effects of slavery's denial of familial bonds in kinship and naming. What changes in the movement from historical trauma to traumatic legacy is the kind of memory forging (and damaging) the link between the subject and social ideology.[3] Instead of the individual "reminiscences" that haunt the subject of Freud's war trauma, we find a complex narrative of communal memory and silences. These narratives circulate within the dominant fiction to structure the process of identification—to determine what is normative, idealized, and shunned—as well as through African American communities formulating alternatives to the identifications made possible by the dominant fiction.

Both Silverman and Cathy Caruth posit literature (and for Silverman the aesthetic realm more generally) as a site of potential reformulation of these narratives of identity. As Caruth notes, "If Freud turns to literature to describe traumatic experience, it is because literature, like psychoanalysis, is interested in the complex relationship between knowing and not knowing. And it is, indeed at the specific point at which knowing and not knowing intersect that the language of literature and the language of psychoanalytic theory of traumatic experience precisely meet" (Caruth 3). Literature and psychoanalysis ask of one another how we can understand the effects of trauma on subject formation in language that can only bear witness to the incomprehensibility of trauma. *High Cotton* complicates Caruth's reading of literature's role in psychoanalytic understandings of trauma by problematizing both the speaking subject and his narrative. Despite his protagonist's initial disavowal of a racial community built around family, work, or politics, Pinckney situates his narrative in dialogue with Ralph Ellison's *Invisible Man* (1947).[4] The text has, in effect, a literary community that the protagonist initially lacks. Sharing tropes of anonymity and invisibility (enforced or desired), the mutability of identity (as Rinehartism or inessentialism), and the need to reach beyond the present to the past (to reconcile oneself to the grandfather's generation), the novels in tandem present a genealogy of African American masculinity spanning more than a century and, significantly, separated by the early years of the Civil Rights Movement. This "kinship" enables the kind of ethical review of subjectivity for which Silverman calls, but it also insists we evaluate the efficacy of the identities portrayed within their historical contexts.

The commonalities between the two novels underscore the power of the traumatic legacy of slavery and the challenges it continues to pose for contemporary African American subjectivity. While *High Cotton* lacks the epic scope of its forebearer, as well as what Eric Sundquist calls *Invisible Man*'s "archaeology of African American identity" (5), the later novel clearly extends Ellison's investigation into the meaning of black invisibility in white America. Pinckney examines how expanded civil rights and access to the middle class and to middle America enable his protagonist to attempt invisibility rather than accept it; at the same time, it is in Pinckney's postmodern rejoinder to Ellison's modernism—as seen in the movement from satire to parody, the rejection of humanism in favor of contingent subjectivity—that Pinckney reaches his most optimistic conclusions.

Both *Invisible Man* and *High Cotton* point to perhaps the central irony of American racism: the desired anonymity and invisibility of identities most frequently denoted by color and voice. *High Cotton* revolves around a crisis in naming on familial and communal levels; it therefore calls into question the efficacy of genealogy and national identity in structuring coherent subjectivity. The narrator's own anonymity would seem to shift the weight of identification from family to race. By emphasizing the changing names of race and his reluctance to claim or be claimed by them, however, he destabilizes this potential community as foundational to subjectivity in any way (as either explicitly empowered or oppressed). This insistence on "un-naming" himself, moreover, reminds us that the crisis in African American subjectivity historically occurs at the intersection of familial and racial identifications. The names initially available to the narrator carry with them a history of racial trauma and erasure.

The narrator reproduces these hegemonic silences by rendering his parents and sisters anonymous and characterizing his own name as nothing more than a "contemporary Dixie-cup quality, and my surname, with its antebellum echo, only barely acceptable" (197). The names that should interpellate and fix, even if temporarily, a subject, instead constitute what Butler terms injurious speech: "To be injured by speech is to suffer a loss of context, that is, not to know where you are. Indeed, it may be that what is *unanticipated* about injurious speech is what constitutes its injury, the sense of putting the addressee out of control" (4). Butler insists that the injurious power of a name lies in its historicity, its circulation within a given set of conventions and at a specific historical moment. She locates the power names have to demean or injure in their ability to reiterate trauma, noting that such speech "works in part through an encoded memory or trauma, one that lives in language and is carried in language" (36). Thus, it is not the language in and of itself but its reiteration that carries with it the force of trauma. Since trauma is, by definition, that which is somehow incomprehensible, its transmission is notable for its curious combination of effects: the muted, disguised, or confusing reiteration of an experience that both momentarily locates the subject and exceeds him or her, that brings the trauma back, so to speak, without bringing it to the fore. "The traumatic event," Butler explains, "is an extended experience that defies and propagates representation at once" (36). While language carries with it the force of trauma, in the process of reiteration it also makes possible a response by interpellating the subject (and the subject is defined as one whose entry into the symbolic order makes him or her capable of speech). As she notes, "The subject of speech who is named becomes, potentially, one who might well name another in time" (29).

In citing Butler's recent work on hate speech, I do not wish to categorize names of black identities as derogatory, serving, at best, to constitute subjects who may one day "talk back." Nor do I want to reduce subjectivity to naming alone. Instead I want to look at the ways in which these identities incorporate traumatic experience and the ability to redefine that experience, and how the psychoanalytic methods used to conceptualize these identities depend upon historical specificity. Butler provides a way of understanding how a given identity simultaneously fixes, exceeds, and fails to account completely for the subject. Appellation and interpellation determine subject formation, bringing the subject into a social context governed by convention and normativity (Butler 135). Butler points out that this process of subject formation in language takes places repeatedly, that the Lacanian "bar" that denotes what may be spoken (and that signals subjectivity) "is reinvoked in political life when the question of being able to speak is once again a condition of the subject's survival" (135). Thus, she insists, and Pinckney evinces through the changing names and contexts of racial identity, that the constitution of the subject in language is an ongoing phenomenon in the subject's life rather than a one-time event in infancy.

While naming momentarily locates the subject within a given social context, and does so through the name's "sedimentary" history, it cannot completely control the subject's response or its own future circulation. Similarly, the name cannot claim exclusive power over the subject's identity. As Butler asks rhetorically, "And what if one were to compile all the names that one has ever been called? Would they not present a quandary for identity?" (30). What Pinckney makes clear is that African

American identities, whose definitions as such synthesize familial and national trauma, do not denote a subject's static relationship to those traumas. The narrator tries desperately to avoid the legacies of traumas that he did not experience yet cannot escape. They have become part of the fabric of social life and language, mutating to adapt to changing historical conditions. In response, he wields both anonymity and self-naming as strategies of self-definition, concluding:

> One day—if it comes—I may be someone's old darky, exercising my fictitious cultural birthright to run off at the mouth, telling someone who may insist on being called a Senufo-American how in my day so many—black, white, and other—were afraid of black teenagers in big sneakers with the laces untied. (309)

Whether labeled a "darky," "black," or "Senufo-American," the protagonist calls for a racial solidarity that, even if it borrows the language of kinship ("fictitious cultural birthright"), recognizes shared experience as its foundation.

If he plays with the language of racial identity, the narrator of *High Cotton* similarly plays with the language of psychoanalysis by continually evoking its models of subjectivity that cannot fully describe him. He uses the language of psychic splitting, for example, to characterize the struggle to see himself according to prevailing codes of identity:

> The ledger of how to be simultaneously yourself and everyone else who might observe you, the captain's log of travel in the dual consciousness, the white world as the deceptive sea and the black world as the armed galley, gave me the comic feeling that I was living alongside myself, that there was a me and a ventriloquist's replica of me on my lap, and that both of us awaited the intervention of a third me, the disembodied me, before we could begin the charade of dialogue. (220)

The image of the two selves, awaiting the intervention of a disembodied third, suggests the Lacanian, poststructuralist subject whose very formation depends upon psychic splitting through entry into language. The danger of this reading is the ease with which it may designate an abstract and ahistorical psychoanalytic theory as the third voice, employing the

black body in the galley to traverse the white consciousness of the encompassing sea. Warning of such slippage into psychoanalytic universalism,
Margaret Homans writes in "'Women of Color' Writers and Feminist
Theory" that too often black bodies "do the work of embodiment or
identification" for white theorists who seek an "alibi" for anti-essentialist positions. Black bodies, in these cases, still figure as the all too familiar "other." Excluded from poststructuralism, they "define it by their
difference from it" (87).

Although *High Cotton* invokes the division between white consciousness and black corporeality, it does so subversively. Pinckney's narrator separates the conflation of the corporeal and the historical by
remaining not only anonymous but virtually absent physically from his
own story. We see the effects of race in various contexts, but rarely its
embodiment. Except for brief glimpses he provides of his thick glasses
or the various sartorial poses he adopts in childhood and adolescence,
he is invisible throughout the novel. Describing his fantasy of joining
the Vienna Choir Boys, for example, he makes this absence explicit: "The
disturbing sign was that in my dream the uniform was visible, but I
wasn't. Even when I pictured myself eating European style, with the knife
in my right hand, the camera cut from the sailor's sleeve to the plate to
get around the thorny problem of there having been no brown wrists
in my prophetic film of the moment, *Almost Angels*" (75). This passage
performs a double gesture: it introduces the terms of a psychoanalytic
reading while asking whether such a reading can have anything at all
to say about subjectivity constituted, at least in part, by racial difference.
Pinckney's adoption of cinematic language and the camera's structuring gaze plays on film theory's psychoanalytic roots as the process of
identification takes place within the frames of the camera's perspective.
Initially assuming control of that perspective ("I pictured myself"), he
seems to be the director, determining what can and cannot be shown.
His authority vanishes in the next clause, however, when he distinguishes
his own desire to see and be seen from what the camera reveals. The
discrepancy between his and the camera's revelations raises the question of how psychoanalytic theories of identification (can) account for
black identities. By presenting blackness only through the space of its
absence, Pinckney warns against any universal application of a set psychoanalytic model and presents his own narrative voice as the media-

tor between the two halves of the self. It is that narrative voice, more-over, that simultaneously erases and constitutes the body in question, thereby privileging the power of literature to exceed trauma over the authority of psychoanalysis to contain it.

No application of psychoanalysis to a literary text devoted to racial identifications and subject formation can be innocent of the history of racial bias within psychoanalytic theories. Recent critical work has shown how coherent subjectivity is predicated upon an assumption of normative whiteness that leaves racial difference inevitably feminized and "other-ed" within the prevailing model of binary sexual opposition. Jean Walton's analysis of early feminist psychoanalytic work makes clear that "theorizations of gender and sexuality . . . depend upon an *unthe-orized racial domain*" (803). Through readings of the foundations of psy-choanalysis, Walton reveals, as does Claudia Tate, both how models of subjectivity assume whiteness and how feminist revisions of these mod-els, even as they undermine the restrictive logic of normative hetero-sexuality, replicate those same racist biases. Feminist and postcolonial psychoanalytic approaches together, however, broaden the range of sub-jectivities theoretically conceivable while insisting on historical specificity.

High Cotton does not simply provide a sample text for a psychoanalysis of contemporary African American subjectivity. It turns the terms of psychoanalytic identifications back on themselves, asking repeatedly how they can make sense of the narrator's own changing definitions of him-self. To return to the language of split subjectivity, for instance, he uses the same image of being separate from himself to characterize his place in black and white communities. Just as a visit to Aunt Clara in Alabama "demanded, like taking a vow, that a part of the self must die" (29), enter-ing the mostly white Westfield Junior High required that "what I was I set aside every morning at 7:45" (85). By repeating the image of the split subject in different contexts, the narrator denies the possibility of static subjectivity available for a psychoanalytic reading. Who he is, and whom he sets apart from himself, depends on the range of images made avail-able by the historical and social moment.

The narrator is continually torn between his desire to identify with dominant (white) images and to reconcile them with his family back-ground. Whether he sees himself as a Vienna Choir boy, a fully inte-grated Westfielder, or the true descendant of the British Romantics, he notes that the "old-timers boasted of their ability to bug you from the grave, saying one day you'd want to talk to them and they wouldn't be there anymore. They'd hint that they'd be watching you closely from wherever they went when they passed on. Your dearest reminded you every morning of the problem that you would never, never get away from" (6). That problem, I suspect, stems from the confusion Ellison's narrator experiences from his grandfather's deathbed speech: "Live with your head in the lion's mouth. I want you to overcome 'em with yeses, undermine 'em with grins, agree 'em to death and destruction, let 'em swoller you till they vomit or bust wide open" (16). To avoid the guilt and confusion Ellison's narrator faces in following his grandfather's advice, Pinckney's protagonist spends much of his childhood rejecting, on grounds of irrelevance, the image of the "Also Chosen" promulgated by his Grandfather Eustace. With his "Holy Land" education at Brown and Harvard and family legacy of professionalism and "good marriages," Grandfather Eustace "took the high road, but because he made the journey in a black body he lived with the chronic dread that maybe he wasn't good enough" (6). To escape the need to be thankful for his opportunities and apologetic for his race, the narrator dismisses his grandfather's would-be lessons: "I spent much of my life running from him, centripetal fashion, because he was, to me, just a poor old darky" (6). While initially his running may appear, however circular, as an improvement upon the conspiracy to "Keep This Nigger-Boy Running" faced by Ellison's invisible man (Ellison 33), that ostensible progress disappears as Pinckney's narrator finds that running from his grandfather does not bring him to his idealized identities. As he describes his entry into Westfield, "Someone was always trying to interrupt, to get between me and the paradise of integration" (82). It is only later that he finds the most he can be in that paradise is "a slave in heaven" (107).

By using references to slavery to describe the characters' attempts to escape its lasting effects, Pinckney underscores the perpetuation of racist ideologies. Both the narrator and his grandfather strive for acceptance according to standards inflected with racism. For Grandfather Eustace this means gaining the degrees and social standing to prove himself acceptable to the white aristocracy he emulates, and then making sure the next generation does the same. As Uncle Castor, Grandfather's brother, quotes Edith Piaf, "Remember where you came from and send the elevator back down" (66). Whereas the older generation maintains a black version of a white social hierarchy, to provide the social mobility forever off-limits to them in white communities, the narrator yearns to melt into the white communities around him. With the family's move to the suburbs and his transfer to Westfield, he sees his chance: "I couldn't allow myself to look back," he comments, "having presented myself to myself as one who had never been anywhere but where I was" (86).

Although the narrator characterizes his bid for social standing as oppositional to his grandfather's, he describes both in images of slaves' plantation lives. The characters attempt to move up a social hierarchy modeled on the plantation in order to come as close as possible to achieving the white father's authority. This strategy necessitates a validation of the slave owner's position that is irreconcilable with historical experiences of the family. Grandfather Eustace, for instance, keeps quiet "about the hardships that he had witnessed, just as his grandfather had thought it wise not to speak too truthfully about his years in bondage" (8); nevertheless, Grandfather Eustace insists that his grandfather had said, "The family [to which he had belonged] was always kind and considerate of its slaves" (9). The narrator uses the same model to characterize his own position in the white suburbs, as when he defines himself according to the "oft-cited genealogy of field niggers and house niggers," adding, "[w]hen I needed to blame a poor performance on something outside myself, I had only to hint that the field niggers were after me again" (107). The reiterations of this trope through five generations attest to the power of racist ideology to define the terms of identity. At the same time, since he uses this language to capture fluctuating rather than fixed identities, Pinckney insists that the images available to contemporary African American subjects need not be restricted to those of black slaves. In the conscious intervention into these recurrent identities, he shows that the terms and the methods used to describe them are malleable. The aesthetic foregrounding of the terms, moreover, makes it impossible to take them for granted; we are asked to recognize their circulation within a given ideology and to reconsider the power dynamics they invoke.

Silverman's model of inessential subjectivity forces us to become conscious of the terms of identity we are willing to recognize and idealize, even as we acknowledge our own dependence upon them. Thus we can see how the discourse of the plantation South sustains itself through generations of the subjects it oppresses. Because phallic power on the plantation included the economic and sexual control of families and property, it conflated masculinity and whiteness. As a continuing metaphor for social "reality," it insists upon that same conflation in setting the terms for valued identities. Pinckney's narrator and Grandfather Eustace find themselves trapped by an unwished for identification with the only levels of social standing permitted in another era (i.e., "the house niggers"). Pinckney intervenes, however, by showing how the reiteration of traumatic experience contains within it the possibility of alternative identifications.

The narrator tries on identities ranging from Vienna Choir Boy to black power activist to bohemian expatriate while keeping an ironic focus on the mirror in his mind's eye. Of his short-lived attempt to join the Heirs of Malcolm, for example, he notes that "there was some unpleasantness between me and another revolutionary about what sort of grammar and spelling the sleeping masses could relate to" (114). Similarly, in England, he tries to relieve his loneliness by joining another revolutionary group, this time hoping that "my blackness would be more prestigious than my politics" (130). These two examples illustrate the ways in which the narrator attempts willfully to deploy "race" rather than be defined by it in his ongoing bids for social acceptance.

High Cotton reinforces the nation-as-family metaphor by articulating the quest for a favored identity in terms of the relationship between the narrator and his grandfather and their strategies for social agency, as a question of genealogy as well as citizenship. Not only does the narrator ultimately try to reconcile his place within his family, African American masculinity, and dominant values, but the potential identities themselves are circumscribed by what is believable within the nation-as-family. While Pinckney indicates the impossibility of stepping outside of the dominant fiction that defines the subject, he also shows that the layers of ideology do not necessarily cohere in every reiteration. The narrator embarks on his journey of self-discovery after hearing ambivalence in the lessons taught him by Grandfather Eustace. Launching his journey is his inability to read the confusing markers of a valuable African American identity:

All men were created equal, but even so, lots of mixed messages with sharp teeth waited under my Roy Rogers pillow. You were just as good as anyone else out there, but they—whoever "they" were—had rigged things so that you had to be close to perfect just to break even. You had nothing to fear, though every time you left the house for a Spelling Bee or a Music Memory Contest the future of the future hung in the balance. You were not an immigrant, there were no foreign accents, weird holidays, or funny foods to live down, but still you did not belong to the great beyond out there; yet though you did not belong it was your duty as the Also Chosen to get up and act as though you belonged, especially when no one wanted you to. (4)

The failure of this racial uplift ideology to interpellate him in a single voice—triggered by the incompatibility of a national and a racial "we"— initiates a process of psychic fragmentation.

The "mixed messages" in *High Cotton* whisper the impossibility of achieving the only identities deemed socially acceptable. At the same time, as interpellations in the Althusserian sense both Butler and Silverman cite, the messages confer subjectivity and make possible a response. For Pinckney's narrator, the unnameable fear he experiences provides him with multiple paths of identification as well as the caveat that some will be more perilous than others. In *High Cotton* multiplicity (even if conflicted) produces options for the ever-changing subject. The only stable subject position in the novel is one of consistent oppression, and it is in learning to accept that subjectivity is always in process and never fixed that the narrator can take an active role in overcoming his fear.

The narrator responds initially to the symptoms rather than the causes of this splitting, and, finding his grandfather's discourse confusing, disavows it by eliding racial and familial markers. In his desire to obtain the coherent subjectivity that the dominant fiction promises its most loyal adherents, he tries to divorce himself from any connections to subjugated subject positions defined by questionable or unstable identifications. Miscegenation, the denial of familial bonds during slavery, and the concomitant crisis of naming refute attempts at genealogical reconstruction. Familial relations are similarly ambiguous: he thinks his Aunt's maid is a cousin, describes relatives in shades and percentages (such as his "beige stepgrandmother"), and notes that "for all I knew as a child Grandfather Eustace came from an Oldsmobile" (17). In mimicking this disavowal of kinship the narrator is still, borrowing from Homi Bhabha, "not quite/not white" (*Location* 92); however, the self-conscious and parodic treatment of these signifiers of paternity and legitimacy undermines their status as the inevitable and only markers of subjectivity.

Freud's approach to overcoming traumatic neurosis shares with Butler's theories of perfomativity an emphasis on the enunciative moment. For Freud, each unwitting repetition of traumatic experience creates a fleeting sense of control over the initial irruption because it is the psyche rather than an outside force that brings back the traumatic event. In transforming the subject's relationship to that event from passivity to action, each repetition, as with Butler's reiteration, interpellates and, thus, constitutes the subject. Even as it defines the subject at that moment (as the recipient of trauma), interpellation makes possible a response, the parameters of which cannot be wholly constrained in advance. This would suggest that since the subject's coherent sense of self is evidently permeable (by the incomprehensible intrusion of the trauma itself), the inevitability and fixity of the trauma are similarly not guaranteed. The effects of traumatic experience, then, present one method of identifying, in Butler's terms, the post-sovereign subject—the subject constituted by and acting within a network of social functions rather than one whose makeup is fixed and who acts solely upon others. While Silverman teaches us that no response can completely free itself from the dominant fiction (since the dominant fiction helps determine what constitutes trauma to begin with), she also shows how trauma expands the range of possible responses. Confronting trauma and its legacies, in other words, may actually alter the dominant fiction, if only in limited ways.[5]

High Cotton insists upon some alterations in trauma theory in order to account for the lasting effect of traumatic legacy on African American masculinity in its changing historical contexts. To begin with, the founding trauma of the Middle Passage and slavery in the United States comprised both physical and psychic violence on individual and collective African Americans. The elements of fright and surprise were present in the wholesale elimination of the subject's control over his or her own corporeal, familial, and productive (in terms of both labor and procreation) integrity. By subordinating the subject's autonomy to a subjugated collective identification, slavery disempowered African Americans on a multitude of levels (while also, of course, enabling a wide range of retaliatory, subversive, and self-protective responses).

Hortense Spillers refers to the trauma of slavery as an "American grammar" composed of a "hieroglyphics of the flesh" passed down through the generations of "various *symbolic substitutions* in an efficacy of meanings that repeat the initiating moments" (67). In *High Cotton*, African American communities are sources of potential identification and strength for the narrator, though they remain marked by the violence that spawned them, and those associations are what initially deter him from claiming membership. On his way to his first Freedom Watch with his family, for instance, he notes that "when Grandfather said 'Negro' he described an abstraction," adding, "synaptic delay prevented my making the connections between Grandfather's parishioners and the offhand 'we' of my parents front-seat talk, talk that concerned the way 'we' were treated at lunch counters on the off-ramps to hell. . . . My nerve endings finally passed on the news when I found myself walled in on all sides by Negroes about to define themselves" (23). Even when he sees pictures of the race riots and attacks of the sixties, he separates himself from their social and political meanings. When he finds that "my friend the television set had begun to send awful pictures from the Old Country" (29), his feeling of betrayal by the TV is assuaged by the thought that the pictures are of the "Old South" as opposed to his "New World." He thus remains loyal to the narrative of the nation as a story of progress and opportunity for all of its members, seeing in the Old Country that which must be forgotten rather than that which remains. At the same time, his invocation of this rhetoric brings it to the fore, eventually enabling a reconsideration of its terms. Despite his overwhelming desire to escape and forget the legacies of the past, echoes of slavery and its traumas reverberate in *High Cotton* both in the language the narrator uses to describe himself and in his social interactions.

Caruth's work on trauma and history, *Unclaimed Experience*, not only expands our conception of trauma to account for its individual and historical attributes, but it fulfills the vital function of insisting on the historicization of psychoanalysis itself. This dual purpose emerges from the central role she ascribes to the literary voice. Since trauma is that which both "defies and demands our witness," it can only be represented in "a language that is always somehow literary: a language that defies, even as it claims, our understanding" (5). She adds that the literary text may be "a parable of psychoanalytic theory itself as it listens to a voice that it cannot fully know but to which it nonetheless bears witness" (7). If subjectivity is achieved through entry into the normativity of language—an entrance that is performed repeatedly throughout the subject's life and that is marked by what must be repetitively excluded at the threshold—then Caruth is, in effect, saying the literary may provide conscious access to that unconscious act of repeated foreclosure.

Silverman makes a parallel argument in *The Threshold of the Visible World*, situating the aesthetic, and its potential to alter the narrative of the dominant fiction, in the liminal space between consciousness and unconsciousness. Aesthetic texts may impact on the identifications we are willing to recognize by implanting "'synthetic' memories—libidinally saturated associative clusters which act like those mnemic elements which, as a result of a psychic working over, have been made the vehicles for the expression of unconscious wishes" (185). While these "'synthetic' memories" also exist within the scope of the dominant fiction, their libidinal charges, or aesthetic properties, enable them to "put marginal elements of the cultural screen in contact with what is most meaningful to a viewer or reader, and thereby validate what would otherwise be neglected or despised" (185). In their psychoanalytic readings of the aesthetic or literary, Caruth and Silverman share the belief that the transformative potential of these texts—their ability to bring to the fore what must be otherwise either repressed, foreclosed, or unconsciously repeated—lies in their ability to show the culturally and historically specific terms of the dominant fiction at work.

Coming to terms with racial trauma and its legacies necessitates the same negotiation between the universal and the historically specific, as does our belief in the value of psychoanalysis in understanding trauma. In order to countermand the obviousness of the dominant fiction and its associative ideologies of national unity, coherent subjectivity, and racial hierarchy, we must insist on historicizing the play of its privileged signifiers as well as our own methods of interpretation. The anxiety that underscores the need to reproduce a racist stereotype parallels the more general need to rearticulate constantly the terms of the dominant fiction and to interpellate its subjects. These addresses and enunciations fulfill two interconnected functions: they enable the dominant fiction and the subjectivities it produces to adapt to changing historical conditions while maintaining a consistent hierarchy, and they keep producing subjects who threaten to disrupt the coherence promised by the dominant fiction.

Pinckney incorporates both forms—oral and visual—of subjectivity into the narrator whose search for identity takes place within and against colonial discourse.[6] *High Cotton* follows the narrator as he recognizes the impossibility of language and race as fixed components of subjectivity and accepts the slippages within them as his inevitable and only foundations. At the same time, he remains firmly rooted to the very models of race, gender, and national identity that launched his search. This duality, of contesting yet never erasing dominant terms of subjectivity, points to the potential uses and limitations of the psychoanalytic approaches that enable this reading.

The narrator's unstable identity fits within the process Fanon outlines of the "black psyche's" differentiation from whiteness. Desire, discourse, and fantasy for the black subject are structured according to valences of "whiteness," such that, "in order to achieve morality, it is essential that the black, the dark, the Negro vanish from consciousness" (194). For Fanon, the problem is one of transforming one's self from an object fixed by a white gaze to a subject no longer confined within the binary of "*turn white or disappear.*" Invisibility, as discussed above, is the first strategy of survival adopted by Pinckney's narrator. At Westfield, to return to an earlier example, he borrows W. E. B. Du Bois's celestial metaphor in trying to blend in, consciously to detach color, as a racial marker, from any content: "I behaved as though I had been among the Westfielders all the while and was finally shedding the protective coloration that had kept me completely unseen. . . . I lived entirely at my surface, passing without reflection from class to class, like someone out for a walk noting whether the clouds either darkened or dissipated" (85–86).[7] As a ghost, the narrator's social agency is circumscribed by the definitions imposed by teachers and classmates. Refusing to acknowledge his own bodily specificity, where others do, renders him prey to the ideologies of the dominant fiction that seek to perpetuate themselves at his expense. In this way, inessential subjectivity alone figures as a

doomed escape from a corporeal self rather than as a means of refor-
mulating its signification.

Although the narrator constantly invokes the traumatic legacy of slavery, he nonetheless strives for acceptance via the (white) nation-as-family model. He articulates this sense of belonging he both wants and
repudiates on explicitly national terms—for example, he describes a conversation with his grandfather as one between *Plessy v. Ferguson* and *Brown
v. Board of Education*. At the same time, Pinckney's invocations of the
nation are frequently parodic, a gesture that opens them up for interrogation and raises the question of how African Americans may fit into,
subvert, or redefine the nation-as-family. Re-signifying terms such as
frontier, immigrant, Pilgrim, and Old Country, the narrator reminds us
of the historical violence that they mask. Attempts to invoke the rhetoric of immigration and the melting pot, for example, repeatedly fail.
"[Grandfather] come[s] from the Old Country," the narrator says. "Not
Lithuania, not Silesia. The Old Country, to us, meant Virginia, Georgia,
the Carolinas, spectral mileposts of cane swamp and pine, remote tide-
water countries swollen with menacing lore" (8). The Old Country as
the plantation South excludes African Americans from the discourse of
national identity as a voluntary communal enterprise, thereby calling
that discourse itself into question. Pinckney's parodies, constructed in
racial terms, force a rereading of the nation-as-family metaphor; they
demand another look at what, in Benedict Anderson's terms, the fantasy of national identity asks us to forget. At the same time, the parodies, ranging from the *Bildungsroman* trope to rhetoric of national identity
to Farrakhan-style rallies, underscore the ambivalence and concurrent
necessity of stereotypes in any form of colonial project. That racial and
sexual stereotypes never completely cohere, however, suggests that parody may be an effective strategy of subverting them. By appropriating
such terms as "nigger" and "Old Country" with the voice of the black
male narrator, Pinckney emphasizes how *inappropriate* they are as
signifiers of his narrator's identity. Whereas Caruth emphasizes the subject's "unwitting" repetition of the language or voice of trauma, Pinckney insists that conscious repetition can simultaneously acknowledge
and invoke the continuation of trauma in order to negotiate the subject's relationship to the dominant fiction.

What parody cannot do is provide a new set of terms with which the narrator can define his self-worth. Although he initially tries to avoid the effects of historical trauma by avoiding racial identifications, he eventually recognizes the need to reconcile his personal and racial background with his current desires. The change ultimately comes after a visit to the South where he finds that even though the "Old Country" has become the "New South," still "people who didn't know me at all opened their doors and hearts, just because I was family" (303). "The graveyards," he adds, "were the last remnants of the Old Country" (301). It is here that the "Gospel Choir sang 'I feel like going home,' with someone, somewhere, letting out a long, low, dry, 'Yes,' and the emotion I'd been looking for all those years finally came" (303). Instead of feeling the past as "cold hands in the dark," he at last recognizes it as a source of strength and direction. It is only by defining his only genealogy in terms of an African American community that he is able to extricate himself from the bind created by self versus other, white versus black identifications.

The literary dimensions of that community resound once again in *High Cotton's* echoes of *Invisible Man*. Although Ellison's narrator does not need to make the journey South, as the separation of Pinckney's "Old Country" from the "New South" has not yet occurred, when he hears at a Harlem funeral procession "an old, plaintive, masculine voice [arise] in song" (441), joined by the marching procession, he realizes, "I was listening to something within myself, and for a second I heard the shattering stroke of my heart. . . . It was not the words, for they were all the same old slave-borne words; it was as though he'd changed the emotion beneath the words while yet the old longing, resigned, transcendent emotion still sounded above, now deepened by that something for which the theory of Brotherhood had given me no name" (442). This momentary connection to the communal past ultimately fails in *Invisible Man*, and the narrator seeks recognition in the humanistic faith that "our fate is to become one" (564). His humanism simultaneously bolsters his belief in the power of that individual, "disembodied voice," whose anonymity is tied to the history of African American letters, yet who may ask rhetorically: "Who knows but that, on the lower frequencies, I speak for you?" (568).

Pinckney rejects this humanism in favor of partial narratives of communal belonging. Despite the seemingly romantic conclusion of his visit South, for instance, Pinckney avoids conflating a return to family and community with a notion of static and coherent selfhood. Pinckney ends the novel with an image, discussed earlier, of historical continuity and contingency with a vision of himself in his grandfather's role, a self-appointed "witness." The quest comes full circle as the narrator imagines his assumption of Grandfather Eustace's familial standing and pedagogical imperative. While the narrator renders the category of race contingent, his primary identification with his grandfather as the embodiment of the hyphenated national identity maintains the image of the nation as family. At the same time, that image is no longer colored white.

What remains for the narrator is to act on the potential alliance between inessential identity and redefined and redeployed racial agency by inscribing the "tribal codes" for himself. As he begins to recognize race as both constructed and un-erasable—a realization that transforms him from a passive to an active subject—he faces the challenge of re-signifying the terms of racial subjectivity in ways that support those codes. Although the narrator holds on to patriarchal metaphors of social grouping and masculine subjectivity, he simultaneously challenges their power by recognizing the lack at the core of subjectivity and, therefore, the possibility of deciding upon the forms of compensation he seeks. In each renewed attempt for a stable and coherent identity, he discovers the instability of his would-be foundations. The novel is most effective here in its portrayal of the tension between the need for signification and the limits on subjectivity necessitated by the signifiers themselves. As the narrator negotiates the ambiguous space between corporeal and psychic markers, he reveals the way in which this ambiguity underlies the prevailing metaphors of social reality. The conscious awareness of lack that results forms the crucial first step in undermining the power of those metaphors without abandoning the communal memories that make his own subjectivity possible.

Notes

1. Diana Fuss's chapter, "Interior Colonies: Frantz Fanon and the Politics of Identification," in *Identification Papers*, provides an excellent analysis of the historical context of Fanon's loyalty to dominant codes of heterosexual masculinity. As she notes, "Fanon's resolutely masculine self-identifications, artic-

ulated through the abjectification of femininity and homosexuality, take shape over and against colonialism's castrating representations of black male sexuality" (160).

2. Silverman builds on Freud's definition of "war trauma" to explain how an "outside" event may trigger neurosis in those who experience it. Her own examples are drawn from films produced just after World War II that show the war's potentially traumatic effects on masculine subjectivity.

3. I use the term "legacy" purposely here to underscore the legitimation of historically denied inheritance and genealogy. Communal memories, then, form the basis for familial identifications, which may be elided on the level of kinship and patronymic markers. As such they constitute a wellspring of possible alternative signifying images.

4. Thanks to Jeanne Follensbee Quinn for a productive discussion of the relationship between *Invisible Man* and *High Cotton* vis-à-vis their specific historical contexts. My discussion of their relationship is meant to be suggestive and exploratory; the topic deserves much fuller analysis. Together the novels portray nearly a two-century-long investigation of African American masculinity.

5. Caruth emphasizes that any response to trauma can only be partially effective in assuaging its effects. Her focus is less on trying to know the unknowable than on coming to terms with it, and hence with one's own fundamental lack.

6. I use "colonial discourse" in the broad sense described by Bhabha: "It is an apparatus that turns on the recognition and disavowal of racial/cultural/historical differences. Its predominant strategic function is the creation of a space for a 'subject peoples' through the production of knowledges in terms of which surveillance is exercised and a complex form of pleasure/unpleasure is incited" (*Location* 70).

7. In *The Souls of Black Folk*, Du Bois describes his initial recognition of being divided from his white classmates by a "vast veil": "I had thereafter no desire to tear down that veil, to creep through; I held all beyond it in complete contempt, and lived above it in a region of blue sky and great wandering shadows" (44).

Works Cited

Benston, Kimberly W. "'I Yam What I Yam': The Topos of (Un)naming in Afro-American Literature." *Black Literature and Literary Theory*. Ed. Henry Louis Gates, Jr. New York: Methuen, 1984. 151–72.

Bhabha, Homi. *The Location of Culture*. New York: Routledge, 1994.

———. *Nation and Narration*. New York: Routledge, 1990.

Butler, Judith. *Excitable Speech: A Politics of the Performative*. New York: Routledge, 1997.

Caruth, Cathy. *Unclaimed Experience: Trauma, Narrative, and History*. Baltimore: Johns Hopkins University Press, 1996.

Du Bois, W. E. B. *The Souls of Black Folk*. 1906. New York: New American Library, 1982.

Ellison, Ralph. *Invisible Man*. New York: Vintage Books, 1972. (Originally published in 1947.)

Fanon, Frantz. *Black Skin, White Masks*. Trans. Charles Lam Markmann. New York: Grove Press, 1967.

Freud, Sigmund. "Beyond the Pleasure Principle." *The Freud Reader*. Ed. Peter Gay. New York: Norton, 1989. 594–626.

———. *Moses and Monotheism*. Trans. Katherine Jones. New York: Knopf, 1939.

Fuss, Diana. *Identification Papers*. New York: Routledge, 1995.

Homans, Margaret. "'Women of Color' Writers and Feminist Theory." *New Literary History* 25.1 (Winter 1994): 73–94.

Laplanche, J., and J.-B. Pontalis. *The Language of Psycho-Analysis*. New York: Norton, 1973.

Pinckney, Darryl. *High Cotton*. New York: Penguin, 1992.

Silverman, Kaja. *Male Subjectivity at the Margins*. New York: Routledge, 1992.

———. *The Threshold of the Visible World*. New York: Routledge, 1996.

Spillers, Hortense J. "Mama's Baby, Papa's Maybe." *Diacritics* 17.2 (Summer 1987): 65–81.

Sundquist, Eric. J., ed. and intro. *Cultural Contexts for Ralph Ellison's* Invisible Man. Boston: Bedford/St. Martin's, 1995.

Tate, Claudia. "Freud and His 'Negro': Psychoanalysis as Ally and Enemy of African Americans." *JPCS: Journal for the Psychoanalysis of Culture and Society* 1.1 (Spring 1996): 53–62.

Walton, Jean. "Re-Placing Race in (White) Psychoanalytic Discourse: Founding Narratives of Feminism." *Critical Inquiry* 21 (Summer 1995): 775–804.

12 Portnoy's Neglected Siblings

A Case for Postmodern Jewish American Literary Studies

DEREK PARKER ROYAL

EWISH AMERICAN FICTION HOLDS A CURIOUS
place in contemporary literary studies. During the 1950s and
1960s it established a dominant position not only within ethnic literary studies, but within postwar American literature as a whole.
Much as Americans in the postwar period were migrating from the
cities to the suburbs, many Jewish American writers were shifting their
focus from the confines of their ethnic communities to the larger realms
of the national culture. Unlike earlier writers such as Abraham Cahan,
Henry Roth, Anzia Yezierska, Michael Gold, and Sholem Asch, these
second- and third-generation Jewish writers concerned themselves not
so much with the Eastern European flavors of the Lower East Side as
with the uptown savvy of Manhattan, the quiet suburbs of New York
and New Jersey, the midwestern sprawl of Chicago, and even the pop
culture capitals of Hollywood and Disney World. Their literary reputations migrated in a similar fashion. In the 1970s both Saul Bellow and
Isaac Bashevis Singer received the Nobel Prize for literature. And
according to Raymond Mazurek, in his survey during the late 1980s of
contemporary literature courses taught throughout the country, Bellow,
Joseph Heller, Norman Mailer, Philip Roth, and Bernard Malamud all

ranked within the top fifteen of the most significant or the most taught novelists. Twentieth-century Jewish American writers had definitely established a formidable canonical presence.

At the same time, this canonical status may have helped to stifle Jewish American literary studies in certain ways. As with any other literature, Jewish American writing has undergone a series of shifts and realignments that reflect not only the place of Jewish culture in particular but also the larger intellectual climates in which it is written. The modernist or largely humanistic emphases of Bellow, Malamud, and Singer are different from those of more contemporary authors who have directly engaged postmodernist issues of language, identity, and authority. Yet despite the notable work of such contemporary writers as Stanley Elkin, Max Apple, Steve Stern, Cynthia Ozick, Thane Rosenbaum, Allegra Goodman, and Philip Roth (especially in his later writings), the critics of Jewish American literature have neglected to focus on the postmodern aspects of their subject matter. This is not to say that certain Jewish writers have never been critically considered within the rubrics of postmodernism (however one chooses to define "postmodern"). Stanley Elkin, Philip Roth, and Joseph Heller have all been read as self-reflexive writers concerned with the deconstruction of reality, texts, and the self. However, while there are a number of journal- and chapter-length studies devoted to various postmodern concerns in individual works or of individual authors (see, for instance, Elizabeth Rose's and Michael Greenstein's essays on Ozick, Alan Wilde's work on Elkin, Michael Dunn's essay on Woody Allen, John Williams's book on E. L. Doctorow, or the substantial body of criticism on Roth's Zuckerman novels), there has been no effort to contextualize the various postmodern strategies among contemporary Jewish American writers *as a whole*. Indeed, most of the extended studies of Jewish American fiction have tended to center on what could be considered the "old guard" of Jewish writers, those following primarily modernist models and/or whose reputations were established soon after the Second World War.[1] All of these works concentrate on authors such as Bellow, Malamud, early Roth, and Singer, while more or less neglecting to highlight the experimental or less conventional side of this literature. This is not to suggest that writers such as Bellow, Singer, Mailer, and Malamud are not significant within the scope of Jewish American literary studies. On the contrary, these writers have helped to lay the foundations of the postwar literary experience, ethnic or otherwise. But certain texts, such as those of Elkin, Ozick, and Roth, have attempted to explore issues of identity within certain postmodernist assumptions. The notion of a core or a center to the ethnic self has been justly questioned by several Jewish writers. Despite the notable interest in the area of Jewish ethnicity and the construction of self, to date there has not been one extended study on the postmodern elements that make up much of contemporary Jewish American writing.[2]

This lack of critical attention to the postmodern elements of this fiction within an American ethnic studies context is unfortunate, and the issue of formulating an understanding of postmodern Jewish ethnicity needs to be addressed. Instead of approaching these primary texts as developing a series of ethnic-specific themes, more emphasis should be placed on the diverse ways many Jewish American writers employ ethnicity to engage issues of identity, community, and textual interpretation. In light of this revealing context, a study of this kind will necessarily foreground two interconnected strategies of interpretation: (1) approaching contemporary Jewish American fiction as an ethnic literature and (2) developing the reading of this literature in terms of postmodern ethnicity. On the surface, the first of these strategies may seem superfluous, if not outright redundant, given the critical history of Jewish American literature. Malamud, Bruce Jay Friedman, Hugh Nissenson, Roth, and Ozick are nothing if not writers highly conscious of their ethnic backgrounds, and critics of American Jewish literature (that is, those who particularize the American Jewish experience) have obviously highlighted this as a major component of their subject's fiction. Yet contemporary critics of ethnic literature in general (especially those involved in defining an ethnic canon) have tended to neglect or at least minimize the importance of American Jewish literature as an ethnic literature. A survey of works on literary ethnicity published in the last ten to fifteen years is highly revealing. Considerations of American Jewish writing as an ethnic representation are conspicuously absent from *The Nature and Context of Minority Discourse* (1990), *Redefining American Literary History* (1990), *All My Relatives: Community in Contemporary Ethnic American Literatures* (1993), *Supernatural Forces: Belief, Difference, and Power in Contemporary Works by Ethnic Women* (1993), *An Other Tongue: Nation and Ethnicity in the Linguistic Borderlands* (1994), and *The Ethnic Canon:*

Histories, Institutions, and Interventions (1995), all of which are concerned with ethnic discourse within larger, and at times hostile, cultural frames.³ (Many of these studies, such as Bonnie TuSmith's *All My Relatives: Community in Contemporary Ethnic American Literatures* (1993), employ the general words "ethnic" and "ethnicity" in their titles, but nonetheless within the text focus only on writers of color. The scope may be rich and necessary, but such a discrepancy between general intentions and specific examination can be misleading to students of ethnic studies.)

These critical works, although needfully opening up (or widening) a space for the study of African American, Native American, Asian American, and Chicano/a literature, all fail to recognize (or at least fail to mention) the similarities between these literatures and Jewish American writing. Perhaps this is because more of an emphasis has been placed on literatures of color than on ethnic literature in general, as is the case in TuSmith's study; or because, in the words of anthropologist Karen Brodkin, Jews have become "white folks" and their ethnic subject positions are not "oppositional" enough; or because some feel that Jewish American writing has already had its time in the critical spotlight; or because many Jewish writers (such as Bellow and Malamud) have become canonized and are in no need of championing; or because their canonical status suggests (perhaps in the eyes of some) a dilution of their ethnic import within the larger scope of "unhyphenated" American literature. Certainly there are differences between literatures of color and Jewish ethnic writing (just as there are differences *among* the various literatures of color), but there are also a number of similarities (such as the prejudicial assumptions placed on a people from both outside and within an ethnic community) that help to highlight the dynamics of this kind of critical analysis. Whatever the reason(s) for neglecting Jewish American writing, literary critics interested in ethnic studies who fail to take into account the undeniable presence of Jewish American literature *as ethnic literature* are not only being remiss, but they are also denying a vibrant and highly relevant community of writers whose work could only benefit their critical projects.

A brief look at some of the issues involved may help to illuminate the politics of constructing a theory of ethnic literature. Werner Sollors, one of the most central, and controversial, theorists of ethnicity, argues that American ethnic identity is caught between an emphasis on old-world hierarchies and a vision of new and self-defining possibility. These conflicting impulses constitute what he calls "the central drama in American culture," and he defines them in terms of "descent" and "consent" relations (6). Descent relations are those that emphasize "our positions as heirs, our hereditary qualities, liabilities, and entitlements." Consent relations, on the other hand, "stress our abilities as mature free agents and 'architects of our fates' to choose our spouses, our destinies, and our political systems" (6). Ethnic literature, then, is largely a dialogue or a negotiation between these two forces, the tension of which reveals to the reader the particular rites and rituals of American newcomers, or as Sollors puts it, "the central codes of Americanness" (8).

Thomas J. Ferraro, while articulating an ethnic model similar to that of Sollors, nonetheless sees the limits of Sollors's arguments. Narrowing his scope from the broad category of ethnicity to the more specific experience of immigration, Ferraro argues that immigrant writers contextualize their lives through a series of "passages" in which they move from confines of the ethnic space to the larger world of letters. Ferraro argues that by choosing to write within the American marketplace, immigrant writers necessarily engage in a dialogue of cultural assimilation:

> The turn to ethnic narrative is an attempt on the part of the writer to negotiate the terms in which the greater freedoms of the United States are to be accepted: on the one hand, to dispel the charge by the clan of having undergone an essential and traitorous assimilation; on the other, to dispel the charge by the culture at large of possessing predispositions of mind and heart inappropriate if not antithetical to the developing concerns of a national literature and culture. (10)

For an ethnic writer, especially one who is an immigrant or an immigrant-offspring, writing becomes a tug of war or a constant negotiation between the world of ancestral definition and the world of possibility.

In contrast to the form of ethnic study espoused by Sollors and Ferraro, Alan Wald argues that these ethnic conceptions fail to account for every discourse at work within all minority fictions. He differentiates between what he calls the "ethnicity school" of Sollors (as well as Mary V. Dearborn and William Boelhower), on the one hand, and the proponents of a class, gender, and race methodology (e.g., Henry Louis Gates Jr.,

Barbara Christian, and Barbara Foley), on the other. What critically limits Sollors's theory, Wald argues, is that he privileges the category "ethnicity" while relegating that of "race" to a mere aspect of certain ethnicities (27–28). For ethnicity theorists, the dynamics at work in the literature of Jewish and Italian Americans are similar in kind to those in African American, Chinese American, Native American, and Chicano writings—regardless of the oppressive and quasi-colonial experiences of people of color. "Class-gender-race" theorists, by contrast, work from the assumption of a "profound distinction—never to be forgotten—between the experience of people of color and the European ethnic immigrants in the *mode and consequences* of their incorporation into the social formation, and their subsequent treatment" (23). In other words, it makes all the difference that one group was coerced into a cultural economy through violent means, while another was more or less assimilated through choice. To people of color, "race" (as socially constructed from without an ethnic group), not "ethnicity" (usually defined from within), is by far the more central category in their American culture.

Henry Louis Gates, Jr., in many ways the most representative of Wald's "race" critics, rightly sees a potential danger in the universalism inherent in Sollor's ethnic model. To approach black literature *only* in terms of European or American theoretical models is to engage in an act of critical neocolonialism. No matter how well-intentioned these egalitarian theories may be, they "somehow always end up lopping off our [black] arms, legs, and pug noses, muffling the peculiar timbres of our voices, and trying to straighten our always already kinky hair" ("Talkin'" 408). Gates's critical distinction between the literature of European ancestry and that of African American descent rests on an internal colonization thesis that highlights the unique linguistic and material obstacles facing people of color. He argues that the distinctiveness of the black text can be found in its language, a dynamic series of codes that function beneath the surface of a work and are recognized by its practitioners as a strategy of community within a culture of oppression. Such a critical emphasis, he concludes, locates the "signifying black difference[s]" ("Talkin'" 407) at work in these texts in ways that a "white"-based criticism cannot.

Both brands of ethnic theory—the "ethnicity school" and the "class-gender-race" approach—taken strictly on their own terms, are not without their limitations. Sollors, for instance, does at times seem too eager to create a universal theory of ethnicity and in the process conflates the historical differences that define a specific group experience.[4] In terms of American Jewish writers, such an emphasis could overlook the fact that "Jewishness" is not only the product of a subject's volition, but also a label placed upon subjects as a means of distancing them from a dominant culture. On the other hand, by focusing exclusively on race-specific codes, one could drastically underemphasize similarities American Jewish writing shares not only with Euro-American traditions, but also with literatures of color (specifically, Hispanic, African, and Asian American)—non-reductive similarities that highlight a text's richness by placing it within a larger ethnic context.[5] What is more, Wald's bifurcated schema of ethnic studies is too Manichean in its categorization and leaves little space for investigations into European ethnicity. In defining the difference between "ethnicity" and "race" as a matter of choice or coercion within an economy, he avoids the danger of universalizing all ethnic groups but falls prey to the tendency to essentialize a particular ethnic group. Not all individuals of European origin came to the United States out of free personal choice; many did so out of economic or political necessity. A Jew who has to flee his or her native soil because of an all-too-real physical threat (whether it be from Nazis, Cossacks, Christians, or Muslims) or from economic strangulation may certainly not share the same history as an African American forced into slavery, but the two do nonetheless share a variety of political, economic, and psychological commonalities that, taken within the context of serious critical comparison, would greatly add to an appreciation of both varieties of ethnic writing. What I would like to suggest is that by approaching American Jewish literature from a larger ethnic perspective, while at the same time acknowledging the limitations to that approach, one need not fall back on an oppressive essentialism that, in Gates's words, "lops off" the vital ethnic- and individual-specific components of that literature.

Such an emphasis on the *construction* of contemporary ethnic theory would naturally lead to a discussion of the postmodern assumptions of ethnicity. Many who have approached Jewish American literature as ethnic literature in the past usually have done so by looking at the "Jewishness" of the writing. A text may be considered "ethnic" to the extent that it articulates the negotiation of Jewish experience within a largely assimilative American culture. These studies attempt to articulate the various cultural and religious signifiers that normally define Jewishness in America. However, such an approach usually posits an authentic or prototypical understanding of American Jewishness without taking into consideration the constructedness of that understanding. A postmodern understanding of Jewishness, on the other hand, would foreground the conditions under which that ethnic identity is conceived. The makeup of ethnic subjectivity, then, could include both an acknowledgment of its engagement within a historical community and a provisional, self-ironizing critique of that engagement. Ozick's *The Messiah of Stockholm* stands as one such example of this postmodern impulse. Lars Andemening, the novel's orphaned protagonist, convinces himself that he is the one and only child of Bruno Schultz, the Polish writer shot dead by the Nazis in 1942, and constructs elaborate scenarios to help explain his unlikely lineage. Ozick uses him both to highlight the arbitrary side of identity formation and to illustrate the high stakes involved in ethnic identification.

However, the postmodern quality of much contemporary Jewish American writing is almost never considered within the contexts of its ethnicity. Authors such as Ozick and Roth are at times read as ethnic writers and at other times as postmodern writers, but almost never as *postmodern ethnic* writers. And while there have been a few attempts at highlighting the common ground between Jewish American ethnicity and postmodernism, such studies are nonetheless limited, usually to one particular work from one individual author. Taking this into account, scholars of ethnic literature should recognize that there is a need to reconceptualize Jewish American literary studies within the larger contexts of contemporary critical thought.

On the surface, at least, the assumptions of postmodernism and of ethnic studies seem antithetical: postmodernism discounts the legitimacy of cultural authenticity, while ethnic literatures usually establish some form of cultural "authenticity," or set of shared assumptions as a means to ensure communal and individual self-assertion. There have been, however, a few critics who have attempted to define a postmodern ethnicity, either by contextualizing one particular ethnic group (usually African Americans) or configuring an abstracted model of what a postmodern reading of ethnicity might look like. Approaching issues of race from a postmodern perspective, bell hooks, for example, has expressed concern over some of the assumptions inherent in certain theories of race or ethnicity. She argues that notions of racial identity may become essentialized, thereby turning repressive, if they are rooted in those master narratives from which marginal subjects have attempted to free themselves. This she sees as a dangerous "modernist" emphasis on points of origin, the search for some "authentic" racial identity that denies difference and stifles alternative voices within that racial or ethnic community. Looking at the possibilities for a black subjectivity, hooks puts it this way:

> The unwillingness to critique essentialism on the part of many African-Americans is rooted in the fear that it will cause folks to lose sight of the specific history and experience of African-Americans and the unique sensibilities and culture that arise from that experience. An adequate response to this concern is to critique essentialism while emphasizing the significance of "the authority of experience." There is a radical difference between a repudiation of the idea that there is a black "essence" and the recognition of the way black identity has been specifically constituted in the experience of exile and struggle. (29)

There are strong political implications here in hooks's critique, ones that extend beyond the African American community. Instead of privileging racial homogeneity, she emphasizes certain psychological conditions shared by a variety of marginalized individuals. This she calls a "radical postmodernism," one that would focus on those "shared sensibilities which cross the boundaries of class, gender, race, etc., that could be fertile ground for the construction of empathy—ties that would promote recognition of common commitment, and serve as a base for solidarity and coalition" (27). Hooks's critical position is more overtly political than the strict ethnic theories of Sollors. He at times tends to reduce or abstract ethnic dynamics for the sake of a single and more formal literary model, whereas hooks, in her emphasis on shared experiences, attempts to locate cohesive differences among rather than solely within individual communities.

Similarly, critics such as R. Radhakrishnan and Ramón Saldívar have theorized ethnic studies as a space where differences are foregrounded and "otherness" is historized. Saldívar discusses the Chicano novel in terms of its "differential structure," that is, the dialectical manner in which it translates the negotiation between two distinct cultures (81). Its subject matter is neither purely Mexican nor purely American, but something else entirely. "This something else," he goes on, "is the *différance* of contemporary Chicano literature, which allows it to retain its special relation to both its Mexican and American contexts, while also letting it be marked by its relation to its own still unconditioned future" (88). In a more extended, yet somewhat more convoluted, analysis, Radhakrishnan similarly establishes difference/*différance* as the centerpiece to a postmodern understanding of ethnicity. He differentiates between universalizing theories of ethnicity—those that lump together all forms of ethnic otherness and in the process erase those differences that distinguish one ethnic experience, or brand of ethnic experience, from another—and theories that are built upon what he calls a need for common ground. Privileging the latter, he takes to task certain forms of poststructuralist criticism, particularly deconstruction, that dehistoricize and reify otherness into a "mystique" ("Common Ground" 12). Instead, he conceives of postmodern ethnicity as a strategy that both particularizes a subject position (defines it in its own right) and finds similarities between that position and other subject positions. Radhakrishnan concludes that such a theory is appropriate within the context of ethnicity "which on the one hand is universal, i.e., insofar as there is no cultural reality that is not subtended by ethnicity (there is nothing called the 'non-ethnic'), and is, on the other hand, the phenomenological and historical expression of a particular group experience from within its *locus*" ("Common Ground" 17). Elsewhere he describes a poststructuralist understanding of ethnicity as one that valorizes the "post-" aspect of identity, or what is left for the subject after it "breaks" from the strictures of representation. An individual ethnic subject stands poised between two potentially constricting language systems: that of an oppressor who uses discourse to disenfranchise the subject, and that of the subject's own community that chooses to define itself strictly on its own terms. In either case there is a fixed and authorized sense of what it means to be ethnic ("Ethnic Identity" 62). The "post-ethnic" subject, by contrast, reflects a sense of Derridean *différance*: ethnic "meaning," or in other words, identity, is defined in terms of its differences from other communities. Yet these distinctions can never be truly essentialized, and ethnic identity as such (what it means to be Italian, what it means to be black, what it means to be a Jew) is always deferred, something that is always already in the making. Such a strategy, according to Radhakrishnan, "conjoins in a relationship of complementarity the twin tasks of semanticizing the indeterminancy of the temporality of the 'post-' and radicalizing the ethnic momentum beyond authoritarian closure" ("Ethnic Identity" 69).

Critics of literatures of color have been particularly insightful in their exploration of the common ground between theories of ethnicity and postmodernism. One illustrative example is David Mikics. He reads Ishmael Reed as a writer who uses ethnicity as an alternative means to resisting the destabilizing nature of postmodern culture. Unlike some earlier African American writers, Reed does not assume there to be one authentic "black" experience counterpoised to a fragmented and largely consumerist late capitalist society. Instead, Mikics argues, Reed turns to certain African myths and folktales that are both subversive and critical of themselves as subversive acts, and uses them as guides to reading and participating in contemporary mass culture (305). This strategy is postmodern in that it denies any monolithic cultural identity and assumes the context of a fragmented and decentered cultural system; yet at the same time it is particularly "ethnic" in that it uses communal experiences and narratives to resist or critique the highly centrifugal nature of postmodern culture.

In light of all of this, the question remains: what might postmodern readings of Jewish American ethnicity look like? Such tendencies are already becoming apparent and can be found in a few small but generalizing studies. Vivian Sobchack, for instance, attempts to define a postmodern ethnicity within the context of contemporary American cinema. She uses the critical frameworks of Linda Hutcheon in postmodern theory and of Werner Sollors in ethnicity to explore three filmmakers, including Woody Allen and Paul Mazursky, who foreground the construction of ethnic consciousness. Her conception of ethnic identity is similar to that of Radhakrishnan in that the differences articulated (as in the case with Leonard "the Human Chameleon" in *Zelig*) are never static, but are always in a constant and unconditional state of flux. What makes these filmmakers' handling of ethnicity so postmodern, Sobchack argues, is that while they acknowledge the cultural power behind the concept of the melting pot, they nonetheless parody and ironize that myth by recontextualizing it in the present and exaggerating its implications. Such a strategy, therefore, highlights the construction of ethnicity as a contradictory and multivalent experience (343). Victoria Aarons presents a more recent and highly impressive example. She emphasizes the long tradition in Jewish literature of bearing witness to the community through the telling of stories. Through her readings of Spiegelman's *Maus*, Gilbert Rogin's "What Happens Next?: An Uncompleted Investigation," and (to a lesser degree) Roth's *The Counterlife*, Aaron asserts that contemporary Jewish American writers—writers who feel cut off from the histories of their parents and grandparents—employ the artifice of the storyteller in order to recreate history, and in doing so, reinvent their fictional selves in terms of their familial pasts (82). Again, the emphasis here is on the fluidity or mutability of identity, but also on identity's grounding in history and communal experience.

All of these considerations—the postmodern aspect of Jewish American writing, the placing of Jewish writers within the larger context of American ethnic writing, and the defining of a postmodern ethnicity— should challenge contemporary critics of Jewish American literature. Given this need to contextualize Jewish American writing within postmodern rubrics, it would perhaps be beneficial to focus on at least one Jewish American writer who foregrounds these theoretical parameters. One such representative of contemporary Jewish American writing, Philip Roth, arguably provides the most illustrative example. This writer, although central within the canon of contemporary Jewish literature, is by no means representative of Jewish American writing as a whole. If, as critics of postmodern ethnicity will argue, authoritative representations of a particular ethnic group are both false and confining, then any attempt to showcase Roth as a "typical" or even "superlative" example of Jewish American writing is not only misleading in the broadest sense, but antithetical to the very goals of this study. What makes Roth so important are the different ways in which he highlights many of the theoretical and cultural issues that define ethnic studies. For instance, in his first series of Zuckerman novels—*The Ghost Writer* (1979), *Zuckerman Unbound* (1981), *The Anatomy Lesson* (1983), and *The Prague Orgy* (1985)—and in his "autobiographical" tetralogy—*The Facts*

(1988), *Deception* (1990), *Patrimony* (1991), and *Operation Shylock* (1993)—
Roth focuses explicitly on the negotiation of a secularized Jewish identity. In this regard, he differs from Cynthia Ozick, who is highly
cognizant of the religious issues involved and explores the place of Jewish faith and the place of the Jewish woman within an assimilated community, as well as from other Jewish American writers—such as Stanley
Elkin and Norman Mailer—who strongly distance themselves from their
Jewish ethnic heritage.

Furthermore, in his American trilogy—*American Pastoral* (1997), *I
Married a Communist* (1998), and *The Human Stain* (2000)—Roth not
only explores the construction of subjectivity but also, and more
significantly here, the ways in which the individual subject constructs
communal history through memory and narrative. Indeed, the third novel
in the trilogy, *The Human Stain*, could serve as a narrative example of
Radhakrishnan's emphasis on "post-ethnic" identity, a subject position
situated between the discourse of the oppressor and that of its own ethnic community. Coleman Silk, the novel's protagonist who is a light-
skinned African American passing as Jewish white, refuses to let either
oppressive system define who he is. In a highly illustrative passage, Silk
gives voice to the kind of arguments found in Radhakrishnan's writings:

> You can't let the big they [the white power structure] impose its bigotry
> on you any more than you can let the little they [the black community]
> become a we and impose its ethics on you. Not the tyranny of the
> we and its we-talk and everything that the we wants to pile on your
> head. . . . Instead the raw I with all its agility. *Self*-discovery—*that* was
> the punch to the labonz. Singularity. The passionate struggle for singu-
> larity. The singular animal. The sliding relationship with everything. Not
> static but sliding. Self-knowledge but *concealed*. What is as powerful as
> that? (108)

But perhaps one of Roth's most revealing texts, especially in its emphasis on postmodern Jewish ethnicity, is *The Counterlife* (1986). More than
any other of his works, this novel vividly illustrates the dynamics
involved in a postmodern articulation of ethnicity. In ways that resem-
ble the fictive play of John Barth, *The Counterlife* is like a Möbius strip
that constantly turns back on itself with no fixed center. Yet Roth's novel

never gets lost in narrative play for its own sake. Its high postmodern aesthetics is always "anchored" to issues of Jewish ethnicity. The entire novel revolves around questions of Jewishness in a variety of contexts: in America, Israel, and England; for secular, practicing, and militantly orthodox Jews; and through the eyes of both Jew and non-Jew alike.[6] Given its emphasis on the cultural issues surrounding Jewish ethnicity, one could rightly approach the fiction of Roth as demonstrating just one, but one highly illustrative, facet of the varied Jewish experience in America.

Another representative of the Jewish American experience, Stanley Elkin, occupies a curious position in Jewish American letters. Although many of his protagonists are Jewish in character or in name, his focus has rarely been overtly ethnic in nature. His fiction is not so much concerned with Jewishness, per se, as it is with the labyrinthine twists and interconnected accidents found in contemporary American society. He is almost never contextualized by critics within the broader scope of Jewish fiction, and whenever he is mentioned in those contexts, he rarely receives more than a passing reference. Only one essay on Elkin has appeared in *Studies in American Jewish Literature*, certainly the most immediate outlet for criticism in Jewish studies, and none have been published in *MELUS*. Indeed, when Elkin is considered at all in the literature it is usually as a representative of postmodern fiction or black comedy. Elkin himself has helped to encourage this critical inclination in interview after interview by refusing the classification of "Jewish writer." But such a refusal, although important in its context, is not grounds for dismissal from the Jewish American canon. In fact, Elkin's apparent lack of interest in Jewish subject matter makes him a particularly appropriate foil to Roth, considered by many to have "Jews on the brain."

For Elkin, the very act of writing itself has become an example of ethnic negotiation within in a broader multicultural society. In *The Franchiser* (1976), for instance, the words and images of mass consumerism help to hide the "core" of Ben Flesh, who zooms across the interconnected artery-like highways of the country to check up on his franchises, establishments devoted to replicating and standardizing experience. It could be argued that Elkin's decision to write in an "assimilative" mode enhances his position, and his importance, as a postmodern ethnic writer.

Regardless of the fact that his fiction reflects many of the central issues in postmodern culture (which it does) he stands as an example of post-modern Jewish writing *because* of his avoidance of ethnic labels, a narrative impulse reminiscent of bell hooks's arguments against ethnic or racial essentialism. Works such as "The Bailbondsman" (1973), *The Franchiser* (1976), *The Living End* (1979), *The Magic Kingdom* (1985), *The MacGuffin* (1991), and *Mrs. Ted Bliss* (1995) all highlight the place of individual identity within a consumer-ridden postindustrial age, but, perhaps just as important, they all provide a unique glimpse at an ethnic author-subject consciously constructing highly assimilated and hybridized subjectivities.

On the other hand, the fiction of Cynthia Ozick stands as one of the most illustrative examples of postmodernism and its relation to Judaic faith. Her narrative structures betray a conflicting series of postulates that refuse any final synthesis. Embedded in such works as "Envy; or, Yiddish in America" (1969), "Usurpation (Other People's Stories)" (1987), *The Cannibal Galaxy* (1983), *The Messiah of Stockholm* (1987), *The Shawl* (1989), and *The Puttermesser Papers* (1997) are both a text and a countertext that vie for dominance but that are ultimately suspended in an uneasy—yet highly revealing—state of irresolution. She takes to heart the Mosaic law against idolatry—one of the most dangerous idols being art—yet is torn between by her place as a Jew and as a writer constantly in the act of creating literary "idols" that approximate existence. This strategy of literary negotiation is particularly significant in that Ozick not only problematizes the postmodern question of the replications of texts, but also places her ethnic subject position in the very center of this controversy. Many of her novels use a series of ironic countertexts to explore the place and function of literature in relation not only to the world at large, but, more precisely, to the world as defined by her Jewish faith.

Finally, the cinema of Woody Allen could stand as one more instance of postmodern ethnic narrative. In addition to the transformations of Leonard Zelig, as discussed by Vivian Sobchack, there are other films that highlight the construction of the self. One of his most notable projects, especially within the scope of this study, is *Deconstructing Harry* (1997). Harry Block, a Philip Roth-like writer who is notorious for using his life and the lives of those around him as grist for his fiction, experiences writer's block (thus the name), and undergoes a process of reimagining himself through his various characters for the purpose of putting his life back into order. By the end of the film, and after experiencing a series of crises, he comes to the realization that his fiction, the multiple recreations of the self, is what actually sustains him. Although here issues of Jewishness are not of central concern, in Allen's works his ethnic position is always an issue, whether remaining in the background or taking center stage. Read within the heretofore mentioned arguments of Radhakrishnan, Saldívar, and hooks, the films of Allen, as well as the fictions of Ozick, stand out as texts exploring the constantly deferred nature of postmodern ethnic identity.

These are just a few illustrative examples of writers who take on their Jewish ethnicity within the various contexts of postmodern thought. A survey of other contemporary Jewish American authors would prove similarly fruitful.[7] There is no shortage of readings on contemporary Jewish American authors, even ones that highlight the postmodern quality of one particular writer or text. However, there has been a short supply of critical attention given to this literature within the more general, and purportedly more inclusive, studies of ethnic texts. Such an absence suggests that critics of Jewish American literature, and of ethnic literature in general, could only benefit by reconceptualizing their subjects in terms of various postmodern constructs, in whatever forms that might take. What is more, an emphasis on the postmodern aspects of ethnic identity would help to foreground what is arguably one of the best defining features of contemporary Jewish American writing: its engagement with the fragmented and commodified state of American culture and the ways in which these secular influences compete with, deny, or give new life to Jewish religious expression. For contemporary Jewish American authors, assimilation is not only a foregone conclusion; its significance as a thematic privileging is by and large outdated. One witnesses in the protagonists of such younger writers as Goodman, Stern, Bukiet, Nathan Englander, Dara Horn, and Aryeh Lev Stollman the need to reevaluate the assimilative impulse, an attitude quite different from that of Bellow's Augie March, Malamud's Morris Bober, or Heller's Yossarian. An emphasis on postmodern Jewish subjectivity would also help to highlight the multifaceted nature—or what one might even call the "nonessentializability"—of recent Jewish American fiction as a whole. Unlike much earlier Jewish American writing, its current form is highly influenced by, among other things, the aftermath of the Holocaust, engagements with Zionism, the growing influence of feminism, the rise in identity politics, and a new emphasis on multicultural or hybridized identity, making it highly difficult to "pin down." Finally, by reading Jewish American literature more within the rubrics of postmodern thought and, at the same time, emphasizing its shared qualities with other American ethnic writing, we would not only be opening up a new space for the study of Jewish texts, but also helping to reinvigorate the already exciting field of American ethnic literary studies.

Notes

1. See, for example, Robert Alter's *After the Tradition: Essays on Modern Jewish Writing* (1969); Max F. Schulz's *Radical Sophistication: Studies in Contemporary Jewish-American Novelists* (1969); Charles Angoff and Meyer Levin's *The Rise of American Jewish Literature* (1970); Ruth R. Wisse's *The Schlemiel as Modern Hero* (1971); Allen Guttmann's *The Jewish Writer in America: Assimilation and the Crisis of Identity* (1971); Louis Harap's *Dramatic Encounters: The Jewish Presence in Twentieth-Century American Drama, Poetry, and Humor and the Black-Jewish Literary Relationship* (1987) and *In the Mainstream: The Jewish Presence in Twentieth-Century American Literature, 1950s-1980s* (1987); Mark Shechner's *After the Revolution: Studies in the Contemporary Jewish American Imagination* (1987); L. S. Dembo's *The Monological Jew: A Literary Study* (1988); Sanford Pinsker's *The Schlemiel as Metaphor: Studies in Yiddish and American Jewish Fiction* (1971, revised 1991) and *Jewish American Fiction, 1917–1987* (1992); Janet Handler Burstein's *Writing Mothers, Writing Daughters: Tracing the Maternal in Stories by American Jewish Women* (1996); Norman Ravvin's *A House of Words: Jewish Writing, Identity, and Memory* (1997); and edited collections such as *Contemporary American-Jewish Literature: Critical Essays* (1973), *On Being Jewish: American Jewish Writers from Cahan to Bellow* (1974), *Jewish Wry: Essays on Jewish Humor* (1987), the *Handbook of American-Jewish Literature: An Analytical Guide to Topics, Themes, and Sources* (1988), and *Semites and Stereotypes: Characteristics of Jewish Humor* (1993). Even Alan L. Berger's and Gloria L. Cronin's recent edited collection, *Jewish American and Holocaust Literature: Representations in the Postmodern World* (2004), despite its self-proclaimed emphasis on the postmodern condition, is by and large comprised of essays devoted to an older generation of Jewish American authors.

2. The one possible exception to this is Andrew Furman's invaluable

study, *Contemporary Jewish American Writers and the Multicultural Dilemma: Return of the Exiled* (2000), a book devoted almost entirely to the younger generation of Jewish American authors (e.g., Melvin Jules Bukiet, Thane Rosenbaum, Allegra Goodman, Steve Stern, and Rebecca Goldstein). However, his concern with postmodernism goes only as far as the topic's links to multiculturalism.

3. Collections such as *Multicultural Autobiography: American Lives* (1992) and *Memory, Narrative, and Identity: New Essays in Ethnic American Literatures* (1994) do include studies of Mary Antin, Henry Roth, Tillie Olsen, Herbert Gold, and Alfred Kazin, but it is important to note, especially within the scope of this study, that these works do not include essays on the more contemporary representatives of American Jewish writing. Here again, Furman's study is notable in that it highlights the absence of Jewish American writing within the larger scope of multiethnic American literary studies. However, his arguments for a more inclusive approach to multiethnic literary studies are quickly dropped after the introduction. But then the book's donnée, after all, is strictly limited to Jewish American fiction.

4. One example of this lies in Sollors's comparative treatment of Charles W. Chesnutt and Abraham Cahan: "One could with some justification talk about '*bluish*' writing in America and thus emphasize the parallels between black and Jewish writings in one appropriate word" (163, emphasis added). Despite the fact that his focus is on structures of similarity, one wonders whether Sollors's treatment of *racial* issues in Chesnutt's work—something not found in Cahan's—is as trite as his phrasing.

5. Wald, in his case for theorizing cultural differences, leaves little room for comparative study. Gates, who at an earlier time vehemently opposed what he has called "the racism of egalitarianism and universalism" ("Talkin'" 409), seems now less inclined to exclude Euro-American critical traditions. See on this point his introduction in *Figures in Black*.

6. For a more detailed analysis of these issues, see my essay, "Postmodern Jewish Identity in Philip Roth's *The Counterlife*."

7. See, for instance, the writings of Joseph Heller, Art Spiegelman, Thane Rosenbaum, S. L. Wisenberg, Allegra Goodman, Melvin Jules Bukiet, and Steve Stern, or the films of Joel and Ethan Coen.

Works Cited

Aarons, Victoria. "Telling History: Inventing Identity in Jewish American Fiction." *Memory and Cultural Politics: New Approaches to American Ethnic*

Literatures. Eds. Amritjit Singh, Joseph T. Skerrett, Jr., and Robert E. Hogan. Boston: Northeastern University Press, 1996. 60–86.

Allen, Woody, dir. *Deconstructing Harry*. Miramax, 1998.

Brodkin, Karen. *How Jews Became White Folks and What That Says about Race in America*. New Brunswick, NJ: Rutgers University Press, 1998.

Dunn, Michael. "*Stardust Memories, The Purple Rose of Cairo*, and the Tradition of Metafiction." *Film Criticism* 12 (1987): 19–27.

Elkin, Stanley. *The Franchiser*. New York: Farrar, 1976.

Ferraro, Thomas J. *Ethnic Passages: Literary Immigrants in Twentieth-Century America*. Chicago: University of Chicago Press, 1993.

Furman, Andrew. *Contemporary Jewish American Writers and the Multicultural Dilemma: Return of the Exiled*. Syracuse, NY: Syracuse University Press, 2000.

Gates, Henry Louis, Jr. *Figures in Black: Words, Signs, and the "Racial" Self*. New York: Oxford University Press, 1987.

———. "Talkin' That Talk." *"Race," Writing, and Difference*. Ed. Henry Louis Gates, Jr. Chicago: University of Chicago Press, 1986. 402–9.

Greenstein, Michael. "Ozick, Roth, and Postmodernism." *Studies in American Jewish Literature* 10 (1991): 54–64.

hooks, bell. *Yearning: Race, Gender, and Cultural Politics*. Boston: South End, 1990.

Mazurek, Raymond. "Courses and Canons: The Post-1945 U.S. Novel." *Critique* 31 (1990): 143–56.

Mikics, David. "Postmodernism, Ethnicity and Underground Revisionism." *Essays in Postmodern Culture*. Ed. Eyal Azmiran and John Unsworth. New York: Oxford University Press, 1993. 295–324.

Ozick, Cynthia. *The Messiah of Stockholm*. New York: Knopf, 1987.

Radhakrishnan, R. "Culture as Common Ground: Ethnicity and Beyond." *MELUS* 14.2 (1987): 5–19.

———. "Ethnic Identity and Post-Structuralist Difference." *The Nature and Context of Minority Discourse*. Eds. Abdul R. JanMohamed and David Lloyd. New York: Oxford University Press, 1990. 50–71.

Rose, Elisabeth. "Cynthia Ozick's Liturgical Postmodernism: *The Messiah of Stockholm*." *Studies in American Jewish Literature* 9 (1990): 93–107.

Roth, Philip. *The Counterlife*. New York: Farrar, 1986.

———. *The Human Stain*. Boston: Houghton, 2000.

———. *Zuckerman Bound: A Trilogy and Epilogue*. New York: Farrar, 1985.

Royal, Derek Parker. "Postmodern Jewish Identity in Philip Roth's *The Counterlife*." *Modern Fiction Studies* 48 (2002): 422–43.

Saldívar, Ramón. "A Dialectic of Difference: Towards a Theory of the Chicano
Novel." *MELUS* 6.2 (1979): 73–92.

Sobchack, Vivian. "Postmodern Modes of Ethnicity." *Unspeakable Images:
Ethnicity and the American Cinema.* Ed. Lester D. Friedman. Urbana: University of Illinois Press, 1991. 329–52.

Sollors, Werner. *Beyond Ethnicity: Consent and Descent in American Culture.*
New York: Oxford University Press, 1986.

TuSmith, Bonnie. *All My Relations: Community in Contemporary Ethnic American Literatures.* Ann Arbor: University of Michigan Press, 1993.

Wald, Alan. "Theorizing Cultural Difference: A Critique of the 'Ethnicity
School.'" *MELUS* 14.2 (1987): 21–33.

Wilde, Alan. *Horizons of Assent: Modernism, Postmodernism, and the Ironic
Imagination.* Philadelphia: University of Pennsylvania Press, 1987.

Williams, John. *Fiction as False Document: The Reception of E. L. Doctorow in
the Postmodern Age.* Columbia, SC: Camden House, 1996.

13 Tension, Conversation, and Collectivity

Examining the Space of Double-Consciousness in the Search for Shared Knowledge

SHEREE MEYER, CHAUNCEY RIDLEY,
AND OLIVIA CASTELLANO

It is a peculiar sensation, this double-consciousness, this sense of always looking at one's self through the eyes of others, of measuring one's soul by the tape of a world that looks on in amused contempt and pity. One ever feels his twoness— an American, a Negro; two souls, two thoughts, two unreconciled strivings; two warring ideals in one dark body, whose dogged strength alone keeps it from being torn asunder.—DU BOIS, *THE SOULS OF BLACK FOLK*

S THE FOLLOWING COLLABORATIVE ANALYSIS demonstrates, W. E. B. Du Bois's concept of double-consciousness in *The Souls of Black Folk* goes to the heart of issues raised by the teaching of, and the scholarship in, multicultural literature. On the one hand, it serves for us as common denominator from which to compare and contrast three important texts, each from three distinct literatures: Jewish American, Chicano, and African American. On the other hand, our use of the concept in these different contexts illustrates how slippery a term it can be.

In our conversations, we have examined the space of double-consciousness and discovered three desires that, in the search for shared knowledge, can undermine the production of a praxis of multicultural criticism and pedagogy. One is the desire to identify with the other, what we have come to refer to as naïve empathy. Another is the tendency to universalize—to move from the troubling differences of multicultural literature to what appears to be "simply" human. Indeed, these two movements often coincide as our desire to identify with characters collapses the particular into the universal. Finally, and of most concern to us in this essay, the movement from theory to praxis raises the danger that an indiscriminate use of theory and its discourse can efface the particularities of a given literary text. Our goal in this essay, therefore, is not to propose a cure for the tensions produced by double-consciousness and in multiculturalism. Rather, it is to anatomize carefully one complex theoretical paradigm, recognizing its potential duplicity—the tendency to impose limits, fix boundaries, and project its own "violent hierarchies"— and applying it in such a way as to respect the particular nuances of these texts and the fluid ethnicities of those who produced them.

Double-consciousness is a diagnosis of one neurosis within the black psyche brought on by the stratification of competing cultures. It articulates a process applicable to other American ethnic minorities insofar as, in order to achieve mainstream success, the minority subject weaves into consciousness ever more advanced theories of prior genetic and cultural depravity. It is also the dilemma of harboring two warring identities seeking very different forms of expression. While Du Bois divides the self in response to a clearly delineated intercultural struggle—one in which the "I" seems forced to choose between two distinct selves that represent two distinct cultures—the texts we consider here are variously more ambiguous. *The Romance Reader, Bless Me, Ultima,* and *Their Eyes Were Watching God* illustrate a continuum of responses to the inter- and intracultural formation of the multicultural subject.

Where the characters in these texts fall on this continuum is sometimes counterintuitive, and putting them in dialogue creates surprising resonances of difference and identity. For the Jewish subject of the Diaspora who clings to the singular consciousness of the *Hasidim,* as does Dov Ber in Pearl Abraham's *The Romance Reader,* there is ideologically no intercultural conflict; he is never a stranger defined in relation to a strange land, never an outsider as long as he remains inside the ideology of Judaism. He is, in some sense, immune to the "amused contempt and pity" of the dominant culture. Yet, for the Jew like Abraham's Rachel, who desires assimilation, double-consciousness produces not only an alienating split (as in Du Bois's original conception) but also a hyperbolic guilt—an intracultural debt to the six million who died and a responsibility to those who would survive as Jews. Antonio, of Rudolfo Anaya's *Bless Me, Ultima*, is already genetically and psychologically marked by the scars of intercultural exchange: "the glory and tragedy of the history of [his] people" (123). Antonio's people are both descendants of the Catholic Spaniards, who conquered Mexico but became priest-haters, and the indigenous people of Mexico, who later embraced Catholicism (123). The character Ultima brings with her a third term—the culturally repressed, indigenous folk ways and belief system of pre-Columbian Mexico. Ironically, given Du Bois's specific address to the African American, Zora Neale Hurston's Janie, the protagonist of *Their Eyes Were Watching God*, most fully rejects the terms of intercultural double-consciousness (not unlike Dov Ber) and, instead, seeks an intracultural reciprocity that will result in a more loving, less paralyzing "split" between her inside and outside selves. Janie's conflict, like Rachel's, is partly an effect of the highly stratified gender politics *within* their closed communities—an effect that Du Bois's focus on race ignores.

Once these three characters are put in dialogue, enabled to "talk" with each other on their own terms, we are able to see how each one— Abraham's Rachel, Anaya's Antonio, and Hurston's Janie—defines, revises, deconstructs, and redefines her/his respective space of tension, while negotiating a sense of cultural and personal identity. All three novels illustrate the process by which multicultural forms provide the grist for narratives; yet each of the narratives we consider here situates its protagonist-narrator at very different stages of that process. Antonio, the youngest of our three protagonists, has been given the historical matter from which to shape a narrative, but at novel's end still lacks a sense of what form it might take. Rachel, perched much closer to adulthood, has come to recognize the deep formal structure of her narrative, its inevitable rising and falling movement. She does not, however, know what its specific dimensions might be. Finally, Janie gains narrative power by mastering the signature forms of African American discourse propagated by the only audiences that matter to her: those as sophisticated in their understanding of these forms as the porch-talkers in Eatonville and the workers of the Jacksonville muck. These characters, theorists of identity in their own right, lovingly affirm the excellence of Janie's retrospective "big story."

How and why does one come to "measure one's soul by the tape of a world that looks on in amused contempt and pity"? If we adopt Rachel's definition of assimilation, "of trying to be like other nations, of wanting to be liked by them" (Abraham 34), then the identification with the dominant culture and the attendant rejection of the minority culture is motivated by desire, and that desire leaves one especially vulnerable to the scornful gaze of the seemingly non-ethnic majority. We can offer a further gloss on the ways in which double-consciousness operates differently in the subject formations of the other protagonists but cannot make a blanket statement about the universality of that desire as characteristic of *the* multicultural subject, a fact that these three novels make evident.

While the protagonists struggle to varying degrees with the lure of assimilation and hence the danger of a paralyzing double-consciousness, as storytellers, they mirror the aesthetic dilemmas of their authors. In Jewish American literature, "Jewishness" could be bleached into apparent universality, but Judaism could not (Glazer 91). Double-consciousness then, for the Jewish American author, is the tension between those cultural qualities that can be "bleached into apparent 'universality'" and those differences that mark the Jew as "other." Situating her novel in the particularity of the *Hasidic* enclave, Pearl Abraham explores that aesthetic tension and, like her protagonist, Abraham, occupies a creative and cultural space that is "home but not home." If "the quest for home is simultaneously a quest for narrative power" (Glazer 85), then *The Romance Reader* is an enactment of *teshuvah*, a turning or returning to a doubled literary tradition in which narrative power is derived from a refusal to escape from the perceived narrowness and limits of ethnic and religious specificity and into the perceived universality of America.

African American cultural forms evince a similar negotiation with the dominant culture, even if "bleaching" per se is not an option within the logic of race in the U.S. Bearing out the psychological splitting of Du Bois's theory were some of the self-appointed "talented tenth" of the Harlem Renaissance. They were not ashamed of representing African

Americans in literature, but of representing the "soul beauty" of the black oral tradition that "set the ruder souls a-dancing and a-singing" (Du Bois 46). Minstrel shows were popular enough and sometimes featured black performers such as Bert Williams, but they were unsubtly contemptuous and demeaning, inspiring many black intellectuals' recoil from all hint of affinity with the backbeat blues phrasing, polyrhythmic dance moves, and vernacular discourses of the "ruder" ninety percent; hence, to be both liked and *respected* by white audiences, these artists felt compelled to display a studied mastery of "high" Anglo American aesthetic strategies.

Zora Neale Hurston's work, on the whole, however, resists this abject compulsion. Unlike Abraham who writes from a space that is "home, but not home," Hurston's best known autobiographical quests are "homeward," to find skilled "Signifiers" and storytellers among the "ruder souls" and to cultivate fluency in these oral discursive strategies (see Hurston 294). The discussion of *Their Eyes* in this collaborative study focuses upon Hurston's fictional protagonist, Janie, and her quest to cultivate such fluency, through which she constructs her own "big story" and achieves control over the gendered, intracultural split between "inside" and "outside," "soul" and "self."

The issues facing Anaya's Chicano protagonist are similarly complicated by a negotiation between the traditional and the dominant cultures, though the resulting split is negotiated in historically and culturally specific ways. In his study of the ways in which Anaya's character, Antonio, represents the Chicano artist, Bruce-Novoa argues that for Chicanos the traditional socioreligious structure, and thus the very culture itself, is under threat of disappearance. Art is a possible response to this "discontinuity of chaotic reality" that the Chicanos in the United States must face; it creates "a space in which structure is imposed on chaos and in which man's images are preserved, outside of sequential time and free of isolating, spatial divisions" ("Portrait" 150). Bruce-Novoa cites Eliade's notion that a human being cannot live except in sacred space and that "when there is no hierophany to reveal it to him, he must construct it for himself" (*Chicano* 3), and Chicano art (the literary text) creates sacred space, a new *axis mundi*, a new connection to the cosmos, which helps to cancel out the threat of disappearance (*Chicano* 5). Just as Anaya the artist has the responsibility of preserving images to help ensure the continuity of Chicano culture, Antonio the adult narrator has taken the material of his childhood and told us his story. Central to this "material" is Antonio's knowledge that the split between Luna and Marez (indigenous and Spanish) at the root of his cultural origins is irresolvable. This story, then, creates a "sacred space" in which the "glory and the tragedy" of conquest continue to influence each other. Anaya has given us a model by which vestiges of the indigenous past continue to be woven with traces of the Spanish culture in infinitely promising, meaningful ways. If assimilation can be defined in positive terms—not in the terms Rachel sets for herself, nor in the terms that threaten the double-consciousness of Du Bois's "talented tenth," but as an endlessly constructive oscillation of energy in the process called self-determination—then, for Anaya, to be Chicano is to learn to tell one's story within the context of an earlier, yet ongoing, historical assimilation. Such a continuous engagement between past and present deconstructs the concept of Chicano identity as fixed. Telling one's story is an unending process in which the "I" is fluid and changing against the backdrop of a fluid and changing cultural past.

In Pearl Abraham's novel, the protagonist Rachel, daughter of a *Hasidic* rabbi, recognizes the double-consciousness through which she will achieve a tenuous subjectivity: "I am guilty, an assimilated American Jew" (34). Interpellated by her father, in the name of God who appears to guarantee a single unified consciousness, Rachel's concession of guilt is, indeed, a precondition of identity, but it is neither a full subjection before the law nor a complete break from it. Instead, the phrase "assimilated American Jew" marks the subject as already doubled, duplicitous, divided. If Rachel's story is paradigmatically a coming-of-age or coming-to-culture tale, it is with a difference, for the narrative, like the Jews who await the messiah, throws its emphasis on a "coming" that has not yet come (and, indeed, may not ever come). Only at that time can the Jew be truly at home in a unified community.

Within the Jewish community, of course, different people experience identity differently. Biale, Galchinsky, and Heschel have argued, in language that recalls the psychic split described by Du Bois, that "as important [as anti-semitism] is the consciousness Jews have of themselves as occupying an anomalous status: insiders who are outsiders and outsiders who are insiders. They represent that boundary case whose very lack of belonging to a recognizable category creates a sense of unease" (5). Yet this definition is inadequate for discussing *The Romance Reader*. As *Hasidim*, pious ones, Rachel and her family have deliberately marked themselves as "outside" by language, clothing, and name; there can be no "inside" cultural position for Rachel in America. For Dov Ber, behavior is not determined by the competing ideologies of a secular society, but by the one Subject that counts, the God of Abraham. In contrast to a "When in Rome, do as the Romans do" philosophy, the *rebbe* asserts, "You will behave in the same way in whatever country or city you're in" (138).

Rachel's name recalls the Rachel in the sacred texts, and, in contrast to the American ideology of individualism that materializes in American literature, the Judaic text constitutes Rachel as one of the "House of Jacob," responsible for the survival of that tribe, its eventual return home to *Eretz Israel*, and its consequent redemption. Isaiah warns that the communal body of Israel is unhealthy and in need of discipline: "Why do you seek further beatings. . . . From head to foot / No spot is sound: / All bruises, and welts, / And festering sores" (*Tanakh* 615). The community and God abandon those who forsake the ways of Israel and assimilate the practices of others. To engage, for example, in the reading of *goyishe* (non-Jewish) texts contaminates the body of the Jewish people.

This single name, Rachel, thus refers to two bodies and implicitly links them together in a single narrative. Du Bois refers to "two warring ideals in one dark body" as though the body is, itself, the signifier of double-consciousness. The body is always imbedded in and constituted by the social. Elizabeth Grosz carefully articulates the system in which bodies matter: "[Bodies] speak social codes. They become intertextualized, narrativized; simultaneously, social codes, laws, norms and ideals become incarnated" (35). One can trace the ways in which Rachel's body and first person narrative (the body as text and the text as body) are sites of conflict between the codes of Judaic texts and the romances of Anglo America. As Rachel acknowledges, textual bodies define bodies as texts (206). But bodies are marked differently: If race marks Du Bois's "dark body," gender marks Rachel's. The ritual shaving of the new wife's head, and the subsequent requirement that it be covered by a wig and a kerchief or hat, inscribes the Book of Isaiah on Rachel's body. "I've never seen my head like this. Round and small. Bumpy. Like Jews in concentration camps. Like Mrs. Sklar" (256). But, here too, her body is "intertextualized," for the historical text of the Holocaust intervenes. Read by Rachel's father, the Holocaust is interpreted in light of Isaiah: "They speak of the sin of assimilation, of trying to be like other nations, of wanting to be liked by them, and of never succeeding" (34). The naked heads of Jewish women are incorporated into the story of the desire for assimilation and its impossibility. "The Jews of Germany thought they could be good Germans first, Yuden second. And what happened? Six million killed by Hitler, may his name forever be erased" (34). If Rachel's statement that "to be assimilated, to be an American Jew, is to be guilty" initially seems hyperbolic—a figure of extension and exaggeration—it seems less so when juxtaposed to the figure of "six million" cited by her father, or to thousands of years of persecution and expulsion that give the lie to the promise of assimilation.

"Trying to be like other nations . . . wanting to be liked by them" beautifully articulates the desire and pain of double-consciousness: "this sense of always looking at one's self through the eyes of others," especially when those eyes at best reflect "amused contempt and pity." Rachel, indeed, is caught up in the gaze of others—the orange-haired lady who "looks [them] up and down every time, as if to let [them] know how strange [they] look" or the bus driver whose eyes make Rachel feel "his hate, his impatience" and make her wish she "looked like the blond girl who works at McDonald's" (25, 33). Unlike her sister, Leah, Rachel cannot return the gaze, refuse its "measure" of her, or give the orange-haired lady or the bus driver "a taste of [their] own medicine." Nor is Rachel comforted by an abstract ideal of God's will when she encounters the "cars with wild or anti-Semitic drivers" who "stare at Father, at his hat and locks . . . [and] laugh" (76).

It is, however, not only the gaze of Americans that marks Rachel as shameful for her desires. "Ma's eyes are on me, on my naked legs and arms" (185). The desiring body—the body that wants to be liked—is already sinful and in need of covering. Rachel is Eve's heir but retains a textual memory of the body before the fall. "Without clothes on, I will be naked Eve in the garden before the sin" (85). Clothing simultaneously inscribes Judaism and modesty on the surface of the female body. In sacred texts, the prophet Isaiah figures the difference between a sinful past and a messianic future in a metaphor of clothing: "Be your sins like crimson / They can turn snow-white; / Be they red as dyed wool, / They can become like fleece" (*Tanakh* 617). While Rachel's father would dress her in the "snow-white" garments of Isaiah and the seamed stockings recommended by the rabbi in Williamsburg, Mr. Gartner (Rachel's composite version of Mr. Rochester and other romance heroes) clothes her as an object of desire. "She brings the red dress, and I step into it with my silky black-stocking feet. . . . It is as if I've painted my naked body red" (164).

Romance novels construct the role of lover/beloved as a possibility for women. Rachel, however, notes the absence of that role from rabbinic Judaism: "In the Talmud, there are three kinds of virtuous women: girl, wife, and mother" (225). The woman of valor (Proverbs 31, "Ayshes chayil") subjects her own desires to the needs of her household. Janice Radway argues that contemporary romance novels appeal to many women because they express "the desire to be loved, cared for, and understood by an adult who is singularly capable of self-abnegating preoccupation with a loved one's needs" (582). Rachel's attraction to both popular romance and Anglo-American quest romance reflects the twin desires of assimilation: an identification with the characters she takes to be representative of the dominant culture and a desire to be loved by members of that culture.

The trajectory of the traditional Judaic narrative differs from the trajectory of romance. "The cyclical narrative of Jewish history . . . might be schematized, then, as follows: Prosperity-Transgression-Diaspora-Repentance-Redemption" (Biale, Galchinsky, and Heschel 196). Rachel reads the quintessential American romance—with its themes of theft, trickery, and escape—into the traditional Judaic narrative. "I stole *Huckleberry Finn* from Waldbaum's, and it was so good I went back and stole Tom Sawyer. . . . This is how Huck would have gotten it. . . . If I ran away like Huck, I wouldn't be hungry" (42). Differences of gender, religion, and ethnicity problematize Rachel's appropriation of Huck's quest. Her problem, indeed, is similar to one Miriyam Glazer identifies in a novel by Anne Roiphe. "When Laura Smith [in Roiphe's novel] imagines herself taking off into the American mythography, leaving the tribe and tribal family behind, she is attempting to live the quest romance of the gentile Huck Finn and his Jewish fellow-travelers. . . . [Roiphe's novel offers a] promise of an escape from the past, but imagines 'no future activities for the liberated self'" (92). Anglo American romance is often predicated on the protagonist's (be it Huck Finn or Jane Eyre) already orphaned status—the severing of ties to the past—and a narrative projected into the "future activities for the liberated self." But Rachel's quest romance is embedded in a Judaic cyclical and tribal narrative, making it impossible to conceptualize a linear pattern of past, present, and future, or a future fully severed from the past.

If the *Hasidic* community seems to reject the structure of the romance narrative Rachel attempts to write for herself, it also denies Rachel an audience willing to hear her voice. Early in the novel, Rachel and her sister Leah raise their voices in song to celebrate Shabbat, "daring each other [to sing] louder and louder." They willfully ignore their brothers' budding patriarchal warnings, "No girls singing" and "It's a sin," in their own vibrant duet until Father (who at first tries to pretend he cannot hear them) "stops singing and slams his hand down on the table . . . then there's silence" (22). Women's voices profane this dialogue with the divine.

The power of Abraham's narrative is in its capture of a double-consciousness born of diverse cultural traditions and in its refusal of the generic romance ending. Rachel's short-lived freedom ends with her poignant "I'm home but not home," signaling a spatial and temporal tension. "I won't be here, on their hands, for long. I watch Ma light candles, and a spreading glowing pain is in my chest. Father's kiddish hurts. . . . I know this is what I'll miss when I go. . . . We stand for kiddish the story of creation" (295–96). Even as Rachel contemplates a future estranged from her past, the rituals of lighting Shabbat candles and kiddish recreate the past in the narrative present. A sacred space is created and maintained by carefully delineated boundaries—the "fence" built around the laws of the Torah to keep its center holy. As a Jew, Rachel feels that the deep structure of her narrative may be inescapable; at novel's end, she seems prepared to live it anyway. As she turns her gaze on the moon and "[hopes] to climb walls," Rachel gives voice to the fear and desire that propel us into narrative: "I wonder how high I will get before I fall" (296).

As Rachel and by extension Pearl Abraham imagine a story in which past and future may, for the female Jewish subject, already be determined by the desire for assimilation and its impossibility, Anaya turns our attention to the historical core of his protagonist, Antonio Juan Luna y Marez, whose very name is a site of conflict. "Luna y Marez" defines the double-consciousness that historically marks him as a mestizo, a hybrid of indigenous and Spanish ancestry. The Lunas (his mother's people) are farmers while the Marezes (his father's) are horsemen who roamed the open plains in search of new dreams. Clearly, the Lunas represent the indigenous cultures of Mexico while the Marezes descend from Spanish conquistadors. Yet, the Lunas are devout Catholics while the Marezes are priest-haters. Early on, Antonio is aware that he carries "two unreconciled strivings" or "two warring ideals" in one body. He wonders why "two people as opposite as my father and my mother had married. . . . Their blood and their ways kept them at odds" (29). The marriage of Luna and Marez already figures as a historical accommodation between two cultures. A negotiated biculturality is at the center of Antonio's identity. It is not a chosen biculturality, but one that history imposed on him and one that his people have been consciously negotiating since the Spanish Conquest of Mexico in 1519.

Antonio's mentor, Ultima, the *curandera* (healer), helps him to historicize his cultural tension, his Luna/Marez dichotomy. When he first meets Ultima, he says, "I knew she held the secret of my destiny" (12). Although she guides him, Ultima never offers a resolution to his story. Antonio explains: "Ultima told me the stories . . . of my people, and I came to understand how that history stirred in my blood" (123). The "glory" of ancient civilizations disrupted by the "tragedy" of conquest is Anaya's way of defining the double-consciousness that is at the heart of being Chicano or mestizo. Ultima helps the boy understand that to be of his "people" is to understand how this history "stirs in his blood." For him there is no outside, no way of stepping beyond his already bifurcated self, without denying that history. Whereas for Abraham's Rachel the stories of the Diaspora tell of the quest for assimilation and thus her own story demands a conscious choice between *Hasidic* and American ways, for Anaya's Antonio, it is a matter of understanding how the assimilation of indigenous and Spanish ways already defines him. Only after he has learned how to manage this internal double-consciousness will he be ready to deal with the triple-consciousness of what it is to be "American."

Not until he is formally introduced to indigenous beliefs, in the form of the Golden Carp, does his sense of self as a "split" being become spiritual malaise—a doubt which plagues him from the moment he learns of the god who loved his people so much that it metamorphosed into a fish to protect them from evil (80). Here, Anaya turns to Aztec cosmology, the indigenous belief system most radically subverted by the arrival of Catholicism; specifically, Anaya revises the fourth cycle of Aztec cosmology. Learning of the Golden Carp causes Antonio to doubt his Catholic beliefs "because the roots of everything I had ever believed in seemed shaken. If the golden carp was a god, who was the man on the cross? The Virgin? Was my mother praying to the wrong God?" (81). As Bruce-Novoa reminds us, to be Chicano is to learn to live in a space of contradiction (*Chicano* 12). The bifurcation between Catholicism, already divided between Christ and Virgin, and the Golden Carp reenacts the cultural crisis and accommodation of the earlier conquest. Faced with competing stories of salvation, Antonio asks his mentor for direction, but Ultima refuses to control his thinking. Instead, she helps him accept the contradiction that marks him as a postcolonial being when she says, "As you grow into manhood you must find your own truths" (119). Though fully aware the Golden Carp is "a miraculous thing . . . a pagan god" that strikes him with "a sudden illumination of beauty and understanding" (114), while the (Catholic) God does not answer his questions during Holy Communion, Antonio never renounces the Catholic God. Rather, he embraces both and accepts the pattern of vulnerability and receptivity that already marks him historically. Integrity, for him, comes from this syncretised spirituality.

In conversation with his father, Antonio asks whether a "new religion" can be made. And he comes to understand that he must take "the llano [valley] . . . the moon and the sea, God and the golden carp—and make something new" (247). His father says that "understanding comes with life" and notes that Ultima "has sympathy for people, and it is so complete that with it she can touch their souls and cure them" (248). The boy is no longer concerned that he cannot resolve his spiritual contradictions. Antonio awaits such syncretism somewhere in the future and believes that sympathy, not naïve empathy, may help structure a working paradigm to guide him in his bicultural existence. While Antonio, the child protagonist, caught inside the web of complications created by his spiritual beliefs, does not extricate himself from his "split" consciousness, Antonio, the adult narrator, comes to terms with it through the power of narrative. For Antonio, stories are a strategy for building and expanding that space of tension between Mexican and American, pushing the two opposing "terms"(i.e., cultures) farther and farther apart. If we read Antonio's narrative as a further gloss of Bruce-Novoa's theory, Antonio must learn to work the space between Luna and Marez. As a Chicano, he must first reinhabit that earlier tension, that historical dichotomy between indigenous and Spaniard. By novel's end, Antonio has not yet arrived at the stage of negotiating between Mexican and American; however, in dealing with the interstices between indigenous and Spaniard, he has proven capable of the task that awaits him. Having taken Ultima's advice, he has turned difference into strength and has begun to weave the disparate strands of conflicting myths into a single story. He says, "From my mother I had learned that man is of the earth. . . . But from my father and Ultima I had learned that the greater immortality is in the freedom of man" (228). Herein lies the strength of the contradiction: Antonio can be both "of the earth" (indigenous) and have "freedom" (the spirit of the conquistador). And his father agrees: "There is power here, a power that can fill a man with satisfaction"—to which Ultima adds: "And there is faith here . . . a faith in the reason for nature being, evolving, growing" (229). In his newly found wisdom, Antonio observes, "And there is also the dark, mystical past, I thought, the past of the people who lived here and left their traces in the magic that crops out today" (229).

By refusing to fall into the predictable and violent hierarchy of Spaniard over indigenous, Antonio finds power and faith. Whether he goes on to become a priest or a folk healer remains ambiguous; however, he has already become a storyteller. He may go on to create a new mythology built on the traditions of his mother's Catholicism, his father's nonsectarian worldview, and Ultima's animism. As if aware that he must venture out into profane space, he begs for Ultima's blessing as she lies dying, a blessing that she grants—a performative speech act that creates the sacred space it invokes: "I bless you in the name of all that is good and strong and beautiful, Antonio. Always have the strength to live. Love life, and if despair enters your heart, look for me in the evenings when the wind is gentle and the owls sing in the hills. I shall be with you" (261).

To be blessed "in the name of all that is good and strong and beautiful" rather than in "the Name of the Father," or any other single pre-existing ideology, invites the subject to live unafraid in the open-ended space of multidimensionality. Anaya revalues the notion of the divided self and implies that for the Chicano, it is a blessing, not a curse. To deny the tension between indigenous and Spaniard is to deny history, foreclosing the space already opened by conflict and contradiction.

As for Janie in Zora Neale Hurston's *Their Eyes Were Watching God*, while her story returns us to some of the issues of gender and romance raised in our discussion of Abraham's novel, it also provides a quite different response to double-consciousness, for neither the *ABC*s she learned from the white folk's school, nor the effort to "articulate the message of another people"—to be like them in order to be liked by them—interests Janie. She is not torn, bewildered, or paralyzed by the aesthetic dilemmas symptomatic of black artists afflicted with Du Boisian double-consciousness:

> The innate love of harmony and beauty that set the ruder souls of his people a-dancing and a-singing raised but confusion and doubt in the soul of the black artist; for the beauty revealed to him was the soul-beauty of a race which his larger audience despised, and he could not articulate the message of another people. (Du Bois 46–7)

Rather, Janie's dream of community complements her dream of marriage. Unlike "men" who pursue horizons that mock their dreams, she pursues her dreams of loving, mutually affirming reciprocity, as illustrated by her vision of bees and pear blossoms: her dreams informing not only her preference in lovers, but also her choice of the horizons that she would rather—and rather not—explore, hence, the forms of discourse that she would rather and rather not cultivate.

Deferring to Henry Louis Gates, Jr.'s "Zora Neale Hurston and the Speakerly Text" for the best account of Hurston's blending of Standard English and black diction within the novel's narrative commentary, this discussion focuses solely on Janie because she represents a third response to double-consciousness within the continuum offered in this collaborative study. Janie chooses neither, like Rachel, to address a larger audience that may despise the perceived narrowness and limits of ethnic and religious specificity, nor, like Antonio, to cultivate an identity wherein the converging trajectories of diverse, even antagonistic traditions produce a divided self that is a blessing not a curse (Gates 191). Instead, at home in segregated, black communities of "Signifiers," big picture talkers, "woofers" and storytellers, Janie cultivates forms of oral, call-and-response discourse among those Du Bois might call "ruder souls," whereby she learns to tell her own "big story" and control the gendered, intracultural split between the soul that dreams identity and the self that performs it.

In pursuit of her dream of marriage, Janie leaves Logan Killicks for Joe Starks. But, once in Eatonville with Joe, she also overhears the porch talkers, emulates their style and improvisational resourcefulness during call-and-response verbal play, and seeks inclusion in that public space of performative reciprocity. Sam Watson and Lige Moss, above all, become her "center," models of her verbal aspirations, two "big picture talkers" who take up "the whole side of the world as a canvas" for their inventive hyperbolas, calls, and responses. Their reciprocal improvisations "never ended" because "there was no end to reach" beyond the exploration of each performer's boundless range and depth of verbal invention, another striking response being the most sincere affirmation of another excellent call (51). Deferring the extensive pleasure of closure via external transcendence in favor of the uninterrupted, *elegant expectancy* of intensive, collaborative, and inventive desire, this dream discourse complements Janie's dream of marriage.

Eager to join in the community narrative, Janie is not split in terms of ethnicity or race. She is, however, ultimately split by the oppression she experiences as a result of her gender. Janie hungrily listens, learns, and performs, yet, just as the porch talkers acknowledge her as a "born orator," Joe forbids her from joining in the fun on the porch or speaking publicly at all. Although Janie "fought back with her tongue," Joe "wanted her submission and would keep fighting until he felt he had it" (67). Over the years, she tires, then, once she submits, "splits" in two: "She had an inside and an outside *now* and *suddenly* she knew how not to mix them" (68, emphasis added). If, as Elizabeth Grosz argues, bodies incarnate codes, laws, norms, and ideals, then Janie's "incarnation" of Joe's law *instantly* engenders her own version of what Judith Butler calls "interiority as an effect and function of public regulation" (172).

Now, Janie's "outside" or "self" is the paltry sum of all allowable gestures by which she may perform a public identity, yet her "inside" or "soul" retains abilities and affinities exceeding Joe's "law," whereupon, instantly, her "soul" escapes the newly inhibited outer boundaries of "self." The soul fleeing outside of her "outside," to be precise if semantically confusing, implies that the soul will not be diminished by the law, although Joe's law can diminish the "self" by inhibiting Janie's responsiveness to the promptings of the soul that dreams. Nevertheless, like an inkling of something forgotten, the soul still beckons Janie to the dream space of the porch talkers, although not as a performer but in the silent and diminished role of eavesdropper upon that "soul-beauty." Recovering a performative role in that dream space and restoring the elegant expectancy of the self's uninhibited responsiveness to the call of the soul entail verbally defeating Joe Starks, the self-proclaimed "big voice" of Eatonville. Yet, even afterward, her soul beckons her still further into "life," new horizons of healthy reciprocity that performatively overwrite the regulatory inscriptions of Joe's law on her "self" and, thus, further enhance her self's responsiveness to the call of the soul.

Rhetorically, a successful call is like a proffered "high five," to which more or less socially and verbally adept individuals respond with more or less grace of style. It is both impolite and slow-witted to leave a speaker's call "hanging" or uninterrupted. A simple, well-timed "amen" or "word" or "sho' you right" will do while chatting. One of the more generally familiar and basic of the larger call-and-response conventions is variously named the dozens or "cappin'" or "snaps." Involving an exchange of hyperbolic insults, the dozens test each speaker's capacity for coolness and invention under agonistic pressure. The best can brand their opponents with stinging, hyperbolic imagery so befitting their opponent's appearance or demeanor that it can "call him out of his name" for an entire lifetime. Less dramatically, the one who first gropes for a reply and/or loses her "cool" has lost the linguistic contest.

The worst mistake Joe Starks makes in his life is to "snap" on Janie in front of the porch talkers who laugh out loud as he invokes "yo' pop eyes" and "yo' rump hangin nearly to yo' knees," after she cuts a ragged plug of tobacco for a customer (74). Janie warns, "stop mixin' my doin's with mah looks," but Joe's failing health has made him irritable: "What de matter wid you? . . . You ain't no young girl to be gettin' all insulted 'bout 'yo looks" (75). Janie offers no response. Her soul prompts but her self is sluggish after years of abjection. The porch is no longer laughing as Joe, again, prods the sleeping bear: "Ain't no use gettin' all mad, Janie. . . . Nobody in heah ain't looking for no wife outa yuh. Old as you is." Then, coolly, Janie blasts him with hyperbole: "Talkin' 'bout me lookin' old! When you pull down yo' britches you look lak the change uh life." Exhilarated, Sam Watson names the discourse: "Great God from Zion! Y'all really playin' de dozens tuhnight." When Starks utters only "Wha- . . . you say?" Walter expectantly urges, "You heard her. You ain't blind" (75). None of the porch talkers doubts for an instant that the "big voice" will verbally rise to the elegant expectancy of the moment, but Starks freezes. Hurston tortuously prolongs the silence in which Starks stammers. A leisurely paragraph minutely details the new cracks in Joe's facade of power. Thereafter, all in Eatonville regard him as one whose power as a "big voice" resides in his material possessions only, not his abilities.

After Joe's death due to an apparent kidney infection, Janie's soul's dreams beckon her into the arms of Tea Cake and wider horizons of "soul-beauty." With Tea Cake in the Jacksonville muck, Janie studies large oral narrative forms: "She got so she could tell big stories herself by listening to the rest." Also, she enjoys the "woofing" and "boogerbooing" of Ed Dockery, Bootyny, and Sop-de-Bottom at cards. And, "because she loved to hear it the men loved to hear themselves" (128). Alert to the intercultural limitations of such fluency, Janie neither speaks nor pays attention at her trial after she is forced to shoot Tea Cake. Her soul stands apart from the authoritarian procedures. "'If you know what's good for you, you better shut your mouth up until somebody calls you,'" barks Mr. Prescott when Sop-de-Bottom chimes in (178).

Nevertheless, following the trial, Janie returns to Eatonville with the skills learned in the muck, ready to tell her own "big story." Silent before her hecklers, she saves the embrace of her well-wrought "call," for one who will "kiss and be kissed," her friend, Pheoby (6). Pheoby's affirmation, "I feel like I growed ten feet taller listenin' tuh you," does not leave Janie hanging (182).

As the narrative frame makes clear, when one sets off for distant horizons only to have one's dreams "mocked to death by Time" (1), it is easy, perhaps instinctive, to recoil from a painful internal dialogue between "two warring impulses" comprising a violent hierarchy. Janie, however, distinguishes between the discourse of destructive double-conscious-ness, "talkin' [that] don't amount tuh uh hill uh beans when yuh can't do nothin' else" (183), and generative, call-and-response reciprocity between self and soul. Her soul dreams horizons of loving reciprocity among the "ruder souls" and calls her "self" there performatively to cultivate the "soul-beauty of a race." Hence, it is with joyful expectation, not fear of what her "larger audience despised," that her self's final call is to her soul: she "pulled in her horizon like a great fish-net . . . from around the waist of the world and draped it over her. . . . So much of life in its meshes. She called in her soul to come and see" (184). The tension between self and soul remains unresolved. The self's call still awaits the soul's response, an elegant expectancy that, in itself, is the defining emphasis of any successful call-and-response reciprocity.

In the primarily secular spaces of American multiculturalism and academe, where we are more likely to interrogate race, gender, and eth-nicity, it is provocative to touch briefly on one theme that emerges in all three texts and further enlarges the paradigm of double-consciousness: the creation of sacred space. While Du Bois's wording sets "one's soul" in opposition to "a world that looks on in amused contempt and pity," Abraham, Anaya, and Hurston—along with their protagonists—seek to maintain the sacred *in* the world. Yet, it is a sacred space as indetermi-nate as the individuals that occupy it. Janie's final, albeit unanswered, call, Ultima's blessing of the young Antonio, and the juxtaposition of Rachel's communal Shabbat with her own unanswered "call" to the moon reveal another aspect of multiethnic literature worthy of further consideration.

In our study of multiethnic literature, this conversation has given us a glimpse of the precarious landscape where the signifier, "American identity," shifts and re-arranges itself in endlessly complex configura-tions that defy easy categories. In an idealistic quest for commonalities, we were not prepared for the nuances of difference that this collabora-tive effort has shown us. Having brought these three texts face to face with each other and having allowed ourselves to listen to them speak, we hear how crucial a role assimilation plays both inside and outside a given culture, but also hear how that process and its alienating effects may vary widely. Regardless of how each story ends, the negotiation that creates narrative deconstructs fixed cultural identity. While all three protagonists seek a loving discourse community that will affirm their newly articulated, but indeterminate, subjectivities, the three authors similarly call out to a less divided, more responsive readership for these multilingual and multi-discourse texts. Thus, this conversation has helped us to understand how the concept of identity (sociocultural or essential), which frequently underpins theories of multiculturalism, needs to be re-figured as an endless process of signification. In productive, open-ended multicultural scholarship, there can be no predictable heuristics for charting the complex terrain that the multicultural subject must travel. We must be prepared, instead, to examine the interstices where characters and texts meet as well as the spaces where their respective cultural matrices make it impossible for them to meet.

Works Cited

Abraham, Pearl. *The Romance Reader*. New York: Riverhead Books, 1995.

Anaya, Rudolfo A. *Bless Me, Ultima*. New York: Warner Books, 1994.

Biale, David, Michael Galchinsky, and Susannah Heschel, eds. *Insider/Outsider: American Jews and Multiculturalism*. Berkeley: University of California Press, 1998.

Bruce-Novoa. *Chicano Poetry: A Response to Chaos*. Austin: University of Texas Press, 1982.

———. "Portraits of Chicano Artists as Young Men: The Narrator in Three Chicano Novels." *Flor y Canto II: An Anthology of Chicano Literature*. Ed. Arnold C. Vento Alurista, José Armas, José F. Pelegrine, and Bernice Zamora. Albuquerque: Pajarito Press, 1979. 150–61.

Butler, Judith. *Gender Trouble*. New York: Routledge, 1990.

Douglass, Frederick. *The Narrative Life of Frederick Douglass*. New York: Dover, 1995.

Du Bois, W. E. B. *The Souls of Black Folk*. New York: Penguin Books/Signet, 1995.

Gates, Henry Louis, Jr. *The Signifying Monkey: A Theory of Afro-American Literary Criticism*. New York: Oxford University Press, 1988.

Glazer, Miriyam. "'Daughters of Refugees of the Ongoing-Universal-Endless-Upheaval': Anne Roiphe and the Quest for Narrative Power in Jewish American Women's Fiction." *Daughters of Valor: Contemporary Jewish American Women Writers*. Ed. Jay L. Halio and Ben Siegel. Newark: University of Delaware Press, 1997. 80–96.

Goodman, Allegra. "Writing Jewish Fiction In and Out of the Multicultural
    Context." *Daughters of Valor: Contemporary Jewish American Women Writ-*
    ers. Ed. Jay L. Halio and Ben Siegel. Newark: University of Delaware
    Press, 1997. 68–274.
Grosz, Elizabeth. *Space, Time, and Perversion.* New York: Routledge, 1995.
Hurston, Zora Neale. *Their Eyes Were Watching God.* New York: Harper and
    Row, 1990.
Radway, Janice. "The Readers and Their Romances." *Feminisms.* Ed. Robyn R.
    Warhol and Diane Price Herndl. New Brunswick, NJ: Rutgers University
    Press, 1991. 551–85.
Tanakh: The Holy Scriptures. Philadelphia: Jewish Publication Society, 1985.

14 When Hybridity Doesn't Resist

Giannina Braschi's Yo-Yo Boing!

JOSÉ L. TORRES-PADILLA

HYBRIDITY, AS AN OPERATIVE CONCEPT today in postcolonial theory, is often presented as a function of diaspora. The economic forces that compel the often violent and disruptive movement of millions of people across boundaries and geopolitical spheres, a phenomenon that still continues, have also had as a consequence the encountering of cultures, languages, and races. In the Western Hemisphere, perhaps more than anywhere else, the various diasporas that accentuate the area's history have had an enormous effect on its people and how they see and interact with the world. The multiplicity of this phenomenon must be emphasized because, although Paul Gilroy's concept of "The Black Atlantic" illustrates the diaspora most influential in informing theories of hybridity, there are other migrations that serve to give a fuller picture of diaspora as a concept and of its relationship to hybridity.[1]

As a Caribbean people, Puerto Ricans share the historic effects of the African diaspora. The slave trade brought to the island's shores ancestors who contributed an indelible part to its racial and cultural makeup. But the Puerto Rican diaspora has led many *compatriotas* to other destinations, notably although not exclusively to the United States. These

Puerto Ricans left the island mainly out of economic need to work in factories or in agribusiness. As American citizens, Puerto Ricans can travel easily between the island and the States and this freedom has facilitated a continual migration that may change in character for different people at different times—for instance, from unskilled workers seeking employment to professionals moving to Orlando for a better standard of living—but is generally underpinned by United States economic power.

The hybrid forms that have developed from this diaspora—and the related reverse migration of Puerto Ricans returning to the island—confront anyone who visits the island or a Puerto Rican enclave in the states. Whether it is Puerto Ricans in winter clothing doing *parandas* (group singing similar to caroling) in New York, the Spanish rap that we hear on the airwaves,[2] or the intermixing of Spanish and English observed in business signs along San Juan streets, it is clear that the traffic of Puerto Ricans between the equally ambiguous "here" and "there" has created an ongoing process of hybrid cultural production.

The most salient manifestation of this hybridity is the intermingling of Spanish and English, often referred to as "Spanglish," the translated version of "Espanglish," a disparaging term introduced and popularized by an island Puerto Rican writer Salvador Tio to label what he saw as the alarming encroachment of English into the Puerto Rican Spanish vernacular.[3] Tio saw Spanglish as a threat to national cultural development, claiming that such abuse of language could not lead to clear thinking and certainly could not create a suitable literature. Frances Aparicio's essay, "La Vida es un Spanglish Disparatero," counters Tio's and other similar commentary by analyzing the poetics of Nuyorican poets and persuasively arguing that only such a hybrid writing could faithfully represent the existing popular culture and social conditions of *puertorriqueños* en El Barrio.[4] Aparicio sees this "poetics of bilingualism" as a form of counterhegemonic cultural production, a response to Anglo American political and cultural dominance (147–48). Some would also argue that the use of "Spanglish" and its poetics undermines the essentialist perceptions of literature and purity in language held by the island's cultural elite. As such, in its ability to reverse colonial authority by unmasking it and showing its ambivalence, Nuyorican poetry represents a hybrid form that adheres to the conventionally held postcolonial position, particularly that of Homi Bhabha, that hybridity works as a resisting force against the colonizer.

Puerto Rico's political situation, however, is too complex and undefined to accept that present postcolonial theories of hybridity explain amply how this concept operates within all facets of Puerto Rican cultural life on the island and in the United States. In Puerto Rico, where the elite has failed to achieve its historically assigned task of constructing a nation-state, what has developed instead is an "illusory nation." Ramon Grosfoguel describes this illusion as "a feeling of nationhood that has not translated into traditional nationalist claims to form a nation-state" (74). Since 1898, when the United States invaded Puerto Rico in its imperialist grab for territory during the Spanish American War, the island has been a possession governed under the Constitution's territorial clause. Despite Puerto Rico's elected Governor and bicameral legislature, United States federal law and power reign supreme, and Puerto Rico's economy (Puerto Ricans use the United States dollar) and every aspect of Puerto Rican society and culture are influenced or shaped by American hegemony. From a historical lack of self-determination and independence, Puerto Ricans have developed a resistance to, some would even say a fear of, traditionally conservative tendencies of nationalism; and what has developed through the island's ideological apparatuses is this particular illusory nation promoted by the *Estado Libre Asociado* (loosely translated as "Associated Free State"), Puerto Rico's ambiguous, neocolonial form of government that misleadingly gives the impression that it has power when real power rests in the hands of the United States President and Congress.

Giannina Braschi's ideological position in *Yo-Yo Boing!*,[5] as outlined below, confirms the realization that, in the relationship between the United States and Puerto Rico, both the colonizer and colonized support the disavowal of which Bhabha writes. In other words, *both* the Puerto Rican colonial government and the United States aim to deny a colonizing intervention that has initiated *Entstellung*, or the "process of displacement, distortion, dislocation, repetition" (Bhabha 105). By not taking a firm stance of resistance against imperialism and hegemony, by actually obscuring this power relationship behind an argument over aesthetics, Braschi's novel in fact supports the continuing colonial status of Puerto Rico and undermines any desire for self-determination that might effect real change.

Unlike the Nuyorican poets' use of Spanish and English to construct an ideologically oppositional text, Giannina Braschi's Pulitzer-nominated novel, *Yo-Yo Boing!*, intentionally merges various registers in the two languages but not in any way that could be typified as resistant or oppositional. The text represents, and argues for, an idealized figure of the Puerto Rican poet, free from the weight of having to make choices for seemingly undecidable situations—in essence, a representation of the traditional, classical aesthete. Thus, the discourse created out of this linguistic performance, decidedly elitist and bourgeois, ultimately defers to political inertia and revels in the status quo, which cannot escape allusions and linkages to the *Estado Libre Asociado*. Indeed, the very form of the novel, with its postmodernist tendencies and features, contributes to a general literary effect that rhetorically supports a political position counter to the desire for Puerto Rican self-determination. In *Yo-Yo Boing!*, we have an example of a text in which hybridity does not resist the colonizer, and therefore a text that raises questions about the present theorization of hybridity, the context from which the concept has emerged, and its validity to assist critics in understanding and interpreting *all* post- (or perhaps more appropriately, neo-) colonial cultural production.

But how precisely does hybridity resist, and why does *Yo-Yo Boing!*, as a hybrid text, fail to resist? Homi Bhabha claims that "hybridity reverses the effects of the colonialist disavowal, so that other 'denied' knowledges enter upon the dominant discourse and estrange the basis of its authority" (114). For Bhabha, "disavowal" refers to the colonizer's denial of his disruptive presence, a strategy operating simultaneously as he attempts to establish an authoritative presence based on difference that is supposed to be assimilated as a constant: "the way it has always been," "the way it should be." The colonial power creates discourse along strict Manichean lines to sustain fabricated differences between itself and the Other, the colonized, and thereby to justify its power based precisely on those differences (JanMohamed). Hybridity undermines the colonizer's rhetorical project by highlighting the falsity of this Manichean premise and showing the ambivalence inherent in attempting to construct a unitary or fixed conception of culture or the corresponding strategy of bifurcating the Self and the Other within that culture.

Resistance, for Bhabha, does not necessarily have to be an "oppositional act of political intention" (110). It is enough for hybridity, as a resisting force, to weaken colonial authority by merely questioning the established discourse that defines and centers the structure of power. Bhabha has been taken to task for this position, which seems to neglect questions of power that go beyond the abstract or the discursive. I mention it here, however, because even this rather feeble resistance eludes Braschi's text. *Yo-Yo Boing!* certainly does not present any outright political opposition to the United States and its power as a colonizer over Puerto Rico. The hybridity in the text consists of an overlaying and interweaving of varying registers in both languages, a consistent deft dialogic playing of one language with and against the other. Braschi contains this hybrid language in the middle part of the book titled "Blow-up," in itself an openly rhetorical decision on the part of the author. The other two parts of the book—"Close-Up" and "Black-out"—are written in sustained formal Spanish. The middle section consists of a series of dialogues, interior monologues, and flashbacks, sometimes without pause and often blending into each other. The writing incorporates all types of linguistic borrowing—loanwords, merged, independent, and phrasal calques—characterized in Puerto Rican Spanglish.[6] There is also intrasentential code-switching or mixing, a mainstay of this hybrid language, although there are not many grammatical borrowings, which both demonstrates Braschi's faithfulness to each language's syntax and grammar and signals her education and social class. In other words, unlike most practitioners of "Spanglish," Braschi is in full command of both languages, and this clearly reaffirms her use of it in this text for artistic effect.

We find these linguistic elements of "Spanglish" across informal and formal registers in the text. For example, in an exchange between the principal character and her lover: "Why do I have to get up para hacerte el gran favor de abrirte la puerta [. . . to do you the favor of opening the door]" (36). Or in this case, which shows the use of a loanword: "I don't want chocolate. It gives me grains" (39). Here, the English word "grains" substitutes the Spanish *granos* meaning pimples. The text is full of other similar examples: "revolting all my gavetas" ("turning over all my drawers"; *revolver* is the Spanish verb for "turn over") (45); and the consistent use of "loose" for lose or "add" for "ad" (as in advertisement). There are Puerto Rican idioms mistranslated into English (purposefully, I suspect), such as, "It's obvious you're missing the shot again," from the Puerto Rican Spanish "disparate," something said without much thought, which comes from the word *disparar*, or to shoot as in a gun, although the noun *disparate* can mean a blunder in formal Spanish (58).

Much of the hybrid language in the novel mimics the conversations of bilingual Puerto Ricans living in the States (and some in the island). Braschi often incorporates these hybridized exchanges in flashbacks, as in this one, in which the protagonist recalls an awkward moment with an ex-lover:

> Relax, no eres el único. [Relax, you aren't the only one]
> —I don't socialize with students.
> —*Esas son las mejores. Son faciles de seducir.* [Those are the best. They're easy to seduce] Listen, it's nothing to be ashamed of.
> —I'm not ashamed of anything. *Sí, vente*—dijo entonces Jabalí irguiéndose como un marajá de la India, y sonriéndose [Yes, come— Jabalí said standing erect like an Indian maharaja, and smiling], pinching my other elbow to the rhythm of: *ya me lo pa-ga-rás* [you'll pay for this]. (65, emphases in original)

Sometimes the exchange between two characters contains literary allusions or imagery, thus crossing into yet another register. In this passage, Braschi has her protagonist go off on a linguistic riff that alludes to T. S. Eliot:

> He really was burned—repressed—and that's why he says:
> *O Lord, Thou pluckest me out.*
> —What does pluckest mean?
> —Oh, Dios, por qué me desplumas [Oh, God, why did you pluck my feathers]. Dios lo desplumó, y por eso se hizo religioso [God plucked his feathers and that's why he turned religious].
> His sexual desire was so repressed hasta que Dios le quito todas sus plumas. Pero que es un poeta sin plumas. Es como un vampiro sin dientes. O una bruja sin escoba. [. . . until God took all of his feathers. But what's a poet without his pens. It's like a vampire without teeth. Or a witch without a broom]. (186)

"Desplumar" means to pluck feathers in Spanish, but here Braschi also alludes to the Puerto Rican characterization of male homosexuals as "patos" (ducks) and thus the plucking of their feathers and Eliot's repressed homosexuality. The colloquial term for a pen is "pluma" and Braschi also uses this denotation of the word in this passage.

Braschi thus applies this hybrid language in registers that run from the vulgar, informal, and conversational to the intellectual, literary, and even the surreal, as in this descriptive passage:

> Faith looked at me con el rabo de su ojo [from the corner of her eye]— the castle swaying on our heads—about to collapse—about to crush us to death. The wagon jutted and a loose beam came tumbling down y toda la estructura cayo perfecta en su lugar [and all of the structure fell into place]. I knew he was going to use our scene. Bright white lights went on, the crowd dispersed and the crew started climbing down scaffolds and girders. Woody turned around to see who had changed his pace. He was panting and sticky, with his face blotchy red. Esperaba que estuviera fascinado. Fellini se hubiera enamorado del runaway train [I expected that he be fascinated. Fellini would have loved the runaway train]. (94)

Braschi even plays with bilingual onomatopoeia:

> Meti una manguera en mi boca [I put a hose in my mouth]—and gulp, gulp, sploosh—ahogado en mi garganta [drowned in my throat]—glup— came a glob, a frog—a tender tadpole which I swallowed whole. (97)

In this example she uses English onomatopoeic language in the middle of a Spanish sentence, then reverts to the more Spanish-sounding "glup" followed by an English sentence. She also transforms an English lullaby into broken English:

> Rocka my baby
>> On the tri tad
>> When the come baby
>> Cris o win blow. (108)

As if these examples do not demonstrate her bilingual virtuosity, towards the end of the middle section Braschi has her protagonist let loose with a Spanglish poetry reading that reaches levels of parody and farce:

Have you thought about me lately?
Thought about you. Or suck about
you. Sucks the smelling stinky
thoughts are sucking wet while
drying—fumes—the smelling stinky
thoughts, away, the dry and stinky
smells of earth, of paradigmas [paradigms] and
chiguaguas [chihuahas] and chinas mias [my sweet oranges]—and
naranjas [oranges]—gandules and beldades [pigeon peas and
    beauties]—
brisas—risas—son risas las mias [breezes—laughter—mine are
    laughter]
son stinkies—las tuyas son finas—[they're stinkies—yours are
    fine]
brisas caidas de la tumba a la nada [breezes fallen from the tomb to
    nothingness]
se caen stinkies son las mias [stinkies fall they are mine]. (150)

Braschi's hybrid linguistic performance, although admirable for its dexterity and range, does not demonstrate the qualities that Bhabha describes in his work. It is precisely this linguistic virtuosity that reveals a hybridity artistically organized—in the Bakhtinian sense—for rhetorical and ideological purposes. Bakhtin calls this type of hybrid "intentional," and it represents "the perception of one language by another language, its illumination by another linguistic consciousness" (359).[7] The intentional hybrid involves, then, two languages represented in two "consciousnesses:" the authorial consciousness and will and the individualized linguistic consciousness and will of the characters represented. In the case of *Yo-Yo Boing!*, the hybridity is not one that somehow surfaces and, by its mere emergence, allows a critical interpretation of the ambivalence created. Braschi has not created a text that through hybridity produces ambivalence, but rather she has consciously created a hybrid text to sustain a point about ambivalence.

The semes in *Yo-Yo Boing!* point to two major sets of contraries, which can be conceptualized in terms of whole and part: monolingualism, identity, and essentialism versus the "part" represented quite often in the text by "the voice" as when the protagonist claims to have "not only brought the hills to life; but the cows to music, to music" with her singing (58); or at the end of part one where she vocalizes vowels in what appears to be slow motion (29–30). Similarly, the author gives us persistent representations of "orifices" set in opposition to the body, which is represented as something dead or uninhabited:

> porque no queria estar metida en mi misma, porque no me encontraba bien corriendo dentro del cuerpo que no poseia, mi cuerpo, si yo quiero ocasionar un fuego, y quemarlo con todos mis recuerdos, con todas las posesiones que me han encarcelado en un cuerpo que ya no soy yo
> [because I didn't want to be within myself, because I didn't feel well being in a body that I did not possess, my body, if I wanted to start a fire, and burn it with all my memories, with all the possessions that have imprisoned me in a body that is no longer me]. (196)

Yo-Yo Boing!, set against Puerto Rico's unsettled political situation, brings us to see the refiguring of the ideal poet in the text, to use Jameson's complex term,[8] as the solution to the island's political impasse inscribed in the imaginary. This poet is bilingual, bicultural, has a voice, and is free from the restraining effects of decision-making and the burden of history. At the end of novel, she proclaims her intent to bury the twentieth century while looking ahead to the twenty-first. More than content to live within ambivalence, the poet revels in it. "My confusion," Braschi's poet/alter-ego states, "is my statement of clarity. I live with plenty of identities within myself. And I want all of them to work" (143). This position on writing somehow becomes a metaphor for political indecision. "Los puertorriqueños," she says, "son puntos y comas. No pueden decidirse por el punto o por la coma [Puerto Ricans are semicolons. They can't decide on the period or the comma]" (182). In an obvious allusion to the island's political status, she asks someone "quien es mas fuerte, la isla que se vende y come bien, o la que se mantiene erecta, y se muere de hambre y de soledad [Which is stronger, the island that sells out and eats well, or the one that stands firm, but dies from hunger and loneliness]." Her answer is noncommittal: "Ninguna de las dos es libre. Todo pertenece [Neither one is free. Everything belongs]" (161).

If Braschi's linguistic repertoire contains various registers and voices, a truly dialogic performance, and thus in Bakhtinian terms, a truly hybrid text, it is nonetheless evident that the sustained discourse belongs to someone from a privileged class. The only glimpse of anyone outside of Braschi's class is of some black muggers who attempt to rob an old Mexican laborer. In presenting "la quijotesca Mishi" as a middle class defender of the old man, Braschi simultaneously racializes the scene and enervates the working class. The protagonist does not grasp the import of Mishi's intervention. She sees it as an opportunity to appropriate the story to entertain friends at a party; in fact, she wants to change the real story's "dismal" ending to make it more aesthetically pleasing (124). The text is rife with bourgeois fetishes, frivolous talk about material things and a cloying concern with name-dropping.

The marginalization of the working class in this text gathers significance when we consider the central, driving ideologeme in this text: that of the traditional, classical aesthete searching for artistic freedom bordering on frivolity: "I want poetry to be a fashion show, to have a taste of frivolity—savoir faire—a taste of time at its peak—Kenzo, Gigli and Gautier. I'm more excited by Bergdorf's windows than the contemporary poetry I've read" (142). Art for art's sake; everything else be damned—this is a position buoyed by the discourse and its rhetoric. Any position differing from this aesthetic is presented as unflattering and rigid; as in the case of Cenci and Olmo-Olmo, both of whom are projected as being socially conscious, but the former is depicted as idealistic and the latter as oafish and insincere. The comments that both of these two characters make about art, and any political or social responsibility or force it may have, are consistently undercut. When Olmo-Olmo criticizes the protagonist's inclination to write about insignificant things such as skin scabs, mucus, and other bodily fluids, and asks "Por que no habla de temas que cambian la condicion humana? [Why not discuss themes that can change the human condition?]," his question's valid authority is subsequently undermined by his silly and amateurish insistence that she write descriptive exercises (162). It is clear by the remarks of other characters that the protagonist's politics are at best frivolous and questionable: "You don't know anything about politics" someone tells her, "Nothing at all. Yet you talk nonsense with such conviction, such hostility. You live in a fantasy world" (157). And later: "You're so self-indulgent, smugly ignorant. You think you're charming the world with your ignorance. You're impeding knowledge" (157). The genuine-ness of her ideals is questioned when someone says, "You dream of palaces for beggars but you wouldn't toss them a dime in the streets" (159). An incident in a restaurant confirms this political passivity. The waiter discriminates against her, and it is her Anglo companion who defends her and in anger tells her: "It was because of your accent. They discriminate against Hispanics. Face it, you know it exists, but when someone slaps your face, you freeze and fall mute" (118). Braschi's polit-ical and aesthetic positions thus become crystallized in a textual ideo-logical representation that ultimately affirms the colonial status quo.

The novel's form, its "experimental format," as a reviewer from *Pub-lisher's Weekly* called it, supports the ideological position outlined above. The novel has a clear postmodernist bent demonstrated by character-istics, or features, usually attributed to such a text: the mixing of pop-ular and high conventions; a commitment to doubleness; parody; the undermining of traditional conventions; reflexivity; the obvious oppo-sition to either/or labeling or thinking. The title itself—*Yo-Yo Boing!*—refers to several of these features. The double and reflexive use of the Spanish singular pronoun for Self ("yo") simultaneously signifies the popular toy as metaphor for ambivalence and the transitionary state of Puerto Ricans. And as Alexandra Vega-Merino mentions in the book's introduction, the title also playfully alludes to the stage name of the famous Puerto Rican comedian and television personality, Luis Anto-nio Rivera (15).

Postmodernism responds to a global multinationalist capitalism that has as a dominant feature the compression of time and space in the ever increasing push to get things done faster to accommodate the demand for more profits.[9] The compression of time and space, through advance-ments in technology (satellite communication, the fax, computer, Inter-net, etc.) is a phenomenon that infiltrates our everyday lives and, of course, informs cultural production. Jameson, who has called post-modernism late capitalism's "cultural logic," has commented on how film is "that medium which will shortly become the hegemonic formal expression of late capitalist society" (160). Narrative, an important cul-tural and rhetorical necessity for what Walter Fisher calls *homo narans* (see *Human Communication*), now becomes filtered through the late cap-italist demands for time and space compression. Postmodernism

stresses "immanence" and "indeterminacy," qualities that film reproduces within its visual compression of time and space. Braschi's novel,
like other postmodernist fiction, seems to have incorporated these
filmic qualities through a grafting of filmic techniques. *Yo-Yo Boing!* contains a continual flow of scenes heavily dependent on dialogue very much
like a film. The filmic influence is also evident in the section titles of
the novel: "Close-Up," "Blow-Up," and "Black-Out."

All of these observations lead one to suspect that Braschi's novel has
bought into the prevailing rhetoric of the postmodernist project. The
text thus affirms postmodernist ideas of immanence, indeterminacy, and
ambivalence. These ideas, though, do not privilege an ideology that could
promote an agenda for Puerto Rico's self-determination. Hybridity,
therefore, in this case cannot be seen as counterhegemonic or resistant. Braschi sees hybridity as part of the ambivalent equation and it does
not necessarily represent a political message against the United States.
Braschi's avant-garde performance embraces postmodernist views; but
once coupled with the island's political context it becomes evident that
these ideas stifle any sense of movement towards a real solution to the
present political limbo. The nonresistant rhetorical position found in
this novel cannot be dismissed as unique to the text; it represents a view
held by many Puerto Ricans living in the island and the United States.
That this text represents such a widely held perspective makes the
remarks on hybridity outlined here all the more pertinent and significant.

In *Culture and Imperialism* (1993), Edward Said discusses the question of resistance from the perspective of the Ariel/Caliban literary
dichotomy. In such a scheme, Ariel represents a "sort of bourgeois native
untroubled by his collaboration with Prospero;" in other words, not only
Braschi's poet, but a good number of Puerto Ricans (214). In Caliban
we see the qualities required for potential effective resistance: an awareness and acceptance of a mongrel past that does not disable future development. And the type of Caliban responsible for radical nationalism is
the one that "sheds his current servitude and physical disfigurements
in the process of discovering his essential, pre-colonial self" (Said 214).
Postmodernist thinking does not accommodate this essentializing move
or strategy. Both bell hooks and Gayatri Spivak have cautioned against
the postmodernist critique of essentialism, which they see as a significant,
perhaps necessary, unifying rhetorical tool, what Spivak calls "strategic

essentialism," in the battle against imperialist and hegemonic power. "You pick up the universal," Spivak writes,

> That will give you the power to fight against the other side, and what you are throwing away is your theoretical purity. Whereas the great custodians of the anti-universal are obliged therefore simply to act in the interest of a great narrative, the narrative of exploitation, while they keep themselves clean by not committing themselves to anything. In fact, they are actually protecting their theoretical purity by repudiating essentialism. (12)

Hooks argues that postmodernist thinking on "essentialism" can actually be useful for oppositional groups because it allows for the affirmation of multiple minority voices and identities that serve to challenge the one-dimensional colonial, imperialist paradigms of such identities (28).

Such an appropriation of discursive strategies once only reserved for the imperialist marks an important juncture in the discussion of postmodernism and its relation to postcolonialism. Commenting on the recent antagonism hurled at neocolonial nationalism, some of which admittedly has lead to horrific consequences, Edward Said nonetheless argues for the power of developing nations to use nationalism as a moving force: "A confused and limiting notion of priority," he writes, "allows that only the original proponents of an idea can understand and use it" (217). Nationalism as concept to unify and politicize a people can be adapted by neocolonial countries without it necessarily, inexorably, leading to "ethnic cleansing." Said, a Palestinian, understands the struggle inherent in resisting a stronger military and hegemonic power, and he personally comprehends that in such a struggle one needs all possible resources.

Said's arguments may be lost amid the critical and theoretical squabble over what precisely "postcolonial" means and represents. As Patrick Williams and Laura Chrisman write in their introduction to *Colonial Discourse and Post-Colonial Theory* (1994), "If colonialism is a way of maintaining an unequal international relation of economic or political power . . . then no doubt we have not fully transcended the colonial . . . we are not yet post-imperialist" (4). Accepting that premise, most Marxist critics would prefer the term "neocolonial" to describe the present situation for many countries in the actual global economy. Puerto Rico's existing situation clearly qualifies it as a "neo-colony" and many would argue that if given independence it would continue to be so. Certainly, postcolonialism or neocolonialism should not be seen as simply a historical post-independence period. Questions of power cannot be easily dismissed or neglected; power cannot be dislodged simply with the signing of a treaty granting a nation's independence or sovereignty. Power is not only manifested in military force; it is also economic, political, ideological, and cultural.

Given all of that, Puerto Ricans may continue to opt for the easier way out, rationalizing that if even sovereignty cannot promise full independence, then why even bother. The answer to such questions centers on how Puerto Ricans want to see themselves, whether such concepts as "dignity" and "self-determination" can hold any liberatory significance in a poststructuralist, postmodern, consumer-mad world. Arguments for the benefits of independence can contain merit even within such a global scenario; and if reaching that goal requires some unifying force that is resistant to the hegemonic power, then essentialist politics cannot be discarded. Such politics and its accompanying rhetorical discourse would need to evaluate the signifying of such terms like "hybridity." Within the present and varying Puerto Rican contexts, "hybridity" must then be consistently signified in a way similar, although not necessarily always the same, as that of the Nuyorican poets if it is to serve as a political and strategic instrument of resistance both in the United States *and* Puerto Rico. Of course, such a project depends on the will of the Puerto Rican people, a questionable factor when we consider that in Puerto Rico the concept of hegemony has evolved to unprecedented dimensions, beyond anything Gramsci could have imagined. In the island, hegemony represents for the United States a highly successful experiment made possible in large part because of the *Estado Libre Asociado*. The United States's colonial strategy in Puerto Rico has been less hands-on than the traditional, classical paradigm would have it. The strength of this strategy depends, as I have already mentioned, on the construction of an illusory sense of nationhood and power. Within this paradigm, the discourse that flows in Puerto Rico, in Spanish (therefore, the strident defense of this language), and seemingly stemming from an indigenous machinery of cultural production, effaces questions of difference more effectively than if there existed an authoritative American cultural presence in the island. What the United States has done brilliantly is to allow the colonial government, run by elected surrogates, to do its cultural dirty work, while the several American military bases on the island speak to the real nature of power. Surely, the real struggle and challenge for *independentistas* is how to de-center or dislodge such a powerfully situated hegemony.

Giannina Braschi's novel serves us with the valuable lesson that present postcolonial theorization of hybridity needs to be evaluated more closely. The concept is theorized from too narrowly drawn a base of knowledge and experience, and therefore it is theoretically limited and limiting. "Hybridity" as signifier has various potential signifieds. The present concept of "hybridity," channeled through postcolonial theory, is based on or shaped by the historical events experienced by former colonies, particularly those of the British Empire. As it stands, this postcolonial theorization of hybridity marginalizes "other" nations and cultures that still, for unfortunate reasons, lag behind in the nationhood continuum. For scholars and critics of United States literature and culture, the analysis of this text, and its use of hybridity, confirms Bruce Simon's idea that we must evaluate this concept within the wider scope of United States and American studies. Simon cautions against the prevailing version of hybridity in the United States, which equates hybridity with pluralism and consequently emphasizes the cultural and minimizes or completely ignores the political and economic (414). The "hybridity" supported by Braschi's text tends towards this particular type. The danger behind this conceptualization of "hybridity" is that it becomes, in Simon's words, "part of diversity management" rather than a hermeneutic or critical tool to analyze the operations of cultural production in the United States and its satellites. Equally important, we cannot disassociate the racial history of hybridity as we consider its cultural manifestations. *Yo-Yo Boing!'s* nomination for a prestigious national award like the Pulitzer must be read as support for its message of bilingualism and biculturalism by those who support an uncritical multicultural or pluralist agenda. Scholars of United States literature and culture should view this development with healthy skepticism, and when using hybridity as a working concept within "American studies," it behooves us to ponder Bruce Simon's suggestion that we think of hybridity "as an invitation to consider ways in which cultural politics matters, the ways that global power relations continue to construct the cultural. It would mean taking hybridity as an opportunity to rethink our own responsibilities as we develop new ways of organizing contemporary literary studies" (432).

Notes

1. Other texts useful to this study were Young, *Colonial Desire*; Ashcroft, Griffiths, and Tiffin, eds., *The Empire Writes Back* and "Hybridity" in *Post-Colonial Studies: The Key Concepts*; Perez-Torres, "Chicano Ethnicity"; and Ekkila, "Ethnicity."

2. Tito Nieves's compact disc, *I Like It Like That*, is a good example of recent Puerto Rican American popular musical hybridity. The album contains a mixture of old boogaloo blues tunes, pop tunes such as Carole King's "It's Too Late" put to salsa rhythms, classic rhythm and blues songs set to bolero arrangements, and bilingual rap.

3. Tio introduces and expounds his ideas on "Spanglish" in four news-paper columns: "Teoría del Espanglish," *Diario de Puerto Rico*, 28 Oct. 1948; "Teoría del Inglañol," *El Mundo*, 27 Mar. 1971; "¿Existe el Bilinguismo?," *El Nuevo Dia*, 25 Nov. 1985; "Espanglish e Inglañol," *El Nuevo Dia*, 24 Dec. 1986.

4. For comments from Puerto Rican diaspora writers on this issue see Costa, "¿Y Que Dicen?" Many of the writers interviewed in Hernandez, *Puerto Rican Voices in English*, speak on similar issues.

5. All future references will be made in parentheses. All translations are mine.

6. For an in-depth analysis of these concepts and other topics related to the bilingual language practice of Puerto Ricans in the United States, see Torres, *Puerto Rican Discourse*.

7. See the essay, "Discourse in the Novel," esp. 358–66.

8. See *The Political Unconscious* 168.

9. For a comprehensive treatment of these ideas, see Harvey, *The Condition of Postmodernity*.

Works Cited

Aparicio, Frances. "La Vida Es un Spanglish Disparatero: Bilingualismo in Nuyorican Poetry." *European Perspectives on Hispanic Literature of the*

United States. Ed. Genevieve Fabre. Houston: Arte Publico, 1998.
147–60.

Ashcroft, Bill, Gareth Griffiths, and Helen Tiffin, eds. *The Empire Writes Back: Theory and Practice in Post-Colonial Literatures.* New York: Routledge, 1989.

———. *Post-Colonial Studies: The Key Concepts.* New York: Routledge, 1998.

Bakhtin, M. M. *The Dialogic Imagination.* Austin: University of Texas Press, 1981.

Bhabha, Homi. *The Location of Culture.* London: Routledge, 1994.

Braschi, Giannina. *Yo-Yo Boing!* Pittsburgh: Latin American Literary Review, 1998.

Costa, Marithelma. "¿Y Que Dicen los Escritores Neorriqueños sobre el Idioma, la Literatura y la Identidad Nacional?" *La Revista del Centro de Estudios Avanzados de Puerto Rico y El Caribe* (Jul.-Dec. 1989): 69–73.

Erkkila, Betsy. "Ethnicity, Literary Theory, and the Grounds of Resistance." *American Quarterly* 47 (1995): 563–94.

Fisher, Walter R. *Human Communication as Narration: Toward a Philosophy of Reason, Value, and Action.* Columbia: University of South Carolina Press, 1984.

Gilroy, Paul. *The Black Atlantic: Modernity and Double Consciousness.* Cambridge, MA: Harvard University Press, 1993.

Grosfoguel, Ramón. "The Divorce of Nationalist Discourses from the Puerto Rican People: A Sociohistorical Perspective." *Puerto Rican Jam: Essays on Culture and Politics: Rethinking Colonialism and Nationalism.* Ed. Frances Negrón-Muntaner and Ramón Grosfoguel. Minneapolis: University of Minnesota Press, 1997. 57–76.

Harvey, David. *The Condition of Postmodernity: An Enquiry into the Origins of Cultural Change.* Cambridge, UK: Blackwell, 1989.

Hernandez, Carmen Dolores. *Puerto Rican Voices in English.* Westport, CT: Praeger, 1997.

hooks, bell. *Yearning: Race, Gender, and Cultural Politics.* Boston: South End, 1990.

Jameson, Fredric. *The Political Unconscious.* Ithaca, NY: Cornell University Press, 1981.

JanMohamed, Abdul R. "The Economy of Manichean Allegory: The Function of Racial Difference in Colonialist Literature." *Critical Inquiry* 12.1 (1985): 59–87.

Nieves, Tito. *I Like It Like That.* Compact disc. RMM Records, 1997.

Perez-Torres, Rafael. "Chicano Ethnicity, Cultural Hybridity, and the Mestizo Voice." *American Literature* 70.1 (1998): 153–76.

Said, Edward. *Culture and Imperialism*. New York: Knopf, 1993.

Simon, Bruce. "Hybridity in the Americas: Reading Conde, Mukherjee, and Hawthorne." *Post-Colonial Theory and the United States: Race, Ethnicity, and Literature*. Ed. Amritjit Singh and Peter Schmidt. Jackson: University Press of Mississippi, 2000. 412–43.

Spivak, Gayatri C. *The Post-Colonial Critic: Interviews, Strategies, Dialogues*. Ed. Sarah Harasym. London: Routledge, 1978.

Torres, Lourdes. *Puerto Rican Discourse: A Sociolinguistic Study of a New York Suburb*. Mahwah, NJ: Lawrence Erlbaum, 1997.

Williams, Patrick, and Laura Chrisman. *Colonial Discourse and Post-Colonial Theory*. New York: Columbia University Press, 1994.

Young, Robert. *Colonial Desire: Hybridity in Theory, Culture and Race*. London: Routledge, 1995.

CONTRIBUTORS

JESSE ALEMÁN is associate professor of English at the University of New Mexico, where he teaches nineteenth-century American and Chicana/o literatures.

ARIEL BALTER has a PhD in English and American literature and has taught at a number of universities and high schools. Currently, she is an independent scholar and writer.

OLIVIA CASTELLANO was a professor of English at California State University, Sacramento, where she taught courses in composition, creative writing, Chicano literature, and multiethnic literature from 1972 until her retirement in 2005. She has written several books of poetry, including *Blue Horses of Madness* (1983), *Mandolin/Yellow Field* (1980), and *The Spaces that Time Missed* (1986).

ANNAMARIE CHRISTIANSEN is an assistant professor of English at Brigham Young University, Hawaii. Her research interests include Oceanic literatures, African American literature, cultural studies, and critical pedagogy. Born in Australia and raised on the U.S. mainland, she is Maori (iwi affiliation: Nga Puhi).

GEORGINA DODGE is assistant vice provost for the Office of Minority Affairs at The Ohio State University, where she collaborates on cross-campus diversity initiatives. Her graduate degrees in English are from UCLA, and her publications focus on multiracial American literatures, autobiography, and immigration.

TRACY FLOREANI is assistant professor of English at Baker University in Baldwin City, Kansas, where she teaches writing and American literature. Her research focuses on ethnicity in post-World War II American culture and immigrant identities in the United States.

DAVID S. GOLDSTEIN earned a PhD in comparative culture from the University of California, Irvine, and teaches American and ethnic studies—primarily literature and film—at the University of Washington, Bothell. He publishes widely on ethnic American literature.

JOE LOCKARD is assistant professor of English at Arizona State University, where he teaches early American and African American literatures. He published *Brave New Classrooms: Democratic Education and the Internet* (co-edited with Mark Pegrum) in 2007. He directs the Antislavery Literature Project, located at http://antislavery.eserver .org, and writes on literatures of race and slavery. His essays have appeared in numerous venues and he was a long-time editor of *Bad Subjects*.

EDWIN J. MCALLISTER received his PhD in American literature from the University of Oregon in 1995. He is currently associate professor of English at Belhaven College in Jackson, Mississippi.

SHEREE MEYER is a professor and current chair of the English Department at the California State University, Sacramento. She teaches courses in early modern literature, literary theory, and theory and pedagogy, as well as the team-taught course in American Identities that generated her collaborative article. Her teaching of *The Romance Reader* has encouraged her to develop a new course in Jewish American literature. She has published articles in *College English*, *College Literature*, and *Pedagogy*.

WILLIAM OVER teaches communication and English literature courses at St. John's University in Queens, New York. His first book, *Human Rights in the International Public Sphere* (1999), won the Best Book Award from the International Division of the National Communication Association in 2000. His second book, *Social Justice in World Cinema and Theatre* (2001), examines human rights issues in mediated forms. His third book, *World Peace, Mass Culture, and National Policy* (2004), concerns notions of peace in an intercultural context. He is particularly interested in the relation of intercultural concerns to democratic agendas globally, and in specific cultural forms that reflect such undertakings.

JEFFREY F. L. PARTRIDGE's articles on Asian American literature and ethnic authorship have appeared in *Studies in the Literary Imagination*, *MELUS*, and other journals. He wrote the introduction to Shawn Wong's second novel, *American Knees*. His most recent book is *Beyond Literary Chinatown* (2007).

CHAUNCEY A. RIDLEY is a professor of literature at California State University, Sacramento. He teaches undergraduate and graduate courses in African American and multiethnic literatures, including the team-taught course in American Identities that generated his collaborative article. He has published articles in *Obsidian II* and *Cultural and Cross-Cultural Studies and the Teaching of Literature*.

DEREK PARKER ROYAL is an assistant professor of English at Texas A & M University-Commerce, founder and current president of the Philip Roth Society, and founder and executive editor of *Philip Roth Studies*. He is the editor of *Philip Roth: New Perspectives on an American Author* (2005) and has published in a variety of scholarly journals. Currently, he is at work on a new book on the short-story cycle in recent Jewish American narrative, an edited collection of essays on the newest generation of Jewish American fiction writers, and the completion of his book, *More Than Jewish Mischief: Narrative and Identity in the Later Fiction of Philip Roth.*

ALEXANDRA W. SCHULTHEIS is assistant professor of post-colonial literature and theory at the University of North Carolina, Greensboro, where she also teaches women's studies and contemporary British and American literature. She is the author of *Regenerative Fictions: Postcolonialism, Psychoanalysis, and the Nation as Family* (2004). She has also published articles on Jamaica Kincaid and Salman Rushdie, and is currently conducting research on Tibetan national identity in diaspora and on subjectivity and human rights.

AUDREY B. THACKER is an adjunct professor of English at the California State University, Northridge, and at California Lutheran University. She received a Ph.D. from Claremont Graduate University, and writes principally on Jewish American literature.

ANDREA TINNEMEYER teaches at the College Preparatory School in Berkeley, California, after having taught at Utah State University. Her most recent book is *Identity Politics and the Captivity Narrative after 1848* (2006).

JOSÉ L. TORRES-PADILLA is associate professor at SUNY Plattsburgh, where he teaches United States ethnic literatures and creative writing. He has published various essays on multiethnic literature as well as poetry and short fiction. He is co-director of the North Country Institute for Writers of Color and managing editor of the *Saranac Review.*

INDEX

Aarons, Victoria, 261
Abraham, Pearl, 275–79
aesthetic texts, 243
African Americans: appellations,
  232–34; racial identity of, 166;
  writers, 50
Africanism, 76
Allen, Woody, 264–65
Almaguer, Tomás, 7
Althusser, Louis, 230
America, defined, xxvi
Anaya, Rudolfo, 279–83
Anderson, Benedict, 17, 245
Aparicio, Frances, 291
Appiah, Anthony, xvi–xvii
Aranda, José F., Jr., 23
Arnold, Matthew, 211–12
Asian Americans, racial identity
  of, 165–66. *See also* Chinese
  Americans

assimilation, 101–2
autobiography: analysis of, 173–
  74; of immigrants, 166–73;
  and race, 159–61; and slavery,
  71
*Autobiography of an Ex-Colored
  Man* (Johnson), 48–70 passim
Aztlán, 171

Baker, Houston A., Jr., 49, 78
Bakhtin, Mikhail, 103, 111, 297
Baldwin, James, 220–22
Baraka, Amiri, 224
Barone, Michael, 175
Barrio Boy (Galarza), 160–73
Basch, Norma, 41
Benston, Kimberly W., 228
Berlant, Lauren, 200
Bernardi, Daniel, 211
Berzon, Judith, 80

head-body race paradigm, 122–24
Hébert, Kimberly G., 82
Hegel, Georg Wilhelm Friedrich, 136
heteroglossia, 103
High Cotton (Pinckney), 227–47 passim
Hispanic, defined, 163, 176
Hispano identity, 5–24
historical romances, 7–16
historical trauma, 230–31
Holocaust, 277
Homans, Margaret, 235
hooks, bell, 258, 264–65, 302
Hopkins, Pauline, 79–82
Hughes, Henry, 124
Hume, David, 123
Hurston, Zora Neale, 49, 274, 283–87
hybridity: Bhabha, Homi, 76–77, 81, 293–94; *Mona in the Promised Land*, 103, 107–11; nonresistance toward, 301; *Paradise*, 91; vs. polyculturalism, 113–15; Puerto Ricans, 290–92, 303–4
hybrid names, 115
hyperbole, 285–86

Ignatiev, Noel, 12–13, 165
I Love Lucy, 185–91
immigration experience: Chinese Americans, 144–47, 152–55; Ellis Island, 157–58; Irish Americans, 165
incest, 34
infectious disease, 147–49
interracial marriage, 34. *See also* marriage
invisibility: Du Bois on, 244–45, 248

Irish Americans: immigration experience, 165; racial identity of, 12–13

Jacobson, Matthew Frye, 159
Jameson, Frederic, 208, 300
Japanese perspective, racial classification, 168
Jazz (Morrison), 86–90
Jen, Gish, 99–115 passim
Jewish ethnicity: and ethnic studies, 256–57; interpretations of, 252; *Mona in the Promised Land*, 106–7; postmodernism, 264–65; *The Turner Diaries*, 129–32
Jewish literature, 250–51, 265–66, 273
Johnson, Charles, 95
Johnson, James Weldon, 48–70 passim
Johnson Act (1924), 124
Jones, Roslyn, 174

Kant, Immanuel, 123
Kawash, Samira, xxvii
Keating, AnnLouise, 222–23
Keppel, Ben, 219
Kinkead, Gwen, 101–2
Koshiro, Yukiko, 168–69

Landay, Lori, 185, 186, 188, 189
Land Law (1851), 17
language: issue of, 191; linguistic borrowing, 294–98; of psychoanalysis, 234–36; Spanglish, 291, 294
"La Raza," 171–72
Latino, defined, 163, 176
Lawson, Benjamin, 51

Simon, Bruce, 304–5
sin razón, 11–12
Skerrett, Joseph, 49
slavery: and autobiography, 71; in *Autobiography of an Ex-Colored Man*, 53–59; literary references to, 237–39; in *The Squatter and the Don*, 22; "tragic" mulatto, 78; trauma of, 242–43, 245; in *Who Would Have Thought It?* 15–16
smallpox epidemic, 147–49
Smith, Valerie, 78
Snyder, William, 34
Sobchack, Vivian, 260–61
social relations, 104, 110, 192–95
Sollors, Werner, 95, 163–64, 253–58, 267
Spanglish, 291, 294
Spigel, Lynn, 183
Spillers, Hortense, 242
spirituality. *See* religion
Spivak, Gayatri, 301–2
The Squatter and the Don (Ruiz de Burton), 16–23
Stepto, Robert, 85
Stout, Arthur B., 147–48
Stuart, Lyle, 121–22
subjectivity, 244, 236
Sugimoto, Etsu, 160–73
Sundquist, Eric, 49–50, 57, 66, 67–68, 231
synthetic memories, 243

Tate, Claudia, 236
Taylor, Clyde, 50
Taylor, Henry Louis, 223
television culture, 182–85
Their Eyes Were Watching God

(Hurston), 283–87. *See also* Hurston, Zora Neale
Tio, Salvador, 291
Todorov, Tzvetan, 135
"tragic" mulatto, 74–95
trauma: Freudian theory of, 230–31, 241, 248; of slavery, 242–43, 245
Treaty of Guadalupe Hidalgo (1848), 10, 39–40, 43, 171
The Turner Diaries (Pierce), 121–35
TuSmith, Bonnie, 253

United States, defined, xxvi
United States–Mexican War, 31–32

Vagrancy Act (1855), 6–7
Vander Zanden, James, 163

Wald, Alan, 254–55, 256
Walker, David, 123–24
Wall, Cheryl, 84
Walton, Jean, 229, 236
Washington, Mary Helen, 196
Werbner, Pnina, 112–13
West, Cornel, 197
westward expansion. *See* Manifest Destiny
white guilt, 145–46
whiteness: analysis of, 222–23; as cultural identity marker, 23; defined, 106, 211; desire for, 82–85; of European immigrants, 159, 164–65; forms of, 17; *Gabriel Conroy*, 44; historicization of, 210; legality of, 35–36; redemption by, 56; re-figuring of, 5–6, 10–11; theory of, 209–12; treat-